MCSD Visual C++ 6.0 Desktop
The Cram Sheet

This Cram Sheet contains the distilled, key facts about the MCSD Visual C++ 6.0 Desktop exam. Review this information last thing before entering the test room, paying special attention to those areas where you feel you need the most review. You can transfer any of the facts onto a blank piece of paper before beginning the exam.

MICROSOFT FOUNDATION CLASS (MFC) FRAMEWORK — DOCUMENT AND VIEW ARCHITECTURE

1. Most MFC classes are derived directly or indirectly from **CObject**. **CObject** supports three major MFC features: runtime class information, serialization, and diagnostic and debugging.

2. **CCmdTarget**, derived from **CObject**, is the base class for the message map architecture. Any class derived from **CCmdTarget** directly or indirectly can contain a message map. **CCmdTarget** performs the actual message map lookup.

3. MFC supports two types of threads: user interface (UI) threads, which have a message pump, and worker threads, which don't. Use **AfxBeginThread()** to launch a new thread. **CWinThread** objects encapsulate threads of execution. **CWinThread** is derived from **CCmdTarget**.

4. **CWinApp**, derived from **CWinThread**, represents the standard Windows application.

5. The AppWizard generated **InitInstance** function in a **CWinApp**-derived class initiates the creation of the main frame window, the document, and the view. The document template ties together these three objects. Each combination of frame window, document, and view types requires a unique document template. Each document template creates and manages all the documents of its type.

6. The AppWizard generated **CMainFrame::OnCreate** function creates and docks the standard status bar and toolbar. Here, you will normally add toolbars and modify the status-bar configuration.

7. **CWnd**, derived from **CCmdTarget,** is the base class for all other window classes. The handle (**HWND**) of the attached Windows window is cached in **CWnd::m_hWnd**.

8. The document object stores the applications data. **CDocument**, derived from **CCmdTarget**, is the base class for document objects.

9. The view object displays a visible representation of the data. **CView**, derived from **CWnd**, is the base class for view objects.

10. Menus, keyboard accelerators, toolbar buttons, and other UI objects generate command messages (**WM_COMMAND**).

11. **WM_COMMAND** messages sent to an SDI frame window are are routed through: the active view object, the active view's document object, the document object's document template, the main frame window object, the application object, and the default window procedure.

12. Regular window messages go directly to the window for which they are intended.

56. The single-thread apartment (STA) requires a Windows message pump.

57. A process can have any number of STAs but only one multithreaded apartment (MTA).

58. Threads within an MTA can use direct interface pointers, but interface pointers that cross apartment boundaries must be marshaled.

59. All MTA-compatible objects must be thread-safe.

60. An object that supports aggregation provides two **IUnknown** implementations—delegating and non-delegating. When it's being created as an aggregated object, it will cache the outer object's **IUnknown** pointer.

61. Know how to create COM components and ActiveX controls by using the SDK, MFC, and ATL.

62. _bstr_t class encapsulates a **BSTR**, _variant_t class encapsulates a **VARIANT**, _com_error class encapsulates a **HRESULT** error code, _com_ptr_t smart pointer encapsulates an interface pointer.

63. ATL provides two smart pointers to manage interface pointers: **CComPtr** and **CComQIptr**. ATL **CComBSTR** encapsulates a **BSTR**.

DATA SERVICES

63. The ADO model consists of seven objects (**Connection**, **Command**, **Recordset**, **Error**, **Property**, **Parameter**, and **Field**) and four collections (**Errors**, **Properties**, **Parameters**, and **Fields**).

64. The ADO **Connection** object manages a physical connection to the database. It allows you to open a connection to a data source, execute SQL statements or database stored procedures, and establish transactions for data updates. The **Connection** object contains an **Errors** collection and a **Properties** collection.

65. You can use the ADO **Command** object to execute SQL statements or stored procedures, define and execute repetitive SQL commands that require a set of SQL parameters, and source a **Recordset**. The **Command** object contains a **Parameters** collection and a **Properties** collection.

66. The ADO **Recordset** object is designed to manipulate data held in a data source. It represents a set of records from the data provider and provides the ability to scroll through the records as well as add, edit, and delete them. The **Recordset** object contains a **Fields** collection and a **Properties** collection.

67. Three ways of creating an ADO recordset: **Recordset::Open()**, **Command::Execute()**, and **Connection::Execute()**.

68. ADO provides four types of record set cursors: Dynamic—Unrestricted movement, allows you to add, modify, or delete records. Keyset—similar to dynamic, additions and deletions made by other users are not visible. Forward—identical to dynamic, but only scrolls forward. Static—like dynamic, but changes made by other users are not visible.

69. Use **MoveFirst()**, **MoveLast()**, **MoveNext()**, and **MovePrevious()** to move the current record position in a **Recordset**.

70. The **Recordset** object and its associated **Fields** collection can be used without a database connection.

71. Some commonly used ADO smart pointers are: **_ConnectionPtr**, **_CommandPtr**, **_RecordsetPtr**, **ErrorsPtr**, **ErrorPtr**, **FieldsPtr**, **FieldPtr**, **_ParameterPtr**, **ParametersPtr**, **PropertiesPtr**, and **PropertyPtr**.

31. Know how to use the resource editors. By able to create static menus, toolbars, dialog boxes, property pages, and form views.

32. Know how to use ClassWizard to create a class for a dialog box, a property page, and a form view.

33. Know how to use ClassWizard to create property sheets. Use **CPropertySheet::AddPage()** to add property pages to a property sheet.

34. Know how to add controls to the resource and handlers to the class.

35. Standard controls, such as **CButton** and **CEdit**, send notifications to their parents by using **WM_COMMAND**.

36. Most common controls, such as **CProgressCtrl** and **CSpinButtonCtrl** enclose their notifications in **WM_NOTIFY**.

37. **CDataExchange** provides dialog data exchange and validation (DDX/DDV).

38. Override **DoDataExchange()** and use **DDX_** functions to transfer data between controls and data members. Use **DDV_** functions to validate the values entered into controls.

39. Register new ActiveX controls by running RegSvr32, passing it the control's filename on the command line.

40. To use ActiveX controls in an MFC application, **AfxEnableControlContainer()** must be called by **InitInstance()**, and #include <afxdisp.h> must be added to StdAfx.h. AppWizard will usually add the code for you.

41. Use the Component Gallery to insert an ActiveX control into your project. ClassWizard, using the type library information, will generate a wrapper class for each of the control's internal **coclass**es.

42. Use the resource editor to add an ActiveX control to a dialog box. Then add event handlers for the control, using ClassWizard or the New Windows Message And Event Handlers dialog box.

43. To create an ActiveX control at runtime, insert the component into the project, add an embedded ActiveX control wrapper class member to the appropriate window class, add an ID for the control, add code to call the control's **Create()** function, add the event sink declaration and definition macros, and add the necessary event message handlers and prototypes.

COMPONENT OBJECT MODEL (COM)

44. All interfaces must be derived directly or indirectly from **IUnknown**, which has three methods: **QueryInterface()**, **AddRef()**, and **Release()**.

45. Standard interfaces are interfaces developed and deployed by Microsoft.

46. Custom interfaces are user-defined interfaces. Custom interfaces use vtable binding.

47. Automation interfaces are derived from **IDispatch**. **IDispatch** exposes four methods: **GetTypeInfoCount()**, **GetTypeInfo()**, **GetIDsOfNames()**, and **Invoke()**.

48. Dual interfaces support both vtable binding and the **IDispatch** interface.

49. In-process servers, which are usually housed in a DLL file, run in the same address space as their clients.

50. Out-of-process servers are housed in EXE files, run in their own address space, and have their own execution context. There are two types of out-of-process servers: local and remote.

51. Register in-process servers by running RegSvr32, passing it the control's file name on the command line. To unregister the server, run RegSvr32 with the /u switch.

52. Register an out-of-process server by running the EXE specifying the /RegServer switch. To unregister the server, use the /UnregServer switch.

53. Out-of-process servers publish a component's class factory dynamically at runtime and revoke it at shut down. It does this by calling the **CoRegisterClassObject()** and **CoRevokeClassObject()** functions.

54. To use the full IDL syntax, define _WIN_DCOM or ensure _WIN32_WINNT is set to a value equal or greater than 0x0400.

55. For a client application to use **CoCreate_InstanceEx()**, either _WIN32_WINNT=0x0400 or _WIN32_DCOM must be defined and objbase.h must be included.

13. A **CView**-derived class overrides **OnDraw**. Whenever the framework receives a **WM_PAINT** it creates a **CPaintDC** object and calls **OnDraw**, passing it a pointer to the **CPaintDC** object.

14. **OnDraw** can be used for displaying to a window, printing, and print previewing.

15. The framework calls five **CView** virtual functions at various stages of the printing process.

- **OnPreparePrinting**—Override to call **DoPreparePrinting()**, which is responsible for displaying the Print dialog box and creating the printer DC. This function is called at the beginning of the print job.
- **OnBeginPrinting**—Override to allocate fonts and other resources needed for the print job. You can also set the maximum page count here. This function is called just before printing starts.
- **OnPrepareDC**—Override to modify the device context. This function is called before each page is printed.
- **OnPrint**—Override to print headers, footers, and other page elements that are not drawn by **OnDraw** or to do all printing here instead of in **OnDraw**. This function is called to print (or preview) one page.
- **OnEndPrinting**—Override to deallocate resources allocated in **OnBeginPrinting**. This function is called when printing ends.

16. A MFC regular DLL exports C-style functions and can be used by Visual Basic, Delphi, and other languages that can call C-style functions. Functions must use the **AFX_MANAGE_STATE** macro.

17. MFC extension DLLs are used to export functions and classes that enhance MFC. Use the **AFX_EXT_CLASS** macro to export a class or function.

18. The preprocessor symbol **_AFXEXT** must be defined for extension DLLs.

19. Compiler switches control the stack construction for function call definitions: /Gd—use **__cdecl**, which specifies the C calling convention (the default setting); /Gr—use **__fastcall**, which specifies that arguments are passed in registers; and /Gz—use **__stdcall**, which specifies that arguments are pushed on the stack from right to left.

20. Compiler switch /GZ can help catch release build errors in debug.

21. The SourceSafe Share command allows a single instance of a component to be used with multiple projects.

22. The SourceSafe Branch command allows tracking the individual directions of a file as a project. The Branch command breaks any sharing links.

23. Pinning a SourceSafe file prevents you from making changes to the file.

24. Use Share, Pin, and Branch to create service pack projects (bug fixes).

25. Use **CreateEx()** to create toolbar objects when extended styles need to be present during the construction of the embedded control.

26. After creating a toolbar, four more actions are required to place a dockable toolbar in your application: load the toolbar resource, enable docking for the toolbar, enable docking for the frame window, and dock the toolbar to the frame window.

27. Add ToolTips to a toolbar by adding **CBRS_TOOLTIPS** to the toolbar style, creating string table resources containing the ToolTip text, and setting the string resource IDs so that they match the toolbar buttons.

28. Use **CStatusbar::SetIndicators ()** to specify the number of panes a status bar will contain.

29. Use **CStatusBar::SetPaneText()** or **CCmdUI::SetText()** to display text in a status bar pane.

30. Know how to use the ClassWizard to create a new class, add member variables, and add message handlers.

MCSD
Visual C++ 6
Desktop

James M. Lacey

MCSD Visual C++ 6 Desktop Exam Cram

Limits Of Liability And Disclaimer Of Warranty

The author and publisher of this book have used their best efforts in preparing the book and the programs contained in it. These efforts include the development, research, and testing of the theories and programs to determine their effectiveness. The author and publisher make no warranty of any kind, expressed or implied, with regard to these programs or the documentation contained in this book.

The author and publisher shall not be liable in the event of incidental or consequential damages in connection with, or arising out of, the furnishing, performance, or use of the programs, associated instructions, and/or claims of productivity gains.

Trademarks

Trademarked names appear throughout this book. Rather than list the names and entities that own the trademarks or insert a trademark symbol with each mention of the trademarked name, the publisher states that it is using the names for editorial purposes only and to the benefit of the trademark owner, with no intention of infringing upon that trademark.

The Coriolis Group, LLC
14455 N. Hayden Road
Suite 220
Scottsdale, Arizona 85260

480/483-0192
FAX 480/483-0193
http://www.coriolis.com

Library of Congress Cataloging-in-Publication Data
Lacey, James, 1943-
    MCSD Visual C++ 6 desktop exam cram / by James Lacey.
        p.   cm.
    ISBN 1-57610-373-0
    1. Electronic data processing personnel--Certification.
2. Microsoft software--Examinations Study guides.   3. Microsoft
Visual C++.   I. Title.
QA76.3.L33   2000
005.26'8--dc21   99-38873
                                                      CIP

President, CEO
Keith Weiskamp

Publisher
Steve Sayre

Acquisitions Editor
Shari Jo Hehr

Marketing Specialist
Cynthia Caldwell

Project Editor
Don Eamon

Technical Reviewer
Nathan Lewis

Production Coordinator
Wendy Littley

Cover Design
Jesse Dunn

Layout Design
April Nielsen

Printed in the United States of America
10 9 8 7 6 5 4 3 2 1

CORIOLIS

14455 North Hayden Road, Suite 220 • Scottsdale, Arizona 85260

Coriolis: The Training And Certification Destination™

Thank you for purchasing one of our innovative certification study guides, just one of the many members of the Coriolis family of certification products.

Certification Insider Press™ has long believed that achieving your IT certification is more of a road trip than anything else. This is why most of our readers consider us their *Training And Certification Destination*. By providing a one-stop shop for the most innovative and unique training materials, our readers know we are the first place to look when it comes to achieving their certification. As one reader put it, "I plan on using your books for all of the exams I take."

To help you reach your goals, we've listened to others like you, and we've designed our entire product line around you and the way you like to study, learn, and master challenging subjects. Our approach is *The Smartest Way To Get Certified ™*.

In addition to our highly popular *Exam Cram* and *Exam Prep* guides, we have a number of new products. We recently launched *Exam Cram Audio Reviews*, which are audiotapes based on *Exam Cram* material. We've also developed *Practice Tests Exam Crams* and *Exam Cram Flash Cards*, which are designed to make your studying fun as well as productive.

Our commitment to being the *Training And Certification Destination* does not stop there. We just introduced *Exam Cram Insider*, a biweekly newsletter containing the latest in certification news, study tips, and announcements from Certification Insider Press. (To subscribe, send an email to **eci@coriolis.com** and type "subscribe insider" in the body of the email.) We also recently announced the launch of the Certified Crammer Society and the Coriolis Help Center— two new additions to the Certification Insider Press family.

We'd like to hear from you. Help us continue to provide the very best certification study materials possible. Write us or email us at **cipq@coriolis.com** and let us know how our books have helped you study, or tell us about new features that you'd like us to add. If you send us a story about how we've helped you, and we use it in one of our books, we'll send you an official Coriolis shirt for your efforts.

Good luck with your certification exam and your career. Thank you for allowing us to help you achieve your goals.

Keith Weiskamp
Keith Weiskamp
President and CEO

Look For These Other Books From The Coriolis Group:

MCSD Architectures Exam Cram
Donald Brandt

MCSD Visual C++ 6 Distributed Exam Cram
James M. Lacey

To my soul mate and wife, Ann, who gave me her love and support during all the many hours I was sitting in front of the computer instead of spending time with her.

About The Author

James M. Lacey is a software developer and technical trainer specializing in C++, COM, Windows, and Client/Server software development. He has over 25 years experience in the computer industry in both hardware and software engineering. This experience includes embedded systems, operating systems, compilers, graphics applications, client/server applications, and database systems.

James is a Microsoft Certified Solution Developer and Trainer. In addition to his own consulting practice, James teaches at Boston University and Worcester Polytechnic Institute. He prefers the challenge of designing and developing total solutions for small- to medium-sized businesses. His consulting practice keeps him abreast of current technology trends and allows him to bring real-world experience to the classroom.

James and his wife, Ann, live in central Massachusetts. He can be contacted at **jlacey@rclink.net**.

Acknowledgments

I would like to acknowledge and say thank you to all the people who supported me and helped me in writing this book. To my team at Coriolis Group, starting with Shari Jo Hehr, acquisitions editor, who recruited me as a new author and gave me the opportunity to write my first book. To Don Eamon, project editor, for his mentoring and quarterbacking through the entire process (Don, the new schedule is in the mail). To Joanne Slike, copyeditor, for her great work and insight, which helped me say what I really wanted to say. To Nathan Lewis, technical reviewer, for his work to ensure technical accuracy.

I'd also like to thank all the people behind the scenes at Coriolis Group who worked their magic in the creation of this book: Wendy Littley, production coordinator; Jesse Dunn, cover designer; April Nielsen, interior designer; and Cynthia Caldwell, marketing specialist.

A special thank you to Gene Olafsen (found by Shari Jo) for his assistance in some of the writing. His contribution helped me finish this book while we are still in the second millennium.

Finally to my wife, Ann, for her encouragement and cheerleading through the birth of my first book.

Contents At A Glance

Table Of Contents

Introduction

Welcome to the *MCSD Visual C++ 6 Desktop Exam Cram*! This book aims to help you get ready to take—and pass—the Microsoft certification test numbered 70-016, "Designing and Implementing Desktop Applications with Microsoft Visual C++ 6.0." This Introduction explains Microsoft's certification programs in general and talks about how the *Exam Cram* series can help you prepare for Microsoft's certification exams.

Exam Cram books help you understand and appreciate the subjects and materials you need to pass Microsoft certification exams. *Exam Cram* books are aimed strictly at test preparation and review. They do not teach you everything you need to know about a topic (such as the ins and outs of C++ programming and database development or all the nitty-gritty details involved in using the Visual C++ 6 integrated development environment (IDE) and Visual Source Safe). Instead, *Exam Cram* books present and dissect the questions and problems we've found that you're likely to encounter on a test. We've worked from Microsoft's own training materials, preparation guides, and tests, as well as from a battery of third-party test preparation tools. Our aim is to bring together as much information as possible about Microsoft certification exams.

Nevertheless, to completely prepare yourself for any Microsoft test, we recommend that you begin by taking the Self-Assessment included in this book immediately following this Introduction. This tool will help you evaluate your knowledge base against the requirements for an MCSD under both ideal and real circumstances.

Based on what you learn from that exercise, you might decide to begin your studies with some classroom training, or that you pick up and read one of the many study guides available. I also strongly recommend that you install, configure, and fool around with the software or environment that you'll be tested on, because nothing beats hands-on experience and familiarity when it comes to understanding the questions you're likely to encounter on a certification test. Book learning is essential, but hands-on experience is the best teacher of all.

The Microsoft Certified Professional (MCP) Program

The MCP program currently includes the following separate tracks, each of which boasts its own special acronym (as a would-be certificant, you need to have a high tolerance for alphabet soup of all kinds):

➤ *MCP (Microsoft Certified Professional)*—This is the least prestigious of all the certification tracks from Microsoft. Passing any of the major Microsoft exams (except the Networking Essentials exam) qualifies an individual for MCP credentials. Individuals can demonstrate proficiency with additional Microsoft products by passing additional certification exams.

➤ *MCP+SB (Microsoft Certified Professional + Site Building)*—This certification program is designed for individuals who are planning, building, managing, and maintaining Web sites. Individuals with the MCP+SB credential will have demonstrated the ability to develop Web sites that include multimedia and searchable content and Web sites that connect to and communicate with a back-end database. It requires passing two of the following three exams: "Designing and Implementing Commerce Solutions with Microsoft Site Server 3.0, Commerce Edition," "Designing and Implementing Web Sites with Microsoft FrontPage 98," and "Designing and Implementing Web Solutions with Microsoft Visual InterDev 6.0."

➤ *MCSD (Microsoft Certified Solution Developer)*—The MCSD credential reflects the skills required to create multitier, distributed, and COM-based solutions, in addition to desktop and Internet applications, using new technologies. To obtain an MCSD, an individual must demonstrate the ability to analyze and interpret user requirements; select and integrate products, platforms, tools, and technologies; design and implement code and customize applications; and perform necessary software tests and quality assurance operations.

To become an MCSD, you must pass a total of four exams: three core exams and one elective exam. Each candidate must choose one of these three desktop application exams—"70-016: Designing and Implementing Desktop Applications with Microsoft Visual C++ 6.0," "70-156: Designing and Implementing Desktop Applications with Visual FoxPro 6.0," or "70-176: Designing and Implementing Desktop Applications with Visual Basic 6.0"—*plus* one of these three distributed application exams—"70-015: Designing and Implementing Distributed Applications with Microsoft Visual C++ 6.0," "70-155: Designing and Implementing Desktop Applications with Visual FoxPro 6.0," or "70-175:

Designing and Implementing Desktop Applications with Visual Basic 6.0." The third core exam is "70-100: Analyzing Requirements and Defining Solution Architectures. "

Elective exams cover specific Microsoft applications and languages, including Visual Basic, Visual C++ (the subject of this book), the Microsoft Foundation Classes, Access, SQL Server, Excel, and more. You cannot use the same exam to satisfy two requirements. For example, if you take and pass "Designing and Implementing Distributed Applications with Microsoft Visual C++ 6.0" to satisfy the core requirement, you cannot also use the exam to satisfy your elective requirement.

If you're on your way to becoming an MCSD and have already taken some exams, visit **www.microsoft.com/train_cert/** for information about how to proceed with your MCSD certification under this new track. Table 1 shows the requirements for the MCSD certification.

➤ *MCDBA (Microsoft Certified Database Administrator)*—The MCDBA credential reflects the skills required to implement and administer Microsoft SQL Server databases. To obtain an MCDBA, an individual must demonstrate the ability to derive physical database designs, develop logical data models, create physical databases, create data services by using Transact-SQL, manage and maintain databases, configure and manage security, monitor and optimize databases, and install and configure Microsoft SQL Server.

To become an MCDBA, you must pass a total of five exams: four core exams and one elective exam. The required core exams are "Administering Microsoft SQL Server 7.0," "Designing and Implementing Databases with Microsoft SQL Server 7.0," "Implementing and Supporting Microsoft Windows NT Server 4.0," and "Implementing and Supporting Microsoft Windows NT Server 4.0 in the Enterprise."

The elective exams that you can choose from cover specific uses of SQL Server and include: "Designing and Implementing Distributed Applications with Visual Basic 6.0," "Designing and Implementing Distributed Applications with Visual C++ 6.0," "Designing and Implementing Data Warehouses with Microsoft SQL Server 7.0 and Microsoft Decision Support Services 1.0," and two exams that relate to NT. These two exams are "Internetworking with Microsoft TCP/IP on Microsoft Windows NT 4.0" and "Implementing and Supporting Microsoft Internet Information Server 4.0."

➤ *MCSE (Microsoft Certified Systems Engineer)*—Anyone who has a current MCSE is warranted to possess a high level of expertise with Windows NT

Table 1 MCSD Requirements*

Core

Choose 1 from the desktop applications development group	
▶ Exam 70-016	Designing and Implementing Desktop Applications with Microsoft Visual C++ 6.0
Exam 70-156	Designing and Implementing Desktop Applications with Microsoft Visual FoxPro 6.0
Exam 70-176	Designing and Implementing Desktop Applications with Microsoft Visual Basic 6.0
Choose 1 from the distributed applications development group	
Exam 70-015	Designing and Implementing Distributed Applications with Microsoft Visual C++ 6.0
Exam 70-155	Designing and Implementing Distributed Applications with Microsoft Visual FoxPro 6.0
Exam 70-175	Designing and Implementing Distributed Applications with Microsoft Visual Basic 6.0
This solution architecture exam is required	
Exam 70-100	Analyzing Requirements and Defining Solution Architectures

Elective

Choose 1 from this group	
Exam 70-015	Designing and Implementing Distributed Applications with Microsoft Visual C++ 6.0
▶ Exam 70-016	Designing and Implementing Desktop Applications with Microsoft Visual C++ 6.0
Exam 70-019	Designing and Implementing Data Warehouses with Microsoft SQL Server 7.0
Exam 70-024	Developing Applications with C++ Using the Microsoft Foundation Class Library
Exam 70-025	Implementing OLE in Microsoft Foundation Class Applications
Exam 70-029	Designing and Implementing Databases with Microsoft SQL Server 7.0
Exam 70-055	Designing and Implementing Web Sites with Microsoft FrontPage 98
Exam 70-057	Designing and Implementing Commerce Solutions with Microsoft Site Server 3.0, Commerce Edition
Exam 70-097	Designing and Implementing Database Applications with Microsoft Access 2000
Exam 70-105	Designing and Implementing Collaborative Solutions with Microsoft Outlook 2000 and Microsoft Exchange Server 5.5
Exam 70-165	Developing Applications with Microsoft Visual Basic 5.0
Exam 70-175	Designing and Implementing Distributed Applications with Microsoft Visual Basic 6.0
Exam 70-176	Designing and Implementing Desktop Applications with Microsoft Visual Basic 6.0
Exam 70-069	Application Development with Microsoft Access for Windows 95 and the Microsoft Access Developer's Toolkit
Exam 70-091	Designing and Implementing Solutions with Microsoft Office 2000 and Microsoft Visual Basic for Applications

(continued)

Choose 1 from this group *(continued)*	
Exam 70-152	Designing and Implementing Web Solutions with Microsoft Visual InterDev 6.0
Exam 70-155	Designing and Implementing Distributed Applications with Microsoft FoxPro 6.0
Exam 70-156	Designing and Implementing Desktop Applications with Microsoft Visual FoxPro 6.0

* This is not a complete listing—you can still be tested on some earlier versions of these products. However, we have tried to include the most recent versions so that you may test on these versions and thus be certified longer. We have not included any tests that are scheduled to be retired.

Core exams that can also be used as elective exams can be counted only once toward certification. The same test cannot be used as both a core and an elective exam.

(version 3.51 or 4) and other Microsoft operating systems and products. This credential is designed to prepare individuals to plan, implement, maintain, and support information systems and networks built around Microsoft Windows NT and its BackOffice family of products.

To obtain an MCSE, an individual must pass four core operating system exams, plus two elective exams. The operating system exams require individuals to demonstrate competence with desktop and server operating systems and with networking components.

You must pass at least two Windows NT-related exams to obtain an MCSE: "Implementing and Supporting Microsoft Windows NT Server" (version 3.51 or 4) and "Implementing and Supporting Microsoft Windows NT Server in the Enterprise" (version 3.51 or 4). These tests are intended to indicate an individual's knowledge of Windows NT in smaller, simpler networks and in larger, more complex, and heterogeneous networks, respectively.

You must pass two additional tests as well. These tests relate to networking and desktop operating systems. At present, the networking requirement can be satisfied only by passing the Networking Essentials test. The desktop operating system test can be satisfied by passing a Windows 95, Windows NT Workstation (the version must match whichever core NT curriculum you are pursuing), or Windows 98 test.

The two remaining exams are elective exams. An elective exam may fall in any number of subject or product areas, primarily BackOffice components. These include tests on Internet Explorer 4, SQL Server, IIS, SNA Server, Exchange Server, Systems Management Server, and the like. However, it's also possible to test out on electives by taking advanced networking tests such as "Internetworking with Microsoft TCP/IP on Microsoft Windows NT" (but here again, the version of Windows NT involved must match the version for the core requirements taken).

Whatever mix of tests is completed toward MCSE certification, individuals must pass six tests to meet the MCSE requirements. It's common for the entire process to take a year or so, and many individuals find that they must take a test more than once to pass. Our primary goal with the *Exam Cram* series is to make it possible, given proper study and preparation, to pass all Microsoft certification tests on the first try.

➤ *MCT (Microsoft Certified Trainer)*—Microsoft Certified Trainers are individuals deemed able to deliver elements of the official Microsoft curriculum based on technical knowledge and instructional ability. Therefore, if you are seeking MCT credentials (which are granted on a course-by-course basis), you need to pass the related certification exam for a course and to take the official Microsoft training on the subject, as well as to demonstrate an ability to teach. MCT candidates must also possess a current MCSE.

The teaching skill criterion may be satisfied by proving that one has already attained training certification from Novell, Banyan, Lotus, the Santa Cruz Operation, or Cisco, or by taking a Microsoft-sanctioned workshop on instruction. Microsoft makes it clear that MCTs are important cogs in the Microsoft training channels. Instructors must be MCTs before Microsoft will allow them to teach in any of its official training channels, including Microsoft's affiliated Authorized Technical Education Centers (ATECs), Authorized Academic Training Programs (AATPs), and the Microsoft Online Institute (MOLI).

Microsoft has announced that the MCP+I and MCSE+I credentials will not be continued when the MCSE exams for Windows 2000 are in full swing because the skill set for the Internet portion of the program has been included in the new MCSE program. Therefore, details on these tracks are not provided here; go to **www.microsoft.com/train_cert/** if you need more information.

Certification is an ongoing activity. Once a Microsoft product becomes obsolete, MCPs typically have 12 to 18 months in which to recertify on current product versions. (If individuals do not recertify within the specified period, their certification becomes invalid.) Because technology keeps changing and new products continually supplant old ones, this should come as no surprise.

The best place to keep tabs on the MCP program and its various certifications is on the Microsoft Web site. The current root URL for the MCP program is at **www.microsoft.com/mcp/**. However, Microsoft's Web site changes frequently, so if this URL doesn't work, try using the search tool on Microsoft's site with either "MCP" or the quoted phrase "Microsoft Certified Professional program" as the search string. This will help you find the latest and most accurate information about the company's certification programs.

Taking A Certification Exam

Alas, testing is not free. Each computer-based MCP exam costs $100, and if you do not pass, you may retest for an additional $100 for each additional try. In the United States and Canada, tests are administered by Sylvan Prometric and Virtual University Enterprises (VUE). Here's how you can contact them:

➤ *Sylvan Prometric*—You can sign up for a test through the company's Web site at **www.slspro.com**. You can also register by phone at 800-755-3926 (within the United States or Canada) or at 410-843-8000 (outside the United States and Canada).

➤ *Virtual University Enterprises*—You can sign up for a test or get the phone numbers for local testing centers through the Web page at **www.microsoft.com/train_cert/mcp/vue_info.htm**.

To sign up for a test, you must possess a valid credit card or contact either company for mailing instructions to send it a check (in the United States). Only when payment is verified, or a check has cleared, can you actually register for a test.

To schedule an exam, call Sylvan or VUE, or sign up online at least one day in advance. To cancel or reschedule an exam, you must call by 7 P.M. (Pacific time) the day before the scheduled test (or you may be charged, even if you don't appear to take the test). When you want to schedule a test, have the following information ready:

➤ Your name, organization, and mailing address.

➤ Your Microsoft test ID. (Inside the United States, this is your Social Security number; citizens of other nations should call ahead to find out what type of identification number is required to register for a test.)

➤ The name and number of the exam you wish to take.

➤ A method of payment. (As already mentioned, a credit card is the most convenient method, but alternate means can be arranged in advance, if necessary.)

After you sign up for a test, you'll be informed as to when and where the test is scheduled. Try to arrive at least 15 minutes early. You must supply two forms of identification to be admitted into the testing room—one of which must be a photo ID.

All exams are completely "closed book." In fact, you will not be permitted to take anything with you into the testing area. However, you will be furnished with a blank sheet of paper and a pen. I suggest that you immediately write down on that sheet of paper all the information you've memorized for the test.

In *Exam Cram* books, this information appears on The Cram Sheet inside the front of each book. You'll have some time to compose yourself, record this information, and even take a sample orientation exam before you must begin the real thing. I suggest you take the orientation test before taking your first exam, but because they're all more or less identical in layout, behavior, and controls, you probably won't need to do this more than once.

When you complete a Microsoft certification exam, the software will tell you whether you've passed or failed. Results are broken into several topic areas. Even if you fail, I suggest you ask for—and keep—the detailed report that the test administrator should print for you. You can use this report to help you prepare for another go-around, if needed.

If you need to retake an exam, you'll have to call Sylvan Prometric or VUE, schedule a new test date, and pay another $100. Microsoft has the following policy regarding failed tests: The first time you fail a test, you are able to retake the test the next day. However, if you fail a second time, you must wait 14 days before retaking that test. If you do fail, I do not recommend taking the exam again the next day unless you just missed a passing grade. To me, a week seems about ideal—it gives you enough time to bone up on those areas in which you had problems while also making sure that the types of questions you encountered are fresh in your mind.

Tracking MCP Status

As soon as you pass any Microsoft exam (other than Networking Essentials), you'll attain Microsoft Certified Professional (MCP) status. Microsoft also generates transcripts that indicate which exams you have passed and your corresponding test scores. You can order a transcript by email at any time by sending an email addressed to **mcp@msprograms.com**. You can also obtain a copy of your transcript by downloading the latest version of the MCT guide from the Web site and consulting the section titled "Key Contacts" for a list of telephone numbers and related contacts.

Once you pass the necessary set of exams (one for MCP, two for MCP+SB, or four for MCSD), you'll be certified. Official certification usually takes anywhere from four to six weeks, so don't expect to get your credentials overnight. When the package for a qualified certification arrives, it includes a Welcome Kit that contains a number of elements:

➤ An MCP, MCP+SB, or MCSD certificate, suitable for framing, along with a Professional Program Membership card and lapel pin.

➤ A license to use the MCP logo, thereby allowing you to use the logo in advertisements, promotions, and documents, as well as on letterhead, business cards, and so on. Along with the license comes an MCP logo sheet, which includes camera-ready artwork. (Note that before using any of the artwork, individuals must sign and return a licensing agreement that indicates they'll abide by its terms and conditions.)

➤ A subscription to *Microsoft Certified Professional Magazine*, which provides ongoing data about testing and certification activities, requirements, and changes to the program.

➤ A one-year subscription to the Microsoft Beta Evaluation program. This subscription will get you all beta products from Microsoft for the next year. (This does not include developer products. You must join the MSDN program or become an MCSD to qualify for developer beta products. To join the MSDN program, go to **http://msdn.microsoft.com/developer/join/**.)

Many people believe that the benefits of MCP certification go well beyond the perks that Microsoft provides to newly anointed members of this elite group. I'm starting to see more job listings that request or require applicants to have an MCP, MCP+SB, MCSD, and so on, and many individuals who complete the program can qualify for increases in pay and/or responsibility. As an official recognition of hard work and broad knowledge, one of the MCP credentials is a badge of honor in many IT organizations.

How To Prepare For An Exam

Preparing for any Microsoft product-related test (including Visual C++ 6 Desktop) requires that you obtain and study materials designed to provide comprehensive information about the product and its capabilities, plus Web site design and maintenance techniques, that will appear on the specific exam for which you are preparing. The following list of materials will help you study and prepare:

➤ The Visual C++ 6 product CD-ROM includes comprehensive online documentation and related materials; it should be a primary resource when you are preparing for the test.

➤ The Microsoft TechNet CD-ROM delivers numerous electronic titles on Visual C++ 6. Its offerings include Product Manuals, Product Facts, Technical Notes, Tips and Techniques, Tools and Utilities, and information on how to access the Seminars Online training materials for Visual C++ 6. A subscription to TechNet costs $299 per year but is well worth the price. Visit **ww.microsoft.com/technet/** and check out the information under the "TechNet Subscription" menu entry for more details.

Don't ignore the Microsoft Developer's Network CD-ROM that comes with the Enterprise edition of Visual C++ 6. You can get the latest version online at **www.msdn.microsoft.com**—the materials include technical articles, tips the Knowledge Base, books, and more.

➤ Find, download, and use the exam prep materials, practice tests, and self-assessment exams on the Microsoft Training And Certification Download page (**www.microsoft.com/train_cert/download/downld.htm**).

In addition, you'll probably find any or all of the following materials useful in your quest for Visual C++ 6 expertise:

➤ *Microsoft Training Kits*—Although there's no training kit currently available from Microsoft Press for Visual C++ 6, many other topics have such kits. It's worthwhile to check to see if Microsoft has come out with anything by the time you need this information.

➤ *Study Guides*—Several publishers (including Certification Insider Press) offer learning materials necessary to pass the tests. The Certification Insider Press series includes:

  ➤ *The* Exam Cram *series*—These books give you information about the material you need to know to pass the tests.

  ➤ *The* Exam Prep *series*—These books provide a greater level of detail than the *Exam Cram* books.

➤ *Classroom Training*—ATECs, AATPs, MOLI, and unlicensed third-party training companies (such as Wave Technologies, American Research Group, Learning Tree, Data-Tech, and others) all offer classroom training on Visual C++ 6. These companies aim to help prepare developers to use Visual C++ 6 to pass the "Designing and Implementing Desktop Applications with Microsoft Visual C++ 6.0." exam. Although such training runs upwards of $350 per day in class, most of the individuals lucky enough to partake (including your humble author, who also teaches such courses) find them to be quite worthwhile.

➤ *Other Publications*—You'll find direct references to other publications and resources in this text, but there's no shortage of materials available about Visual C++ 6. To help you sift through some of the publications out there, I end each chapter with a "Need To Know More?" section that provides pointers to more complete and exhaustive resources covering the chapter's information. This should give you an idea of where I think you should look for further discussion.

By far, this set of required and recommended materials represents a nonpareil collection of sources and resources for Visual C++ 6 and related topics. I anticipate that you'll find that this book belongs in this company. In the section that follows, I explain how this book works, and I give you some good reasons why this book counts as a member of the required and recommended materials list.

About This Book

Each topical *Exam Cram* chapter follows a regular structure, along with graphical cues about important or useful information. Here's the structure of a typical chapter:

➤ *Opening Hotlists*—Each chapter begins with a list of the terms, tools, and techniques that you must learn and understand before you can be fully conversant with that chapter's subject matter. I follow the hotlists with one or two introductory paragraphs to set the stage for the rest of the chapter.

➤ *Topical Coverage*—After the opening hotlists, each chapter covers a series of topics related to the chapter's subject title. Throughout this section, I highlight topics or concepts likely to appear on a test using a special Exam Alert layout, like this:

This is what an Exam Alert looks like. Normally, an Exam Alert stresses concepts, terms, software, or activities that are likely to relate to one or more certification test questions. For that reason, I think any information found offset in Exam Alert format is worthy of unusual attentiveness on your part. Indeed, most of the information that appears on The Cram Sheet appears as Exam Alerts within the text.

Pay close attention to material flagged as an Exam Alert; although all the information in this book pertains to what you need to know to pass the exam, I flag certain items that are really important. You'll find what appears in the meat of each chapter to be worth knowing, too, when preparing for the test. Because this book's material is very condensed, I recommend that you use this book along with other resources to achieve the maximum benefit.

In addition to the Exam Alerts, I have provided tips that will help you build a better foundation for Visual C++ 6 knowledge. Although the information may not be on the exam, it's certainly related and will help you become a better test-taker.

This is how tips are formatted. Keep your eyes open for these, and you'll become a Visual C++ 6 guru in no time!

➤ *Practice Questions*—Although I talk about test questions and topics throughout each chapter, this section presents a series of mock test questions and explanations of both correct and incorrect answers. I also try to point out especially tricky questions by using a special icon, like this:

Ordinarily, this icon flags the presence of a particularly devious inquiry, if not an outright trick question. Trick questions are calculated to be answered incorrectly if not read more than once—and carefully at that. Although they're not ubiquitous, such questions make regular appearances on the Microsoft exams. That's why I say exam questions are as much about reading comprehension as they are about knowing your material inside out and backwards.

➤ *Details And Resources*—Every chapter ends with a section titled "Need To Know More?". These sections provide direct pointers to Microsoft and third-party resources offering more details on the chapter's subject. In addition, these sections try to rank or at least rate the quality and thoroughness of the topic's coverage by each resource. If you find a resource you like in this collection, use it, but don't feel compelled to use all the resources. On the other hand, I recommend only resources I use on a regular basis, so none of my recommendations will be a waste of your time or money (but purchasing them all at once probably represents an expense that many network administrators and would-be MCSDs might find hard to justify).

The bulk of the book follows this chapter structure slavishly, but there are a few other elements I'd like to point out. Chapter 24 is a sample test that provides a good review of the material presented throughout the book to ensure you're ready for the exam. Chapter 25 is an answer key to the sample test that appears in Chapter 24. Additionally, you'll find a glossary that explains terms and an index that you can use to track down terms as they appear in the text.

Finally, the tear-out Cram Sheet attached next to the inside front cover of this *Exam Cram* book represents a condensed and compiled collection of facts, figures, and tips that I think you should memorize before taking the test. Because you can dump this information out of your head onto a piece of paper before taking the exam, you can master this information by brute force—you need to remember it only long enough to write it down when you walk into the test room. You might even want to look at it in the car or in the lobby of the testing center just before you walk in to take the test.

How To Use This Book

If you're prepping for a first-time test, I've structured the topics in this book to build on one another. Therefore, some topics in later chapters make more sense after you've read earlier chapters. That's why I suggest you read this book from front to back for your initial test preparation. If you need to brush up on a topic or you have to bone up for a second try, use the index or table of contents to go straight to the topics and questions that you need to study. Beyond helping you prepare for the tests, I think you'll find this book useful as a tightly focused reference to some of the most important aspects of Visual C++ 6.

Given all the book's elements and its specialized focus, I've tried to create a tool that will help you prepare for—and pass—Microsoft Exam 70-016, "Designing and Implementing Desktop Applications with Microsoft Visual C++ 6.0." Please share your feedback on the book with us, especially if you have ideas about how I can improve it for future test-takers. I'll consider everything you say carefully, and I'll respond to all suggestions.

Please send your questions or comments to me at **jlacey@rclink.net** or the publisher at **cipq@coriolis.com**. Please remember to include the title of the book in your message; otherwise, we'll be forced to guess which book you're writing about. And we don't like to guess—we want to *know*! Also, be sure to check out the Web pages at **www.certificationinsider.com**, where you'll find information updates, commentary, and certification information.

Thanks, and enjoy the book!

Self-Assessment

Based on recent statistics from Microsoft, as many as 400,000 individuals are at some stage of the certification process but haven't yet received an MCP or other Microsoft certification. Three or four times that number may be considering whether or not to obtain a Microsoft certification of some kind. That's a huge audience!

The reason this Self-Assessment is included in this *Exam Cram* book is to help you evaluate your readiness to tackle MCSD certification. It should also help you understand what you need to master the topic of this book—namely, Exam 70-016, "Designing and Implementing Desktop Applications with Microsoft Visual C++ 6.0." But before you tackle this Self-Assessment, let's discuss concerns you may face when pursuing an MCSD, and what an ideal MCSD candidate might look like.

MCSDs In The Real World

In the next section, we describe an ideal MCSD candidate, knowing full well that only a few real candidates will meet this ideal. In fact, our description of that ideal candidate might seem downright scary—but take heart: Although the requirements to obtain an MCSD may seem formidable, they are *not* impossible to meet. However, you should be keenly aware that it does take time, requires some expense, and consumes substantial effort to get through the process.

You can get all the real-world motivation you need from knowing that many others have gone before, so you will be able to follow in their footsteps. If you're willing to tackle the process seriously and do what it takes to obtain the necessary experience and knowledge, you can take—and pass—all the certification tests involved in obtaining an MCSD. In fact, we've designed these *Exam Crams*, and the companion *Exam Preps*, to make it as easy on you as possible to prepare for these exams. But prepare you must!

 There is currently no *Exam Prep* for the Visual C++ Desktop exam.

The same, of course, is true for other Microsoft certifications, including:

➤ MCSE, which is aimed at network engineers and requires four core exams and two electives for a total of six exams.

➤ Other Microsoft certifications, whose requirements range from one test (MCP or MCT) to many tests (MCP+SB, MCDBA).

The Ideal MCSD Candidate

Just to give you some idea of what an ideal MCSD candidate is like, here are some relevant statistics about the background and experience such an individual might have. Don't worry if you don't meet these qualifications, or don't come that close—this is a far from ideal world, and where you fall short is simply where you'll have more work to do.

➤ Academic or professional training in application design and development as well as relevant database design and usage.

➤ Typically, six years of professional development experience (33% of MCSDs have less than four years of experience, 20% have five to eight years of experience, and 48% have eight plus years of experience). This experience includes development tools such as Visual Basic, Visual C++, and so on. This must include application design, requirements analysis, debugging, distribution, and an understanding of the Microsoft Services Model.

➤ Three-plus years in a relational database environment designing and using database tools such as SQL Server and Access. The ideal MCSD will have performed both logical and physical database designs from entity modeling through normalization and database schema creation.

➤ A thorough understanding of issues involved in the creation and deployment of distributed applications to include knowledge of COM and DCOM, issues involved in the usage of in-process and out-of process components, and the logical and physical design of those components.

➤ An understanding of both operating system architectures (Windows 9x, NT) as they relate application as well as network issues to include Internet architectures. (You will not, of course, be expected to demonstrate the level of knowledge that a network engineer needs to have. Instead, you want to be familiar with the issues that networks—particularly the Internet—raise in client/server applications.)

Fundamentally, this boils down to a bachelor's degree in computer science, plus at least three to four years of development experience in a networked environment, involving relational database design and usage, and application architecture design, development, and deployment. Given the relative newness of the technologies involved, there are probably few certification candidates that meet these requirements. Particularly in the area of multi-tiered applications, most meet less than half of these requirements—at least, when they begin the certification process. But because those who have already achieved their MSCD certification have survived this ordeal, you can survive it too—especially if you heed what our Self-Assessment can tell you about what you already know and what you need to learn.

Put Yourself To The Test

The following series of questions and observations is designed to help you figure out how much work you must do to pursue Microsoft certification and what kinds of resources you may consult on your quest. Be absolutely honest in your answers, or you'll end up wasting money on exams you're not yet ready to take. There are no right or wrong answers, only steps along the path to certification. Only you can decide where you really belong in the broad spectrum of aspiring candidates.

Two things should be clear from the outset, however:

➤ Even a modest background in applications development will be helpful.

➤ Hands-on experience with Microsoft development products and technologies is an essential ingredient to certification success.

Educational Background

1. Have you ever taken any computer-programming classes? [Yes or No]

   If Yes, proceed to Question 2; if No, proceed to Question 5.

2. Have you taken any classes on applications design? [Yes or No]

   If Yes, you will probably be able to handle Microsoft's architecture and system component discussions. You will be expected, in most of the exams, to demonstrate core COM concepts. This will include an understanding of the implications of in-process and out-of process components, cross-process procedure calls, and so forth.

   If No, consider some basic reading in this area. The "Component Tools Guide" in the Visual Basic documentation is actually quite good and covers the core concepts. Third party COM books can also be helpful.

3. Have you taken any classes oriented specifically toward Visual Basic or C++? [Yes or No]

If Yes, you will probably be able to handle the programming related concepts and terms in the "Desktop Applications" and "Distributed Applications" portions of the MCSD track. Each section allows you to choose between a Visual Basic, a Visual FoxPro, or a Visual C++ exam. If you feel rusty, brush up on your VB or VC++ terminology by going through the Glossary in this book and the product documentation.

If No, and if you don't have a good deal of on-the-job experience, you might want to read one or two books in this topic area. *Visual Basic 6 Black Book*, by Steven Holzner, (Coriolis Group, 1998, ISBN 1-576109-283-1) is really quite good and is at an appropriate level.

4. Have you taken any database design classes? [Yes or No]

   If Yes, you will probably be able to handle questions related to general data access techniques. If you do not have experience specific to Microsoft Access or Microsoft SQL Server, you will want to touch up on concepts specific to either of those two products.

   If No, you will want to look over the exams that you can take from the "Elective Exams" portion of the MSCD. There include a wide variety covering topics such as SQL Server and FrontPage. You may have expertise in one of these areas and should, therefore, aim to take one of those exams. All in all, whether you take the SQL Server (or Access) exam, you should consider reading a book or two on the subject. I like *Microsoft SQL Server 6.5 Unleashed*, by David Solomon, Ray Rankins, et al., (Sams Publishing, ISBN 0-672-39856-4), although this book is older and covers some of the concepts more appropriate to a DBA.

5. Have you done any reading on application design and development? [Yes or No]

   If Yes, go onto the next section, "Hands-On Experience."

   If No, be particularly alert to the questions asked in the next section, "Hands-On Experience." Frequently, a little experience goes a long way. For any areas where you may be weak, consider doing extra reading as outlined in questions 2, 3, and 4 above. Carefully review the Glossary in this book and take unfamiliar terms as cues to areas you need to brush up on. Look at the "Terms you'll need to know" and "Techniques you'll need to master" lists at the front of each chapter. Again, for any terms or techniques that are unfamiliar, consider boning up in those areas.

Hands-On Experience

The most important key to success on all of the Microsoft tests is hands-on experience, especially with the core tool on which you are testing (Visual Basic, Visual FoxPro, or Visual C++), as well as an understanding of COM and ADO. If we leave you with only one realization after taking this Self-Assessment, it should be that there's no substitute for time spent developing real world applications. The development experience should range from both logical and physical design to the creation of remote COM services and to database programming. The recurring theme through nearly all of the tests will be COM and database techniques.

6. Have you created COM components?

    If Yes, you will probably be prepared for Exam 70-100, "Analyzing Requirements and Defining Solution Architectures." This satisfies the "Solutions Architecture" section of the MCSD requirements. Go to Question 7.

    If No, you need to bone up on COM concepts as outlined in Question 2 earlier.

7. Have you done database programming?

    If Yes, go to Question 8.

    If No, you will be in a weak position on all the tests. You need to consult a book such as the one recommended in Question 3 above.

8. Have you done ADO development?

    If Yes, go to Question 9.

    If No, you need to consult an ADO reference. Use the MSDN library on your product's (Visual Basic, Visual C++, or Visual Studio) CD-ROM and review the ADO articles. Additionally, check out a book such as the one recommended in Question 4.

9. Have you developed with Visual Basic?

    If Yes, you should be prepared to take Exam 70-176, "Designing and Implementing Desktop Applications with Microsoft Visual Basic 6.0." This will satisfy the Desktop Applications Development requirement. Go to Question 10.

    If No, go to Question 10.

10. Have you developed with Visual C++?

    If Yes, you should be prepared to take Exam 70-016, "Designing and Implementing Desktop Applications with Microsoft Visual C++ 6.0." If you also answered yes to Question 9, you can use Exam 70-016 as your Elective requirement (see Question 12). Go to Question 11.

    If No and if you also answered No to Question 9, then you probably should consider getting some real-world experience with either Visual Basic or Visual C++. (If you answered Yes to Question 9 and No to this question, you will want to take Exam 70-176.)

11. Have you developed Distributed applications with either Visual Basic or Visual C++?

    If Yes, you should be prepared to take either Exam 70-175, "Designing and Implementing Distributed Applications with Microsoft Visual Basic 6.0" or Exam 70-015, " Designing and Implementing Distributed Applications with Microsoft Visual C++ 6.0." Either exam will satisfy the Distributed Applications requirement of the MSCD. Go to Question 12.

    If No, consult the book recommended in Question 3.

12. Have you used one of the products listed in the "Elective Exams" section of the MCSD?

    If Yes, go ahead and take that exam after consulting the Microsoft Web site for a list of the MCSD requirements (see Chapter 1).

    If No, consider boning up on Microsoft Access or Microsoft SQL Server, as outlined in Question 4 above, and taking one of those exams. If you are qualified in both Visual Basic and Visual C++, consider taking Exam 70-016 (Visual C++ Desktop) for the Desktop Applications Development section and Exam 70-176 (Visual Basic Desktop) for the Elective.

Testing Your Exam-Readiness

Whether you attend a formal class on a specific topic to get ready for an exam or use written materials to study on your own, some preparation for the Microsoft certification exams is essential. At $100 a try, pass or fail, you want to do everything you can to pass on your first try. That's where studying comes in.

We have included practice questions at the end of each chapter. If you do well, take the practice exam in Chapter 15 to see how you do.

For any given subject, consider taking a class if you've tackled self-study materials, taken the test, and failed anyway. The opportunity to interact with an instructor and fellow students can make all the difference in the world, if you can afford that privilege. For information about Microsoft classes, visit the Training and Certification page at **www.microsoft.com/train_cert/** (use the "Find a Course" link).

If you can't afford to take a class, visit the Training and Certification page anyway, because it also includes pointers to free practice exams. And even if you can't afford to spend much at all, you should still invest in some low-cost practice exams from commercial vendors, because they can help you assess your readiness to pass a test better than any other tool. The following links may be of interest to you in locating practice exams:

➤ *SelfTest Software (www.stsware.com)*—At the time of this writing, the cost for the first test ordered was $79. The Visual Basic 6 exam was not yet ready. The VB5 exam included 390 questions.

➤ *MeasureUp (www.measureup.com)*—At the time of this writing, tests cost $99. The Visual Basic 6 exam was not yet ready. The Visual Basic 5 test included 180 practice questions.

13. Have you taken a practice exam on your chosen test subject? [Yes or No]

   If Yes and you scored 70 percent or better, you're probably ready to tackle the real thing. If your score isn't above that crucial threshold, keep at it until you break that barrier. (If you scored above 80, you should feel pretty confident.)

   If No, obtain all the free and low-budget practice tests you can find (see the list above) and get to work. Keep at it until you can break the passing threshold comfortably.

 When it comes to assessing your test readiness, there is no better way than to take a good-quality practice exam and pass with a score of 70 percent or better. If you pass an exam at 80 percent or better, you're probably in great shape.

Assessing Readiness For Exam

Beyond the general exam-readiness information in the previous section, you can do several things to prepare for the Visual Basic 6 Desktop exam. As you're getting ready for Exam 70-176, you should cruise the Web looking for "braindumps" (recollections of test topics and experiences recorded by others) to help you anticipate topics you're likely to encounter on the test. A good place to start is Durham Software's Web site (**www.durhamsoftware.com/cert**).

> You can't be sure that a braindump's author can provide correct answers. Thus, use the questions to guide your studies, but don't rely on the answers in a braindump to lead you to the truth. Double-check everything you find in any braindump.

Microsoft exam mavens also recommend checking the Microsoft Knowledge Base (available on its own CD as part of the TechNet collection, or on the Microsoft Web site at **http://support.microsoft.com/support/**) for "meaningful technical support issues" that relate to your exam's topics. Although we're not sure exactly what the quoted phrase means, we have also noticed some overlap between technical support questions on particular products and troubleshooting questions on the exams for those products.

One last note: It might seem counterintuitive to talk about hands-on experience in the context of the Visual Basic Desktop exam. But as you review the material for that exam, you'll realize that real-world, Visual Basic development experience will be invaluable. While there will undoubtedly be some "paper-MCSDs" emerging from the examination process, the exams are increasingly being designed to pose real-world problems. For these types of questions, book learning simply can't replace having actually "done it."

Onward, Through The Fog!

Once you've assessed your readiness, undertaken the right background studies, obtained the hands-on experience that will help you understand the products and technologies at work, and reviewed the many sources of information to help you prepare for a test, you'll be ready to take a round of practice tests. When your scores come back positive enough to get you through the exam, you're ready to go after the real thing. If you follow our assessment regime, you'll not only know what you need to study, but when you're ready to make a test date at Sylvan or VUE. Good luck!

Microsoft
Certification Exams

Terms and concepts you'll need to understand:

√ Radio button

√ Checkbox

√ Exhibit

√ Multiple-choice question formats

√ Careful reading

√ Process of elimination

√ Adaptive tests

√ Fixed-length tests

√ Simulations

Techniques you'll need to master:

√ Assessing your exam-readiness

√ Preparing to take a certification exam

√ Practicing (to make perfect)

√ Making the best use of the testing software

√ Budgeting your time

√ Saving the hardest questions until last

√ Guessing (as a last resort)

Exam taking is not something that most people anticipate eagerly, no matter how well prepared they may be. In most cases, familiarity helps offset test anxiety. In plain English, this means you probably won't be as nervous when you take your fourth or fifth Microsoft certification exam as you'll be when you take your first one.

Whether it's your first exam or your tenth, understanding the details of exam taking (how much time to spend on questions, the environment you'll be in, and so on) and the exam software will help you concentrate on the material rather than on the setting. Likewise, mastering a few basic exam-taking skills should help you recognize—and perhaps even outfox—some of the tricks and snares you're bound to find in some of the exam questions.

This chapter, besides explaining the exam environment and software, describes some proven exam-taking strategies that you should be able to use to your advantage.

Assessing Exam-Readiness

Before you take any more Microsoft exams, I strongly recommend that you read through and take the Self-Assessment included with this book (it appears just before this chapter). This will help you compare your knowledge base to the requirements for obtaining an MCSD, and it will also help you identify parts of your background or experience that may be in need of improvement, enhancement, or further learning. If you get the right set of basics under your belt, obtaining Microsoft certification will be that much easier.

Once you've gone through the Self-Assessment, you can remedy those topical areas where your background or experience may not measure up to an ideal certification candidate. But you can also tackle subject matter for individual tests at the same time, so you can continue making progress while you're catching up in some areas.

Once you've worked through an *Exam Cram*, read the supplementary materials, and taken the practice test, you'll have a pretty clear idea of when you should be ready to take the real exam. I strongly recommend that you keep practicing until your scores top the 70 percent mark; 75 percent would be a good goal to give yourself margin for error in a real exam situation (where stress will play more of a role than when you practice). When you hit that point, you should be ready to go. However, if you get through the practice exam in this book without attaining that score, you should keep taking practice tests and studying the materials until you get there. You'll find more information about other practice test vendors in the Self-Assessment, along with even more pointers on how to study and prepare. But now, on to the exam!

The Exam Situation

When you arrive at the testing center where you scheduled your exam, you'll need to sign in with an exam coordinator. He or she will ask you to show two forms of identification, one of which must be a photo ID. After you've signed in and your time slot arrives, you'll be asked to deposit any books, bags, or other items you brought with you. Then, you'll be escorted into a closed room. Typically, the room will be furnished with anywhere from one to half a dozen computers, and each workstation will be separated from the others by dividers designed to keep you from seeing what's happening on someone else's computer.

You'll be furnished with a pen or pencil and a blank sheet of paper, or, in some cases, an erasable plastic sheet and an erasable pen. You're allowed to write down anything you want on both sides of this sheet. Before the exam, you should memorize as much of the material that appears on The Cram Sheet (in the front of this book) as you can, so you can write that information on the blank sheet as soon as you are seated in front of the computer. You can refer to your rendition of The Cram Sheet anytime you like during the test, but you'll have to surrender the sheet when you leave the room.

Most test rooms feature a wall with a large picture window. This permits the exam coordinator to monitor the room, to prevent exam-takers from talking to one another, and to observe anything out of the ordinary that might go on. The exam coordinator will have preloaded the appropriate Microsoft certification exam—for this book, that's Exam 70-016—and you'll be permitted to start as soon as you're seated in front of the computer.

All Microsoft certification exams allow a certain maximum amount of time in which to complete your work (this time is indicated on the exam by an onscreen counter/clock, so you can check the time remaining whenever you like). The fixed-length Visual C++ Desktop exam consists of 43 randomly selected questions. You may take up to 90 minutes to complete the exam.

All Microsoft certification exams are computer generated and use a multiple-choice format. Although this may sound quite simple, the questions are constructed not only to check your mastery of basic facts and figures of Visual C++ and related tools and technologies, but also to require you to evaluate one or more sets of circumstances or requirements. Often, you'll be asked to give more than one answer to a question. Likewise, you might be asked to select the best or most effective solution to a problem from a range of choices, all of which technically are correct. Taking an exam is quite an adventure, and it involves real thinking. This book shows you what to expect and how to deal with the potential problems, puzzles, and predicaments.

Some Microsoft exams employ more advanced testing capabilities than might immediately meet the eye. Although the questions that appear are still multiple choice, the logic that drives them is more complex than older Microsoft tests, which use a fixed sequence of questions (called a *fixed-length* computerized exam). Other exams employ a sophisticated user interface (which Microsoft calls a *simulation*) to test your knowledge of the software and systems under consideration in a more or less "live" environment that behaves just like the original.

For upcoming exams, Microsoft is turning to a well-known technique, called *adaptive testing*, to establish a test-taker's level of knowledge and product competence. These exams look the same as fixed-length exams, but an adaptive exam discovers the level of difficulty at and below which an individual test-taker can correctly answer questions. At the same time, Microsoft is in the process of converting all its older fixed-length exams into adaptive exams as well.

Test-takers with differing levels of knowledge or ability therefore see different sets of questions; individuals with high levels of knowledge or ability are presented with a smaller set of more difficult questions, whereas individuals with lower levels of knowledge are presented with a larger set of easier questions. Both individuals may answer the same percentage of questions correctly, but the test-taker with a higher knowledge or ability level will score higher because his or her questions are worth more.

Also, the lower-level test-taker will probably answer more questions than his or her more knowledgeable colleague. This explains why adaptive tests use ranges of values to define the number of questions and the amount of time it takes to complete the test.

Adaptive tests work by evaluating the test-taker's most recent answer. A correct answer leads to a more difficult question (and the test software's estimate of the test-taker's knowledge and ability level is raised). An incorrect answer leads to a less difficult question (and the test software's estimate of the test-taker's knowledge and ability level is lowered). This process continues until the test targets the test-taker's true ability level. The exam ends when the test-taker's level of accuracy meets a statistically acceptable value (in other words, when his or her performance demonstrates an acceptable level of knowledge and ability) or when the maximum number of items has been presented (in which case, the test-taker is almost certain to fail).

Microsoft tests come in one form or the other—either they're fixed-length or they're adaptive. Therefore, you must take the test in whichever form it appears—you can't choose one form over another. However, if anything, it pays off even more to prepare thoroughly for an adaptive exam than for a fixed-length one: The penalties for answering incorrectly are built into the test itself on an adaptive exam, whereas the layout remains the same for a fixed-length test, no matter how many questions you answer incorrectly.

The biggest difference between an adaptive test and a fixed-length test is that, on a fixed-length test, you can revisit questions after you've read them over one or more times. On an adaptive test, you must answer the question when it's presented, and you'll have no opportunities to revisit that question thereafter. As of this writing, the Visual C++ Desktop exam is a fixed-length exam, but this can change at any time. Therefore, you must prepare as if it were an adaptive exam to ensure the best possible results.

In the section that follows, you'll learn more about what Microsoft test questions look like and how they must be answered.

Exam Layout And Design

Some exam questions require you to select a single answer, whereas others ask you to select one or more correct answers. The following multiple-choice question requires you to select a single correct answer. Following the question is a brief summary of each potential answer and why it is either right or wrong.

Question 1

You are implementing an in-process COM component that has a ProgID of "MathComponent". In which subkey of HKEY_CLASSES_ROOT is the fully qualified path and DLL name of your server located?

○ a. CLSID\InprocServer32

○ b. CLSID\{*clsid*}\InprocServer32

○ c. InprocServer32

○ d. ProgID\InprocServer32

The correct answer is b. COM classes are registered beneath the **HKEY_CLASSES_ROOT\CLSID** key. Because answer b is the only correct answer, answers a, c, and d are incorrect. Each class is a subkey of **HKEY_CLASSES_ROOT\CLSID**, where the name of the class subkey corresponds to the class **GUID**. The class subkey has several critical subkeys hanging off it, which vary depending on the type of server. In this case, the COM component is an in-process server, so the path and DLL name are located in the **InProcServer32** subkey. The complete entry would look like this: HKEY_CLASSES_ROOT\CLSID\{*clsid*}InprocServer32 = "C:\My Components\MathComponent.dll".

This sample question format corresponds closely to the Microsoft certification exam format—the only difference on the exam is that questions are not followed by answer keys. To select an answer, position the cursor over the radio button next to the answer. Then, click the mouse button to select the answer.

Let's examine a question where one or more answers are possible. This type of question provides checkboxes rather than radio buttons for marking all appropriate selections.

Question 2

Which statements are true? [Check all the correct answers]

❑ a. A CFile object provides an actual connection to a physical file.

❑ b. MFC always provides version checking on embedded objects derived from CObject.

❑ c. MFC provides the CArchive class to facilitate transferring a document's data to a storage medium.

❑ d. CFile provides buffered file I/O.

Answers a and c are correct. **CFile** and **CArchive** objects work together to provide serialization of MFC objects. The **CFile** object provides unbuffered, binary disk I/O to and from a physical file. The **CArchive** object provides a type-safe buffering mechanism for writing or reading serializable objects to or from a **CFile** object. The insertion and extraction operators are overloaded both as member functions of **CArchive** and as global functions for a number of different data types. These overloads provide version checking. However, MFC does not provide an overload for **CObject** embedded objects. Therefore, answers b and d are incorrect.

For this type of question, more than one answer may be required. As far as can be determined (and Microsoft won't comment), such questions are scored as wrong unless all the required selections are chosen. In other words, a partially correct answer does not result in partial credit when the test is scored. For Question 2, you have to check the boxes next to items a and c to obtain credit for a correct answer. Notice that picking the right answers also means knowing why the other answers are wrong.

Although these two basic types of questions can appear in many forms, they constitute the foundation on which all the Microsoft certification exam questions rest. More complex questions include exhibits, which are usually screenshots of various Visual C++ tools or utilities. For some of these questions, you'll be asked to make a selection by clicking on a checkbox or radio button on the screenshot itself. For others, you'll be expected to use the information displayed therein to guide your answer to the question. Familiarity with the underlying tool or utility is your key to choosing the correct answer(s).

Other questions involving exhibits use charts or network diagrams to help document a workplace scenario that you'll be asked to troubleshoot or configure. Careful attention to such exhibits is the key to success. Be prepared to toggle frequently between the exhibit and the question as you work.

Recognizing Your Test Type: Fixed-Length Or Adaptive

When you begin your exam, the software will tell you the test is adaptive, if in fact the version you're taking is presented as an adaptive test. If your introductory materials fail to mention this, you're probably taking a fixed-length test. However, when you see the first question, you'll be able to tell for sure: If it includes a checkbox that lets you mark the question (for later return and review) you'll know you're taking a fixed-length test, because adaptive test questions can only be visited (and answered) once, and they include no such checkbox.

The Fixed-Length Test-Taking Strategy

A well-known principle when taking fixed-length exams is to first read over the entire exam from start to finish while answering only those questions you feel absolutely sure of. On subsequent passes, you can dive into more complex questions more deeply, knowing how many such questions you have left. On adaptive tests, you get only one shot at the question, which is why preparation is so crucial for such tests.

Fortunately, the Microsoft exam software for fixed-length tests makes the multiple-visit approach easy to implement. At the top-left corner of each question is a checkbox that permits you to mark that question for a later visit. (Note that marking questions makes review easier, but you can return to any question if you're willing to click the Forward or Back buttons repeatedly.) As you read each question, if you answer only those you're sure of and mark for review those that you're not sure of, you can keep working through a decreasing list of questions as you answer the trickier ones in order.

There's at least one potential benefit to reading the exam over completely before answering the trickier questions: Sometimes, information supplied in later questions will shed more light on earlier questions. Other times, information you read in later questions might jog your memory about Visual C++ facts, figures, or behavior that also will help with earlier questions. Either way, you'll come out ahead if you defer those questions about which you're not absolutely sure.

Here are some question-handling strategies that apply only to fixed-length tests. Use them if you have the chance:

➤ When returning to a question after your initial read-through, read every word again—otherwise, your mind can fall quickly into a rut. Sometimes, revisiting a question after turning your attention elsewhere lets you see something you missed, but the strong tendency is to see what you've seen before. Try to avoid that tendency at all costs.

➤ If you return to a question more than twice, try to articulate to yourself what you don't understand about the question, why the answers don't appear to make sense, or what appears to be missing. If you chew on the subject for awhile, your subconscious might provide the details that are lacking, or you might notice a "trick" that will point to the right answer.

As you work your way through the exam, another counter that Microsoft thankfully provides will come in handy—the number of questions completed and questions outstanding. For fixed-length tests, it's wise to budget your time by making sure that you've completed one-quarter of the questions one-quarter of the way through the exam period (or the first 18 questions in the first 26 minutes) and three-quarters of the questions three-quarters of the way through (54 questions in the first 78 minutes).

If you're not finished when 100 minutes have elapsed, use the last 5 minutes to guess your way through the remaining questions. Remember, guessing is potentially more valuable than not answering, because blank answers are always wrong, but a guess may turn out to be right. If you don't have a clue about any of the remaining questions, pick answers at random, or choose all a's, b's, and so on. The important thing is to submit an exam for scoring that has an answer for every question.

When you near the end of your exam period, you're better off guessing than leaving questions unanswered.

The Adaptive Test-Taking Strategy

If one principle applies to taking an adaptive test, it could be summed up as "Get it right the first time." You cannot elect to skip a question and move on to the next one when taking an adaptive test, because the testing software uses your answer to the current question to select whatever question it plans to present to you next. Also, you cannot return to a question once you've moved on, because the software only gives you one chance to answer the question.

When you answer a question correctly, you are presented with a more difficult question next to help the software gauge your level of skill and ability. When you answer a question incorrectly, you are presented with a less difficult question, and the software lowers its current estimate of your skill and ability. This continues until the program settles into a reasonably accurate estimate of what you know and can do, and it takes you through somewhere between 25 and 35 questions, on average, as you complete the test.

The good news is that if you know your stuff, you'll probably finish most adaptive tests in 30 minutes or so. The bad news is that you must really, really know your stuff to do your best on an adaptive test. That's because some questions are so convoluted, complex, or hard to follow that you're bound to miss one or two, at a minimum, even if you do know your stuff. Therefore, the more you know, the better you'll do on an adaptive test, even accounting for the occasionally weird or unfathomable question that appears on these exams.

As of this writing, Microsoft has not advertised which tests are strictly adaptive. You'll be best served by preparing for the exam as if it were adaptive. That way, you should be prepared to pass no matter what kind of test you take (that is, fixed-length or adaptive). If you do end up taking a fixed-length test, remember our tips from the preceding section. They should help you improve on what you could do on an adaptive test.

If you encounter a question on an adaptive test that you can't answer, you must guess an answer. Because of the way the software works, you may have to suffer for your guess on the next question if you guess right, because you'll get a more difficult question next.

Exam-Taking Basics

The most important advice about taking any exam is this: Read each question carefully. Some questions are deliberately ambiguous, some use double negatives, and others use terminology in incredibly precise ways. I have taken numerous exams—both practice and live—and in nearly every one have missed at least one question because I didn't read it closely or carefully enough.

Here are some suggestions on how to deal with the tendency to jump to an answer too quickly:

➤ Make sure you read every word in the question. If you find yourself jumping ahead impatiently, go back and start over.

➤ As you read, try to restate the question in your own terms. If you can do this, you should be able to pick the correct answer(s) much more easily.

Above all, try to deal with each question by thinking through what you know about Visual C++ as well as the design and implementation of Win32 desktop applications—the characteristics, behaviors, facts, and figures involved. By reviewing what you know (and what you've written down on your information sheet), you'll often recall or understand things sufficiently to determine the answer to the question.

Question-Handling Strategies

Based on exams I have taken, some interesting trends have become apparent. For those questions that take only a single answer, usually two or three of the answers will be obviously incorrect, and two of the answers will be plausible—of course, only one can be correct. Unless the answer leaps out at you (if it does, reread the question to look for a trick; sometimes those are the ones you're most likely to get wrong), begin the process of answering by eliminating those answers that are most obviously wrong.

Things to look for in obviously wrong answers include spurious menu choices or utility names, nonexistent software options, and terminology you've never seen. If you've done your homework for an exam, no valid information should be completely new to you. In that case, unfamiliar or bizarre terminology probably indicates a totally bogus answer.

Numerous questions assume that the default behavior of a particular utility is in effect. If you know the defaults and understand what they mean, this knowledge will help you cut through many Gordian knots.

Mastering The Inner Game

In the final analysis, knowledge breeds confidence, and confidence breeds success. If you study the materials in this book carefully and review all the practice questions at the end of each chapter, you should become aware of those areas where additional learning and study are required.

Next, follow up by reading some or all of the materials recommended in the "Need To Know More?" section at the end of each chapter. The idea is to become familiar enough with the concepts and situations you find in the sample questions that you can reason your way through similar situations on a real exam. If you know the material, you have every right to be confident that you can pass the exam.

After you've worked your way through the book, take the practice exam in Chapter 24. This will provide a reality check and help you identify areas to study further. Make sure you follow up and review materials related to questions you miss on the practice exam before scheduling a real exam. Only when you've covered all the ground and feel comfortable with the whole scope of the practice exam should you take a real one.

If you take the practice exam and don't score at least 75 percent correct, you'll want to practice further. Although one is not available for Visual C++ Desktop yet, Microsoft usually provides free Personal Exam Prep (PEP) exams and the self-assessment exams from the Microsoft Certified Professional Web site's download page (its location appears in the next section). If you're more ambitious or better funded, you might want to purchase a practice exam from a third-party vendor.

Armed with the information in this book and with the determination to augment your knowledge, you should be able to pass the certification exam. However, you need to work at it, or you'll spend the exam fee more than once before you finally pass. If you prepare seriously, you should do well. Good luck!

Additional Resources

A good source of information about Microsoft certification exams comes from Microsoft itself. Because its products and technologies—and the exams that go with them—change frequently, the best place to go for exam-related information is online.

If you haven't already visited the Microsoft Certified Professional site, do so right now. The MCP home page resides at **www.microsoft.com/mcp** (see Figure 1.1).

> *Note: This page might not be there by the time you read this, or it might have been replaced by something new and different, because things change regularly on the Microsoft site. Should this happen, please read the sidebar, "Coping With Change On The Web."*

The menu options on this site point to the most important sources of information in the MCP pages. Here's what to check out:

➤ **Certifications** Use this menu entry to pick whichever certification program you want to read about.

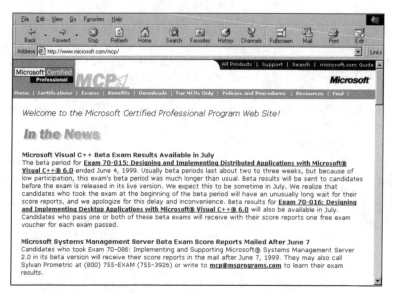

Figure 1.1   The Microsoft Certified Professional Web site.

➤ **Exams** Use this menu entry to pull up a search tool that lets you list all Microsoft exams and locate all exams relevant to any Microsoft certification (MCP, MCP+SB, MCSD, and so on) or those exams that cover a particular product. This tool is quite useful not only to examine the options but also to obtain specific exam preparation information, because each exam has its own associated preparation guide.

➤ **Downloads** Use this menu entry to find a list of the files and practice exams that Microsoft makes available to the public. These include several items worth downloading, especially the Certification Update, the PEP exams, various assessment exams, and a general exam study guide. Try to make time to peruse these materials before taking your first exam.

These are just the high points of what's available in the Microsoft Certified Professional pages. As you browse through them—and I strongly recommend that you do—you'll probably find other informational tidbits mentioned that are every bit as interesting and compelling.

Coping With Change On The Web

Sooner or later, all the information I've shared with you about the Microsoft Certified Professional pages and the other Web-based resources mentioned throughout the rest of this book will go stale or be replaced by newer information. In some cases, the URLs you find here might lead you to their replacements; in other cases, the URLs will go nowhere, leaving you with the dreaded "404 File not found" error message. When that happens, don't give up.

You can always find what you want on the Web if you're willing to invest some time and energy. Most large or complex Web sites—and Microsoft's qualifies on both counts—offer a search engine. On all of Microsoft's Web pages, a Search button appears along the top edge of the page. As long as you can get to Microsoft's site (it should stay at **www.microsoft. com** for a long time), use this tool to help you find what you need.

The more focused you can make a search request, the more likely the results will include information you want. For example, search for the string "training and certification" to produce a lot of data about the subject in general. If, however, you're looking for a preparation guide for Exam 70-016, "Designing and Implementing Desktop Applications with Microsoft Visual C++ 6.0," you'll be more likely to get there quickly if you use a search string similar to the following:

```
"Exam 70-016" AND "preparation guide"
```

Likewise, if you want to find the Training and Certification downloads, try a search string such as this:

```
"training and certification" AND "download page"
```

Finally, feel free to use general search tools—such as **www.search.com**, **www.altavista.com**, and **www.excite.com**—to look for related information. Although Microsoft offers great information about its certification exams online, there are plenty of third-party sources of information and assistance that need not follow Microsoft's party line. Therefore, if you can't find something where the book says it lives, intensify your search.

The Development Environment

Terms you'll need to understand:

√ Project workspace

√ Preprocessor definitions

√ Compiler switches

√ Libraries

√ Source control management system

√ Shadow folder

√ Cloaked project

Techniques you'll need to master:

√ Installing Visual C++ and supplemental products

√ Using AppWizard and ClassWizard

√ Modifying project settings

√ Installing SourceSafe, giving permission to users, and managing projects

Visual C++

Microsoft's Visual C++ product features both a sophisticated programming editor, in the form of the Integrated Development Environment (IDE), and powerful machine-code-generation tools, with an optimizing compiler and incremental linker. The IDE offers a number of wizards that can generate common template code for you, and a drag-and-drop metaphor is employed in constructing user interface components.

Editions And Features

Visual C++ is offered in three editions: Standard, Professional, and Enterprise. The following list describes your choices:

➤ *Standard*—The Standard Edition was formerly known as the Learning Edition. This edition only allows static linking to the MFC libraries.

➤ *Professional*—The Professional Edition supports the creation of applications, services, and controls for both the Windows and NT operating systems. This edition does not offer SQL debugging, Visual Modeler, or Internet Information Server (IIS).

➤ *Enterprise*—The Enterprise Edition supports all of the tools necessary to develop and debug n-tier architecture solutions. In addition, this product includes MTS and SQL Server.

Installation Issues

You have several drawbacks to consider at the installation stage. The following list covers these drawbacks:

➤ Side-by-side installation is not supported

➤ Dual-boot computer installs must be to different locations

NT Option Pack

The NT Option Pack is part of the distribution media, which ships with Visual Studio Enterprise Edition, or it may be downloaded separately from Microsoft.

Installation

The NT Option Pack requires NT 4.0, Server or Workstation, and Service Pack 3 to be installed. Alpha or beta versions of IIS must be uninstalled prior to Option Pack installation.

Components

The following components are distributed in the NT Option Pack. The custom setup option allows you to install only those components you require.

➤ *Internet Information Server (IIS)*—Microsoft's Internet Information Server is a Web application server for Windows NT.

➤ *Data Access Components (MDAC)*—The Option Pack supplies the most recent data access components. These components provide access to a variety of data sources, including those that support the ODBC and/or SQL standards, as well as nonrelational stores. The MDAC package provides support for ActiveX Data Objects (ADO), OLE DB, and ODBC drivers and services.

➤ *Management Console (MMC)*—The Microsoft Management Console offers a single-point enterprise management that is both extensible and intelligible. The MMC offers an Explorer-like view of systems and services that are "snapped in." From a developer perspective, ATL offers excellent support for the construction of MMC snap-in components.

➤ *Message Queue Server (MSMQ)*—A message queue offers cost-based message routing and resilience to systems operating over unreliable communication links.

➤ *Transaction Server (MTS)*—Microsoft's transaction server is a component-based, scalable transaction engine.

➤ *SNA Server*—Microsoft's SNA Server implements an SNA-compatible data transport that connects the local type 2.1 node to a remote host (PU4/5) and/or peer (PU2.1) system.

Integrated Development Environment— Wizards

Visual C++ offers a number of code generators, in the guise of wizards, to help you during initialization and development of your software project.

Wizards

You can display the AppWizard selection list by selecting File|New from the menu and displaying the Projects tab. Important AppWizards include the following:

➤ *MFC AppWizard* (DLL and EXE)

➤ *MFC ActiveX ControlWizard*

➤ *ISAPI Extension Wizard*

➤ *ATL COM AppWizard*

➤ *Custom AppWizard*

➤ *ClassWizard*—The most commonly used wizard when developing MFC- or ATL-based applications is the ClassWizard. It is almost essential when you want to define a message handler, create a class, respond to ActiveX events, and define an Automation interface.

➤ *ATL Object Wizard*—The ATL Object Wizard offers code-generation support based on C++ templates as opposed to ClassWizard's generation of classes, functions, and macros utilizing MFC's object hierarchy. ATL objects may be added to either ATL- or MFC-based projects. If you are using ATL in your MFC project, you must make sure that the project has been configured for ATL support.

Integrated Development Environment— Workspace

The Workspace pane is a dockable window, which provides three tabbed panes: ClassView, ResourceView, and FileView. Each pane contains a tree control whose root node is the *project workspace*. The project workspace may contain information for one or more projects.

In the Workspace pane, the default project's folder name is represented with bold type.

➤ *ClassView*—The first level of the tree includes the project's classes, interfaces, and globals. Globals and classes can be expanded to reveal their functions and variables, whereas an interface can be expanded to reveal its methods and properties.

The context menu for classes offers access to many ClassWizard functions, including adding a member function or variable and adding a Windows message handler. The corresponding menu for interfaces allows creation of methods and properties.

The context menu for functions and variables allows navigation to the corresponding definition and/or declaration. Whereas the context menu for interface methods and properties simply offers to navigate to the declaration, ActiveX control interfaces allow the definition of new events.

➤ *ResourceView*—The ResourceView tree is arranged such that each resource category, such as Accelerator Table, Cursor, Dialog, and Menu, is given a top-level folder. Expansion of a resource folder displays the resources of that type.

The context menu for the resource view allows the import of resources contained within other files. Insert Copy and Export menus round out the powerful resource management functions offered by this view.

➤ *FileView*—FileView displays a logical representation of the projects and files in the workspace. This logical view does not necessarily reflect their physical disk organization.

This tab also displays the source control management's state for each file, if you have SourceSafe installed on your computer and the project(s) in your workspace have been introduced to source management.

➤ *Output*—Similar to the Workspace window, the Output window offers a number of tabs that aid in a program's creation and debugging. These tabs include Build, Find Results, Debug, Results, and SQL Debugging.

Using Visual C++

In Visual C++, the project workspace contains one or more projects. Construction of each project may be the result of creating a project with a different AppWizard (MFC AppWizard, ISAPI Extension Wizard, ATL COM AppWizard, and so on). When you create a project workspace, a DSW file is created to store workspace-related information. The workspace also creates default DSP and OPT files for a single project. The project section contains more information regarding these files.

A Visual C++ project contains all of the files that are necessary to compile, link, and debug your application. When you start a project in Visual C++, AppWizard generates the files shown in Table 2.1.

Important Preprocessor Definitions

The following are preprocessor terms and definitions with which you should become familiar:

➤ _WIN32—This symbol identifies the application as one that requires the Win32 runtime to execute.

➤ _DEBUG/_NDEBUG—The compiler defines the _DEBUG symbol when specifying the /MTd or /Mdd option.

➤ _WINDOWS—The compiler defines the _WINDOWS symbol for all source files in the project. This definition is not appropriate for console applications.

Table 2.1 Working files needed to complete a Visual C++ application.

File/Extension	Description
DSW	The workspace file organizes all the projects in a single workspace.
OPT	The workspace options file contains individual user settings; as such, this file is generally not introduced into source management.
DSP	The project's makefile information is stored in this file. For previous releases of Visual C++, this information was present in a MAK file.
CLW	The Visual C++ ClassWizard stores its information in this file.
ODL	The Object Description Language file contains OLE interface and type library definitions.
NCB	This extension stands for "No Compile Browser." The file contains information useful for the Component Gallery, ClassView, and the WizardBar.
README.TXT	Visual C++ generates a text file that describes each of the generated files and its purpose.

➤ _AFXDLL/_USRDLL—MFC offers support for two types of DLLs: those that contain a **CWinApp** object and those that share an existing **CWinApp** object. An _AFXDLL shares the MFC library with an application; therefore, it doesn't require its own instance of **CWinApp**. Such a DLL requires a special version of **LibMain()** and a DLL initialization export.

➤ _MBCS/_UNICODE—The Visual C++ compiler supports three character-mapping modes: single byte (default), multibyte (_MBCS), and Unicode (_UNICODE).

Important Compiler Switches

Before you can distribute release builds of your program, you need to be aware of Visual C++'s compiler switches and the importance they have to your programming needs. The following sections provide details about these switches.

Calling Conventions (/Gd/Gr/Gz)

A number of compiler switches determine the order of stack construction for function call definitions. This information is used to determine who is responsible for removing arguments from the stack (the caller or the callee) and the name-decorating convention. The following list explains each of these calling switches:

➤ **/Gd**—The **/Gd** option is the default compiler setting, using the **_cdecl** naming convention, specify the C calling convention for all functions that are not members of a C++ class.

➤ **/Gr**—The **/GR** option instructs the compiler to use the **_fastcall** specification, passing some arguments in the microprocessor's registers. This calling convention is specific to Intel platform builds only.

➤ **/Gz**—The **_stdcall** convention pushes arguments on the stack from right to left and requires C prototype definitions for all functions.

Disable/Debug (/Od)

This option suppresses all code optimizations, speeding the compilation process. It is only available in the Professional and Enterprise Editions (the Standard Edition does not support optimization switches). With the **/Od** switch, code movement is suppressed and the debugging process is simplified.

Runtime Library (/MD/ML/MT/LD)

These compiler options identify the runtime library to be associated with the produced module. The lowercase "d" at the end of the switch specifies the debug version of the library and additionally defines the **_DEBUG** symbol.

➤ **/MD** and **/MDd**—This switch indicates that the multithreaded DLL runtime libraries should be used. This switch also defines the **_MT** and **_DLL** symbols. The MSVCRT.LIB is used to resolve externals and requires the presence of the MSVCRT.DLL or MSVCRTD.DLL to be present at runtime.

➤ **/ML** and **/MLd**—This switch indicates that the single-threaded LIBC.LIB will be used to resolve runtime externals.

➤ **/MT** and **/MTd**—The multithreaded versions of the statically linked runtimes are selected with this switch. The **_MT** symbol is defined.

➤ **/LD** and **/LDd**—This switch passes the **/DLL** option to the linker, linking the startup code, and is used to create a DLL.

Warning Level (/Wn)

The compiler defines warning levels from 0 to 4. **/W0** instructs the compiler not to issue warnings (even if they exist); **/W4** is the lowest warning level and **/W1** is the highest.

Minimal Rebuild (/Gm)

This option speeds the build/debug cycle by allowing the compiler to maintain a database of C++ method signatures and not recompile header (H) files if only the body of such functions change.

Preprocessor Definition (/D)

This option defines symbol or constant preprocessor definitions as command-line arguments to the compiler. This affects code generation in a manner that is identical to **#define** statements contained in the actual code.

Precompiled Header (/Yc/Fp/Yu)

The first option, **/Yc**, instructs the compiler to generate a precompiled header (PCH) file. Without a file name provided, the compiler compiles code in the specified source file. If the **/Yc** option is followed by a file name, such as /Yc stdafx.h (as is the default Visual C++ setting), the compiler compiles the code up to and including the specified header file. The **/Fp** option allows you to specify the name and path for the precompiled header file. To instruct the compiler to use the existing precompiled header, specify **/Yu**.

Program Database (/Fd)

The **/Fd** compiler option requires a file name to follow, specifying the name for the PDB file (other than the default).

Catch Release-Build Errors In Debug Build (/GZ)

It is common to write code that works fine during development (in debug builds) and has problems (stack or otherwise) when built for release. The **/Gz** option changes code generation in the following three ways:

➤ Auto-initialization of local variables fills all memory used by variables not explicitly initialized with 0xCC.

➤ Function pointer call stack validation makes sure that the stack pointer (ESP) is the same before and after calls through a function pointer.

➤ Call stack validation checks the stack pointer at the end of a function to see that the stack pointer has not been changed.

Debug Info (/Zd/Z7/Zi/ZI)

The compiler offers a number of debug options that determine the type of debug information to create and where the debug information resides. Debug information may either be stored in a program database (PDB) or in the compiled object (OBJ).

➤ **/Zd**—This option reduces the amount of debug information that is contained in the compiled object by storing line numbers only. The **/Zd** option does not include symbolic information; therefore, the debugger's expression evaluator will not operate.

➤ **/Z7**—Use this option to produce object files that contain C 7.0-compatible debug information, including line numbers and all symbolic debug information.

➤ **/Zi**—This option stores all debug information in a program database file, thus offering a small object file while still supporting debugging efforts.

➤ **/ZI**—New to Visual C++ 6.0, this option also stores debug information in a program database file; however, it supports a format that allows operation of the Edit and Continue feature.

File Dependencies (/FD)

The Update Dependencies function is no longer available in the 6.0 compiler. Instead, the **/FD** switch ensures that the most reliable dependency information is used to build your project.

As a side note: Visual C++ 6.0 now supports dependency information placed in a separate, editable text file.

Libraries

A number of C runtime libraries exist that form the foundation of Visual C++ applications. These libraries fall into two primary categories: debug and nondebug. In each of these categories are three libraries:

➤ *LIBC.LIB*—Supports single-threaded applications and is statically linked to the module.

➤ *LIBCMT.LIB*—Supports multithreaded applications and is statically linked to the module.

➤ *MSVCRT.LIB*—Supports multithreaded applications and is dynamically linked to the module. This file contains the import library for the MSVCRT.DLL.

➤ *Debug*—Corresponding sets of debug libraries exist. The file names of libraries that contain debug information end with the letter "D": LIBCD.LIB, LIBCMTD.LIB, and MSVCRTD.LIB.

Project Settings

The Project Settings dialog box, available either from the Project menu or by right-clicking on a file in the FileView tab of the Workspace window, offers a dialog-based approach to identifying and configuring compiler and linker settings.

SourceSafe

Microsoft's SourceSafe can be used to manage document changes produced by any application, language, or tool. The following sections present an overview of this software.

Purpose

One of the best and most important software practices is employing a *source control management system*. Source control is a critical tool for the release management process and to ensure a level of safety and accountability in multiprogrammer development projects.

In more recent years, source control has become a highly popular method of maintaining Web site information. SourceSafe has always provided the capability to store files of any type; for a Web site, these include many file types, including HTM, JPG, GIF, and so on. With the release of version 6.0, the product is able to verify hyperlinks and publish content to your Web server.

Platforms And Requirements

Microsoft recommends a Pentium-class computer for either the client or server components of SourceSafe. Minimum operating system requirements are either Windows 95/98 or NT 4 with Service Pack 3. Both Unix and Macintosh variants are available through Microsoft partners. Additionally, a product called SourceOffSite offers an add-on product to SourceSafe that provides secure access to a SourceSafe database over the Internet.

Configuration Files

There are two configuration files that are important for SourceSafe operation. These two files are described in the following list:

➤ *SS.INI*—The SS.INI file contains information specific to an individual developer.

➤ *SRCSAFE.INI*—The SRCSAFE.INI file contains information for Visual SourceSafe's global variables.

Installation

SourceSafe is a typical client/server application. In a common configuration, the server-side install is performed on a different machine from those machines on which the client software is installed. It's possible to install the client and server components on one machine, thereby negating a client install on individual user machines. (Of course, the proper licensing conditions must be met.)

Client

The client installation may either be performed from the SourceSafe distribution media or from a network drive. For a client installation from disk, you should select the Client option from the Setup.exe program. The client software may also be installed by double-clicking on the Netsetup.exe program in the directory from which VSS is installed.

Server

A server installation of SourceSafe requires you to simply select the Server option from the Setupe.exe program that is part of the VSS distribution media.

User Interface

SourceSafe offers two ways for creating projects and maintaining files. The first is a standalone utility, and the second involves integration with your Visual Studio environment.

Standalone

SourceSafe offers a standalone file management program called Microsoft Visual SourceSafe Explorer. This client application can be deployed on every developer's desktop, allowing the rights assigned by an administrator to scope access to managed files.

The Visual SourceSafe Administrator is another application, generally only installed on the machines of those in charge of configuration management, that allows creation of source control databases, creation of user accounts, and privilege management of existing accounts. In addition, the administrator program allows you to archive and restore source databases.

IDE Integration

You should not put workspace option (OPT) files into SourceSafe when you introduce the project to source control, because these files contain information that is specific to each user's computer. This file contains information regarding IDE window and toolbar layouts, which generally differ among developers.

Common Operations

Many of the source management functions you will perform on a daily basis using SourceSafe are intuitive and can be accomplished easily with the graphical tools. Although you probably won't perform the following advanced functions very often, they do require additional explanation.

Creating A Project

The SourceSafe hierarchy of file management places projects directly below the database. When logging in to SourceSafe, you select the database to which you wish to connect. By default, the name given to this database is Common and its label designator is "$/". To create a project, simply use the Create Project option under the File menu. You must have the Add access privilege (on the parent object) to perform this operation.

Projects may also be added to the SourceSafe database by displaying a project's context menu from the FileView tab of the Workspace window and selecting Add To Source Control.

Checking Files In And Out

Files under source control require a checkout process in order for changes to be made. Checking out a file places a writeable copy of the file on your computer.

Sharing

SourceSafe offers a powerful attribute to facilitate *reuse* with the **Share** command. This allows a single instance of a component to be used with multiple projects in the SourceSafe environment. In this manner, changes made to the component from one project are immediately made available to other projects.

Branching

It is common in the software development process to take a file in two different directions. This may be as the result of a localization effort or for product stratification. Visual SourceSafe provides the **Branch** command, tracking the individual directions of the file as a project.

> *Note: The **Branch** command breaks any link that you established using the **Share** command.*

Merging/Multiple Checkouts

Visual SourceSafe is capable of combining multiple changed copies of a file into a single file, either visually or manually. Additionally, the multiple checkout option allows more than one user at a time to check out a file for change. Visual SourceSafe automatically merges the contents of files when they are checked back in. If the automatic merge detects conflicts, a visual merge tool is displayed.

Binary Files

SourceSafe is capable of versioning *binary* files—those that do not only contain character information. By default, Visual SourceSafe assigns the binary file attribute to those files containing NULL characters. You may override this assignment if necessary.

Shadow Folders

A *shadow folder* is an optional view of the contents of a SourceSafe project containing the most recently checked-in version of each file in a project. A person with administrator privileges may initialize a centralized folder containing all of the files of a project. The shadow folder does not contain a master copy of the project files, nor should it be confused with a user's local working copy of the project files.

Cloaked Projects

A *cloaked project* is one where the operations **Get, Check In, Check Out, Undo Check Out,** and **Project Difference** are not processed if attempted indirectly (such as in the result of a recursive operation). A cloaked project may have subprojects that are not cloaked; as such, a recursive **Get** command performed on the root project will only result in the acquisition of files in those subprojects that are not cloaked.

Practice Questions

Question 1

> ActiveX control events may be easily added from the context menu of which window?
>
> ○ a.   The ClassView pane of the Workspace window.
>
> ○ b.   The FileView pane of the Workspace window.
>
> ○ c.   The ResourceView pane of the Workspace window.
>
> ○ d.   The Build pane of the Output window.

The correct answer is a. Only the ClassView pane allows you to add functions and variables to a class, as well as respond to ActiveX events. FileView and ResourceView are also panes of the Workspace window; however, they don't offer object manipulation menus. The Build pane contains output from the compiler and linker.

Question 2

> The Visual C++ compiler allows the specification of various calling conventions using command-line switches. Which switch allows argument passing via registers?
>
> ○ a.   /Gd
>
> ○ b.   /Gr
>
> ○ c.   /Od
>
> ○ d.   /Zi

The correct answer is b. The **/Gr** option allows arguments to be passed using processor registers. This convention is also known as **_fastcall**.

Question 3

In situations where a release build of an application causes a stack fault and the corresponding debug build does not, which compiler switch would you invoke to allow this condition to be observed in debug builds?

○ a. /GZ

○ b. /Fd

○ c. /Od

○ d. /Z7

The correct answer is a. The **/GZ** compiler switch instructs the compiler to insert code to initialize variables and perform stack verification.

Question 4

Which library supports multithreaded applications, dynamically linked to a module?

○ a. LIBC.LIB

○ b. MSVCRT.LIB

○ c. LIBCD.LIB

○ d. LIBCMT.LIB

The correct answer is b. The MSVCRT.LIB file resolves runtime externals for a dynamically linked library whose name is MSVCRT.DLL.

Question 5

The preprocessor switch identifying that the code shares an existing CWinApp object is as follows:

○ a. _WIN32

○ b. _AFXDLL

○ c. _USRDLL

○ d. _SYSDLL

The correct answer is b. The **_AFXDLL** directive ensures that a new **CWinApp** object is not created for the DLL.

Question 6

> What SourceSafe operation modifies the behavior of the following operations:
> Get, Check In, and Check Out?
>
> ○ a. Branching
>
> ○ b. Sharing
>
> ○ c. Cloaking
>
> ○ d. Checking in

The correct answer is c. The cloaking operation ignores the specified operations if they are performed via indirect means (as in part of a recursive operation).

Need To Know More?

 Kruglinski, David J., George Shepherd, and Scot Wingo. *Programming Microsoft Visual C++*. 5th ed. Microsoft Press, Redmond, WA, 1998. ISBN 1-57231-857-0. This book strikes a good balance between theory and practical application. It is divided into six parts and covers nearly every aspect of MFC programming, from the basics to database management and the Internet. The first chapters offer solid coverage of the development environment.

Menus

Terms you'll need to understand:

- √ ON_COMMAND_RANGE
- √ ON_UPDATE_COMMAND_ UI_RANGE
- √ CCmdUI
- √ CCmdUI::SetCheck()
- √ CCmdUI::Enable()
- √ CCmdUI::SetRadio()
- √ CCmdUI::SetText()
- √ CWnd::GetMenu()
- √ CMenu::GetSubMenu()
- √ ON_COMMAND_EX

- √ CMenu::CreatePopupMenu()
- √ CMenu::DeleteMenu()
- √ CMenu::RemoveMenu()
- √ CMenu::AppendMenu()
- √ CMenu::InsertMenu()
- √ CMenu::ModifyMenu()
- √ CWnd::OnMeasureItem()
- √ CWnd::OnDrawItem()
- √ CMenu::MeasureItem()
- √ CMenu::DrawItem()

Techniques you'll need to master:

- √ Implementing dynamic menus
- √ Implementing cascading menus
- √ Implementing owner-drawn menus

Menus are an important part of most Windows applications and are probably the most widely recognized user interface component existing. Well-designed menus allow users to quickly and easily move through the high-level structure of the user interface. Because they are such an important element of the user interface, both Windows and Microsoft Foundation Classes (MFC) provide a lot of support to applications that use them.

Most of the time, you will use the Resource Editor to create menus. However, what if you need to make changes to a menu at runtime? You cannot use the Resource Editor then. Instead, you need to add the required code to your application.

In this chapter, you will see three ways that a menu might be changed at runtime. First, you will look at how one might implement a dynamic menu. Dynamic menus allow you to present the user with a different set of choices, depending on the context. Then you will look at how you might implement cascading menus at runtime. Cascading menus enable you to provide the user with a level of depth that is easy to follow and understand.

In the final topic, you will explore owner-drawn menus. Owner-drawn menus enable you to display graphical items in a menu instead of just text. For example, you can create an owner-drawn menu to display color palettes and drawing objects in menus.

Dynamic Menus

Normally, you use the Resource Editor during design time to define the menus for your application. Menus defined at design time are static. But what about the times that you would like to provide menu options based on system, user, or data settings? To do this, you need to add and delete menu items at runtime. These kinds of menus are known as *dynamic menus*.

Consolidating Command Handlers Into A Command Range

Before creating dynamic menus, you need to look at a couple of macros that make the task a little easier. Often, a menu allows the user to change a specific attribute of the application by selecting one item from a list. Examples include menus for selecting colors, zoom levels, and dimensions. Because there are many menu items, there are also many command handlers that are nearly identical in their functionality. To provide a more maintainable and elegant solution, you can use the **ON_COMMAND_RANGE** macro to map all the messages with similar functionality to a single handler. There is also an **ON_UPDATE_ COMMAND_UI_RANGE** macro that allows you to map a contiguous range of command IDs to a single update message handler. Update message handlers update the state of menu items and toolbar buttons associated with the command. ClassWizard does not support message map ranges, so you must place these macros yourself. Be sure to put them outside the ClassWizard's comments. You must also add the function prototype entry to the class's header file in the **DECLARE_MESSAGE_MAP** section.

Building The Application

In this section, you will build an application called Dynamic.exe that uses dynamic menus. Before you start writing code, first specify what Dynamic.exe should look like and what it will do.

➤ When you start Dynamic.exe, it will display a simple line of text in the center of the window, as shown in Figure 3.1.

➤ As you can see in Figures 3.2 and 3.3, the Colors menu allows you to select one of four or one of seven different colors. When you select one of the colors from the Colors menu, the text in the center of the window will change to the color you selected.

➤ The colors shown on the Colors menu are controlled by the Options menu, as shown in Figure 3.4.

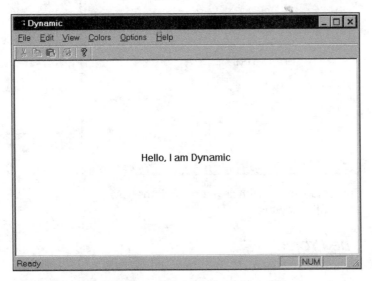

Figure 3.1   The window of the Dynamic.exe program.

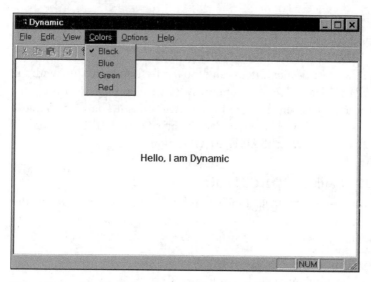

Figure 3.2 The Colors menu with four color items (RGB and black) showing.

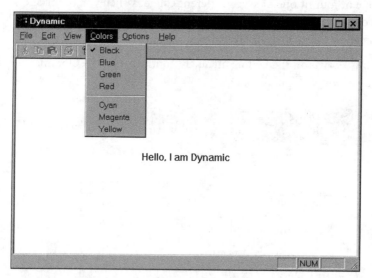

Figure 3.3 The Colors menu with seven color items (CMYK and RGB) showing.

Creating The Project

Run AppWizard to generate a single-document interface (SDI) project without document/view architecture support. Name the project "Dynamic" and create it in \ExamCram\Dynamic. The options and the default class names are shown in Figure 3.5.

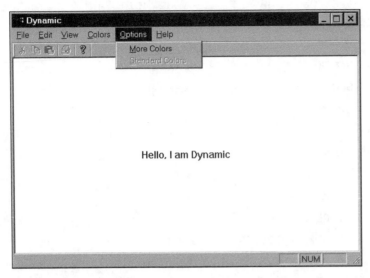

Figure 3.4 The Options menu of the Dynamic.exe program.

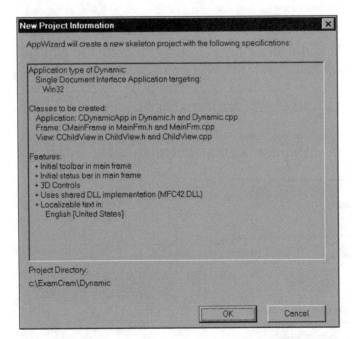

Figure 3.5 The New Project Information dialog box, which shows the options and default class names of the Dynamic project.

Table 3.1 Resource symbols.	
Symbol	**ID**
ID_COLORS_BLACK	0x9000
ID_COLORS_BLUE	0x9001
ID_COLORS_GREEN	0x9002
ID_COLORS_RED	0x9003
ID_COLORS_CYAN	0x9004
ID_COLORS_MAGENTA	0x9005
ID_COLORS_YELLOW	0x9006
ID_OPTIONS_MORE_COLORS	0x9010
ID_OPTIONS_STANDARD_COLORS	0x9011

Creating The Resource Symbols

You need a resource symbol for each of your menu items. Choose View|Resource Symbols, and then enter the symbols as shown in Table 3.1.

Notice how **ID_COLORS_BLACK** through **ID_COLORS_YELLOW** are sequential. This is necessary when consolidating command handers.

Adding The Colors And Options Menus

Using the Resource Editor, add the Colors and Options top-level menu items and their associated submenus so that they look like Figures 3.6 and 3.7.

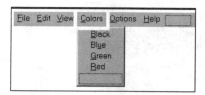

Figure 3.6 The Colors menu.

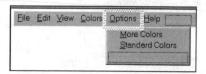

Figure 3.7 The Options menu.

The terminology used to describe menus can be confusing. At the top level of the hierarchy is the *menu bar*; menus drop down from the menu bar, and at the lower levels are *submenus*. A menu bar is sometimes called a *top-level menu*. The menu that appears when a top-level menu item is clicked is a *drop-down menu,* and items in that menu are referred to as *menu items,* Because the resource editor uses POPUP statements to define top-level menu items and the associated submenus, drop-down menus are also known as *pop-up menus.*

Windows also provides *shortcut menus.* A shortcut menu is not attached to the menu bar; it can pop up anywhere on the screen. Because shortcut menus can be popped up anywhere on the screen, they too are known as pop-up menus. A shortcut menu is typically associated with a portion of a window, such as the client area, or with a specific object, such as an icon. For this reason, these menus are also called *context menus.*

Many applications will use the same pop-up menu as both a drop-down menu and a context menu.

If you build and run the program, you will see that Colors and Options have been added to the menu bar, but the items on the drop-down menu are all disabled. So let's add some basic functionality to the program. After you get that working, you will then tackle the dynamic menu portion.

Adding The Basic Functionality

In this section, you will first add the code needed to get the text to display on screen. Then you will add the menu items needed to change its color.

1. Use the Resource Editor to add a text string to the **STRINGTABLE**. The string's ID is **IDS_HELLO_MESSAGE,** its value is 0xE000 and the caption is "Hello, I am Dynamic".

2. Add two member variables to the **CChildView** class:

```
private:
    CString m_strHelloMessage;
    UINT m_uColor;
```

3. At the top of **ChildView.cpp**, add the following shaded code:

```
COLORREF COLORS[] = { RGB(0,    0,    0),    // Black
                      RGB(0,    0, 255),    // Blue
                      RGB(0,  255,    0),    // Green
                      RGB(255,  0,    0),    // Red
                      RGB(  0, 255, 255),    // Cyan
                      RGB(255,  0, 255),    // Magenta
                      RGB(255, 255,    0) }; // Yellow
/////////////////////////////////////////////////////////////
// CChildView

CChildView::CChildView()
  : m_uColor( ID_COLORS_BLACK )
{
  m_strHelloMessage.LoadString(IDS_HELLO_MESSAGE);
}
```

4. Now, modify the **OnPaint** handler to draw the text in the center of the window. The argument to **SetTextColor()** specifies the color of the text as an RGB value. Here is what the code might look like:

```
void CChildView::OnPaint()
{
    CPaintDC dc(this); // device context for painting
    CRect rect;
    GetClientRect (&rect);
    dc.SetTextColor( COLORS[m_uColor - ID_COLORS_BLACK] );
    dc.DrawText(m_strHelloMessage, -1, &rect,
        DT_SINGLELINE | DT_CENTER | DT_VCENTER);
    // Do not call CWnd::OnPaint() for painting messages
}
```

5. Your program can now display the text and center it in the window. Now, let's give it the capability of changing the color. First, add an **ON_COMMAND_RANGE** entry to the message map. This macro takes three arguments. The first two specify the beginning and ending numbers of the range, and the third specifies the handler. Although only black through red can be selected, just use yellow for the ending color. Next, add a function to handle the message. Its prototype is as follows:

```
afx_msg void OnColors(UINT nID);
```

Following is what the code should look like:

```
BEGIN_MESSAGE_MAP(CChildView,CWnd )
    //{{AFX_MSG_MAP(CChildView)
    ON_WM_PAINT()
    //}}AFX_MSG_MAP
    ON_COMMAND_RANGE(ID_COLORS_BLACK, ID_COLORS_YELLOW, OnColors)
END_MESSAGE_MAP()
```

```
void CChildView::OnColors(UINT nID)
{
    m_uColor = nID;
    Invalidate();
}
```

ClassWizard cannot add the **ON_COMMAND_RANGE** macro to the message map. You must type it in yourself.

6. Now add the code needed to place a checkmark next to the menu item that was last selected. The **ON_UPDATE_COMMAND_UI_ RANGE** macro is used to specify the update command handler. This handler, **OnUpdateColors()**, will be called for each item on the Colors menu. A pointer to a **CCmdUI** object, which represents the item, is passed to the handler. This object can be used to change the menu item's appearance by calling its member functions. This handler calls the **SetCheck()** member function to place a checkmark next to the last item the user selected, which is stored in **m_uColors**. Here again you must type in the entry to the message map:

```
BEGIN_MESSAGE_MAP(CChildView,CWnd )
    //{{AFX_MSG_MAP(CChildView)
    ON_WM_PAINT()
    //}}AFX_MSG_MAP
    ON_COMMAND_RANGE(ID_COLORS_BLACK, ID_COLORS_YELLOW, OnColors)
    ON_UPDATE_COMMAND_UI_RANGE(ID_COLORS_BLACK, ID_COLORS_YELLOW,
        OnUpdateColors)
END_MESSAGE_MAP()
```

```
void CChildView::OnUpdateColors(CCmdUI *pCmdUI)
{
    pCmdUI->SetCheck(pCmdUI->m_nID == m_uColor);
}
```

SetCheck() is one of four functions the **CCmdUI** class provides for changing the appearance of menu items. The other three are **Enable()**, **SetRadio()**, and **SetText()**. **Enable()** is used to enable and disable a menu item. **SetRadio()** works like **SetCheck()** but adds and removes a bullet rather than a check mark. **SetText()** allows you to set the text of the menu item.

7. Add the prototype for **OnUpdateColors()** to your header file.

Adding The Dynamic Menu Capability

This section shows how to add and delete the additional selections to the Colors menu. The Options menu controls which color selections are available on the Colors menu. Like the Colors menu, the Options menu also uses a composite command handler and an update handler.

1. Add the code for the composite command handler. This handler first uses **GetMenu()** to retrieve a pointer to the top-level menu. It then uses this pointer to call **GetSubMenu()** to retrieve a pointer to the Colors menu. The argument supplied to **GetSubMenu()** specifies the position of the desired submenu. Colors is the fourth menu item; however, because position values start at 0 for the first menu item, a 3 is passed. Next, the number of items in the Colors menu is obtained. Then based on the number, items are either added to or removed from Colors. If items are removed, the color is set to black. When items are added, a separator is first added before the items. Either way, **Invalidate()** is called to ensure that the window gets repainted. Here is what the code might look like:

```
void CChildView::OnOptionColors(UINT nID)
{
  CMenu *pTopMenu = AfxGetMainWnd()->GetMenu();
  ASSERT(pTopMenu);
  CMenu *pColorsMenu = pTopMenu->GetSubMenu(3);
  ASSERT(pColorsMenu);
  UINT count = pColorsMenu->GetMenuItemCount();
  ASSERT(count == 4 || count == 8);

  switch(nID)
  {
  case ID_OPTIONS_STANDARD_COLORS:
    // adjust the count for 0-base
    for(count-; count > 3; count-)
```

```
        pColorsMenu->RemoveMenu(count, MF_BYPOSITION);
    m_uColor = ID_COLORS_BLACK;
    break;
  case ID_OPTIONS_MORE_COLORS:
    pColorsMenu->AppendMenu(MF_SEPARATOR);
    for(int i = ID_COLORS_CYAN; i <= ID_COLORS_YELLOW; i++)
    {
      CString prompt;
      prompt.LoadString(i);
      pColorsMenu->AppendMenu(MF_STRING, i, prompt);
    }
    break;
  }
  Invalidate();
}
```

2. Now add an **ON_COMMAND_RANGE** macro to the message map:

```
BEGIN_MESSAGE_MAP(CChildView,CWnd )
  //{{AFX_MSG_MAP(CChildView)
  ON_WM_PAINT()
  //}}AFX_MSG_MAP
  ON_COMMAND_RANGE(ID_COLORS_BLACK, ID_COLORS_YELLOW, OnColors)
  ON_UPDATE_COMMAND_UI_RANGE(ID_COLORS_BLACK, ID_COLORS_YELLOW,
    OnUpdateColors)
  ON_COMMAND_RANGE(ID_OPTIONS_MORE_COLORS,
    ID_OPTIONS_STANDARD_COLORS, OnOptionColors)
END_MESSAGE_MAP()
```

MFC also provides the **ON_COMMAND_EX(ID, FUNC)** macro, which could have been used here. Like the **ON_COMMAND_ RANGE** macro, the **ON_COMMAND_EX** macro allows several menu commands to be mapped to the same handler. However, because a distinct **ON_COMMAND_EX** macro must be pro- vided for each menu item, nonsequential IDs can be used.

3. Now add code to keep the Options menu in sync. Use the ClassWizard to add a function to handle the **ON_UPDATE_COMMAND_UI** message for both **ID_OPTIONS_MORE_COLORS** and **ID_ OPTIONS_STANDARD_COLORS**. Each time the wizard presents the suggested name, change it to **OnUpdateOptions**. Then add the

following code. The **Enable()** function (see the following code for an example) is used to enable or disable the items on the Options menu, depending on the number of items on the Colors menu.

```
void CChildView::OnUpdateOptions(CCmdUI *pCmdUI)
{
    CMenu *pTopMenu = AfxGetMainWnd()->GetMenu();
    ASSERT(pTopMenu);
    CMenu *pColorsMenu = pTopMenu->GetSubMenu(3);
    ASSERT(pColorsMenu);

    UINT standard = ID_COLORS_RED - ID_COLORS_BLACK + 1;

    switch(pCmdUI->m_nID)
    {
    case ID_OPTIONS_STANDARD_COLORS:
        pCmdUI->Enable(pColorsMenu->GetMenuItemCount() != standard);
        break;
    case ID_OPTIONS_MORE_COLORS:
        pCmdUI->Enable(pColorsMenu->GetMenuItemCount() == standard);
        break;
    }
}
```

Updating The String Table

Now add the menu prompts that will be needed when the extra items are added to the Colors menu. Also, add the text to be displayed on screen.

If you pin down the String Properties dialog box, it stays on the screen until you close it. This will allow you to enter all of the strings at one time.

When finished, your string table should look like Figure 3.8.

ID	Value	Caption
IDR_MAINFRAME	128	Dynamic
ID_COLORS_BLACK	36864	Black
ID_COLORS_BLUE	36865	Blue
ID_COLORS_GREEN	36866	Green
ID_COLORS_RED	36867	Red
ID_COLORS_CYAN	36868	Cyan
ID_COLORS_MAGENTA	36869	Magenta
ID_COLORS_YELLOW	36870	Yellow
IDS_HELLO_MESSAGE	36871	Hello, I am Dynamic
AFX_IDS_APP_TITLE	57344	Dynamic

Figure 3.8 Updated string table.

Cascading Menus

Cascading menus allow you to display your menu items in a multitier arrangement. This technique can be very useful when you have a lot of menu items and you want to reduce clutter. They also can be used to organize your menus as submenus that contain related selections, such as colors, pen widths, and fonts.

Although there is no practical limit to the number of menus that you can nest by cascading, keep in mind, of course, that additional levels means additional complexity. For this reason, the user interface guidelines suggest no more than four levels of nesting be used. The guidelines also recommend that cascading menus be avoided for frequent, repetitive commands. However, that said, such menus can be beneficial when applied judiciously.

In this section, you will look at how a cascading menu might be added at runtime. You will do this by making changes to the Dynamic.exe program.

Adding A Member Variable And A String Resource

You will need two data elements. The first will be used to hold the pointer to the cascade menu item. The second will be the text needed for the menu prompt.

1. Add a private data member to **CChildView** and initialize it:

   ```
   private:
       CMenu * m_pMoreColors;
       CString m_strHelloMessage;
       UINT m_uColor;

   CChildView::CChildView()
     : m_uColor(ID_COLORS_BLACK)
     , m_pMoreColors(0)
   {
     m_strHelloMessage.LoadString(IDS_HELLO_MESSAGE);
   }
   ```

2. Add a string resource. Name it **IDS_MORE_COLORS** and make the text "More Colors".

Adding The Menu

Locate the **OnOptionsColors** function and modify it as shown below. In this code, the additional colors are added using a **CMenu** class object. After the object is instantiated, **CreatePopupMenu()** is called to create a pop-up menu. The additional color items are then appended to the pop-up, which is then appended to the Colors menu. The additional colors are removed by calling **DeleteMenu()**. Then the **CMenu** object is deleted, and the pointer is set to null.

Normally you would probably create the **CMenu** object on the stack and **Detach()** it when you **AppendMenu()** it. However, the stage is being set here for an easy transition to owner-drawn menus, so it is being created as a member variable.

```
void CChildView::OnOptionColors(UINT nID)
{
  CMenu *pTopMenu = AfxGetMainWnd()->GetMenu();
  ASSERT(pTopMenu);
  CMenu *pColorsMenu = pTopMenu->GetSubMenu(3);
  ASSERT(pColorsMenu);

  UINT count = pColorsMenu->GetMenuItemCount();
  ASSERT(count == 4 || count == 5);

  switch(nID)
  {
  case ID_OPTIONS_STANDARD_COLORS:
    // adjust the count for 0-base
    pColorsMenu->DeleteMenu(-count, MF_BYPOSITION);
    delete m_pMoreColors;
    m_pMoreColors = 0;
    m_uColor = ID_COLORS_BLACK;
    break;
  case ID_OPTIONS_MORE_COLORS:

    m_pMoreColors = new CMenu;
    m_pMoreColors->CreatePopupMenu();
    CString prompt;
    for(int i = ID_COLORS_CYAN; i <= ID_COLORS_YELLOW; i++)
    {
      prompt.LoadString(i);
      m_pMoreColors->AppendMenu(MF_STRING, i, prompt);
    }
    prompt.LoadString(IDS_MORE_COLORS);
    VERIFY( pColorsMenu->AppendMenu( MF_STRING | MF_POPUP,
                           (UINT) m_pMoreColors->m_hMenu,
                           prompt )
        );
```

```
    break;
  }
  Invalidate();

}
```

 Notice here that **DeleteMenu()** was used, whereas previously **RemoveMenu()** was used. The difference between the two can be confusing. Use **DeleteMenu()** when the item to be removed has an associated pop-up menu.

Destroying The CMenu Object

Use the ClassWizard to add a function to handle **WM_DESTROY**. Then add the following code to ensure that the **CMenu** object is deleted when the window is destroyed.

```
void CChildView::OnDestroy()
{
  CWnd ::OnDestroy();
  delete m_pMoreColors;
}
```

Owner-Drawn Menus

Up to now, all of the menu items have been presented to the user in the form of text. This is fine for most applications, but sometimes something more is needed. At these times, a picture really can be worth a thousand words. Depicting menu items with bitmap images is easy and straightforward. You simply create a **CBitmap** object for each of the menu items and call **CMenu::AppendMenu()** to append it to the menu. Windows then displays the bitmap when the menu is displayed. Unfortunately, bitmaps are fixed in size and not easy to adapt to changes in screen metrics.

Fortunately, however, Windows provides a more flexible way to replace the text with graphics: It allows you to draw your own menu items. This kind of menu is called an *owner-drawn menu*. Being more flexible, it requires a little more work on your part. Here are the three steps that you must follow when implementing an owner-drawn menu:

1. Label each menu item as owner-drawn with the **MF_OWNERDRAW** flag. This must be done at runtime using **AppendMenu()**, **InsertMenu()**, or **ModifyMenu()**.

2. Provide an **OnMeasureItem** handler and associated message map entry. The **OnMeasureItem** handler is passed a control ID and a **MEASURE ITEMSTRUCT**. In OnMeasureItem(), set the *itemWidth* and *itemHeight* fields of **MEASUREITEMSTRUCT** with the menu item's width and height in pixels.

3. Provide an **OnDrawItem** handler and associated message map entry. The **OnDrawItem** handler's job is to draw the menu item on the screen.

 Windows only sends the **WM_MEASUREITEM** message once for each owner-drawn menu prior to it being displayed the first time. The **WM_DRAWITEM** is, of course, sent to the owner of the menu every time a menu item should be drawn.

Handling the the **WM_ MEASUREITEM** and **WM_DRAWITEM** messages is the job of the window that owns the menu. However, a more elegant and object-oriented method for implementing owner-drawn menus is to derive a class from **CMenu** and override the **MeasureItem()** and **DrawItem()** virtual functions. That is how you will do it here; you will continue to build on the Dynamic.exe program.

Adding A New Class Derived From CMenu

First, use File|New to add a new header file to your project. Here is what it should look like:

```
// ColorMenu.h : header file

#if !defined(COLORMENU_H_INCLUDED_)
#define COLORMENU_H_INCLUDED_

#if _MSC_VER > 1000
#pragma once
#endif // _MSC_VER > 1000

class CColorMenu : public CMenu
{
// Construction
public:
  CColorMenu(bool = true);
// Operations
public:
  void AppendColorMenu(UINT id1, UINT id2, COLORREF * cr);
```

```
// Implementation
public:
    virtual void MeasureItem(LPMEASUREITEMSTRUCT lpMIS);
    virtual void DrawItem(LPDRAWITEMSTRUCT lpDIS);
    virtual ~CColorMenu();
};
#endif // COLORMENU_H_INCLUDED_
```

The following listing shows the implementation. All of the interesting action occurs in **MeasureItem()** and **DrawItem()**. **MeasureItem()** just contains two statements, but without them, **DrawItem()** won't work properly. The first statement specifies the width of each menu item, and the second specifies the height.

DrawItem() is a bit more complicated. For each menu item, there are potentially four things to do. First, you have to determine if a checkmark needs to be drawn. If it does, you create a bitmap and draw it using the **BitBlt** function. **OBM_CHECK** is the bitmap ID.

Next, you need to determine if the entire item needs to be drawn. This is simply a matter of selecting a brush and filling the rectangle. Notice that the rectangle is to the left of the area needed for the checkmark.

Then you should check to see if an item's selection state has changed and if it is now selected. If both of these conditions are true, you highlight its frame. By also checking for **ODA_DRAWENTIRE**, you force the first item in the menu to be selected when it is drawn.

Finally, if an item's selection state has changed and that change is to *not selected*, you need to remove the highlighting frame.

```
// ColorMenu.cpp : implementation file
//

#define OEMRESOURCE

#include "stdafx.h"
#include ""ColorMenu.h"

#ifdef _DEBUG
#define new DEBUG_NEW
#undef THIS_FILE
static char THIS_FILE[] = __FILE__;
#endif

/////////////////////////////////////////////////////////////////
// CColorMenu
```

```
CColorMenu::CColorMenu(bool create)
{
  if(create)
    VERIFY(CreateMenu());
}


CColorMenu::~CColorMenu()
{
  Detach();
  ASSERT(m_hMenu == NULL);
    // default CMenu::~CMenu will destroy
}


void CColorMenu::MeasureItem(LPMEASUREITEMSTRUCT lpMIS)
{
  lpMIS->itemWidth = ::GetSystemMetrics(SM_CXMENUCHECK) * 5;
  lpMIS->itemHeight = ::GetSystemMetrics(SM_CYMENUCHECK);
}


void CColorMenu::DrawItem(LPDRAWITEMSTRUCT lpDIS)
{
  CDC* pDC = CDC::FromHandle(lpDIS->hDC);
  CRect rect(lpDIS->rcItem);

  if(lpDIS->itemState & ODS_CHECKED)
  {
    CBitmap bmCheck;
    bmCheck.LoadOEMBitmap(OBM_CHECK);
    BITMAP  bmStruct;
    bmCheck.GetObject(sizeof(BITMAP), &bmStruct);
    CSize sizeBM(bmStruct.bmWidth, bmStruct.bmHeight);

    CDC dcMem;
    dcMem.CreateCompatibleDC(pDC);
    CBitmap * pOldBitmap = dcMem.SelectObject(&bmCheck);
    pDC->BitBlt(rect.left, rect.top,
                sizeBM.cx, sizeBM.cy,
                &dcMem, 0, 0, SRCCOPY );
    dcMem.SelectObject(pOldBitmap);
  }
  rect.left += ::GetSystemMetrics(SM_CXMENUCHECK);

  COLORREF cr = (COLORREF)lpDIS->itemData;
  if(lpDIS->itemAction & ODA_DRAWENTIRE)
  {
    CBrush br(cr);
```

```
      pDC->FillRect(&rect, &br);
   }
   if( (lpDIS->itemAction & (ODA_SELECT | ODA_DRAWENTIRE))
       && (lpDIS->itemState & ODS_SELECTED) )
   {
      COLORREF crHighLight = cr ^ 0xFFFFFF;
      CBrush br(crHighLight);
      pDC->FrameRect(&rect, &br);
   }
   if( (lpDIS->itemAction & ODA_SELECT)
       && !(lpDIS->itemState & ODS_SELECTED))
   {
      CBrush br(cr);
      pDC->FrameRect(&rect, &br);
   }
}

void CColorMenu::AppendColorMenu(UINT id1, UINT id2, COLORREF * cr)
{
   for(UINT i = id1; i <= id2; i++)
   {

      VERIFY( AppendMenu( MF_ENABLED | MF_OWNERDRAW, i,
                          (LPCTSTR)*cr++) );
   }
}
```

To use **OBM_CHECK**, you need to place a **#define** OEMRESOURCE before the **#include** **<afxwin.h>** statement in your **StdAfx.h** file.

```
. . .
#define VC_EXTRALEAN    // Exclude rarely-used stuff from . . .
#define OEMRESOURCE

#include <afxwin.h>      // MFC core and standard components
#include <afxext.h>      // MFC extensions
#include <afxdtctl.h>    // MFC support for Internet . . .
. . .
```

Modifying CChildView

First, modify **ChildView.h** to include the **CColorMenu** header file (**Color Menu.h**). Then provide the prototype for **AttachColorMenu()**. This function will create and attach your owner-drawn (**CColorMenu**) menu to the menu bar.

```
#if _MSC_VER > 1000
#pragma once
#endif // _MSC_VER > 1000
#include "ColorMenu.h"
///////////////////////////////////////////////////////////////////
// CChildView window
class CChildView : public CWnd
```

Next, add **m_mnuColors** and change the type of **m_pMoreColors**:

```
private:
  void AttachColorMenu();
  CColorMenu m_mnuColors;
  CColorMenu * m_pMoreColors;
  CString m_strHelloMessage;
  UINT m_uColor;
```

Now modify **ChildView.cpp**. First, add a call to **AttachColorMenu()** in **PreCreateWindow()**:

```
cs.lpszClass =
   AfxRegisterWndClass(CS_HREDRAW|CS_VREDRAW|CS_DBLCLKS,
     ::LoadCursor(NULL, IDC_ARROW), HBRUSH(COLOR_WINDOW+1), NULL);

  AttachColorMenu();
  return TRUE;
}
```

Then change the section of **OnOptionColors()** that adds the extra color to the Colors menu:

```
case ID_OPTIONS_MORE_COLORS:
    m_pMoreColors = new CColorMenu(false);
    m_pMoreColors->CreatePopupMenu();

    m_pMoreColors->AppendColorMenu(
                ID_COLORS_CYAN, ID_COLORS_YELLOW,
                &COLORS[ID_COLORS_CYAN -ID_COLORS_BLACK] );

    CString prompt;

    prompt.LoadString(IDS_MORE_COLORS);
    VERIFY( pColorsMenu->AppendMenu( MF_STRING | MF_POPUP,
                            (UINT) m_pMoreColors->m_hMenu,
                            prompt )
         );
    break;
```

Now add the **AttachColorMenu()** function:

```
void CChildView::AttachColorMenu()
{
  m_mnuColors.AppendColorMenu( ID_COLORS_BLACK,
                               ID_COLORS_RED,
                               COLORS );
  // Replace the specified menu item with a color popup
  CMenu* pMenuBar = AfxGetMainWnd()->GetMenu();
  ASSERT(pMenuBar != NULL);

  TCHAR szString[256];
  // Colors menu
  pMenuBar->GetMenuString(3, szString, sizeof(szString),
                          MF_BYPOSITION);

  // Make the newly created menu become the Colors menu's popup.
  pMenuBar->ModifyMenu(3, MF_BYPOSITION | MF_POPUP,
                       (UINT)m_mnuColors.m_hMenu, szString);
}
```

Modifying The Menu Resource

Open the Resource Editor and delete the color selections from the Colors menu. Because you are using **AttachColorMenu()**, you no longer need these entries in the resource file.

Note: All of the examples above were non-document/view MFC applications, and the menu commands were mapped to member functions of the window class that owns the menu. Alternately, the menu commands could be handled in the application class. In document/view applications, menu commands can be handled just about anywhere—in the view class, the frame class, the application class, or even the document class.

Practice Questions

Question 1

> Which macro is used to map a contiguous range of command IDs to a single message handler function?
>
> ○ a. ON_UPDATE_COMMAND_UI_RANGE
>
> ○ b. ON_CONTROL_RANGE
>
> ○ c. ON_COMMAND_RANGE
>
> ○ d. ON_COMMAND_EX

The correct answer is c, **ON_COMMAND_RANGE**. Answer a maps a contiguous range of command IDs to a single update message handler function. Answer b maps a contiguous range of control IDs to a single message handler function for a specified Windows notification message, such as **BN_CLICKED**. Answer d maps several distinct menu commands to the same handler without constraining their respective IDs.

Question 2

> Which function adds menu items to a cascading menu?
>
> ○ a. CMenu::AppendMenuItems()
>
> ○ b. CMenu::AppendMenu()
>
> ○ c. CMenu::AddPopupItems()
>
> ○ d. CMenu::AddMenu()

The correct answer is b, **AppendMenu()**. Answers a, c, and d are not members of the **CMenu** class.

Question 3

Using ClassWizard, the following code was added to the view:

```
void CDrawView::OnContextMenu(CWnd* pWnd, CPoint
    point)
{

  // TODO: Add your message handler code here
}
```

Which snippet of code should be added to provide a pop-up menu?

○ a.
```
CMenu mnuTop;
    mnuTop.LoadMenu(IDR_CONTEXT);
    mnuTop.Popup(TPM_RIGHTBUTTON,
                 point.x, point.y,
                 AfxGetMainWnd());
```

○ b.
```
CMenu menubar;
    if(menubar.LoadMenu(IDR_POPUPMENUS))
    {
    CMenu *pPopup = menubar.GetSubMenu(0);
    ASSERT(pPopup != NULL);
    pPopup->Popup(TPM_RIGHTBUTTON,
                             point.x, point.y,
                             this);
    }
```

○ c.
```
CMenu mnuTop;
    if(mnuTop.CreatePopupMenu())
     {
     CString prompt;
      for(int i = ID_COLORS_CYAN;
        i <= ID_COLORS_YELLOW;
        i++)
     {
     prompt.LoadString(i);
     mnuTop.AppendMenu(MF_STRING, i, prompt);
     }
```

(continued)

Question 3 *(continued)*

```
            mnuTop.Popup(TPM_RIGHTBUTTON,
                         point.x, point.y,
                         pWnd);
      }
  d. CMenu mnuContext;
     if(mnuContext.LoadMenu(IDR_CONTEXT))
     {
     CMenu *pContext =
     mnuContext.GetSubMenu(0);
     ASSERT_VALID(pContext);
     pContext->TrackPopupMenu(TPM_RIGHTBUTTON,
                      point.x, point.y,
                      this);
     }
```

The correct answer is d. Answers a, b, and c all use **Popup()**. This is to confuse you; **Popup()** is not a member of **CMenu**. To add more confusion, answer d uses variable names that refer to context menus rather than pop-up menus. It's important to remember that a pop-up menu is sometimes called a context menu. Context menu are designed to pop up when the user right-clicks an object in a window. If **Popup()** is changed to **TrackPopupMenu()**, answers b and c will work correctly.

Question 4

Which one of the following statements is true?

○ a. Windows sends the WM_MEASUREITEM message to the owner of the menu once for each owner-drawn item before it is drawn. Windows sends the WM_DRAWITEM message to the owner of the menu the first time an owner-drawn menu item is to be drawn.

○ b. Windows sends the WM_MEASUREITEM message for each owner-drawn menu prior to it being displayed. Windows sends the WM_DRAWITEM message to the owner of the menu the first time an owner-drawn menu item is to be drawn.

○ c. Windows sends the WM_MEASUREITEM message to the owner of the menu once for each owner-drawn menu prior to it being displayed the first time. Windows sends the WM_DRAWITEM to the owner of the menu every time an owner-drawn menu item should be drawn.

○ d. Windows sends the WM_MEASUREITEM message for each owner-drawn menu prior to it being displayed. The WM_DRAWITEM is, of course, sent to the owner of the menu every time a menu item should be drawn.

The correct answer is c. The **WM_MEASUREITEM** message need only be sent once for each owner-drawn menu, because the dimensions only need to be determined one time. The **WM_DRAWITEM** message is sent every time a visual aspect of the menu has changed to ensure that the owner-drawn menu is redrawn correctly.

Need To Know More?

 Kruglinski, David J., George Shepherd, and Scot Wingo. *Programming Microsoft Visual C++*. 5th ed. Microsoft Press, Redmond, WA, 1998. ISBN 1-57231-857-0. This book strikes a good balance between theory and practical application. It is divided into six parts and covers nearly every aspect of MFC programming, from the basics to database management and the Internet. Chapter 13 covers menus.

 Prosise, Jeff. *Programming Windows with MFC*. Microsoft Press, Redmond, WA, 1999. ISBN 1-57231-695-0. This updated version of the author's popular *Programming Windows 95 with MFC* book is excellent. It's divided into four parts: Fundamentals of Windows and MFC; The Document/View Architecture; Beyond the Basics; and COM, OLE, and ActiveX. The author's approach is to first present a number of fundamental concepts, using snippets of code where appropriate, then present a completed program that employs the concepts followed by an explanation of the code. After you have worked through the book, not only will you know how to use MFC to write 32-bit applications, you will understand the code that AppWizard, ClassWizard, and other code generators produce. Chapter 4 provides a good description of menus and contains two example programs.

 MSDN Library, Technical Articles\Visual Tools\Visual C++\ MFC Self-Drawing Menus

 Visual C++ Documentation, MFC Sample Program— "DYNAMENU." This is a MFC sample program that illustrates dynamic modification of menus and status bars regardless of whether handling commands are known at compile time. This sample program uses the document/view architecture.

Toolbars And Status Bars

Terms you'll need to understand:

√ CControlBar

√ CToolBar

√ LoadToolBar

√ EnableDocking

√ DockControlBar

√ FloatControlBar

√ CToolBarCtrl

√ CStatusBar

√ CStatusBarCtrl

Techniques you'll need to master:

√ Creating a toolbar

√ Adding a custom toolbar to an application

√ Understanding when to use **CFrameWnd::EnableDocking**

√ Understanding when to use **CControlBar::EnableDocking**

√ Writing code that docks a toolbar

√ Creating a status bar

√ Adding panes to a status bar

√ Writing code that keeps a status bar updated

This chapter looks at two basic parts of the Windows user interface: toolbars and status bars. A *toolbar* is a child window with buttons and—sometimes—other types of controls, such as combo boxes. These controls allow the user to issue commands with a simple mouse click. A *status bar* is a child window positioned at the bottom of the main window. It is used to display context-sensitive help messages for menu items and toolbar buttons. It also displays text messages, such as "NUM" to tell the user that Num Lock is on.

The basic MFC classes for toolbars and status bars are **CToolBar** and **CStatusBar**. Both of these classes are derived from **CControlBar**. **CControlBar** is derived from **CWnd**. **CControlBar** windows are positioned inside frame windows and have the ability to resize and reposition themselves as the parent window's size and position changes.

Toolbars

Most applications use toolbars to provide instant access to commonly used commands. Toolbars normally consist of a number of buttons, where each button serves as a shortcut to a menu item. Then, rather than navigating through menus or needing to remember keystrokes, the user can simply click a toolbar button. Like a menu item, when a toolbar button is clicked, a **WM_COMMAND** message is created. By assigning the same command ID to a menu item and a toolbar button, the same command and update handlers will serve both the menu item and the toolbar button. Although not nearly as frequent in occurrence, toolbars can also operate as standalone objects.

If you create a single-document interface (SDI) or multiple-document interface (MDI) application using the AppWizard and accept the default toolbar setting in Step 4, the code to create the standard toolbar window, load the button images, and attach it to the main frame window will be generated. This standard toolbar provides buttons for the commonly used File and Edit menu commands, as well as a button for the About dialog box. This is a good start, but as your application design evolves, you will quickly discover that the standard toolbar does not satisfy the unique requirements of your application.

Understanding The Standard Toolbar

When AppWizard generates your skeleton MFC application, it adds a **CToolBar** object, **m_wndToolBar**, to the **CMainFrame** class definition. It also adds code to **CMainFrame::OnCreate()** that creates the toolbar as a child window of the frame window and loads the associated resources:

```
if (!m_wndToolBar.CreateEx(this, TBSTYLE_FLAT, WS_CHILD | WS_VISIBLE
          | CBRS_TOP | CBRS_GRIPPER | CBRS_TOOLTIPS | CBRS_FLYBY
```

```
              | CBRS_SIZE_DYNAMIC) ||
              !m_wndToolBar.LoadToolBar(IDR_MAINFRAME))
{
  TRACE0("Failed to create toolbar\n");
  return -1;      // fail to create
}
```

The function used to create the toolbar's window is **CreateEx()**. This function is new to Visual C++ 6.0. Its second parameter allows you to set the new toolbar style flags. Here, **TBSTYLE_FLAT** is used to create a flat toolbar where both the toolbar and the buttons are transparent. **TBSTYLE_FLAT** is one of three styles that affect the "3D" aspect of the toolbar buttons. If you want to create a toolbar that resembles the Internet Explorer 4 toolbars, use **TBSTYLE_FLAT | TBSTYLE_TRANSPARENT**. Changing it to 0 creates the old-look "raised buttons" style. Here are the descriptions of all three 3D-toolbar styles:

➤ **TBSTYLE_FLAT** Flat toolbar where both the toolbar and the buttons are transparent, and the button text appears under the button bitmap. The button underneath the cursor is automatically highlighted.

➤ **TBSTYLE_TRANSPARENT** Like **TBSTYLE_FLAT**, except only the toolbar is transparent. Buttons appear raised.

➤ **TBSTYLE_LIST** Similar to **TBSTYLE_TRANSPARENT**, except text is to the right of the button bitmap.

The third parameter specifies the control bar style. This parameter can be a combination of the appropriate standard window styles, such as **WS_CHILD** and **WS_VISIBLE**, and any of the following:

➤ **CBRS_TOP** Docks the toolbar to the top of the client area of a frame window and draws a border on the bottom edge

➤ **CBRS_BOTTOM** Docks the toolbar to the bottom of the client area of a frame window and draws a border on the top edge

➤ **CBRS_ALIGN_LEFT** Docks the toolbar to the left side of the client area of a frame window and draws a border on the right edge

➤ **CBRS_ALIGN_RIGHT** Docks the toolbar to the right side of the client area of a frame window and draws a border on the left edge

➤ **CBRS_ANY** Docks the toolbar to any side of the client area of a frame window

➤ **CBRS_FLOAT_MULTI** Allows multiple toolbars to be floated in one mini-frame window

➤ **CBRS_TOOLTIPS** Displays tooltips for the toolbar

➤ **CBRS_FLYBY** Updates the message text at the same time as tooltips

➤ **CBRS_GRIPPER** Adds a gripper bar

➤ **CBRS_SIZE_DYNAMIC** Allows the user to resize the floating toolbar

➤ **CBRS_SIZE_FIXED** Keeps the user from resizing the floating toolbar

After the toolbar window is created, the toolbar resource is loaded by calling **LoadToolBar()** and passing the ID of the toolbar to be loaded. For the default toolbar, **IDR_MAINFRAME** is used.

Following the creation and loading of the toolbar, three additional actions are necessary to place a dockable toolbar in your application:

1. Enable docking for the toolbar.

2. Enable docking for the frame window.

3. Dock the toolbar to the frame window.

Here is the code the AppWizard generates for the standard toolbar:

```
m_wndToolBar.EnableDocking(CBRS_ALIGN_ANY);
EnableDocking(CBRS_ALIGN_ANY);
DockControlBar(&m_wndToolBar);
```

The first line enables the toolbar to dock to any edge of the frame window. By combining the flags in Table 4.1, you can specify that the toolbar can only dock to specific edges. Alternately, to make the toolbar float, pass a 0. For example, to allow the standard toolbar to dock on the top and left edges, you would change the line of code to the following:

```
m_wndToolBar.EnableDocking(CBRS_ALIGN_TOP | CBRS_ALIGN_LEFT);
```

The next line of code calls **EnableDocking**, a member function of the frame window. This function specifies the edges of the frame window that allows docking. You pass this function the same combination of flags shown in Table 4.1.

The **DockControlBar** function is then called to specify the initial edge of the frame window where the toolbar will be docked. The prototype for the function is as follows:

```
void DockControlBar( CControlBar * pBar,
                     UINT nDockBarID = 0,
                     LPCRECT lpRect = NULL );
```

Table 4.1 Docking styles.	
Docking Style	**Description**
CBRS_ALIGN_TOP	Allows docking at the top of the client area
CBRS_ALIGN_LEFT	Allows docking at the left of the client area
CBRS_ALIGN_RIGHT	Allows docking at the right of the client area
CBRS_ALIGN_BOTTOM	Allows docking at the bottom of the client area
CBRS_ALIGN_ANY	Allows docking on any side of the client area

The first parameter points to the toolbar to be docked. The second parameter, *nDockBarID*, specifies which sides of the frame window to consider for docking. It can be 0, or one or more of the values shown in Table 4.2. If 0, the control bar can be docked to any side enabled for docking in the destination frame window. The third parameter determines, in screen coordinates, where the toolbar will be docked in the nonclient area of the destination frame window. If you replace **DockControlBar** with **FloatControlBar**, the toolbar will initially not be docked to the frame window.

Adding Your Own Toolbar

Now that you understand the standard toolbar, let's look at what it takes to add one of your own design. The steps are as follows:

1. Make certain that there is a command ID and a handler for every control that you place on your toolbar. Normally, you will use the same IDs and handlers that you use for your menu items.

2. Use the Resource Editor to create your toolbar resource. Associate each toolbar button with the appropriate command ID.

3. Add a menu item that will allow the user to make the toolbar visible and invisible.

Table 4.2 nDockBarID values.	
Value	**Description**
AFX_IDW_DOCKBAR_TOP	Dock to the topside of the frame window
AFX_IDW_DOCKBAR_BOTTOM	Dock to the bottom side of the frame window
AFX_IDW_DOCKBAR_LEFT	Dock to the left side of the frame window
AFX_IDW_DOCKBAR_RIGHT	Dock to the right side of the frame window

4. Add a **CToolBar** variable to the appropriate header file. Normally, this will be your **CMainFrame** class header file. This variable can be an object or a pointer; it's your choice. If you do make it a pointer, ensure that it is initialized to 0 in the **CMainFrame** constructor.

5. If you haven't already done so, provide the implementation code to support each of the toolbar buttons.

6. Write the code for the menu item specified in Step 3. Here, you need to provide code that will make the toolbar visible and invisible. Additionally, if in Step 4 you choose to use a pointer, you must create the toolbar before you use it. And don't forget to add a **WM_DESTROY** message handler so that you can delete it. If in Step 4 you decided to use an object, provide code to your frame window's **OnCreate** function to create your toolbar.

7. Add a UI handler to the frame window.

Creating The Project

Run AppWizard to generate an SDI project with document/view architecture support. Deselect Printing and Print Preview in Step 4. Name the project, and create it in \ExamCram\Toolbars. The options and the default class names are shown in Figure 4.1.

Adding Resource IDs And Menu Items

Using Table 4.3 as a guide, add the resource IDs to your application.

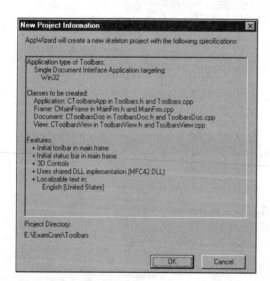

Figure 4.1 New project information.

Table 4.3 Resource IDs.	
ID	Value
IDR_COLOR_TOOLBAR	130
IDS_WELCOME_MESSAGE	0x7000
ID_COLORS_BLACK	0x9000
ID_COLORS_BLUE	0x9001
ID_COLORS_GREEN	0x9002
ID_COLORS_RED	0x9003
ID_VIEW_COLORTOOLBAR	0x9004

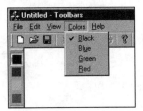

Figure 4.2   Colors menu.

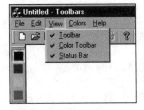

Figure 4.3   View menu.

Using the Resource Editor, update the menu to look like Figures 4.2 and 4.3. Now add the code needed to handle the Color menu items and to display a message in the center of the view window. Ensure that selecting a different color on the menu will cause the color of the text to change. Because the Document/View architecture is now being used, you should separate the data and the view of the data appropriately. Here is what the code might look like:

```
// ToolbarsDoc.h
. . .
public:
  virtual ~CToolbarsDoc();
  CString GetWelcomeMessage();
  COLORREF GetColor();
#ifdef _DEBUG
  virtual void AssertValid() const;
  virtual void Dump(CDumpContext& dc) const;
#endif

protected:
// Generated message map functions
protected:
  //{{AFX_MSG(CToolbarsDoc)
  //}}AFX_MSG
```

```
  afx_msg void OnColors(UINT nID);
  afx_msg void OnUpdateColors(CCmdUI* pCmdUI);
  DECLARE_MESSAGE_MAP()
private:
  CString m_strWelcomeMessage;
  static COLORREF theColors[4];
  UINT m_uColor;
};
```

```
// ToolbarsDoc.h
. . .
// CToolbarsDoc
COLORREF CToolbarsDoc::theColors[4] =
                { RGB(  0,   0,   0), // Black
                  RGB(  0,   0, 255), // Blue
                  RGB(  0, 255,   0), // Green
                  RGB(255,   0,   0) }; // Red
```

```
IMPLEMENT_DYNCREATE(CToolbarsDoc, CDocument)

BEGIN_MESSAGE_MAP(CToolbarsDoc, CDocument)
  //{{AFX_MSG_MAP(CToolbarsDoc)
  //}}AFX_MSG_MAP
  ON_COMMAND_RANGE(ID_COLORS_BLACK, ID_COLORS_RED, OnColors)
  ON_UPDATE_COMMAND_UI_RANGE(ID_COLORS_BLACK, ID_COLORS_RED,
OnUpdateColors)
END_MESSAGE_MAP()
```

```
///////////////////////////////////////////////////////////////////
// CToolbarsDoc construction/destruction

CToolbarsDoc::CToolbarsDoc()
  : m_uColor(ID_COLORS_BLACK)
{
  // TODO: add one-time construction code here
  VERIFY( m_strWelcomeMessage.LoadString(IDS_WELCOME_MESSAGE) );
}
```

```
. . .


void CToolbarsDoc::OnColors(UINT nID)
{
  m_uColor = nID;
  UpdateAllViews(NULL);
}
```

```
void CToolbarsDoc::OnUpdateColors(CCmdUI* pCmdUI)
{
   pCmdUI->SetCheck(pCmdUI->m_nID == m_uColor);
}

COLORREF CToolbarsDoc::GetColor()
{
   return theColors[m_uColor - ID_COLORS_BLACK];
}

CString CToolbarsDoc::GetWelcomeMessage()
{
   return m_strWelcomeMessage;
}


// ToolbarsView.doc
. . .

// CToolbarsView drawing

void CToolbarsView::OnDraw(CDC* pDC)
{
   CToolbarsDoc* pDoc = GetDocument();
   ASSERT_VALID(pDoc);
   // TODO: add draw code for native data here
   CRect rect;
   GetClientRect(&rect);
   pDC->SetTextColor(pDoc->GetColor());
   pDC->DrawText(pDoc->GetWelcomeMessage(), -1, &rect,
                 DT_SINGLELINE | DT_CENTER | DT_VCENTER);
}
```

Adding The Toolbar Resource

Use the Resource Editor to add a toolbar that contains four buttons. From left to right, make the buttons black, blue, green, and red. Make sure that the toolbar button IDs match the Color menu items. See Figure 4.4.

 The Toolbar Button Properties dialog box's Prompt property allows you to enter text that will appear in the status line when the cursor passes over a Toolbar button or when the menu item with the matching ID is selected. You can also add a ToolTip by adding the ToolTip string after a \n separator code.

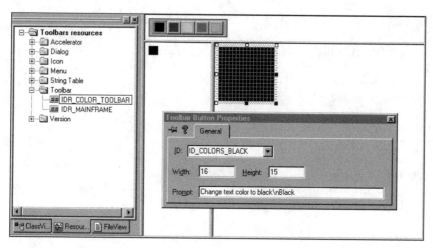

Figure 4.4 Toolbar resources.

Creating The Color Toolbar

Now modify the **CMainFrame** class. Add a **CToolBar** variable to the header file. Then modify **CMainFrame::OnCreate** to create the toolbar as a child window of the frame window and to load the associated resources:

```
// MainFrm.h
protected:  // control bar embedded members
        CStatusBar  m_wndStatusBar;
        CToolBar    m_wndToolBar;
        CToolBar    m_wndColorToolBar;
// Generated message map functions


// MainFrm.cpp
// TODO: Delete these three lines if you don't want the toolbar to
//  be dockable
m_wndToolBar.EnableDocking(CBRS_ALIGN_ANY);
EnableDocking(CBRS_ALIGN_ANY);
DockControlBar(&m_wndToolBar);
// Create the color toolbar
if (!m_wndColorToolBar.CreateEx(this, TBSTYLE_FLAT,
            WS_CHILD | WS_VISIBLE | CBRS_TOP | CBRS_GRIPPER
            | CBRS_TOOLTIPS | CBRS_FLYBY | CBRS_SIZE_DYNAMIC) ||
  !m_wndColorToolBar.LoadToolBar(IDR_COLOR_TOOLBAR))
{
  TRACE0("Failed to create toolbar\n");
  return -1;      // fail to create
}
m_wndColorToolBar.EnableDocking(CBRS_ALIGN_ANY);
DockControlBar(&m_wndColorToolBar, AFX_IDW_DOCKBAR_LEFT);
return 0;
```

This code is essentially the same as that used for the standard toolbar. The only differences are as follows:

➤ The resource ID passed to **LoadToolBar()** is for the color toolbar.

➤ Because **CFrameWnd::EnableDocking** was called when establishing the standard toolbar, there is no need to call it again.

➤ **AFX_IDW_DOCKBAR_LEFT** is passed as the second parameter to **DockControlBar()**. See Table 4.2.

If you run your application at this point, it creates a flat-style toolbar that initially docks to the left of the frame. The toolbar should have four buttons that, when clicked, change the color of the text. It also has a gripper bar for repositioning.

Adding Code For The View\Color Toolbar Item

Add **ON_COMMAND** and **ON_UPDATE_COMMAND_UI** entries to the message map for the View\Color Toolbar item. Then add the necessary code:

```
void CMainFrame::OnViewColorToolBar()
{
  if(m_wndColorToolBar.IsWindowVisible() == TRUE)
    // Hide the toolbar
    ShowControlBar(&m_wndColorToolBar, FALSE, FALSE);
  else
    // Show it.
    ShowControlBar(&m_wndColorToolBar, TRUE, FALSE);
}


void CMainFrame::OnUpdateViewColorToolBar(CCmdUI* pCmdUI)
{
  pCmdUI->SetCheck(m_wndColorToolBar.IsWindowVisible());
}
```

Don't confuse **CToolBar** and **CToolBarCtrl**. **CToolBar**, inherited from **CControlBar**, is a control bar that has a row of bitmapped buttons and optional separators. **CToolBarCtrl**, inherited from **CWnd**, provides the internal control of the **CToolBar** object. **CToolBarCtrl** is available only for programs running under Windows 95 and Windows NT 3.51 and later. **CToolBar::GetToolBarCtrl** allows you to obtain a reference to the **CToolBarCtrl** object.

Make sure that you understand the difference between these two toolbar classes. Test writers love questions about controls that are specific to or different among operating systems.

Status Bars

Most modern Windows programs include a status bar that displays—without interrupting the user's work—various kinds of status information. Typically displayed at the bottom of a parent window, it is a horizontal window that can be divided into one or more areas. These areas are commonly referred to as *panes*, *panels*, or *indicators*. Each pane is a rectangular area that can be set individually, so one pane might be used to display context-sensitive help for a menu item or toolbar, whereas another displays the current line and column number in a document.

The default MFC status bar, created by the AppWizard, displays the state of the Caps Lock, Num Lock, and Scroll Lock keys in the rightmost panes and the currently selected menu item or toolbar button in the leftmost pane (pane 0), commonly referred to as the "message pane."

In this section, the default status bar will first be examined. Then you will look at how you can add a new pane to a status bar and keep it updated. After that, you will see one way to draw in a status bar pane.

Understanding The Standard Status Bar

When AppWizard generates your skeleton MFC application, it adds a **CStatusBar** object, **m_wndStatusBar**, to the **CMainFrame** class definition. It also adds code to **CMainFrame::OnCreate()** that creates the status bar (see Figure 4.5) as a child window of the frame window and sets the indicators or panes:

```
if (!m_wndStatusBar.Create(this) ||
    !m_wndStatusBar.SetIndicators(indicators,
      sizeof(indicators)/sizeof(UINT)))
  {
    TRACE0("Failed to create status bar\n");
    return -1;      // fail to create
  }
```

The default AppWizard generated indicators array is defined at the top of **MainFrm.cpp**:

```
static UINT indicators[] =
{
  ID_SEPARATOR,             // status line indicator
  ID_INDICATOR_CAPS,
  ID_INDICATOR_NUM,
  ID_INDICATOR_SCRL,
};
```

Except for the first, each of the entries specifies a string resource that is to be displayed when the pane is enabled. The first entry, **ID_SEPARATOR**, is a

Figure 4.5   Default status bar generated by AppWizard.

special ID value meaning there is no string resource associated with it. The framework will display the menu item and toolbar button prompts in this area. The other three entries are IDs that are handled by the framework to display the current status of the Caps Lock, Num Lock, and Scroll Lock keys:

```
STRINGTABLE DISCARDABLE
BEGIN
    ID_INDICATOR_EXT        "EXT"
    ID_INDICATOR_CAPS       "CAP"
    ID_INDICATOR_NUM        "NUM"
    ID_INDICATOR_SCRL       "SCRL"
    ID_INDICATOR_OVR        "OVR"
    ID_INDICATOR_REC        "REC"
END
```

The framework positions all panes after the first to the far right of the status bar. It sizes the width of each of these panes for the text string assigned to them and draws them "indented," so that they are visible even when they are blank. The first pane is stretched to fill the remaining space.

Adding A New Pane

Now that you understand the status bar AppWizard provides, you will add a new pane to it. As you will see, adding a new pane to the standard status bar is not very difficult. It only entails three steps:

1. Define the pane's command ID.

2. Create a new string resource to be displayed in the pane.

3. Add the pane to the indicators array.

Here are the changes to make to your Toolbars application:

```
// resource.h
#define ID_COLORS_RED               0x9003
#define ID_VIEW_COLORTOOLBAR        0x9004
#define ID_INDICATOR_COLOR          0x9005

// Toolbars.rc
STRINGTABLE DISCARDABLE
BEGIN
    ID_COLORS_BLACK     "Change text color to black\nBlack"
    ID_COLORS_BLUE      "Change text color to blue\nBlue"
    ID_COLORS_GREEN     "Change text color to green\nGreen"
```

```
     ID_COLORS_RED              "Change text color to red\nRed"
     ID_VIEW_COLORTOOLBAR       "Show or hide the color toolbar\n
       Toggle Color Toolbar"
     ID_INDICATOR_COLOR         "Black "
END


// MainFrm.cpp
static UINT indicators[] =
{
  ID_SEPARATOR,              // status line indicator
  ID_INDICATOR_COLOR,
  ID_INDICATOR_CAPS,
  ID_INDICATOR_NUM,
  ID_INDICATOR_SCRL,
};
```

Notice that the string "Black " has a space after the "k". MFC uses this string to
determine the size of the status bar pane. The added space ensures that the
string "Green" will be displayed properly.

Displaying The Text

Many developers use **CStatusBar::SetPaneText()** to display the text. Although
you can do it this way, it is not the best approach. The best way is to call
CCmdUI::SetText in an update handler function for the pane. The Class-
Wizard won't help you here. Add the following code:

```
// ToolbarsDoc.h
afx_msg void OnColors(UINT nID);
afx_msg void OnUpdateColors(CCmdUI* pCmdUI);
afx_msg void OnUpdateColorPanel(CCmdUI* pCmdUI);


// ToolbarsDoc.cpp

ON_COMMAND_RANGE(ID_COLORS_BLACK, ID_COLORS_RED, OnColors)
ON_UPDATE_COMMAND_UI_RANGE(ID_COLORS_BLACK, ID_COLORS_RED,
OnUpdateColors)
ON_UPDATE_COMMAND_UI(ID_INDICATOR_COLOR, OnUpdateColorPanel)


. . .


void CToolbarsDoc::OnUpdateColorPanel(CCmdUI* pCmdUI)
{
  CString color;
  color.LoadString(m_uColor);
```

```
// Extract name of the color
int idx = color.Find(_T('\n'));
ASSERT(idx >= 0);
color.Delete(0, idx + 1);
// Set the color into the text of the user-interface
pCmdUI->SetText(color);
}
```

This code loads the string resource that contains the name of the current color. It then extracts the second substring, which is the name of the color. To finish, it sets the color into the text of the user-interface item—in this case, the new pane you added.

Drawing In A Pane

You now have everything in place so that with a few simple changes, you can display the actual color, rather than the name, in the status bar. All you need to do is change the handler so that it fills the pane with color rather than with text, as follows:

```
void CToolbarsDoc::OnUpdateColorPanel(CCmdUI* pCmdUI)
{
  pCmdUI->SetText("");
  CStatusBar *pSB = static_cast<CStatusBar *>(pCmdUI->m_pOther);

  CRect rect;
  pSB->GetItemRect(pCmdUI->m_nIndex, &rect);
  rect.DeflateRect(1, 1);

  CBrush brush(theColors[m_uColor - ID_COLORS_BLACK]);

  CClientDC dc(pSB);
  CBrush * pOldBrush = dc.SelectObject(&brush);

  dc.PatBlt(rect.left, rect.top,
            rect.Width(), rect.Height(),
            PATCOPY);
  dc.SelectObject(pOldBrush);
}
```

First, ensure that there is no text to draw in the pane. Then, get a pointer to the status bar object. Next, determine the area that will be colored, and create a brush of the proper color. After that, create a dc, give it your brush, and fill the area using the **PatBlt()** function. Last, restore the old brush.

At this point, if you compile and run the program, you'll see that the status bar appears to work as expected. However, when you resize the window, you will notice that the color pane doesn't maintain its color. Your system must be set up to "Show window contents while dragging" to display this effect.

Maintaining The Color While Resizing

The standard status bar repaints itself when it receives a **WM_PAINT** message. However, the color pane is refreshed when the **UPDATE_COMMAND_UI** is triggered, and because **CStatusBar:: OnPaint()** doesn't trigger **UPDATE_COMMAND_UI**, it doesn't get refreshed. Luckily, fixing the problem isn't a big deal. A custom class derived from **CStatusBar** will do the trick.

Creating A Custom Status Bar

Create a class named **CCustomStatusBar**, and override the **OnPaint()** handler to send **WM_IDLEUPDATECMDUI** message to itself. Because ClassWizard doesn't provide **CStatusBar** as a base class, use generic **CWnd** as the base class, and then manually change all of the references to **CWnd** in your header and CPP files. Here are the critical lines of code for the **CCustomStatusBar** class:

```
// CustomStatusBar.h
class CCustomStatusBar : public CStatusBar
{
// Construction


protected:
  //{{AFX_MSG(CCustomStatusBar)
  afx_msg void OnPaint();
  //}}AFX_MSG

// CustomStatusBar.cpp
#include "stdafx.h"
#include "Toolbars.h"
#include "CustomStatusBar.h"
#include <afxpriv.h>  // For WM_IDLEUPDATECMDUI message
#ifdef _DEBUG


BEGIN_MESSAGE_MAP(CCustomStatusBar, CStatusBar)
      //{{AFX_MSG_MAP(CCustomStatusBar)
      ON_WM_PAINT()
      //}}AFX_MSG_MAP
```

```
END_MESSAGE_MAP()
```

```
////////////////////////////////////////////////////////////////
// CCustomStatusBar message handlers
```

```
void CCustomStatusBar::OnPaint()
{
  CStatusBar::OnPaint();
  SendMessage(WM_IDLEUPDATECMDUI);
}
```

Now modify your frame window to use **CCustomStatusBar** instead of
CStatusBar:

```
// MainFrm.h
#endif // _MSC_VER > 1000
#include "CustomStatusBar.h"
class CMainFrame : public CFrameWnd
{
```

```
. . .
```

```
protected:  // control bar embedded members
  CCustomStatusBar  m_wndStatusBar;
  CToolBar          m_wndToolBar;
  CToolBar          m_wndColorToolBar;
```

The examples in this chapter show how the **CToolBar** and **CStatusBar** classes work with **CFrameWnd** to lay themselves out within the frame window. However, if you need a toolbar or status bar to work with a dialog box or pop-up window, you need to use the **CToolBarCtrl** and **CStatusBarCtrl** classes. Because each of these classes wrap a Windows common control, they are more complicated to use and significantly increase the amount of code required. For information on using **CToolBarCtrl** and **CStatusBarCtrl**, see Technical Note 60 online.

Practice Questions

Question 1

Which of the following statements regarding toolbars and status bars is true? [Check all the correct answers]

- ❏ a. CToolBar and CStatusBar inherit directly from CWnd.
- ❏ b. CToolBar inherits directly from CWnd, and CToolBarCtrl inherits directly from CControlBar.
- ❏ c. CStatusBar inherits directly from CControlBar.
- ❏ d. CToolBarCtrl inherits directly from CWnd.

The correct answers are c and d. **CToolBar** and **CStatusBar** inherit directly from **CControlBar**. **CToolBarCtrl** and **CStatusBarCtrl** inherit directly from **CWnd**.

Question 2

Which of the following statements are false regarding the creation of a dockable toolbar? [Check all the correct answers]

- ❏ a. You only need to enable docking for the frame window.
- ❏ b. You do not need to enable docking for the frame window; however, you must enable docking for each toolbar you want to be dockable, and you must add code to dock the toolbar to a frame window.
- ❏ c. You must enable docking for the frame, enable docking for each toolbar you want to be dockable, and dock the toolbar to the frame.
- ❏ d. You must enable docking for the frame and add code to dock the toolbar to the frame, but you do not need to enable docking for the toolbar you want to dock.

The correct answers are a, b, and d (they are the false statements). To create a dockable toolbar, you must complete all three steps: enable docking for the frame, enable docking for each toolbar you want to dock, and add code to dock the toolbar to the frame window.

Question 3

> You have created a toolbar and have placed three buttons on it. Now you want to
> add a text label to each button. Which of the following functions would you use?
>
> ○ a. CToolBar::SetButtonLabel()
>
> ○ b. CToolBar::SetText()
>
> ○ c. CToolBar::SetCaption()
>
> ○ d. CToolBar::SetButtonText()

Answer d is correct. **SetButtonText()** is the only function of the four listed
that is a member of the **CToolBar** class. **SetButtonText()** is called to set the
text on a toolbar button. You need to be careful when you use **SetButtonText()**,
because the pane will not automatically resize. To resize the pane, you must use
CToolBar::SetSizes(). It should be pointed out that you must not use these
functions if you want your toolbars to follow the *Windows Interface Guidelines*
for Software Design recommendations for button and image sizes.

Question 4

> Which of the following functions is used to place text in a status bar panel?
> [Check all the correct answers]
>
> ❑ a. CStatusBar::SetPaneInfo()
>
> ❑ b. CStatusBar::SetPaneText()
>
> ❑ c. CCmdUI::SetText()
>
> ❑ d. CStatusBar::SetText()

Answers b and c are correct. **CCmdUI::SetText()** in conjunction with
UPDATE_COMMAND_UI is the best method to use. **CStatusBar::**
SetPaneText() can be used; however, because the status bar belongs to the
frame window and the code needing to update the text can be anywhere, such
as in a document or view, this is not the preferred method. **CStatusBar::**
SetPaneInfo() is used to set the specified indicator pane to a new ID, style, and
width. **SetText()** is not a member of **CStatusBar**.

Need To Know More?

 Kruglinski, David J., George Shepherd, and Scot Wingo. *Programming Microsoft Visual C++*. 5th ed. Microsoft Press, Redmond, WA, 1998. ISBN 1-57231-857-0. This book strikes a good balance between theory and practical application. It is divided into six parts and covers nearly every aspect of MFC programming, from the basics to database management and the Internet. Chapter 14 covers toolbars and status bars.

 Prosise, Jeff. *Programming Windows with MFC*. Microsoft Press, Redmond, WA, 1999. ISBN 1-57231-695-0. This is the updated version of the author's popular book, *Programming Windows 95 with MFC*. Chapter 12 covers **CToolBar** and **CStatusBar**.

Dialog Boxes And Property Sheets

5

Terms you'll need to understand:

√ Modal

√ Modeless

√ **CDialog**

√ **DoModal**

√ **EndDialog**

√ Dialog Data Exchange (DDX)

√ **DoDataExchange**

√ **CDataExchange**

√ **UpdateData**

√ Dialog Data Validation (DDV)

√ **CDialogBar**

√ **CCommonDialog**

√ **CPropertySheet**

√ **CPropertyPage**

Techniques you'll need to master:

√ Understanding when and how to use DDX and DDV

√ Understanding how to write custom DDX and DDV functions

√ Creating a modeless dialog box

√ Writing code that properly instantiates, manipulates, and destroys a modeless dialog box

√ Creating and using a dialog bar

√ Understanding how to customize a common dialog box

√ Creating property sheets and property pages

√ Writing code that employs both modal and modeless property sheets

Dialog Boxes

Dialog boxes are one of the primary methods that Windows programs use to display information and receive input from users. They promote good user interface design by providing a standard way for the application programmer to put controls up for the user. Because the way dialog boxes work is consistent from one Windows program to the next, users know how to navigate between the controls. This uniformity among Windows programs means that users—whether they are new, infrequent, or regular users—will be more productive in both speed of action and speed of thought.

Dialog boxes come in two basic varieties: modal and modeless. *Modal dialog boxes* require the user to respond before the application continues. These modal dialog boxes can be stacked so that one dialog box starts another, thus forcing control to the most recent dialog box and returning to the calling dialog box when closed. *Modeless dialog boxes*, on the other hand, behave much more like normal windows, allowing the user to do other work within the application. A user might open a modeless dialog box and carry out some action; then for convenience, rather than closing it, the user might just move it out of the way and continue working with the application.

Modal dialog boxes are the most common and easiest to program, but they are also the most restrictive for the user. For your application, the choice of modal or modeless will depend on a number of factors. In general, however, modal dialog boxes are usually employed for detail windows required to complete a command: which file to save to, how to format the selected text, and so on. These boxes are used to ask questions of the user, to collect details, and to confirm actions. By contrast, modeless dialog boxes are generally used to implement "tools" that may be used alongside documents. Examples of these tools are the Spelling and Grammar checker and Find and Replace provided with Microsoft Word. Modeless dialog boxes are, in general, more complex both to design and implement than modal dialog boxes. Unfortunately, it seems that in many applications, the programmer placed ease of programming over convenience for the user and used a modal dialog box when a modeless would be more appropriate.

Creating A Modal Dialog Class

Developing a dialog box, whether modal or modeless, entails two basic steps: create a dialog template using the Resource Editor and then use ClassWizard to create a **CDialog**-derived class to handle the dialog box's functionality. Your new class, as created by ClassWizard, will know what template is associated with it and may have member variables that reflect the state of the controls in the template. By using ClassWizard and hand-coding, you can then add specialized code to initialize, reset, validate, or process information and a message map and message handlers so that your dialog box can react to the user.

Modal dialog boxes are constructed by using one of two constructors:

```
CDialog(LPCTSTR lpszTemplateName, CWnd* pParentWnd = NULL);

CDialog(UINT nIDTemplate, CWnd* pParentWnd = NULL);
```

With both of these constructors, the first argument specifies the template resource and the second specifies the parent window. If you do not specify a parent window, MFC automatically uses the application's top-level window as the dialog box's parent.

ClassWizard provides a default constructor for your **CDialog**-derived dialog box that initializes the base class using the second of the above two constructors. If you look at the constructor ClassWizard provides you will see code similar to this:

```
CMyDialog::CMyDialog(CWnd* pParent /*=NULL*/)
    : CDialog(CMyDialog::IDD, pParent)
```

After constructing the **CDialog**-derived object, you then call **CDialog:: DoModal()** to display the dialog box. **DoModal()** blocks the calling function until the dialog box is closed, normally, by the user clicking the OK or Cancel button. Both **CDialog::OnOK()** and **CDialog::OnCancel()** call **CDialog:: EndDialog()**, which terminates the dialog box. When **EndDialog()** is called, it is passed one argument, which is the value returned to the caller of **DoModal()**. The value passed to **EndDialog()** by **OnOK()** is **IDOK**, and the value passed by **OnCancel()** is **IDCANCEL**. You can override this behavior by calling **CDialog::EndDialog()** and specifying the value that should be returned. Here are the prototypes for **DoModal()** and **EndDialog()**:

```
virtual int DoModal();
void EndDialog(int nResult);
```

Constructing and displaying a modal dialog box using the **CDialog**-derived class might look like this:

```
CMyDialog dlg;
  switch(dlg.DoModal())
  {
  case IDOK:
    // user clicked the OK button
    break;
```

```
case IDCANCEL:
  // user clicked the Cancel button, press the escape key, or
  break;
case -1:
  // couldn't create the dialog box
  break;
case IDABORT:
  // some other error occurred
  break;
default:
  // unknown value
  break;
}
```

Dialog Data Exchange (DDX)

DDX is an easy way to move data to and from a dialog box control. Once you have everything in place, the framework transfers the initial value to the control when the dialog box is created and transfers the contents of the control back when the dialog box is dismissed. Let's look "under the covers" to understand how this works.

Using ClassWizard, create a data member in the dialog box class that is associated with the control on the dialog template. When ClassWizard creates the data memory, it also adds a **DDX_** function call between the **// AFX_DATA_ MAP** lines inside the dialog box's **DoDataExchange()** function. There are several of these **DDX_** functions that handle the various types of controls and data types. Some of the more common functions are shown in Table 5.1. You can also add your own entries manually at the end of the **DoDataExchange()** function after the ClassWizard map.

Table 5.1   DDX functions.

Name	Control	Associated Data Types
DDX_Check	Checkbox	**int**
DDX_CBIndex	Combo box	**int**
DDX_CBString	Combo box	**CString**
DDX_LBIndex	Drop list box	**int**
DDX_LBString	Drop list box	**CString**
DDX_Radio	Radio button group	**int**
DDX_Text	Edit box	**BYTE, short, int, UINT, long, DWORD, CString, float, double, COleDateTime, COleCurrency**

DoDataExchange() is called by the framework to exchange and validate dialog data. It is passed a pointer to a **CDataExchange** object that holds context information needed for DDX to take place. **CDataExchange** contains two data members:

➤ **m_bSaveAndValidate** indicates the direction of a dialog data exchange operation

➤ **m_pDlgWnd** is a pointer to the CWnd object for which dialog data exchange is taking place.

Here's what a simple example of **DoDataExchange()** looks like, where a single edit control has a DDX value variable defined:

```
void CNameDlg::DoDataExchange(CDataExchange* pDX)
{
        CDialog::DoDataExchange(pDX);
        //{{AFX_DATA_MAP(CMyDialog)
        DDX_Text(pDX, IDC_NAME, m_strName);
        //}}AFX_DATA_MAP
}
```

DoDataExchange() is never called directly. Instead, **CWnd::UpdateData()** is called. **CWnd::UpdateData()** creates a **CDataExchange** object and calls **DoDataExchange()**. **UpdateData()** takes one parameter:

```
BOOL UpdateData(BOOL bSaveAndValidate = TRUE);
```

If the value of **bSaveAndValidate** is **TRUE**, then the DDX value member variable associated with the control is updated with the data that is in the control on the dialog box. For the example above, if the edit control **IDC_NAME** had a value of "Ann" and **UpdateData(TRUE)** was called, the **m_strName** would also contain the value "Ann". However, if the value of **bSaveAndValidate** is **FALSE**, then the control would be updated with the value of the member variable.

UpdateData() is called twice automatically by the framework. The first time it is called is by **CDialog::OnInitDialog()**. **CDialog::OnInitDialog()** is a virtual function that is invoked when the dialog box is initialized and before it is displayed. **CDialog::OnInitDialog()** calls **UpdateData(FALSE)**, so as long as your derived class calls (or fails to override) **CDialog::OnInitDialog()**, the controls on your dialog box will be initialized. The second time **UpdateData()** is automatically called by the framework is in **CDialog::OnOK()**, but here the argument passed is **TRUE**.

Once everything is in place, the client code to initialize dialog box controls and receive user input is straightforward. For a modal dialog box, you can write code like this:

```
CNameDlg dlg;
dlg.m_StrName = "";
if(dlg.DoModal() == IDOK)
{
  m_theName = dlg.m_StrName;
}
```

Dialog Data Validation (DDV)

DDV is an easy way to validate dialog box information entered by the user. Typically, this means checking for boundaries, such as the maximum length for string values in an edit box control or the minimum or maximum values when you expect a number to be entered. Like DDX, the easy way to set this up is with ClassWizard. As you add some types of variables to a dialog box, you can also supply validation parameters. When you specify a validation parameter, ClassWizard will place, in the **DoDataExchange()** function, a **DDV_** function call directly after the corresponding **DDX_** function call. Table 5.2 shows the types of DDV functions supported by ClassWizard.

Here's a simple example where a couple of edit controls are used to obtain an employee's name and ID: The name is limited to 50 or fewer characters, and the ID must be a number between 1 and 99,999.

```
void CEmployee::DoDataExchange(CDataExchange* pDX)
{
        CDialog::DoDataExchange(pDX);
        //{{AFX_DATA_MAP(CEmployee)
        DDX_Text(pDX, IDC_EMPLOYEE_ID, m_nID);
        DDV_MinMaxUInt(pDX, m_nID, 1, 99999);
        DDX_Text(pDX, IDC_EMPLOYEE_NAME, m_strName);
        DDV_MaxChars(pDX, m_strName, 50);
        //}}AFX_DATA_MAP
}
```

You can add your own validation code immediately after //}}AFX_DATA_ MAP to check for conditions not covered by the **DDV_** functions. This code can, of course, be in line statements or function calls. Either way, if the validation fails, you need to inform the user, call **CDataExchange::PrepareCtrl()** or **CDataExchange::PrepareEditCtrl()** so that the focus can return to the correct control, and then call **CDataExchange::Fail()** to fail the validation. If you chose to use a function, it needs to accept a pointer to the **CDataExchange**

Table 5.2 DDV variable types.		
Variable Type	Data Validation	Example DDV Function
CString	Maximum length	DDV_MaxChars
Numeric	Minimum value, maximum value	DDV_MinMaxDouble

object (pDX), a reference to the mapped variable to be tested, and any additional custom parameters you might need. Here's an example:

```
if (pDX->m_bSaveAndValidate)
{
  if (m_strName.GetLength() == 0)
  {
    AfxMessageBox("Name cannot be empty!");
    pDX->PrepareEditCtrl(IDC_EMPLOYEE_NAME);
    pDX->Fail();
  }
}
```

Unfortunately, from a user's viewpoint, DDV doesn't quite measure up to expectations. As you probably realize, the problem is that validation occurs along with control-to-variable data transfer. This usually means that validation doesn't occur until the user clicks the OK button. If this becomes a problem, you can add code to validate the data on a keystroke-by-keystroke basis by employing a customized edit control or intercept the **EN_KILLFOCUS** command and validate the data in the handler.

Adding Custom DDX/DDV

By making special entries in DDX.CLW or in your project's CLW file you can integrate your own DDX_ and DDV_ routines into the ClassWizard user interface. The instructions on how you can do this are specified in MFC Technical Note 26.

Using A Modeless Dialog Box

Unlike a modal dialog box, a modeless dialog box is asynchronous. It doesn't take over the application's input and output. Instead, it is usually displayed to complement the normal running of the application by passing information back to the client window.

Creating And Destroying A Modeless Dialog Box

When creating modeless dialog boxes, you use **CDialog** as the base class just as you do for modal dialog boxes. However, because **CDialog** assumes it will be modal, you will need to override the default behavior if you want your dialog box to be modeless.

This means that the **DoModal()** function is not used to create, display, and terminate the dialog box. Instead, three functions must be called: **CDialog::Create()** to create the dialog box, **CWnd::ShowWindow()** to display it, and **CWndDialog::DestroyWindow()** for termination. It's possible to eliminate calling **ShowWindow()**. If the dialog template's **Visible** property is set to **TRUE**, the dialog box will be displayed by **Create()**. Much of the time, the calls to **Create()** and **ShowWindow()** are added to the **CDialog**-derived class constructor.

```
CModeless::CModeless(CWnd* pParent /*=NULL*/)
  : CDialog(CModeless::IDD, pParent)
{
  //{{AFX_DATA_INIT(CModeless)
    // NOTE: the ClassWizard will add member initialization here
  //}}AFX_DATA_INIT

  if(Create(CModeless::IDD, pParent))
  {
    ShowWindow(SW_SHOW);
  }
}
```

Because modeless dialog boxes have a longer life than modal dialog boxes, you will normally instantiate the object on the heap and maintain a pointer to it as a protected or private data member. This does, however, present a problem. A dialog box does not automatically free its memory. This problem is usually solved in one of two ways: The client uses the **delete** operator to delete the object, or the object deletes itself.

Let's look at the case where you want the object to delete itself. To set this in motion, you need to override **OnOK()** and **OnCancel()**. Rather than calling **CDialog::EndDialog**, **OnOK()** and **OnCancel()** must call **CDialog::DestroyWindow()**. **DestroyWindow()** sends appropriate messages to the window to deactivate it and remove the input focus. It sends **WM_DESTROY** and **WM_NCDESTROY** messages to the window. MFC knows that **WM_NCDESTROY** is the last message sent to a window, so after it handles the message, it calls **PostNcDestroy()**. This is where the object will delete itself. Here's what the code might look like:

```
// Modeless.cpp
. . .
```

//

```
// CModeless message handlers

void CModeless::OnOK()
{
  UpdateData(TRUE);
  DestroyWindow();
}

void CModeless::OnCancel()
{
  DestroyWindow();
}

void CModeless::PostNcDestroy()
{
  delete this;
}
```

Data Exchange Between A Modeless Dialog Box And Its Client

The client can set values and call member functions of the modeless dialog box at any time during its lifetime through its access pointer. The client can also call **UpdateData(FALSE)** to transfer the contents of the member variables to the controls.

But how does the dialog box inform the client about user input? One way is for the dialog box to post or send messages to the client. To do this, the dialog box needs a pointer to the client, and the client and the dialog box must share one or more user-defined messages. Additionally, the dialog box's **OnClose()** and **OnOK()** functions need to be changed. Actually, because this is a modeless dialog box, you probably want to replace the OK button with an Apply button. Or you could leave the OK button and add an Apply button. Here's what the code for the modeless dialog box might look like:

```
// Modeless.h : header file
//
#define ML_APPLY  WM_APP
#define ML_CANCEL WM_APP + 1

/////////////////////////////////////////////////////////////////
// CModeless dialog

class CModeless : public CDialog
{
// Construction
```

```
public:
  CModeless(CWnd* pParent);    // standard constructor

. . .


// Modeless.cpp
. . .
/////////////////////////////////////////////////////////////////
// CModeless dialog

CModeless::CModeless(CWnd* pParent )
  : CDialog(CModeless::IDD, pParent)
{
  //{{AFX_DATA_INIT(CModeless)
    // NOTE: the ClassWizard will add member initialization here
  //}}AFX_DATA_INIT

  if(Create(CModeless::IDD, pParent))
  {
    ShowWindow(SW_SHOW);
  }
}
. . .
/////////////////////////////////////////////////////////////////
// CModeless message handlers

void CModeless::OnApply()
{
  UpdateData(TRUE);
  m_pParentWnd->SendMessage(ML_APPLY);
}

void CModeless::OnCancel()
{
  m_pParentWnd->SendMessage(ML_CANCEL);
  DestroyWindow();
}

void CModeless::PostNcDestroy()
{
  delete this;
}
```

In the header file, two messages are defined that the dialog box will send to the parent window. **ML_APPLY** is used to inform the parent window that the user has clicked the Apply button. At this point, the parent should retrieve the information from the dialog box and apply it as appropriate for the application. **ML_CANCEL** is sent to inform the parent that the "Cancel" has been clicked and the dialog box will delete itself. Now look at the constructor's prototype. To ensure that a pointer to the parent window is available, the default parameter has been removed. This pointer is used by the **OnApply()** and **OnCancel()** functions to send the messages to the parent.

In the implementation file, the constructor creates and shows the dialog box window. **OnApply()** calls the **UpdateData()** member function with the argument **TRUE** and then sends the **ML_APPLY** message to the parent window. **OnCancel()** sends the **ML_CANCEL** message to the parent window and calls **DestroyWindow()**.

On the client side, when the modeless dialog box is instantiated, a pointer to the client must be passed to the constructor. Handlers must also be added for the user-defined messages:

```
/////////////////////////////////////////////////////////////////
// CUseModeless

IMPLEMENT_DYNCREATE(CUseModeless, CView)

BEGIN_MESSAGE_MAP(CUseModeless, CView)
  //{{AFX_MSG_MAP(CUseModeless)
  ON_COMMAND(ID_MODELESS, OnStartModeless)
  ON_MESSAGE(ML_APPLY, OnModelessApply)
  ON_MESSAGE(ML_CANCEL, OnModelessCancel)
  //}}AFX_MSG_MAP
END_MESSAGE_MAP()


. . .
CUseModeless:: CUseModeless ()
  : m_pModeless(NULL)
{
  // TODO: add construction code here
}


. . .
void CUseModeless::OnStartModeless()
{
  if(m_pModeless == NULL)
    m_pModeless = new CModeless(this);
}

LRESULT CUseModeless::OnModelessCancel(WPARAM wParam,
                                       LPARAM lParam)
```

```
{
  m_pModeless = NULL;
  return 1L;
}

LRESULT CUseModeless::OnModelessApply(WPARAM wParam,
                                      LPARAM lParam)
{
  // Retrieve the information from the dialog box
  m_strName = m_pModeless->m_strName;
  . . .
  return 1L;;
}
```

A member variable, **m_pModeless**, is used to hold a pointer to the modeless dialog. This pointer is initially set to **NULL** by the constructor. **OnStartModeless()** checks **m_pModeless** for **NULL** to ensure that there is never more than one instance of the dialog box. When the **ML_CANCEL** message is received **OnModelessCancel()** sets m_pModeless to **NULL**. **OnModelessApply()** handles the **ML_APPLY** message. Here you would retrieve the information from the dialog box and use it as appropriate for your application.

Dialog Bars

Dialog bars, a close relative to dialog boxes, are like toolbars. Instead of having an array of bitmap buttons like a toolbar, a dialog bar uses a dialog template, which allows you to use all of the controls that you can use with a dialog box.

The easiest way to add a dialog bar to your program is through the Components and Controls Gallery. Just go to the Project|Add to Project|Components and Controls... menu item. When the Components and Controls Gallery dialog box comes up, open the Visual C++ Components folder, select the Dialog Bar shortcut, and click Insert. This will add a dialog bar to a frame window in your project. Your project must have at least one **CFrameWnd**-derived class to use this component.

MFC's **CDialogBar** class implements the dialog bar. The dialog bar component declares a member variable of type **CDialogBar** in your frame window class. The dialog bar is initialized during the creation of the frame window. All you then need to do is add a menu item for displaying the dialog bar, add controls to the template, and add the necessary handlers.

You can manually add message map entries to respond to the dialog bar's notification messages. You can also use ClassWizard by using the following procedure:

1. In ResourceView, open the dialog template that corresponds to the dialog bar.

2. Invoke ClassWizard (CTRL+W). ClassWizard displays the Adding A Class dialog box.

3. Choose Select An Existing Class and click on the OK button. ClassWizard asks you to select a class.

4. Choose the name of the frame window class that you specified when creating the dialog bar, and click the Select button. ClassWizard warns you that the class is not a dialog class and asks whether you want to link the class to the dialog resource anyway.

5. Click the Yes button. The identifiers of the controls on your dialog bar appear in the Object IDs list on ClassWizard's Message Maps page.

6. Assign command handlers to the controls as usual.

You can, of course, also use the Resource Editor to add a new dialog template resource for a dialog bar. In the ResourceView pane, right-click the top-level item, and select Insert from the drop-down menu to display the Insert Resource dialog box (see Figure 5.1). Then simply select IDD_DIALOGBAR and insert it as a new resource.

Customizing Common Dialog Boxes

Windows provides a number of standard dialog boxes to gather information from the user. These common dialog boxes provide advantages for both the programmer and the user. For you, the programmer, they allow you to easily incorporate into your program dialog boxes that you often need, and they are

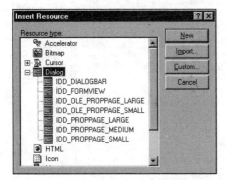

Figure 5.1   Insert Resource dialog box.

easy to use. Users like them because, from one program to the next, they carry out the same common tasks in the same way. All of these common dialog box classes are derived from a common base, **CCommonDialog**. A list of these classes is shown in Table 5.3.

Usually, you can use these common dialog box classes directly. Sometimes, however, you will need to make minor behavior changes. To change only the behavior of a common dialog box, first consult the Windows Software Development Kit (SDK). You can customize each common dialog box class to perform in different ways, depending on flags or settings in the construction of the object. For example, you can customize the File Open dialog box to hide the read-only checkbox that appears by default. However, on rare occasions, you might need to make more drastic changes. If major changes are needed, consider starting with the dialog box template and making whatever changes you need—adding controls, deleting controls, and deriving a unique class from **CDialog**. You can make these changes to the template, but the resulting dialog box will not be a common dialog box.

Between the two extremes is another method whereby you "nest" one dialog box inside of another so that multiple dialog boxes appear as one seamless whole. Here are the basic steps you need to follow:

1. Create a dialog resource template. Size it appropriately, and set the Style property to Child and its Border property to None. Then select its Clip Siblings and Visible properties.

2. Place a control with an ID of **stc32** (=0x045f). This control will normally be a static text or a group. This ID has a special purpose: to let the

Table 5.3 Common dialog box classes.	
Class	**Purpose**
CColorDialog	Allows the user to select or create a color
CFileDialog	Allows the user to open or save a file
CFindReplaceDialog	Allows the user to substitute one string for another
CPageSetupDialog	Allows the user to input page measurement parameters
CFontDialog	Allows the user to select a font
CPrintDialog	Allows the user to set up the printer and print documents
COleDialog	Provides common functionality for a number of **COleDialog**-derived classes

common dialog handler know where to place all of the standard controls. If there is no **stc32** control, the common dialog handler assumes all new controls added by the application-defined template should be placed below the standard controls. If the developer includes the **stc32** control, the common dialog handler will look at the size of this control. If it is too small to hold all the standard controls, the common dialog handler will move the controls to the right of or below the **stc32** control to make room for the new controls.

3. Add other controls as needed.

4. Use ClassWizard to create a class derived from **CDialog**, add data members as needed, and specify DDX/DDV appropriately.

5. By hand, change the base class to the appropriate common dialog class; that is, change **CDialog** to one of the classes listed in Table 5.3.

6. Change the signature of the constructor from what ClassWizard provided to the signature required for the common dialog box you are using.

7. Change the constructor so that the correct base class is invoked.

8. In the body of the constructor, customize the underlying Windows structure. As a minimum, you will need to add *xx*_ENABLETEMPLATE (where *xx* is the correct prefix for the dialog type) to **Flags**, set **lpTemplateName** to the resource ID, and set **hInstance** using AfxGetInstanceHandle.

 The **CHOOSECOLOR** structure defines its **hInstance** as a **HWND** instead of an **HINSTANCE**, so you will need to cast your instance handle to an **HWND**.

9. Add initialization code to **OnInitDialog** as appropriate.

10. Add the necessary handlers and code.

11. Add code to the client as needed. Remember, the common dialog box just gathers data.

That's all there is to it. Sounds simple enough, right? It is, provided you are customizing **CFileDialog**. As soon as you try one of the others, however, you're going to encounter some problems. They all have their own unique idiosyncrasies.

Property Sheets

Dialog boxes are useful for displaying and receiving small amounts of information. However, users become frustrated quickly when they are required to navigate through many dialog boxes to accomplish what is a single logical task. A better way to handle this situation is to use a dialog box that contains tabs. Each tab corresponds to a related page of controls. In MFC terminology, this type of dialog box is known as a *property sheet*, with *property page*s. Property sheets represent the actual dialog box, and property pages represent the tabs. The user can flip from one property page to another by clicking on the tab control that is hosted by the property sheet. As a Visual C++ user, you'll recognize Figure 5.2, the Options dialog box, reached from the Options command in the Tools menu.

MFC supports property sheets and property pages through the **CPropertySheet** and **CPropertyPage** classes. Surprisingly, **CPropertySheet** is derived from **CWnd**, not **CDialog**. However, with a little thought, this makes sense. **CDialog** provides a programmatic interface to a Windows dialog box, and Windows dialog boxes are closely tied to a dialog template resource that specifies the dialog box's controls and their placement. **CPropertySheet** has nothing do with dialog templates; instead, the controls on a property sheet are maintained in one or more overlapping property pages, each containing controls for setting a group of related properties. Because the property pages maintain the controls and are intimately related to dialog template resources, it is the **CPropertyPage** class that is derived from **CDialog**.

Creating Property Page Resources

You create property page resource templates in the Resource Editor in nearly the same way that you create dialog bar resource templates. The only thing

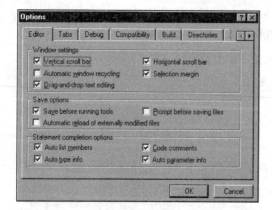

Figure 5.2 Visual C++ Options dialog box.

different is that instead of selecting **IDD_DIALOGBAR,** you need to select **IDD_PROPPAGE_SMALL, IDD_PROPPAGE_MEDIUM,** or **IDD_ PROPPAGE_LARGE.** The only difference between the three is the initial size of the property sheet. If you have different-size property pages, the largest one will determine the size of the property sheet.

Creating A CPropertyPage-Derived Class

After designing a property page template, you can use ClassWizard to create a **CPropertyPage**-derived class. You do this in very much the same way that you create a **CDialog**-derived class. Be careful, though. ClassWizard will default the base class to **CDialog.**

Creating And Displaying A Modal CPropertySheet

Although **CPropertySheet** objects are not derived from **CDialog,** they are constructed and displayed in the same way that **CDialog** objects are constructed and displayed. For example, to create and display a modal property sheet, you would normally declare a **CPropertySheet** object and call **DoModal().** However, you also need to make an instance of each **CPropertyPage**-derived class and attach them to the property sheet using **CPropertySheet::AddPage().** You can use ordinary DDX calls on the **CPropertyPage** objects to initialize and retrieve control data. Here's an example:

```
CPropertySheet sheet("Example Property Sheet");
// instantiate the CPropertyPage-derived objects
CPropPage1 page1;
CPropPage2 page2;
CPropPage3 page3;
// attach the pages to the sheet
sheet.AddPage(&page1);
sheet.AddPage(&page2);
sheet.AddPage(&page3);
// initialize the controls via DDX
page1.m_Name = "Ann";
page1.m_ID = 1234;
. . .
page2.m_Dept = 100;

if(sheet.DoModal() == IDOK)
{
   // retrieve the information via DDX
   m_strName = page1.m_Name;
   . . .
}
```

As you can see, the only difference between the code above and an ordinary dialog box is that there are three "dialogs" (actually **CPropertyPage** objects) instead of one.

There are a number of interesting member functions. For a list of some of them, see Tables 5.4 and 5.5.

To simplify property sheet creation and to enhance encapsulation, you can derive your own property sheet class from **CPropertySheet** and include data members for the property pages so that the pages are constructed automatically when the sheet is instantiated. This means the sheet will need to initialize and retrieve the DDX information and accessor functions must be provided for the exchange of information between the sheet and the client. Here's what the class might look like:

```
// Sheet.h : header file
//
/////////////////////////////////////////////////////////////////
// CSheet

class CSheet : public CPropertySheet
{
        DECLARE_DYNAMIC(CSheet)
. . .
public:
  void AttachPages();
  // accessor functions would go here
. . .
private:
  CPropPage1 page1;
  CPropPage2 page2;
  CPropPage3 page3;
};

// Sheet.cpp : implementation file
//
. . .
/////////////////////////////////////////////////////////////////
// CSheet

IMPLEMENT_DYNAMIC(CSheet, CPropertySheet)

CSheet::CSheet(UINT nIDCaption, CWnd* pParentWnd, UINT iSelectPage)
        : CPropertySheet(nIDCaption, pParentWnd, iSelectPage)
{
```

```
  AttachPages();
}


CSheet::CSheet(LPCTSTR pszCaption, CWnd* pParentWnd,
                UINT iSelectPage)
        :CPropertySheet(pszCaption, pParentWnd, iSelectPage)
{
  AttachPages();
}


void CSheet::AttachPages()
{
  AddPage(&page1);
  AddPage(&page2);
  AddPage(&page3);
  // code to initialize the pages could go here
}
```

Table 5.4   CPropertyPage operations.

Name	Description
CancelToClose	Changes the OK button to read "Close" and disables the Cancel button after an unrecoverable change in the page of a modal property sheet
SetModified	Activates or deactivates the Apply Now button
QuerySiblings	Forwards the message to each page of the property sheet

Table 5.5   CPropertyPage overrideables.

Name	Description
OnCancel	Called by MFC when the Cancel button is clicked.
OnKillActive	Called by MFC when the current page is no longer the active page. Perform data validation here.
OnOK	Called by MFC when the OK, Apply Now, or Close button is clicked.
OnSetActive	Called by MFC when the page is made the active page.
OnApply	Called by MFC when the Apply Now button is clicked.
OnReset	Called by MFC when the Cancel button is clicked.
OnQueryCancel	Called by MFC when the Cancel button is clicked, and before the cancel has taken place.

Creating And Displaying A Modeless CPropertySheet

The major difference between displaying a modeless property sheet and a modal property sheet is what you might suspect. Instead of using the **DoModal()** function to display the property sheet, you use the **CPropertySheet::Create()** function. When using modeless property sheets, you must exercise the same care as when using modeless dialog boxes. Avoid constructing the property sheet and property pages on the stack, as shown in the following code:

```
// client code
// display the property sheet
m_pPropertySheet = new CMyPropertySheet;

CPropPage1 * pPage1 = new CPropPage1;
m_pPropertySheet->AddPage(pPage1);

CPropPage2 * pPage1 = new CPropPage2;
m_pPropertySheet->AddPage(pPage2);

CPropPage1 * pPage3 = new CPropPage3;
m_pPropertySheet->AddPage(pPage3);

m_pPropertySheet->Create();

// more client code in some other function.
delete m_pPropertySheet;
m_pPropertySheet = 0;


// Property sheet code
CMyPropertySheet::PostNcDestroy()
{
  for(int pn = 0; pn < GetPageCount(); pn++)
  {
    CPropertyPage * pPage = GetPage(pn);
    ASSERT(pPage);
    delete pPage;
  }
  CPropertySheet::PostNcDestroy();
}
```

Practice Questions

Question 1

Which is the base class of CPropertySheet?

○ a. CDialog

○ b. CWnd

○ c. CCommonDialog

○ d. CView

The correct answer is b. Almost all of the controls (except for OK, Cancel, Apply, and Help) associated with a property sheet are maintained in one or more overlapping property pages. Each property page contains some number of controls and is intimately related to a dialog template resource. Each property page provides a programmatic interface that displays information and receives input from the user. Thus, **CPropertyPage** class is derived from **CDialog**. Property sheets, however, have nothing to do with dialog templates; therefore, it makes more sense that they be a generic window, **CWnd**, derivative and not a **CDialog** derivative. However, as a point of interest, if you pull back the covers and look inside, you will see that **CPropertySheet** uses the Win32 property sheet implementation (which uses the common tab control) from the Windows common controls.

Question 2

Which statement below is true?

○ a. Modal dialog boxes are invoked with CDialog::DoModal(), and modeless dialog boxes are invoked with CDialog::Create().

○ b. Modal dialog boxes are invoked with CDialog::Create(), and modeless dialog boxes are invoked with CDialog::Create().

○ c. Modal dialog boxes are invoked with CDialog::Create(), and modeless dialog boxes are invoked with CDialog::DoModeless().

○ d. Modal dialog boxes are invoked with CDialog::DoModal(), and modeless dialog boxes are invoked with CDialog::DoModeless().

Answer a is correct. After constructing a **CDialog** object, **CDialog::DoModal()** is called to display a modal dialog box. **DoModal()** blocks the calling function until the dialog box is closed, normally, by the user clicking the OK or Cancel button. However, the purpose of a modeless dialog box is to complement the normal running of the application, which means it cannot block the calling function. Instead, a modeless dialog box must operate like a normal window. And like most windows, three functions are used to create, display, and terminate the modeless dialog box. These functions are **CDialog::Create()** to create the dialog box, **CDialog::ShowWindow()** to display it, and **CDialog::Destroy Window()** to terminate it.

Question 3

What is the advantage of using common dialog boxes?

○ a. Runtime performance of your application is improved.

○ b. Your code can be easily transported to other operating systems.

○ c. Your application's user interface is consistent with other Windows-based applications.

○ d. The development time needed for property sheets and tabbed dialog boxes is reduced.

Answer c is correct. Common dialog boxes are Win32 system dialog boxes that programmers can use for implementing operations that are common to many applications. Because many applications are using the same set of standard dialog boxes, the user is able to carry out the same common tasks in the same way as he or she moves from one application to another.

Question 4

CDialogBar is derived from which class?

○ a. CDialog

○ b. CControlBar

○ c. CCommonDialog

○ d. CDlgCtrl

Answer b is correct. **CControlBar** is the base class for the control-bar classes **CDialogBar, CStatusBar, CToolBar, CReBar,** and **COleResizeBar.**

A dialog bar is a control bar, based on a dialog template resource, with the functionality of a modeless dialog box. They behave like toolbars, but because they are based on dialog templates, they can have any control that a dialog box can. Dialog bars can contain any Windows control. As in a dialog box, the user can tab among the controls. Dialog bars can be docked to the top or bottom of a frame window, or they can be floated to any desired location on the screen.

Question 5

Which function does the framework call to initialize data in a dialog box or to retrieve and validate dialog data?

O a. CWnd::DoDataExchange()

O b. CDataExchange::UpdateData()

O c. CWnd::OnInitDialog()

O d. CWnd::UpdateData()

Answer a is correct. Answers c and d are added to confuse you. Note, the question asks which function does the framework call. When a dialog box is created, **CDialog::OnInitDialog** calls **UpdateData()** (inherited from **CWnd**) with a **FALSE** parameter to initialize the dialog box controls. **UpdateData()** creates a **CDataExchange** object and calls the dialog's **DoDataExchange()** function, passing it a pointer to the **CDataExchange** object. **DoDataExchange()**, in turn, calls one or more **DDX_** functions to initialize the dialog box controls. Later, when the user clicks OK, **CDialog::OnOK()** calls **UpdateData()** with a **TRUE** parameter, causing the **DDX_** functions to transfer the data from the controls to the member variables. The **DDV_** functions will also validate the data values. If a data value fails the validation, a warning message is displayed and the dialog box remains on the screen with the input focus on the control that failed the validation.

Need To Know More?

 Kruglinski, David J., George Shepherd, and Scot Wingo. *Programming Microsoft Visual C++*. 5th ed. Microsoft Press, Redmond, WA, 1998. ISBN 1-57231-857-0. This book strikes a good balance between theory and practical application. It is divided into six parts and covers nearly every aspect of MFC programming, from the basics to database management and the Internet. Chapter 6 provides a good example on how to customize the File Open and Save As dialog boxes.

 Prosise, Jeff. *Programming Windows with MFC*. Microsoft Press, Redmond, WA, 1999. ISBN 1-57231-695-0. This excellent book is divided into three parts: MFC Basics, the Document/View Architecture, and Advance Topics. Chapter 8 covers dialog boxes, property sheets, and common dialog boxes. Nine example programs are provide.

 Williams, Al. *MFC Black Book*. The Coriolis Group, Scottsdale, AZ, 1998. ISBN 1-57610-185-1. Chapter 5 provides practical cookbook-style solutions to problems programmers will encounter when implementing modeless dialog boxes and when using DDX and DDV.

 MFC Technical Note 26 describes the DDX and DDV architecture. It also describes how to write a **DDX_** or **DDV_** procedure and how to extend ClassWizard to use the routines.

 Visual C++ Documentation, MFC Sample Program— "MODELESS." This is an MFC sample program that demonstrates the use of an MFC **CDialog** object as a modeless dialog. MODELESS is a very simple dialog-based application that manages a list box in its main dialog box, while providing a modeless dialog that allows you to add strings to the list box in the main window.

Multiple Views And Multiple Documents

6

Terms you'll need to understand:

√ Single-document interface (SDI)

√ Multiple-document interface (MDI)

√ Splitter window

√ Document object

√ View object

√ **CDocument**

√ **CView**

√ Frame window object

√ **CFrameWnd**

√ **CMDIFrameWnd**

√ **CMDIChildWnd**

√ Document template

√ **CRuntimeClass** object

√ **RUNTIME_CLASS**

√ **CSingleDocTemplate**

√ **CMultiDocTemplate**

√ **CSplitterWnd**

√ Static splitter

√ Dynamic splitter

√ **CCreateContext**

Techniques you'll need to master:

√ Understanding the purpose of documents, views, templates, and frames within the document/view architecture, and explaining how they interact

√ Creating and using static splitters

√ Creating and using dynamic splitters

√ Writing code that employs both static and dynamic splitters

√ Creating SDI and MDI applications that employee multiple views

√ Creating MDI applications that employees multiple document types

This chapter looks at the various view classes available in MFC. The chapter begins with a general overview of various components of the document/view architecture and how they fit together. In turn, each of the two categories of document/view applications, single-document interface (SDI) and multiple-document interface (MDI), are presented. SDI applications support just one open document at a time. MDI applications allow the user to have two or more documents open concurrently. Windows WordPad is an example of an SDI application. Word and Excel are MDI applications.

Document/view applications aren't limited to just one view of a document's data. Using splitter windows, an application can present two or more views of the same document in resizable "panes" that subdivide the frame window's client area. How to employ splitter windows will be sandwiched between the SDI and MDI sections.

Document/View Components

The document/view architecture is one of the cornerstones of the MFC library. Central to this architecture is the concept of a document object and a corresponding view window. The document object is responsible for storing, loading, and saving the data associated with the application, whereas the view object renders the data onscreen and provides a user interface for manipulating the data. This separation of the data from the user interface supports and encourages the use of modular and object-oriented development techniques, thus allowing you to produce applications that are easier to enhance and maintain.

There are four main components to the MFC document/view architecture: documents, views, document/view frames, and document templates. The following sections address each component.

The Document Object

The *document object* conceptually holds the data used by the application. Usually, the data is stored internal to the program, but this does not need to be the case. The data could be in a database or some other remote data source. The important thing is that the document object serves as a data source and provides data management for the application. As you would expect, being in charge of data management, the document object is responsible for reading and writing its data to and from persistent storage.

In MFC, the document object is constructed from a class derived from **CDocument**. When you implement a document within your application, you will usually add data members to hold the data and public member functions that other objects can use to query and edit the document's data. How the data storage is implemented in the document is the programmer's responsibility.

Table 6.1 Noteworthy CDocument member functions.	
Function Name	**Description**
AddView	Attaches a view to the document.
GetFirstViewPosition	Returns a **POSITION** value that can be passed to **GetNextView()**.
GetNextView	Returns a **CView** pointer of the next view in the list of views associated with the document.
GetPathName	Returns the path (which includes the file name) of the document's data file. Returns an empty string if the document has not been saved or does not have a disk file associated with it.
GetTitle	Retrieves the document's title.
IsModified	Indicates whether the document has been modified since it was last saved. It returns nonzero if the document has been modified since it was last saved.
SetModifiedFlag	Sets or clears the document's modified flag, which indicates whether the document contains unsaved data.
UpdateAllViews	Updates all views associated with the document by calling each view's **OnUpdate()** function.

A **CDocument**-derived class provides a number of important functions, a few of which are shown in Table 6.1.

A document object can have any number of views associated with it and maintains a list of the views. **AddView()**, as its name implies, adds a view to the list. **UpdateAllViews()** commands all the views attached to the document to update themselves by calling each view's **OnUpdate()**. In an SDI application with just one view, **UpdateAllViews()** usually isn't used, because the single view often updates itself in response to user input either before or after updating the document's data. But in multiple-view applications, **UpdateAllViews()** is called whenever the document is modified to keep all the other views in sync.

The **CDocument** class also has a number of virtual functions that can be overridden to customize a document's behavior. Four of these virtual functions are almost always overridden in a derived document class. These four are shown in Table 6.2.

The View Object

As mentioned above, the view class renders the document object's data onscreen and enables the user to modify the data. Documents and views are tightly interrelated, and information flows in both directions.

Table 6.2 Commonly overridden CDocument virtual member functions.	
Function Name	**Description**
OnNewDocument	Called by the framework during the process of document object creation. The default implementation of this function calls **DeleteContents()** to tidy any existing document data and then sets the document's modified state to **FALSE**. Override this function to initialize the data object before a new document is created.
OnOpenDocument	Called by the framework during the process of opening an existing file. The default implementation of this function calls **DeleteContents()** to delete any data in the document, opens, and reads the file, and then sets the document's modified state to **FALSE.** Override this function if the default implementation (which calls **Serialize()**) is not adequate for your application.
DeleteContents	Deletes the document's contents without actually destroying the document object itself. You need to override this function to free any memory or resources you allocated for the document.
Serialize	Called by the framework to both load and store the document to disk. You need to override this function to serialize each of your application's objects.

In an SDI application, the document object is constructed just once and reused each time a document is created or opened. This being the case, one-time initialization code should be put in **OnNewDocument()** and **OnOpenDocument()**, rather than in the document object's constructor.

The *view object* keeps a pointer to the document object, which it uses to access the document's member variables in order to display and modify them. This pointer is exposed through the view's **GetDocument()** member function. When AppWizard generates the source code for a view class, it hides the **CView::GetDocument()** function with one that casts the pointer to the appropriate document type and returns the result.

CView is an abstract class that defines the basic properties of a view. You will normally derive your view class from **CView**. MFC provides a number of view classes derived from **CView**. Some of these classes are used directly. Others, like **CView**, are abstract base classes used for deriving view classes of your own. Chapter 7 presents these **CView**-derived classes.

CView and its derivatives include several virtual member functions that can be overridden to customize a view's operation. The more important ones are shown in Table 6.3. **OnDraw()**, which is the most important, is called by the framework whenever the view needs to be updated. **OnDraw()** receives one argument, a pointer to a device context. Because the GDI is a device-independent graphics system, **OnDraw()** can produce identical (or nearly identical) output on two difference devices if it is passed two different device contexts. This means that **OnDraw()** can be used to render to the screen or to a printer.

Views, like documents, are constructed once and then reused repeatedly in SDI applications. Use **OnInitialUpdate()** to perform all view-related initialization on a per-document basis.

 As a minimum, you should be familiar with all the overrideable functions listed in Table 6.3.

The Frame Window Object

The *frame window object* defines the application's physical workspace on the screen and serves as a container for a view. SDI applications use just one frame window—a **CFrameWnd** that serves as the application's top-level window and frames the view of the document. MDI applications use several frame windows—a **CMDIFrameWnd** that acts as a top-level window and a **CMDIChild Wnd** child window that frames views of the application's documents. A frame window orchestrates much of what goes on behind the scenes in a document/

Table 6.3	Key CView overrideables.
Function Name	**Description**
OnDraw	**CView::OnPaint()** creates a **CPaintDC** object and then calls this function, passing it the **CPaintDC** object. This function renders the document image on the screen. **CView::OnDraw()** is a pure virtual function, and implementation is required in your **CView**-derived class.
OnInitialUpdate	Called by the framework just before the first time the view is displayed.
OnUpdate	Called by the framework so that the view can be updated when the document's data has changed. It is called by **CDocument::UpdateAllViews()** and by the default implementation of **OnInitialUpdate()**.

view application. Its main role is to host one or more views, as well as various user-interface elements: toolbars, status bars, and dialog bars.

The Document Template

It is the *document template* that ties the other three components together. Your application has one document template for each type of document that it supports. The document template is responsible for creating and managing all the documents of its type.

The document template object provides the means whereby MFC can dynamically create instances of the document, view, and frame window classes that you define in your code. It is able to do this because it stores pointers to the **CRuntimeClass** objects associated with each of your document, view, and frame window classes. Using the **RUNTIME_CLASS()** macro, you specify these **CRuntimeClass** objects when constructing a document template.

MFC defines two document template classes that can be used in your application: **CSingleDocTemplate** and **CMultiDocTemplate**. Both of these classes are derived from **CDocTemplate**, which is an abstract base class that defines the basic functionality for document templates. You usually create one or more document templates in the implementation of your application's **InitInstance()** function. After creating a document template, you call **CWinApp::AddDocTemplate()** to add it to the list of available document templates that the application maintains. Here's an example of what the code might look like for an SDI application:

```
CSingleDocTemplate* pDocTemplate;
pDocTemplate = new CSingleDocTemplate(
    IDR_MAINFRAME,
    RUNTIME_CLASS(CMySDIDoc),
    RUNTIME_CLASS(CMainFrame),        // main SDI frame window
    RUNTIME_CLASS(CMySDIView));
AddDocTemplate(pDocTemplate);
```

 You need to understand and be able to explain the Document/ View architecture. You should know the objects that make up the architecture, the purpose of each, and how they relate.

Multiple Views

As you already know, a view can be attached to only one document, but a document can have multiple views attached to it at the same time, as when the contents of the document appear in a splitter window or in multiple child windows in an

MDI application. To help you implement multiple views, a document object keeps a list of its views, provides member functions for adding and removing views, and supplies the **UpdateAllViews()** member function, which sends a message to the views when the user changes the data in a document.

Single-Document Interface

This section shows how to create multiple views of the same document for an SDI application. In the sample application, multiple views share a single frame window. The views are constructed from different classes, each view providing a different way to display the same document. In this example, one view shows the text in a document in a normal mode, while the other view shows the text in italics. Here are the steps needed to create a multiple-view SDI application:

1. Create an SDI application, named "MultiViewSDI", the way you usually would using AppWizard, except in Step 6 of the wizard, change the name of the view class to "CDefaultView" (refer to Figure 6.1). Add the necessary code so that the program displays a single line of text in the middle of the window and the user can change the color of the text by menu selections. Place the command handlers in the **CMainFrame** class. This ensures that they will be available, no matter which view is active. If you place the command handlers in the view class, the handlers will not be available unless that view object is active. (It's also possible to put them in the document object.)

2. Make a copy of DefaultView.cpp and DefaultView.h. Rename the copies to ItalicsView.cpp and ItalicsView.h.

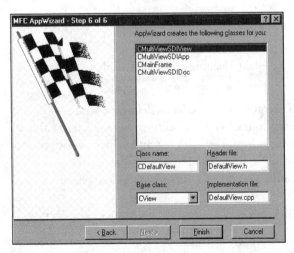

Figure 6.1   MFC AppWizard—Step 6 of 6 for the MultiViewSDI application.

3. Edit both files, changing all references to **CDefaultView** to read **CItalicsView**.

4. In ItalicsView.h, change **#include** "DefaultView.h" to **#include** "ItalicsView.h". Also, change the include guard so that it is unique.

5. Make the constructor public.

6. Modify the **OnDraw** event of the new view class so that italics are used. Here is what the code might look like:

```
void CItalicsView::OnDraw(CDC* pDC)
{
  CMultiViewSDIDoc* pDoc = GetDocument();
  ASSERT_VALID(pDoc);

  CFont * pOldFont = pDC->GetCurrentFont();
  LOGFONT lf;
  pOldFont->GetLogFont(&lf);
  lf.lfItalic = TRUE;
  CFont font;
  font.CreateFontIndirect(&lf);
  pOldFont = (CFont*) pDC->SelectObject(&font);

  CRect rect;
  GetClientRect (&rect);
  pDC->SetTextColor( pDoc->GetColor() );
  pDC->DrawText(pDoc->GetTextMessage(), -1, &rect,
        DT_SINGLELINE | DT_CENTER | DT_VCENTER);

  pDC->SelectObject(pOldFont);
}
```

7. Include the header files for the document class and both view classes in Mainfrm.cpp.

8. Add two private data members to the **CMainFrame** class. These variables will be pointers to the two view objects your application uses. Provide forward references for **CDefaultView** and **CItalicsView** prior to the **CMainFrame** definition. Initialize these pointers to 0 in the constructor of **CMainFrame**, as shown in the following example code:

```
class CDefaultView;
class CItalicsView;
class CMainFrame : public CFrameWnd
```

```
{
// ...
private:
  CDefaultView * m_pDefaultView;
  CItalicsView * m_pItalicsView;
// ...
}

CMainFrame::CMainFrame()
  : m_pItalicsView(0)
  , m_pDefaultView(0)
{
}
```

9. Add two menu selections to permit the application to switch between the two views. The View menu is a good place to insert the menu selections, but you can choose any of the drop-down menus.

10. Add command handlers to **CMainFrame** for the two new menu items. Here's the sample code:

```
void CMainFrame::OnDefault()
{
  ChangeView(m_pDefaultView, m_pItalicsView);
}

void CMainFrame::OnItalics()
{
  // Only do this the first time through
  if(!m_pItalicsView)
  {
    m_pDefaultView = static_cast<CDefaultView*>(GetActiveView());

    m_pItalicsView = new CItalicsView;
    m_pItalicsView->Create(NULL, NULL, AFX_WS_DEFAULT_VIEW,
      rectDefault, this, AFX_IDW_PANE_FIRST + 1);
  }

  ChangeView(m_pItalicsView, m_pDefaultView);
}

void CMainFrame::ChangeView(CView * pAdd, CView * pRemove)
{
  ASSERT(pAdd);
  ASSERT(pRemove);
```

```
// Set the child id of the active view to AFX_IDW_PANE_FIRST,
// so that CFrameWnd::RecalcLayout will allocate to this
// "first pane" that portion of the frame window's client area
// not allocated to control bars.  Set the child id of the
// other view to anything other than AFX_IDW_PANE_FIRST; here
// the child id's of the two views are switched.

int nSwitchChildID = pAdd->GetDlgCtrlID();
pAdd->SetDlgCtrlID(AFX_IDW_PANE_FIRST);
pRemove->SetDlgCtrlID(nSwitchChildID);

pAdd->ShowWindow(SW_SHOW);
pRemove->ShowWindow(SW_HIDE);

CDocument * pDoc = GetActiveDocument();
pDoc->AddView(pAdd);
pDoc->RemoveView(pRemove);

SetActiveView(pAdd);
RecalcLayout();
}
```

You can choose to leave the inactive view in the application, or you can remove the inactive view from your application. The previous sample code uses **CDocument::RemoveView()** to remove the inactive view. Removing it means that when the document object is changed and **CDocument::UpdateAllViews()** is called, the inactive view object's **OnDraw()** function will not be called.

Removing the inactive view is not required, but it makes the application more efficient. If the inactive view is not removed from the document object's list of attached views, nothing detrimental will happen when the inactive view's **OnDraw** function executes. In an application with only two views, each with simple **OnDraw** functions, you will not be able to tell much difference.

11. Enable and disable the two menu items, as shown in the following example code:

```
void CMainFrame::OnUpdateDefault(CCmdUI* pCmdUI)
{
  pCmdUI->Enable(
    GetActiveView()->IsKindOf(RUNTIME_CLASS(CItalicsView)));
}
```

```
void CMainFrame::OnUpdateItalics(CCmdUI* pCmdUI)
{
  pCmdUI->Enable(
    GetActiveView()->IsKindOf(RUNTIME_CLASS(CDefaultView)));
}
```

You now have an example of how an SDI application can switch the view back and forth, allowing the user to see the same information, but in a different format.

 Command routing is one of the noteworthy features of the Document/View architecture. Command messages can be handled almost anywhere. Make sure that you understand and can explain the routing of command messages from the user interface through the various Document/View objects.

CSplitterWnd

This section shows a way in which an SDI application can present two or more views of data at the same time. Fortunately, MFC provides a class, **CSplitterWnd**, that does most of the work for you.

A *splitter window* is a basic window that can be divided vertically or horizontally—or both vertically and horizontally—into two or more panes by movable splitter bars. Each pane is a child of the splitter window, and the splitter window itself is a child of the frame window.

There are two types of splitter window: static and dynamic. Table 6.4 presents their similarities and differences.

Dynamic Splitter Windows

Dynamic splitter windows are the easier of the two types to create and initialize. Doing so only requires three steps:

1. In the frame window class, define a **CSplitterWnd** member variable.

2. Use ClassWizard to override the frame window's virtual **OnCreateClient()** function.

3. Call **CSplitterWnd::Create()** from inside **OnCreateClient()**. Doing so creates a dynamic splitter window in the frame window's client area.

Table 6.4   Static versus dynamic splitter windows.

Attribute	Static Splitter	Dynamic Splitter
Maximum number of rows and columns	16 x 16	2 x 2
Is row and column configuration changeable by the user?	No, the number of rows and columns are specified at creation and can't be changed by the user.	Yes, the number of rows and columns can be split and unsplit interactively.
Can each pane provide a different type of view of the data?	Yes.	No, unless you derive from **CSplitterWnd** and modify the default behavior.
Horizontal scroll bar	Each pane has its own.	Columns share a vertical scroll bar.
Vertical scroll bar	Each pane has its own.	Rows share a horizontal scroll bar.

Let's look at the prototype for **CSplitterWnd::Create()**:

```
BOOL Create( CWnd* pParentWnd, int nMaxRows, int nMaxCols,
SIZE sizeMin, CCreateContext* pContext, DWORD dwStyle = WS_CHILD
| WS_VISIBLE |WS_HSCROLL | WS_VSCROLL | SPLS_DYNAMIC_SPLIT,
UINT nID = AFX_IDW_PANE_FIRST );
```

The second and third parameters are used to specify the maximum number of rows and columns the splitter can have. Because this is a dynamic splitter, which can support a maximum of two rows and two columns, these will be 1 or 2. The fourth parameter specifies the minimum width and height in pixels for each pane. The fifth parameter is a pointer to a **CCreateContext** structure. In most cases, this can be the *pContext* passed to the parent frame window.

The framework uses the **CCreateContext** structure when it creates the frame windows and views associated with a document. When creating a window, the values in this structure provide information used to connect the components that make up a document and the view of its data. You will only need to create your own **CCreateContext** object if you are overriding parts of the creation process. A **CCreateContext** structure contains pointers to the document, the frame window, the view, and the document template. It also contains a pointer to a **CRuntimeClass** that identifies the type of view to create. The runtime class information and the current document pointer are used to create a new view dynamically. Refer to Table 6.5 to see how and when each **CCreateContext** member might be used.

Table 6.5	CCreateContext data members.
Member	**What It Is For**
m_pNewViewClass	Points to a **CRuntimeClass** object that's used to create a new view.
m_pCurrentDoc	Points to the current document that's to be associated with the new view.
m_pNewDocTemplate	Points to the **CDocumentTemplate** object that's to be used when creating MDI children.
m_pLastView	Points to the view to use as an example when creating additional views.
m_pCurrentFrame	Points to the current frame window object.

Notice that **CSplitterWnd::Create**'s last parameter defaults to **AFX_IDW_PANE_FIRST**, the same value that you saw in the MultiViewSDI application above. This value is one of the "magic numbers" that specifies parts of the main frame. **AFX_IDW_PANE_FIRST** specifies that the default child window is to be the first pane. You only need to modify this value if you create a second splitter in a frame window that already contains a splitter.

After you create a dynamic splitter window, the framework takes care of the rest. If you know ahead of time that you are going to want a dynamic splitter, you don't even need to go through the trouble of overriding **OnCreateClient()**. You can have AppWizard provide it during Step 4. At Step 4 of 6, simply click the Advanced button, then on the Advanced Options property box, pick the Windows Styles tab and select Use Split Window. Refer to Figures 6.2 and 6.3.

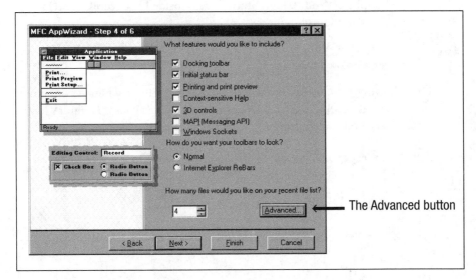

Figure 6.2   MFC AppWizard—Step 4 of 6.

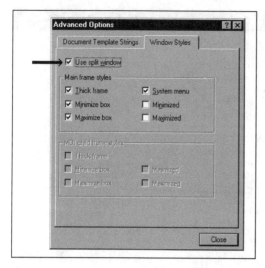

Figure 6.3 MFC AppWizard—Advanced Options property box.

Static Splitter Windows

Static splitter windows require a little more work than dynamic splitter windows—one whole step. This one extra step provides one important advantage: You control the kind of view you want to use. Here are the steps required to add a static splitter window to a frame window:

1. In the frame window class, define a **CSplitterWnd** member variable.

2. Use ClassWizard to override the frame window's virtual **OnCreateClient()** function.

3. Call **CSplitterWnd::CreateStatic()** from inside **OnCreateClient()** to create a static splitter window.

4. Use **CSplitterWnd::CreateView()**. This creates a view in each of the splitter window's panes.

The following **OnCreateClient()** creates a static splitter window containing one row and two columns in a frame window and adds your **CDefaultView** to the left pane and your **CItalicsView** to the right pane.

```
BOOL CMainFrame::OnCreateClient(LPCREATESTRUCT lpcs,
                                CCreateContext* pContext)
{
  if(!m_wndSplitter.CreateStatic(this, 1,2))
  {
```

```
    return FALSE;
  }
  if(!m_wndSplitter.CreateView(0,0,RUNTIME_CLASS(CDefaultView),
    CSize(256,0), pContext))
  {
    return FALSE;
  }
  if(!m_wndSplitter.CreateView(0,1,RUNTIME_CLASS(CItalicsView),
    CSize(0,0), pContext))
  {
    return FALSE;
  }

  return TRUE;
}
```

Add the above code to the MultiViewSDI application, and remove the command handlers that switch the view. After you have made the changes, when you run the application, it should look like Figure 6.4.

Recommended Configurations

Microsoft's recommended configurations and usage for static splitters are as follows:

➤ 1 row × 2 columns for displaying two dissimilar panes side by side

➤ 2 rows × 1 column for displaying two dissimilar panes, one on top of the other

➤ 2 rows × 2 columns for displaying similar panes, usually in four side-by-side squares

Figure 6.4   MultiViewSDI with a 1 x 2 splitter.

Microsoft's recommended configurations and usage for dynamic splitters are as follows:

➤ 1 row × 2 columns for displaying columnar data

➤ 2 rows × 1 column for displaying textual or other data

➤ 2 rows × 2 columns for displaying grid- or table-oriented data

Multiple-Document Interface

The major difference between single- and multiple-document interfaces is that MDI applications allow you to have more than one document open at the same time. In fact, subject to limits on memory and resources, you can open as many documents as you want. When we think of MDI applications, Word, Excel, and similar applications usually come to mind, which might lead one to believe that an MDI application can only handle one type of document. But this is not the case. MDI applications can support multiple document types.

Like SDI applications, MDI applications store their data in a document object derived from **CDocument** and present views derived from **CView** or one of its many derived classes. However, in MDI applications, the main window is derived from **CMDIFrameWnd** instead of **CFrameWnd**. The client area of the frame window contains a special client window created by the frame window. View windows are wrapped with "document frames" that are derived from **CMDIChildWnd**. These **CMDIChildWnd**-derived windows float within the workspace defined by the client area.

In an MDI application, the client window is a child of the top-level frame window. Moving on down the hierarchy, the **CMDIChildWnd**-derived windows are children of the MDI client window, and views are children of the document frames. Document objects, of course, contain the data displayed in the views.

Combinations Of Documents And Views MDI Supports

Think about the various relationships between document objects and view objects that you might want to implement in an application. Simply saying "multiple views and multiple documents" isn't quite specific enough. More specifically, the relationships are as follows:

➤ Single view on a single document type

➤ Multiple views on a single document type

➤ Single views on multiple document types

➤ Multiple views on multiple document types

Now that the various relationships have been spelled out, let's examine the support MFC provides through MDI.

Single View On A Single Document Type

Like SDI, for an MDI application, single view on a single document type is the standard relationship of a document, its view, and its frame window. The difference here between an SDI application and an MDI application is that the MDI application can have multiple documents open at the same time. However, the relationship is what should be considered, not the number of documents that can be open. This relationship can be described in a relatively straightforward manner: a one-to-many relationship between documents and views, and a one-to-one relationship between each view and a frame window. Notice that the one-to-many relationship is between documents and views, not document types and views. Although the application might have many documents open, they are all of the same document type.

Multiple Views On A Single Document Type

For this relationship you need to look at three basic models. These three models are described in the following list:

➤ The user is able to view objects of the same class, each in a separate MDI document frame window. AppWizard provides a New Window option on the Window menu that the user can use to open additional frames with a view of the same document.

➤ The user is able, in the same document frame window, to look at multiple views of the same document object. AppWizard Step 4 of 6 will include a dynamic splitter as part of the view class. Remember that a dynamic splitter splits the view space of a single document window into multiple separate views of the same document.

➤ The user is able to view objects of different classes in a single frame window. In this model, each view provides the user with a different way to view the same document. This functionality must be hand-coded by the programmer. The easy way, of course, is to use the **CSplitterWnd** class.

Keeping each of the views current as the content of the document changes is an important matter. Two functions, **CDocument::UpdateAllViews()** and **CView::OnUpdate()**, are key in providing the necessary functionality. You should know when and by whom these functions are called.

Single Views On Multiple Document Types

AppWizard creates a single document class for you. However, occasionally you may need to support more than one document type. Remember, this discussion is about document types, not document objects. Let's say you are building a simple ASCII text file viewer that can read files with extensions such as .TXT, .ASC, or .INI, and you want all of these to map to the same document and view class. When the user chooses the New option from the File menu, the framework displays a dialog box (see Figure 6.5) that lists the application's supported document types. After the user chooses a document type, the framework creates the proper type of document, view, and frame window objects. The algorithm used is based on the *filterExt* substring of the string resource of each registered document template. This string resource is composed of seven substrings separated by the \n character. Except for trailing substrings, the \n character must be used as a placeholder if a substring is not included. These substrings describe the document type. Table 6.6 describes these substrings.

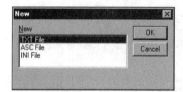

Figure 6.5   New option dialog box.

Table 6.6	Document template string resource.
Substring	**Description**
windowTitle	Frame window's title. It's only used in SDI applications.
docName	Default name assigned to new documents of this type. This name, plus a number, appears in the frame window's title and in the Save As dialog box for new documents.
fileNewName	Descriptive name for documents of this document type. It is displayed in the FileNew dialog box.
filterName	Descriptive name for documents of this type and an associated default file name extension.
filterExt	Default file extension for documents of this type.
regFileTypeId	The identifier that is stored in the Registry. It's used to associate the *filterExt* file extension with the application.
regFileTypeName	Descriptive name for documents of this type.

Unfortunately, each document template object can be associated with only one resource string and, therefore, with no more than one file extension. This means you need to create one distinct document template object for each file extension that you want to use in your application. Each of the document template objects that you create will share the same arguments for the document, view, and frame window classes. However, each document template object will have a distinct resource ID. The following snippet of code demonstrates how this is done:

```
BOOL CTextViewerApp::InitInstance()
{
  // . . .
  CMultiDocTemplate* pDocTemplate;
  pDocTemplate = new CMultiDocTemplate(
                   IDR_TXT_DOCTYPE,
                   RUNTIME_CLASS(CTextViewerDoc),
                   RUNTIME_CLASS(CChildFrame),
                   RUNTIME_CLASS(CTextViewerView));
     AddDocTemplate(pDocTemplate);

  pDocTemplate = new CMultiDocTemplate(
                   IDR_ASC_DOCTYPE,
                   RUNTIME_CLASS(CTextViewerDoc),
                   RUNTIME_CLASS(CChildFrame),
                   RUNTIME_CLASS(CTextViewerView));
     AddDocTemplate(pDocTemplate);

  pDocTemplate = new CMultiDocTemplate(
                   IDR_INI_DOCTYPE,
                   RUNTIME_CLASS(CTextViewerDoc),
                   RUNTIME_CLASS(CChildFrame),
                   RUNTIME_CLASS(CTextViewerView));
     AddDocTemplate(pDocTemplate);
  // ...

}
```

Multiple Views On Multiple Document Types

Assume that you now need to develop an application that supports both worksheet and chart documents. Here, you will probably represent each document type with its own document class and its own view class, which means you will need to create a unique **CDocument**-derived class and **CView**-derived class for each document type. You will also need to register each document type, like you did above, but now each document template object will have unique document and view classes. The following code provides an example:

```
BOOL CTextViewerApp::InitInstance()
{
  // . . .
  CMultiDocTemplate* pDocTemplate;
  pDocTemplate = new CMultiDocTemplate(
                 IDR_SHEET_DOCTYPE,
                 RUNTIME_CLASS(CWorksheetDoc),
                 RUNTIME_CLASS(CChildFrame),
                 RUNTIME_CLASS(CWorksheetView));
      AddDocTemplate(pDocTemplate);

  pDocTemplate = new CMultiDocTemplate(
                 IDR_GRAPH_DOCTYPE,
                 RUNTIME_CLASS(CGraphDoc),
                 RUNTIME_CLASS(CChildFrame),
                 RUNTIME_CLASS(CGraphView));
      AddDocTemplate(pDocTemplate);

  // ...

}
```

Practice Questions

Question 1

Which of the following statements are true? [Check all the correct answers]

❏ a. An MDI application can have two documents of the same type open at the same time.

❏ b. MDI applications can only handle one type of document.

❏ c. An MDI can have two documents of dissimilar types open at the same time.

❏ d. An MDI application can have any number of documents open at the same time.

The correct answers are a and c. Answer d is a trick answer. The actual number of documents that can be open at one time is *not* unlimited but will always be limited by the availability of memory and system resources. Therefore, answer a is correct, and answer d is incorrect.

Although AppWizard only provides support for a single document type, you can add support for additional document types by creating a **CDocument**-derived class and **CView**-derived class for each document type you wish your application to support. The types of documents MDI applications can have open are specific to each application. Depending on the application, it might support one, two, or more document types. Therefore, answer c is correct, and answer b is incorrect.

Question 2

Which statements are true? [Check all the correct answers]

❏ a. A view object can be attached to multiple documents.

❏ b. A document object can have multiple views attached to it.

❏ c. OnDraw() can be used for output to a window, for printing, and for print previewing.

❏ d. A document template object can support more than one document type.

The correct answers are b and c. A document object can have more than one view associated with it, but a view always relates to a one specific document object. Therefore, answer a is incorrect. A unique document template instance is required for each document, view, and frame window combination. Therefore, answer d is incorrect.

In a document/view application, the framework fields the **WM_PAINT** message and calls the view's **OnDraw()** function, passing it a paint DC pointer for drawing. When a document is printed, the framework calls the same **OnDraw()** function, passing it a pointer to a printer DC.

Question 3

Which statement is true?

○ a.   A dynamic splitter can have up to 8 rows and 8 columns.

○ b.   The user can change a static splitter's row and column configuration.

○ c.   A static splitter can have up to 16 rows and 16 columns.

○ d.   A splitter window pane is usually derived from CFrameWnd.

The correct answer is c. The **CSplitterWnd** class provides the functionality of a splitter window, which is a window that contains multiple panes. A pane is usually an application-specific object derived from **CView**, but it can be any **CWnd** object that has the appropriate child window ID. Therefore, answer d is incorrect. In static splitters, the panes are created when the splitter window is created, and the order and number of panes never change. In dynamic splitters, additional panes are created and destroyed as the user splits and unsplits new views. The maximum number of panes you can specify for static splitters is 16 rows by 16 columns. Therefore, answer c is correct, and answer b is incorrect.

A dynamic splitter starts out with a single view, and splitter boxes are provided to initiate splitting. When creating either kind of splitter window, you must specify the maximum number of rows and columns that the splitter will manage. For a static splitter, panes must be created to fill all the rows and columns. For a dynamic splitter, the first pane is automatically created when the **CSplitterWnd** is created. The maximum number of panes you can specify for dynamic splitters is 2 rows by 2 columns. Therefore, answer a is incorrect.

Question 4

What is the function of the following code? [Check all the correct answers]

```
pDocTemplate = new CMultiDocTemplate(
                IDR_DRAW,
                RUNTIME_CLASS(CMyDoc),
                RUNTIME_CLASS(CChildFrame),
                RUNTIME_CLASS(CDrawView));
     AddDocTemplate(pDocTemplate);
pDocTemplate = new CMultiDocTemplate(
                IDR_FORM,
                RUNTIME_CLASS(CMyDoc),
                RUNTIME_CLASS(CChildFrame),
                RUNTIME_CLASS(CFormView));
     AddDocTemplate(pDocTemplate);
```

❑ a. Attach two views to the same document object.

❑ b. Register two different views on the same document type.

❑ c. Register two different views on two different document types.

❑ d. Insufficient information is provided.

The correct answer is d. Either b or c could be correct, if you knew the value of the *filterExt* substring of the string resource. However, because the string resource is not provided, you do not know the value of the *filterExt* substring. Not knowing the value of *filterExt* means you cannot determine if you are dealing with one or two document types. Answer a is incorrect because the question is dealing with document types, not document objects. Answer b is a trick. Both function calls are using the same document object class, **CMyDoc**, to trick you. Remember that it is the contents of the *filterName* substring that determines the document type, not the document class.

Need To Know More?

Kain, Eugene. *The MFC Answer Book: Solutions for Effective Visual C++ Applications.* Addison-Wesley, Reading, MA, 1998. ISBN 0-201-18537-7. This is a real "how-to" book. The author devotes three chapters—almost half of the book—to the document/view architecture. Chapter 1 is all theory, Chapter 2 deals with documents and document templates, and Chapter 3 covers views. The author also provides an appendix that includes a number of very useful utility functions and classes. This book uses a question-and-answer format, is very well written, and is easy to follow. If you find yourself asking, "How do I ...?", then this book is for you.

Prosise, Jeff. *Programming Windows with MFC* Microsoft Press, Redmond, WA, 1999. ISBN 1-57231-695-0. This is the updated version of the author's popular book, *Programming Windows 95 with MFC.* Chapter 9 provides a good description of the document/view architecture and builds a simple SDI application to demonstrate the significant points. Chapter 11 presents splitters and MDI. The author uses the application for Chapter 9 as a starting point and adds splitters to it, showing how to embed one splitter inside another.

Shepherd, George and Scot Wingo. *MFC Internals: Inside the Microsoft Foundation Class Architecture.* Addison-Wesley, Reading, MA, 1996. ISBN 0-201-40721-3. This book's focus is on how MFC works. Chapters 7 and 8 cover the document/view architecture. Chapter 7 alone probably provides more about the workings of the document/view architecture than most programmers care to know. Chapter 9 includes a very detailed section on splitters. This book is not for everyone, but those who want to know what goes on under the covers should study this book. The authors really know MFC and present it well.

Visual C++ Programmer's Guide. MSDN Library Visual Studio 6.0.

View Classes

Terms you'll need to understand:

- √ CScrollView
- √ CFormView
- √ CCtrlView
- √ CEditView
- √ CRichEditView
- √ CHARFORMAT
- √ CListView
- √ CTreeView
- √ LVCOLUMN

Techniques you'll need to master:

- √ Implementing applications that use the **CScrollView** class
- √ Implementing applications that use the **CFormView** class
- √ Implementing applications that use the **CEditView**, **CFormView**, **CListView**, **CScrollView**, and **CTreeView** classes
- √ Understanding the advantage of using a **CEditView** class instead of a **CEdit** class
- √ Understanding the advantage of using a **CRichEditView** class instead of a **CEditView** class
- √ Modifying **CListView**'s style property
- √ Modifying **CTreeView**'s style property

In the last chapter, you saw where the **CView** class provides the basic function-ally for user-defined view classes and how, by deriving your view classes from **CView**, you can render images of your documents on the screen as appropriate for your applications. MFC provides a number of classes derived directly or indirectly from **CView** that provide unique functionality. Some of these classes are used directly. Others, like **CView**, are abstract base classes used for deriving view classes of your own. Figure 7.1 shows the derivation chain. Table 7.1 provides a summary description of each of these classes.

CCtrlView and its derivatives adjust the document/view architecture to the new common controls supported by Windows 95 and Windows NT versions

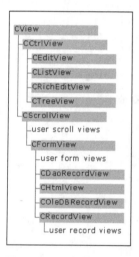

```
CView
  └CCtrlView
      ├CEditView
      ├CListView
      ├CRichEditView
      └CTreeView
  └CScrollView
      ├user scroll views
      └CFormView
          ├user form views
          ├CDaoRecordView
          ├CHtmlView
          ├COleDBRecordView
          └CRecordView
              └user record views
```

Figure 7.1 MFC view class hierarchy.

Table 7.1	MFC CView-derived classes.
Class	**Description**
CCtrlView	Derived from **CView**, this is the base class for the specialized view classes that apply the document/view architecture to the 32-bit Windows common controls.
CEditView	Derived from **CCtrlView**, this class provides a simple view based on the Windows edit box control. Since it allows entering and editing text, it can be used as the foundation for a simple text editor application. See also **CRichEditView**.
CRichEditView	Derived from **CCtrlView**, this view contains a **CRichEditCtrl** object. This class is similar to **CEditView**, but better. **CRichEditView** handles formatted text, fonts, colors, and embedded OLE objects.

(continued)

Table 7.1	MFC CView-derived classes (continued).
Class	**Description**
CListView	Derived from **CCtrlView**, this view contains a **CListCtrl** object. Displays icons and strings in a manner similar to the right-hand pane of the Windows 95 Explorer.
CTreeView	Derived from **CCtrlView**, this view contains a **CTreeCtrl** object. Displays icons and strings arranged in a hierarchy in a manner similar to the left-hand pane of the Windows 95 Explorer.
CScrollView	Derived from **CView**, this class provides basic scrolling capabilities.
CFormView	A form view—that is, a view that contains controls. Derived from **CScrollView**, it is the base class for more specialized views containing controls. The form layout is based on a dialog box resource.
CHtmlView	A Web browser view with which the application's user can browse sites on the World Wide Web, as well as folders in the local file system and on a network. The Web browser view can also work as an Active document container. This class is derived from **CFormView**.
CRecordView	Derived from **CFormView**, this view displays ODBC database records in controls. If you select ODBC support in your project, the view's base class is **CRecordView**. The view is connected to a **CRecordset** I object.
CDaoRecordView	Derived from **CFormView**, this view displays DAO database records in controls. If you select DAO support in your project, the view's base class is **CDaoRecordView**. The view is connected to a **CDaoRecordset** object.
COleDBRecordView	Derived from **CFormView**, this view displays OLE DB records in controls. If you select OLE DB support in your project, the view's base class is **COleDBRecordView**. The view is connected to a **CRowset** object.

3.51 and later. **CFormView** and its derivatives support Dialog Data Exchange and can be used like you would a **CDialog**-derived class.

This chapter covers **CScrollView**, **CFormView**, and **CCtrlView** and its derivatives. The remaining **CView**-derived classes will be covered in later chapters. Most of these views are available at MFC AppWizard Step 6 of 6. Refer to Figure 7.2.

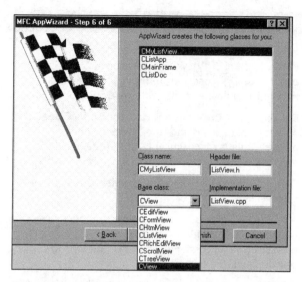

Figure 7.2   MFC AppWizard - Step 6 of 6—selecting the view's base class.

CScrollView

By deriving a class from **CView** and overriding the message-mapped **OnHScroll()** and **OnVScroll()**, you can handle standard scrolling yourself. However, there is an easier way: Derive your view class from **CScrollView** instead of from **CView**. In fact, **CScrollView** comes with even more capabilities:

➤ It controls the sizing of windows and viewports and manages mapping modes.

➤ It handles scroll bar messages, appropriately scrolling the view.

➤ It handles keyboard, nonscrolling mouse, and IntelliMouse wheel messages appropriately.

In order for **CScrollView** to correctly depict the scroll bars on the view, it needs to know how big the entire document is and the current position of the scroll bars. The view can set its scrollable size by calling **SetScrollSizes()**. The call to **SetScrollSizes()** sets the view's mapping mode, the total dimensions of the scroll view, and the amounts to scroll horizontally and vertically. All sizes are in logical units. Two convenient places for your application to call **SetScrollSizes()** are the **OnUpdate()** and **OnInitialUpdate()** members of your view.

When the user clicks a scroll bar shaft outside of the scroll box, **CScrollView** scrolls a "page." When a scroll arrow at either end of a scroll bar is clicked,

CScrollView scrolls a "line." By default, a page is 1/10 the total size of the view, and a line is 1/10 of the page size. You can change the page size and line size by calling **SetScrollSizes()**.

Before calling **OnDraw()** of your derived view class, **CScrollView** automatically adjusts the viewport origin for the **CPaintDC** device-context object that it passes to **OnDraw()**. To adjust the viewport origin for the scrolling window, **CScrollView** overrides **CView::OnPrepareDC()**. This adjustment is automatic for the **CPaintDC** device context that **CScrollView** passes to **OnDraw()**, but you must call **CScrollView::OnPrepareDC()** yourself for any other device contexts you use, such as a **CClientDC**. You can override **CScrollView::OnPrepareDC()** to set the pen, background color, and other drawing attributes, but call the base class to do scaling.

Instead of scrolling, **CScrollView** can automatically scale the view to the current window size. In this mode, the view has no scroll bars, and the logical view is stretched or shrunk to exactly fit the window's client area. To use this scale-to-fit capability, call **SetScaleToFitSize()**. (Call either **SetScaleToFitSize()** or **SetScrollSizes()**, but not both.)

CFormView

A *form view* is really just a view that contains controls. These controls are laid out based on a dialog template resource. Choosing **CFormView** as the base class for your application in Step 6 of MFC AppWizard provides a "blank" form, which you can customize with the appropriate controls. Because controls are able to paint themselves, you normally do not need to override **OnDraw()**. Also, because **CFormView** is derived from **CScrollView**, your **CFormView**-derived class will automatically support scrolling as needed.

You can also insert new forms into document/view-based applications, even if your application did not initially support forms, by selecting Insert|New Form. In an SDI or MDI application, which implements the default document/view architecture, when you choose File|New, the framework will prompt you to choose from the available views.

Although, the MFC AppWizard and the Insert|New Form command are the preferred methods for creating forms-based applications, you can create a view based on **CFormView** by taking the following steps:

1. Use the Dialog Box Editor to design the template.

2. Set the appropriate properties: Style = Child, Border = None, Visible = Cleared, Titlebar = Cleared, ID = IDD_MYNEWFORM.

3. With the Dialog Editor open, run ClassWizard and create a **CFormView**-derived class.

4. Add data members to your view class that correspond to the controls.

5. Override **OnUpdate()** and **OnInitialUpdate()** as appropriate for your application. Use **OnInitializeUpdate()** to initialize member variables and the form's controls. Use **OnUpdate()** to update the form's member variables controls.

6. Add message handlers in the view class to respond to messages generated by the controls.

7. Implement a member function to move data from your view to your document.

8. In **InitInstance()** of your **CWinApp**-derived class, associate your view class with a document class and frame window using a document template.

9. Optionally, override **OnPaint()** in your view class as required.

In summary, if you want a dialog-style interface but still want the benefits of the document/view architecture, then you should probably build your application with the **CFormView** as the base class for your view window and use the SDI application model.

CCtrlView

CCtrlView is the base class for all of the view classes that work by containing a Windows control. That is, the client area of the view window is actually filled by a control. The control does all the work. If you need to access the control directly, you call the appropriate member function to obtain a reference that can be used to manipulate the control. When you might need to create a view based on your own control or combination of controls, **CCtrlView** is a good base class to use. For a more specialized base class use one of the **CCtrlView**-derived classes.

A key overrideable function is **PreCreateWindow()**. Overriding this function allows you to adjust the style bits of your control. Call the base class implementation of the function to initialize default settings before setting your style bits. Here's what the code might look like for a **CListView**-derived class:

```
BOOL CMyListView::PreCreateWindow(CREATESTRUCT& cs)
{
```

```
    if(!CListView::PreCreateWindow(cs))
    return FALSE;

 cs.style |= LVS_SORTASCENDING | LVS_REPORT;

 return TRUE;
}
```

It's also possible to adjust the style bits by overriding **OnInitialUpdate()**. The following code accomplishes the same as the preceding code:

```
void CMyListView::OnInitialUpdate()
{
    // ...

    // Get a reference to the list control
    // embedded in the view
    CListCtrl & clc = GetListCtrl();

    // Use the reference to call member functions
    // of the embedded control
    clc.ModifyStyle(0, LVS_SORTASCENDING | LVS_REPORT);

    // ...do rest of initialization steps

}
```

Each **CCtrlView**-derived class has its own set of style bits. Some of these style bits need to be set prior to the creation of the Windows window; others can be set after the Windows window is created but before it is visible; and still others can be set after the window is visible. Depending on when the style bits need to be set, you can specify then in the **Create** function, in the override of **PreCreateWindow()**, **OnCreate()** or **OnInitialUpdate()**, or in some other manner, such as in a menu.

All of the classes derived from **CCtrlView** handle most of the drawing for you in their customized versions of **OnDraw()**. Typically, the only time that you will override **OnDraw** is for printing/print preview. Place code in the appropriate message handlers to handle updates by the user in a view.

You should never use **CCtrlView** directly in your code but instead use one of the derivatives: **CEditView, CListView, CRichEditView,** and **CTreeView**.

CEditView

CEditView uses a Windows edit control to hold the entire text document in memory while the user edits the document's contents. Text size is limited to 64K, and you cannot mix fonts.

CEditView extends the functionality of the edit control by handling the Edit menu Cut, Copy, Paste, Clear, Select All, Find, Replace, Repeat, and Undo commands and the File menu Print command. However, the support for Select All, Find, Replace, and Repeat are not obvious. For example, to employ the Select All capability you would add a menu item to the Edit menu and use the **CEditView** message map by assigning an ID of **ID_EDIT_SELECT_ ALL**. **ID_EDIT_SELECT_ALL** and others are defined in afxres.h. Aternatively, you can use your own IDs and add handlers like the following:

```
//////////////////////////////////////////////////////////////
// CMyEditView message handlers

void CMyEditView::OnEditSelectAll()
{
  CEditView::OnEditSelectAll();
}
void CMyEditView::OnUpdateEditSelectAll(CCmdUI* pCmdUI)
{
  CEditView::OnUpdateNeedText(pCmdUI);
}
```

CRichEditView

In the preceding section, I mentioned two problems with **CEditView**: Text size is limited to 64K, and you cannot mix fonts. The **CRichEditView** over-comes these two problems. It also supports OLE. Figure 7.3 shows a very simple word processor implemented with **CRichEditView**. AppWizard wrote almost everything. All I did was run AppWizard, selecting Container support, added a menu and a small amount of code. The program handles ASCII and RTF files and is able to bold and italicize the text. Here's the code:

```
void CWPView::OnInitialUpdate()
{
  CRichEditView::OnInitialUpdate();
  // Set the printing margins (720 twips = 1/2 inch).
  SetMargins(CRect(720, 720, 720, 720));

  CHARFORMAT cf;
  memset(&cf, 0, sizeof(cf));
```

```
cf.cbSize = sizeof(cf);
cf.dwMask = CFM_FACE | CFM_SIZE | CFM_BOLD | CFM_ITALIC;
cf.yHeight = 12 * 20; // character height in twips,
                      // 1 twip is 1/20 of a printer's point
cf.bPitchAndFamily = DEFAULT_PITCH | FF_DONTCARE;
strcpy(cf.szFaceName, "Arial");

SetCharFormat(cf);
}

// . . .

//////////////////////////////////////////////////////////////////
// CWPView message handlers

void CWPView::OnBold()
{
  OnCharEffect(CFM_BOLD, CFE_BOLD);
}
void CWPView::OnUpdateBold(CCmdUI* pCmdUI)
{
  OnUpdateCharEffect(pCmdUI, CFM_BOLD, CFE_BOLD);
}
void CWPView::OnItalics()
{
  OnCharEffect(CFM_ITALIC, CFE_ITALIC);
}
void CWPView::OnUpdateItalics(CCmdUI* pCmdUI)
{
  OnUpdateCharEffect(pCmdUI, CFM_ITALIC, CFE_ITALIC);
}
```

It doesn't require much effort to add support that allows the user to change the font and to align the text. The secret to changing the font without having to convert between **LOGFONT** and **CHARFORMAT** structures is an undocumented **CFontDialog** constructor, as in the following code:

```
CHARFORMAT cf;
cf = GetCharFormatSelection();
CFontDialog dlg(cf,
    CF_FORCEFONTEXIST | CF_INITTOLOGFONTSTRUCT | CF_SCREENFONTS);
if(dlg.DoModal() == IDOK)
{
  dlg.GetCharFormat(cf);
  SetCharFormat(cf);
}
```

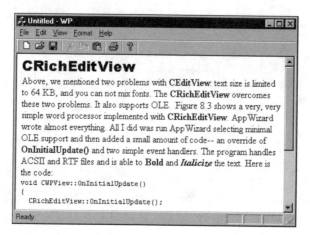

Figure 7.3 A very simple word processor.

Alignment of text is accomplished by calling **CRichEditView::OnParaAlign()** passing a value of **PFA_LEFT**, **PFA_RIGHT**, or **PFA_CENTER**. To keep your menu or style bar buttons updated, map them to an update handler that calls **CRichEditView::OnUpdateParaAlign()**.

The **CHARFORMAT** structure contains information about character formatting in a rich edit control. The **dwMask** member contains a bit mask that specifies which of the other members contain valid information or attributes to be set. The mask can be zero or a combination of the values shown in Table 7.2. The character effects are contained in **dwEffects**. For example, when **CFM_BOLD** is set in **dwMask** it indicates that the value of **CFE_BOLD** in **dwEffects** is valid. The **dwEffects** member can be zero or a combination of the values shown in Table 7.3. There is also a **CHARFORMAT2** structure, which is a Rich Edit 2.0 extension of the **CHARFORMAT** structure.

CListView

The **CListView** class simplifies the use of **CListCtrl**, the class that encapsulates list control functionality, with the MFC document/view architecture. A *list control* displays a collection of items, each consisting of an optional icon and a label. The default list view style shows the items across the page. Fortunately, list views provide several ways of arranging items and displaying individual items. For example, additional information about each item can be displayed in columns to the right of the icon and label. Table 7.4 shows the available list view styles.

Table 7.2 CHARFORMAT's dwMask values.

Value	Meaning
CFM_BOLD	**CFE_BOLD** is valid.
CFM_CHARSET	The **bCharSet** member is valid.
CFM_COLOR	The **crTextColor** member and **CFE_AUTOCOLOR** are valid.
CFM_FACE	The **szFaceName** member is valid.
CFM_ITALIC	**CFE_ITALIC** is valid.
CFM_OFFSET	The **yOffset** member is valid.
CFM_PROTECTED	**CFE_PROTECTED** is valid.
CFM_SIZE	The **yHeight** member is valid.
CFM_STRIKEOUT	**CFE_STRIKEOUT** is valid.
CFM_UNDERLINE	**CFE_UNDERLINE** is valid.

Table 7.3 CHARFORMAT's dwEffects values.

Value	Meaning
CFE_AUTOCOLOR	**GetSysColor(COLOR_WINDOWTEXT)** will return the text color.
CFE_BOLD	Characters are bold.
CFE_ITALIC	Characters are italic.
CFE_STRIKEOUT	Characters are struck.
CFE_UNDERLINE	Characters are underlined.
CFE_PROTECTED	Characters are protected.

You can override **OnInitialUpdate()** in order to set the style and to initialize the list view. The following code shows a report style with three line items. Any real-world application should keep its data in the document class separate from the view. However, for simplicity, the following example embeds the data in the code:

```
void CRptLstView::OnInitialUpdate()
{
  CListView::OnInitialUpdate();

  CListCtrl & rClv = GetListCtrl();
  // modify the style
```

```
rClv.ModifyStyle(NULL, LVS_SORTASCENDING | LVS_REPORT);
LVCOLUMN lv;    // a struct that contains information
                      about a column
lv.mask = LVCF_FMT          // The fmt member is valid
          | LVCF_TEXT       // The pszText member is valid
          | LVCF_WIDTH;     // The cx member is valid
lv.fmt = LVCFMT_LEFT;       // Text is left-aligned

// Create 3 columns and give each column a header.
static char * header[3] = { "Name", "Phone', "Email" };
lv.cx = 100;
lv.pszText = header[0];
rClv.InsertColumn(0, &lv);

lv.cx = 120;
lv.pszText = header[1];
rClv.InsertColumn(1, &lv);

lv.cx = 250;
lv.pszText = header[2];
rClv.InsertColumn(2, &lv);

// Now add some information
rClv.InsertItem(0, "Mary Smith");
rClv.SetItemText(0, 1, "404 555-1192");
rClv.SetItemText(0, 2, "msmith@BigBear.com");

int indx = rClv.InsertItem(1, "Don Adams");
rClv.SetItemText(indx, 1, "502 555-8982");
rClv.SetItemText(indx, 2, "DonAdams@HotOne.com");

indx = rClv.InsertItem (2, "Ann Johnson");
rClv.SetItemText(indx, 1, "518 555-7776");
rClv.SetItemText(indx, 2, "ann@worldwide.com");

SetRedraw();
}
```

The preceding code creates a window that looks like the one shown in Figure 7.4.

One of the reasons you might use a list view is to enable users to specify a selection of items. You can use **GetNextItem()** to search a list view item that has the specified properties and that bears the specified relationship to a given item. Here's its prototype:

```
int GetNextItem( int nItem, int nFlags ) const;
```

Table 7.4 List view styles.	
Style	**Description**
LVS_ALIGNLEFT	Aligns to the left in icon view and small icon view.
LVS_ALIGNTOP	Aligns to the top in icon view and small icon view.
LVS_AUTOARRANGE	Keeps icons automatically arranged in icon view and small icon view.
LVS_EDITLABELS	Enables editing in place of item text.
LVS_ICON	Arranges large icons (32x32 pixels) from left to right, then down.
LVS_LIST	Vertical list view.
LVS_NOCOLUMNHEADER	In report view, turns off column header.
LVS_NOLABELWRAP	In icon view, displays item text on a single line.
LVS_NOSCROLL	Disables scrolling.
LVS_NOSORTHEADER	Disables the ability of column headers to work like buttons.
LVS_OWNERDRAWFIXED	In report view, enables the owner window to paint items.
LVS_REPORT	Specifies report view.
LVS_SHAREIMAGELISTS	Allows the same image lists to be used with multiple list view controls.
LVS_SHOWSELALWAYS	If the control does not have the focus, always shows the selection.
LVS_SINGLESEL	Allows only one item at a time to be selected.
LVS_SMALLICON	Arranges small icons (16x16 pixels) from left to right, then down.
LVS_SORTASCENDING	Sorts items based on item text in ascending order.
LVS_SORTDESCENDING	Sorts items based on item text in descending order.

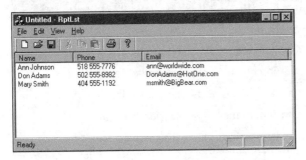

Figure 7.4   The list view with column headers.

GetNextItem() returns the index of the next item if successful, or –1 otherwise. The first parameter, *nItem*, specifies the index of the item to begin the searching with, or –1 to find the first item that matches the specified flags. The second parameter is a flag value that specifies the particular items you want to find. A list of these flags is shown is Table 7.5.

After you have an index, you can call **GetItemText()** to retrieve the text for the item. **GetItemText()** takes the index and the column for the requested text and returns a **CString**. Here's a snippet of code that finds and retrieves the selected items:

```
// . . .
m_strList.RemoveAll();     // m_strList is a CStringList
int nSelected = -1;
do
{
  nSelected = GetListCtrl().GetNextItem(nSelected,
              LVNI_SELECTED);
  if(nSelected != -1)
  {
    CString str = GetListCtrl().GetItemText(nSelected, 0);
    m_strList.AddTail(str);
  }
} while(nSelected != -1);
// . . .
```

CTreeView

CTreeView encapsulates tree control functionality within the document/view architecture. The **CTreeView** will occupy the entire client area of a frame window or splitter window and will be automatically resized when its parent window is resized. Like all view classes, it can process command messages from menus, accelerator keys, and toolbars. The tree control itself contains

Table 7.5   Flag values used by CListView::GetNextItem().

Flag Value	Description
LVNI_ABOVE	Finds an item that is above the specified item
LVNI_ALL	Finds a subsequent item by index (the default value)
LVNI_BELOW	Finds an item that is below the specified item
LVNI_TOLEFT	Finds an item to the left of the specified item
LVNI_TORIGHT	Finds an item to the right of the specified item

the data necessary to display the tree, so the corresponding document object can be relatively simple.

You can use AppWizard to automatically create an SDI framework that supports a tree view. In AppWizard Step 6 of 6, you select **CTreeView** for the view's base class. After the framework is in place, you need to customize the properties of the tree control and populate it. If you want to display images in the tree view, you must build an image list and associate it with the view.

Tree views, like list views, have a number of style flags. However, unlike list views, some tree view flags are used to add horizontal and vertical lines in the tree control that link the parent and child items and buttons that open and close hierarchies. There are also flags that allow the user to edit the items directly and others that disable drag-and-drop. Table 7.6 shows the six tree view style flags available on Windows 95 and Windows NT versions 3.51 and later systems.

Normally, you will override **OnInitialUpdate()** so that you can use **Modify Style()** to set the style flags. In **OnInitialUpdate()** is where you might also create an image list and associate the list with the tree control. You might also want to initialize the data in the control at this time, but usually you will place the code to populate the control in **OnUpdate()**.

To display images with the nodes, you must complete the following steps:

1. Use the Resource Editor to create an image list of like-sized bitmaps, and add it to your project.

Table 7.6   Tree view styles.

Style Flag	Description
TVS_DISABLEDRAGDROP	Inhibits the tree view control from sending **TVN_BEGINDRAG** notification messages.
TVS_EDITLABELS	Permits the user to edit the labels.
TVS_HASBUTTONS	Adds plus (+) and minus (-) buttons next to parent items.
TVS_HASLINES	Adds lines to link child items to their corresponding parent item.
TVS_LINESATROOT	Adds lines to link items at the root of the tree view control. This value is only valid if **TVS_HASLINES** is also specified.
TVS_SHOWSELALWAYS	Stipulates that a selected item is to remain selected when the tree view control loses focus.

2. Build an image list.

3. Associate the image list with the tree control.

4. As you insert a node, select an image to use for each of the two states of a node: selected and unselected.

Populating the tree control in **OnUpdate** consists of two steps:

1. Delete all data from the tree control.

2. Populate the tree control (with the updated items).

As the user interacts with the control, handle each of the messages you want to by adding an **ON_NOTIFY_REFLECT** macro in your control window's message map or by adding an **ON_NOTIFY** macro to your parent window's message map. By calling the various Set member functions, you can change the indentation and the text, image, or data associated with an item. You can also traverse the contents of the tree control with functions that allow you to retrieve handles to parents, children, and siblings of a specified item. You can even sort the children of a particular node.

One way to find the selected node of a tree view is by using **GetSelectedItem()**, which returns the **HTREEITEM** handle of the selected item. Alternatively, **CTreeView** has a **GetNextItem()** function that is analogous to the list view's **GetNextItem()** function. The flags to use with the tree view's **GetNextItem()** function are shown is Table 7.7.

Table 7.7   Flag values used by CTreeView::GetNextItem().

Flag Value	Description
TVGN_CARET	GetNextItem() returns the currently selected tree view item.
TVGN_CHILD	GetNextItem() returns the first child tree view item. The *hItem* parameter must be NULL.
TVGN_DROPHILITE	GetNextItem() returns the tree view item that is the target of a drag-and-drop operation.
TVGN_FIRSTVISIBLE	GetNextItem() returns the first visible tree view item.
TVGN_NEXT	GetNextItem() returns the next sibling tree view item.
TVGN_NEXTVISIBLE	GetNextItem() returns the next visible tree view item that follows the specified item.

(continued)

Table 7.7	Flag values used by CTreeView::GetNextItem() (continued).
Flag Value	**Description**
TVGN_PARENT	GetNextItem() returns the parent of the specified tree view item.
TVGN_PREVIOUS	GetNextItem() returns the previous sibling tree view item.
TVGN_PREVIOUSVISIBLE	GetNextItem() returns the first visible tree view item that precedes the specified item.
TVGN_ROOT	GetNextItem() returns the first child item of the root tree view item of which the specified item is a part.

The following example code displays a window as shown in Figure 7.5.

```
void CMyTreeView::OnInitialUpdate()
{
  CTreeView::OnInitialUpdate();

  CTreeCtrl & tree = GetTreeCtrl();

  HTREEITEM hDivision = tree.InsertItem("Indo-European");
  HTREEITEM hClass = tree.InsertItem("Centum Languages",
                                     hDivision);
  HTREEITEM hGroup  = tree.InsertItem("Germanic", hClass);
  tree.InsertItem("East Germanic (Gothic)", hGroup);
  HTREEITEM hFamily  = tree.InsertItem("West German", hGroup);
  HTREEITEM hType = tree.InsertItem("High German", hFamily);
  tree.InsertItem("Modern High German", hType, TVI_SORT);
  tree.InsertItem("Yiddish", hType, TVI_SORT);
  hType    = tree.InsertItem("Low German", hFamily);
  tree.InsertItem("Afrikaans", hType, TVI_SORT);
  tree.InsertItem("Dutch", hType, TVI_SORT);
  tree.InsertItem("Flemish", hType, TVI_SORT);
  tree.InsertItem("Modern Low German", hType, TVI_SORT);
  tree.InsertItem("Frisian", hType, TVI_SORT);
  tree.InsertItem("English", hType, TVI_SORT);
  hFamily  = tree.InsertItem("North Germanic", hGroup);
//
// code to add the remaining branches of the tree view goes here
//
```

```
   // Set style to lines with buttons.
   tree.ModifyStyle(0,
              TVS_HASLINES | TVS_HASBUTTONS | TVS_LINESATROOT);

   SetRedraw();
}
// . . .
/////////////////////////////////////////////////////////////////////
// CMyTreeView message handlers

// Place the text of the selected item in the Windows title bar
void CMyTreeView::OnSelchanged(NMHDR* pNMHDR, LRESULT* pResult)
{
   NM_TREEVIEW* pNMTreeView = (NM_TREEVIEW*)pNMHDR;

   CTreeCtrl & tree = GetTreeCtrl();
   HTREEITEM hSelected = tree.GetSelectedItem();

   if(hSelected >= 0)
   {
     CString strSelected = tree.GetItemText(hSelected);
     GetDocument()->SetTitle(strSelected);
   }

   *pResult = 0;
}
```

Figure 7.5   An expanded tree view.

Practice Questions

Question 1

> Which of the following statements are true? [Check all correct answers]
>
> ❑ a. CScrollView::SetScrollSizes() sets the amounts to scroll horizontally and vertically.
>
> ❑ b. CScrollView::SetScrollSizes() scales the viewport size to the current window size automatically.
>
> ❑ c. CScrollView::SetScrollSizes() sets the view's mapping mode.
>
> ❑ d. CScrollView::SetScrollSizes() sets the total dimensions of the scroll view.

The correct answers are a, c, and d. **CScrollView::SetScrollSizes()** takes four parameters. The first parameter, **nMapMode**, is an **int** that specifies the mapping mode to set for the view. The possible values are **MM_TEXT, MM_HIMETRIC, MM_TWIPS, MM_HIENGLISH, MM_LOMETRIC,** and **MM_LOENGLISH.** The second parameter, **sizeTotal**, is a **SIZE** that specifies the total size of the scroll view. The **cx** member contains the horizontal extent, and the **cy** member contains the vertical extent. The third parameter, **sizePage**, is a **const SIZE&** that specifies the horizontal (**cx**) and vertical (**cy**) amounts to scroll in each direction in response to a mouse-click in a scroll bar shaft. The fourth parameter, **sizeLine**, is a **const SIZE&** that specifies the horizontal (**cx**) and vertical (**cy**) amounts to scroll in each direction in response to a mouse-click in a scroll arrow. Answer b is incorrect because the function **CScrollView::SetScaleToFitSize()** is used to scale the viewport size to the current window size automatically, not **CScrollView::SetScrollSizes()**.

Question 2

> To adjust the viewport origin for the scrolling window, CScrollView overrides which function?
>
> ○ a. CView::OnDraw().
>
> ○ b. CView::OnPrepareDC().
>
> ○ c.   CView::OnEndDraw().
>
> ○ d. CView::OnUpdate().

The correct answer is b. **CView::OnPrepareDC()** is called by the framework before the **OnDraw()** member function is called. Classes derived from **CView** override **CView::OnPrepareDC()** to adjust attributes of the device context. **CScrollView** overrides **CView::OnPrepareDC()** to adjust the viewport origin for the scrolling window. **CView::OnDraw()** is called to render an image of the document. Because **CView::OnDraw()** is a pure virtual function, it must be implemented in the derived class. **CView::OnUpdate()** is called to notify a view that its document has been modified. This function has nothing to do with adjusting the device context's attributes. **CView::OnEndDraw()** is not a legal function.

Question 3

> Which statement is correct?
>
> O a. Because CFormView is derived from CDialog, its constructors must identify a dialog resource either by name or by its ID.
>
> O b. Because CFormView is derived from CScrollView, you must provide an override from OnDraw().
>
> O c. Because CFormView is derived from CDialog, it can use DDX and DDV.
>
> O d. Because CFormView is derived from CScrollView, it will automatically support scrolling.

The correct answer is d. Answers a and c are incorrect because **CFormView** is derived from **CScrollView**, not **CDialog**. However, **CFormView**'s constructors must identify a dialog resource and **CFormView** can use **DDX** and **DDV**, but you must call **UpdateData()** yourself at the appropriate times. Answer b is incorrect because **CScrollView** provides an **OnDraw** override, which **CForm View** inherits.

Question 4

Which function would you override to adjust the style bits of the edit control associated with CEditView?

○ a. OnUpdate()

○ b. OnCreateWindow()

○ c. OnPrepareDC()

○ d. PreCreateWindow()

The correct answer is d. Some edit control style bits need to be set prior to the creation of the Windows window, others can be set after the Windows window is created but before it is visible, and still others can be set after the window is visible. **PreCreateWindow()** occurs before the framework calls the operating system to create the Windows window. In the override of **PreCreateWindow()** the style bits are available in the **CREATESTRUCT** argument and change be changed. Answers a and c are incorrect because **OnUpdate()** and **OnPrepareDC()** have nothing to do with the creation or style of the **CEditView** window. **OnCreateWindow()** is wrong because there is no such function.

Need To Know More?

 Bates, Jon and Tim Tompkins. *Using Visual C++ 6.* Que Corporation, Indianapolis, IN: 1998. ISBN 0-7897-1635-6. This book is aimed at the beginning-to-intermediate programmer and—in typical Que style—its focus is on "how-to." Chapters 18 and 19 provide examples, one each, for **CScrollView**, **CListView**, **CTreeView**, and **CRichEditView**.

 Prosise, Jeff. *Programming Windows with MFC.* Microsoft Press, Redmond, WA: 1999. ISBN 1-57231-695-0. This is the revision of the author's popular book, *Programming Windows 95 with MFC.* Chapter 10 provides coverage of scroll views, tree views, and list views. An example program for each type of view is covered.

 Visual C++ Programmer's Guide, MSDN Library Visual Studio 6.0.

Common Controls

Terms you'll need to understand:

- √ Control styles
- √ Notification messages and notification codes
- √ WM_NOTIFY
- √ NMHDR
- √ NM_CHAR
- √ NMCHAR
- √ NMUPDOWN
- √ UDN_DELTAPOS
- √ ON_NOTIFY
- √ ON_NOTIFY_RANGE

- √ LRESULT
- √ CProgressCtrl
- √ CIPAddressCtrl
- √ CSpinButtonCtrl
- √ Buddy window
- √ CDateTimeCtrl
- √ CMonthCalCtrl
- √ CSliderCtrl
- √ CImageList

Techniques you'll need to master:

- √ Describing the basic functionality of each of the common controls
- √ Adding Windows common controls to MFC applications
- √ Creating controls dynamically
- √ Setting control attributes
- √ Processing notification messages

Since the first version of Windows, there have been push buttons, checkboxes, and edit boxes that developers could use in their applications. However, some programmers found the standard controls limiting, so they implemented their own controls. Microsoft noticed this and decided to include the more popular ones as part of the operating environment of Windows 95. Collectively known as the *common controls*, these controls range from a simple slider to an edit control that provides character and paragraph formatting. Most of these controls belong to a window class implemented in comctl32.dll. The window class and the corresponding window procedure define the properties, appearance, and behavior of the control.

Since the release of Windows 95, additional common controls have been added to the list, resulting in new versions of comctl32.dll. Table 8.1 outlines the different DLL versions. MSDN online help covers all versions, marking elements above version 4.00 with a version number. This chapter assumes version 4.72.

MFC provides classes to wrap nearly all the common controls. Table 8.2 shows the common controls, the **WNDCLASS**es on which they're based, their alias as defined in Commctrl.h, their corresponding MFC wrapper classes, and a short description.

This chapter covers many of the common controls, but by no means all of them. The toolbar and status bar controls are covered in Chapter 4. The list, tree, and rich edit controls are covered in Chapter 7. (In this chapter, you will

Table 8.1   Comctl32.dll versions.

Version	Distribution Platform
4.00	Windows 95 and Windows NT 4.0
4.70	Internet Explorer 3.x
4.71	Internet Explorer 4.0
4.72	Internet Explorer 4.01 and Windows 98
5.80	Internet Explorer 5
5.81	Windows 2000

Table 8.2   The common controls.

Control	MFC Class	Description
Animation	**CAnimateCtrl**	This control displays an audio video interleaved (AVI) clip.
Date and time picker	**CDateTimeCtrl**	This control provides a simple and intuitive interface to exchange date and time information with a user.

(continued)

Table 8.2   The common controls (continued).

Control	MFC Class	Description
Extended combo box	**CComboBoxEx**	This control provides an extension of the combo box control that provides native support for item images.
Header	**CHeaderCtrl**	This control displays headings at the top of columns of information and lets the user sort the information by clicking the headings.
Hotkey	**CHotKeyCtrl**	This control lets the user define hot keys.
IP Address	**CIPAddressCtrl**	Similar to an edit control but these controls allow you to enter a numeric address in Internet Protocol (IP) format.
List	**CListCtrl**	This control displays a collection of items, each consisting of an icon and a label, and provides several ways to arrange the items.
Month calendar	**CMonthCalCtrl**	This control provides a simple and intuitive way for a user to select a date from a familiar interface.
Progress	**CProgressCtrl**	This control indicates the progress of a lengthy operation.
Rebar	**CRebarCtrl**	This control acts as a container for child windows.
Rich edit	**CRichEditCtrl**	This control generates a window in which user can edit with character and paragraph formatting.
Slider	**CSliderCtrl**	This control lets the user select from a range of values by moving a slider.
Spin button	**CSpinButtonCtrl**	This control uses a pair of arrows that can be clicked by the user. Usually used with a companion edit or static control, in which case clicking an arrow increments or decrements the value in the companion control.
Status bar	**CStatusBarCtrl**	This control displays status information in a horizontal window.
Tab	**CTabCtrl**	This control defines multiple pages for the same area of a window or dialog box. Each page consists of a set of information or a group of controls that an application displays when the user selects the corresponding tab.

(continued)

Table 8.2   The common controls (continued).

Control	MFC Class	Description
Toolbar	**CToolBarCtrl**	This control contains buttons that carry out menu commands.
ToolTip	**CToolTipCtrl**	This control displays a small pop-up window that contains a line of text that describes the purpose of a tool in an application.
Tree	**CTreeCtrl**	This control displays a hierarchical list of items. Each item consists of a label and an optional bitmap.

see how the list and tree controls use images.) You first look at some common features that are shared by most of the controls and then you'll look at a number of controls one at a time.

You should be familiar with all of the common controls. The MSDN library contains a wealth of information and provides a number of sample programs that demonstrates how to use most of the common controls.

Common Features

As an MFC programmer, there are two ways that you normally create a common control. First, you can add a control to a dialog template and let the Visual C++ Dialog Editor write a **CONTROL** statement for you. Or, you can instantiate the MFC class and then call **Create()**. The following statements create an IP address control using the second method:

```
// . . .
CIPAddressCtrl ipAddress;
ipAddress.Create(WS_CHILD | WS_VISIBLE | WS_BORDER,
    CRect(x1, y1, x2, y2), this, IDC_IPADDRESS);
// . . .
```

The **Create()** function's four arguments are the control's style flags, the control's position and size (as a **CRect** object), a pointer to the control's parent window, and the control's ID. The style flags must include **WS_CHILD**, because common controls, like other controls, are child windows used in conjunction with other windows to provide user interaction. In addition to the standard window styles, each type of common control has a set of control styles that can be used to vary the appearance and behavior of the control. There is also a set of styles that are used by two or more types of common controls. Table 8.3 shows these common styles.

In addition to sharing a number of window styles, common controls also share the means by which they send notifications to their parents. Unlike the standard controls, which send notifications to their parents using **WM_COMMAND** messages, most common controls enclose their notifications in **WM_NOTIFY**

Table 8.3   Common control styles.

Style	Description
CCS_ADJUSTABLE	Enables a toolbar's built-in customization features. The user can add, delete, and rearrange toolbar buttons.
CCS_BOTTOM	Places the control at the bottom of the parent window's client area and sets it to the same width as the parent window. This is the default style for status windows.
CCS_LEFT	Places the control vertically on the left side of the parent window.
CCS_NODIVIDER	Prevents a 2-pixel highlight from being drawn at the top of the control.
CCS_NOMOVEX	In response to a **WM_SIZE** message, the control will resize and move itself vertically but not horizontally.
CCS_NOMOVEY	In response to a **WM_SIZE** message the control will resize and move itself horizontally but not vertically. By default, header windows have this style.
CCS_NOPARENTALIGN	Causes the control to keep its position within the parent window despite changes to the size of the parent.
CCS_NORESIZE	Prevents the control from using the default width and height when setting its initial size or a new size. Instead, the control uses the width and height specified in the request for creation or sizing.
CCS_RIGHT	Causes the control to display vertically on the right side of the parent window.
CCS_TOP	Causes the control to position itself at the top of the parent window's client area and sets it to the same width as the parent window's width. Toolbars use this style by default.
CCS_VERT	Causes the control to display vertically.

messages. A **WM_NOTIFY** message's **wParam** holds the child window ID of the control that sent the message, and **lParam** holds a pointer to either an **NMHDR** structure or a structure that's a superset of **NMHDR**. **NMHDR** is defined as follows:

```
typedef struct tagNMHDR {
  HWND hwndFrom;
  UINT idFrom;
  UINT code;
} NMHDR;
```

hwndFrom holds the window handle to the control sending the message. **idFrom** is the identifier to the control, and **code** is the notification code. The notification code can be control-specific, or it can be one of the common notification codes shown in Table 8.4.

Table 8.4 Common notification codes.	
Notification	**Sent When**
NM_CHAR	A character key is processed.
NM_CLICK	The user clicks the left mouse button.
NM_DBLCLK	The user double-clicks the left mouse button.
NM_HOVER	The mouse hovers over an item.
NM_KEYDOWN	The control has the keyboard focus and the user presses a key.
NM_KILLFOCUS	The control has lost the input focus.
NM_NCHITTEST	The control receives a **WM_NCHITTEST** message.
NM_OUTOFMEMORY	The control cannot complete an operation because not enough memory was available.
NM_RCLICK	The user clicks the right mouse button within the control.
NM_RDBLCLK	The user double clicks the right mouse button within the control.
NM_RELEASEDCAPTURE	The control is releasing mouse capture.
NM_RETURN	The control has the input focus and the user presses Enter.
NM_SETCURSOR	The control is setting the cursor in response to a **WM_SETCURSOR** message.
NM_SETFOCUS	The control has received the input focus.
NM_TOOLTIPSCREATED	The control has created a ToolTip control.

A number of the preceding notifications define a structure that starts with an **NMHDR**-type variable. For instance, **NM_CHAR** passes the address of an **NMCHAR** structure that contains additional information about the character that caused the notification message. **NMCHAR** is defined as follows:

```
typedef struct tagNMCHAR {
  NMHDR hdr;
  UINT ch;
  DWORD dwItemPrev;
  DWORD dwItemNext;
} NMCHAR ;
```

The **ch** member contains the character being processed. The **dwItemPrev** and **dwItemNext** members are specific to the control that is sending the notification.

In addition to the preceding notification codes, many of the common controls define their own unique codes to signify control-specific events. For example, the parent of an up-down control is notified when the position of the control is about to change. The parent is sent a **WM_NOTIFY** message with a code of **UDN_DELTAPOS**. **lParam** points to an **NMUPDOWN** structure that contains information about the position change. **NMUPDOWN** is defined as follows:

```
typedef struct _NM_UPDOWN {
    NMHDR hdr;
    int   iPos;
    int   iDelta;
} NMUPDOWN;
```

The **iPos** member represents the up-down control's current position, and **iDelta** represents the proposed change in the up-down control's position.

In addition to the **UDN_DELTAPOS** notification, the up-down control can also notify the parent that it is releasing mouse capture. Look at the following snippet of code that determines which notification was sent, and if it was **UDN_DELTAPOS**, retrieve **iPos** from the **NMUPDOWN** structure:

```
NMHDR * pNMH = (NMHDR *) lParam;
switch(pNMH->code)
{
  case NM_RELEASEDCAPTURE:
    // process the notification
    break;
  case UDN_DELTAPOS:
  {
```

```
    NMUPDOWN * pUpDown = (NMUPDOWN *) pNMH;
    int pos = pUpDown->iPos;
    // process the notification
    break;
  }
}
```

First, you cast **lParam** to a **NMHDR** pointer so that you can access the notification code. If the code is **UDN_DELTAPOS**, you recast the pointer to a **NMUPDOWN** pointer, which allows you to access the **iPos** and **iDelta** members.

If the window that processes these notifications contains two or more up-down controls, it can examine the **hwndFrom** or **idFrom** field of the **NMHDR** structure to determine which control sent the notification. Here's an example that handles two controls:

```
NMHDR * pnmh = (NMHDR *) lParam;

  switch(pnmh->code)
  {
  case UDN_DELTAPOS:
    if(pnmh->idFrom == IDC_UPDOWN_ONE}
    {
      // process the notification from the first up-down control
    }
    else
    {
      // process the notification from the other up-down control
    }
    break;
  case NM_RELEASEDCAPTURE:
    if(pnmh->idFrom == IDC_UPDOWN_ONE}
    {
      // process the notification from the first up-down control
    }
    else
    {
      // process the notification from the other up-down control
    }
    break;
  }
```

As you can see, it would not take very many controls before this became an unwieldy situation. Fortunately, MFC provides message map macros to encapsulate **WM_NOTIFY** messages: **ON_NOTIFY** and **ON_NOTIFY_RANGE**. The following message map entries map **UDN_DELTAPOS** and **NM_ RELEASEDCAPTURE** notifications from an up-down control whose ID is **IDC_UPDOWN_ONE** to a pair of handling functions named **OnDeltaPosUDOne** and **OnReleasedCaptureUDOne**:

```
ON_NOTIFY(UDN_DELTAPOS, IDC_UPDOWN_ONE, OnDeltaPosUDOne)
ON_NOTIFY(NM_RELEASEDCAPTURE, IDC_UPDOWN_ONE,
          OnReleasedCaptureUDOne)
// . . .
void CMyView::OnDeltaPosUDOne(NMHDR * pnmh, LRESULT * pResult)
{
  NMUPDOWN * pUpDown = (NMUPDOWN *) pnmh;
  // process the notification
}

void CMyView::OnReleasedCaptureUDOne(NMHDR * pnmh,
          LRESULT * pResult)
{
  // process the notification
}
```

The **pResult** parameter points to a 32-bit **LRESULT** variable that receives the handler's return value. The return value is control- and notification-specific. For **UDN_DELTAPOS**, return nonzero to prevent the change in the control's position, or zero to allow the change. For **NM_RELEASEDCAPTURE**, like many notifications, the return value is ignored.

In the following sections, you'll explore a number of individual controls. For each control, you'll look at how it is created, what its unique window styles and notification codes are, and how it is used.

The Progress Bar Control

This control is probably the easiest of all the common controls to use. It is normally used to inform the user about the progress of a task. It consists of a rectangle that is gradually filled with the system highlight color as an operation progresses. When the progress bar is completely filled in, the task associated with the progress is also complete. A progress bar control has a range, which represents the entire duration of the operation, and a current position, which corresponds to the progress the application has made toward completing the operation.

The following code shows how a progress bar is created and initialized:

```
// header file
CProgressCtrl m_progressBar;

// cpp file
// . . .
m_progressBar.Create(WS_CHILD | WS_VISIBLE | WS_BORDER,
    CRect(x1, y1, x2, y2), this, IDC_PROGRESSBAR);
m_progressBar.SetRange(0,10);
m_progressBar.SetStep(1);
m_progressBar.SetPos(0);
```

The progress bar control's styles can be any combination of window styles, plus the two shown in Table 8.5. After creating and initializing the control, **CProgressCtrl::StepIt()** is called to advance the current position by the step increment and to redraw the bar to reflect the new position.

The IP Address Control

This control is almost as easy to use as the progress bar control. The IP address control is similar to an edit control but allows the user to enter and manipulate a numerical address in IP format. This format consists of four 3-digit fields (see Table 8.6). Each field is treated individually; the field numbers are zero-based and proceed from left to right. Once three digits have been entered in a given field, keyboard focus is automatically moved to the next field. If filling the entire field is not required, the user can enter fewer than three digits. For example, if the field should only contain 21, typing "21" and pressing the right arrow key will take the user to the next field. The default range for each field is 0 to 255. The control also allows the application to obtain the address in numeric form rather than its text form.

The IP address control was introduced in Microsoft Internet Explorer 4.0. MFC wraps this control in the **CIPAddressCtrl** class.

The IP address control doesn't have any style flags of its own, but it does have a single notification code, and it can send three edit control notifications (see Table 8.6) through the **WM_COMMAND** message.

Table 8.5	Progress bar styles.
Style	**Description**
PBS_SMOOTH	Displays progress status in a smooth scrolling bar instead of the default segmented bar
PBS_VERTICAL	Displays progress status vertically, from bottom to top

Table 8.6	IP address control notifications.
Notification	**Sent When**
IPN_FIELDCHANGED	The user changes a field in the control or moves from one field to another.
EN_SETFOCUS	The IP address control gains the keyboard focus.
EN_KILLFOCUS	The IP address control loses the keyboard focus.
EN_CHANGE	Any field in the IP address control changes. Received after the screen has been updated.

The following code shows how to create and use an IP address control:

```
// header file
// ...
afx_msg void OnIPAddressFieldChanged(NMHDR * pnmh,
    LRESULT * pResult);
CIPAddressCtrl m_ipAddress;
// IP Address fields
BYTE m_byField0;
BYTE m_byField1;
BYTE m_byField2;
BYTE m_byField3;
// Number of non-blank IP Address fields
int m_nFields;
// ...

// cpp file
// ...
  //}}AFX_MSG_MAP
  ON_NOTIFY(IPN_FIELDCHANGED, IDC_IPADDRESS,
        OnIPAddressFieldChanged)
END_MESSAGE_MAP()
// ...

m_nFields = 0;
m_ipAddress.Create(WS_CHILD | WS_VISIBLE | WS_BORDER,
    CRect(x1, y1, x2, y2), this, IDC_IPADDRESS);
// ...
void CMyIPAddressView::OnIPAddressFieldChanged(NMHDR * pnmh,
    LRESULT * pResult)
{
  m_nFields = m_ipAddress.GetAddress(m_byField0, m_byField1,
                        m_byField2, m_byField3);
}
// ...
```

The Up-Down Control

The up-down control is a pair of arrow buttons that the user can click to incre-ment or decrement a value, such as a scroll position or a number displayed in a companion control. The value associated with an up-down control is called its "current position." An up-down control is most often used with a companion control, called a *buddy window*. The more common name for the up-down control is *spin button control*, which is why the MFC class that wraps the con-trol is named **CSpinButtonCtrl**.

The up-down control has a number of style flags, shown in Table 8.7.

Here's how you might create and use an up-down control:

```
// header file
// ...
// Spinner or Up-Down and its buddy
CSpinButtonCtrl m_upDown;
CEdit m_buddyEdit;

afx_msg void OnUpDown(NMHDR * pnmh, LRESULT * pResult);

// cpp file
// ...
  ON_NOTIFY(UDN_DELTAPOS, IDC_UPDOWN, OnUpDown)
// ...
m_buddyEdit.Create(WS_CHILD | WS_VISIBLE | WS_BORDER,
   CRect(x1, y1, x2, y2), this, IDC_BUDDYEDIT);
m_upDown.Create(WS_CHILD | WS_VISIBLE | WS_BORDER |
   UDS_ALIGNRIGHT | UDS_SETBUDDYINT | UDS_ARROWKEYS,
    CRect(0,0,0,0), this, IDC_UPDOWN);
m_upDown.SetBuddy(&m_buddyEdit);
m_upDown.SetRange(1,100);
m_upDown.SetPos(50);

// ...
void CMyView::OnUpDown(NMHDR * pnmh, LRESULT * pResult)
{
  NMUPDOWN * pUpDown = (NMUPDOWN *) pnmh;

  int nPos1 = pUpDown->iPos;
  int nPos2 = m_upDown.GetPos();
  if(HIWORD(nPos2))
  {
    // error occurred if high-order word is nonzero
  }
```

```
CString str1;
m_upDown.GetBuddy()->GetWindowText(str1);

CString str2;
m_buddyEdit.GetWindowText(str2);

*pResult = 0;  // allow the change
}
```

In this example, three unique style flags are used with **Create()**. They position the spinner on the right of the edit control, allow the user to use the arrows to manipulate the spinner, and turn on the feature whereby the spinner automatically updates the buddy control. **CSpinButtonCtrl::SetBuddy()** sets the buddy window for a spin button control. **CSpinButtonCtrl::SetRange()** and **CSpinButtonCtrl::SetPos()** establish the control's range and its initial value.

The code in **OnUpDown()** shows how to retrieve the information from both the up-down control and the buddy control. All four methods return the current position. The **iDelta** member of the **NMUPDOWN** structure is a signed integer that contains the proposed change in position. If the user has clicked the up button, this is a positive value. If the user has clicked the down button, this is a negative value.

Table 8.7 Up-down control styles.

Style	Description
UDS_ALIGNLEFT	Causes the up-down control to be aligned next to the left edge of the buddy window.
UDS_ALIGNRIGHT	Causes the up-down control to be aligned next to the right edge of the buddy window.
UDS_ARROWKEYS	The up-down control will automatically increment and decrement the position when the up arrow and down arrow keys are pressed.
UDS_AUTOBUDDY	Causes the up-down control to automatically select the previous z-order window as its buddy window.
UDS_HORZ	Causes the up-down control's arrows to point left and right instead of up and down.
UDS_NOTHOUSANDS	Inhibits the insertion of the thousands separator between every three decimal digits.
UDS_SETBUDDYINT	The up-down control will update its buddy window when the position changes.
UDS_WRAP	If the position is incremented or decremented beyond the ending or beginning of the range it will automatically wrap.

The Date And Time Picker Control

As a user, would you rather enter a date by typing it, picking it from a calendar, or using the up and down arrow buttons? Well, **CDateTimeCtrl** provides all three methods. Table 8.8 shows the special styles to be used with the date and time picker controls. Table 8.9 shows a few of the notification codes the control can sent to its parent.

There are a number of member functions that allow you to change the colors and fonts for this control, but the most important function is **GetTime()**, which returns the date and time entered by the user. It fills in a **COleDateTime** or **CTime** object, or a SYSTEMTIME structure, which can be accessed by individual members.

Table 8.8	Date and time picker control styles.
Style	**Description**
DTS_APPCANPARSE	Allows the user to press the F2 key and then edit within the client area.
DTS_LONGDATEFORMAT	Causes the date to be shown in long format.
DTS_RIGHTALIGN	Causes the drop-down month calendar to be right-aligned with the control. The default is left-aligned.
DTS_SHORTDATEFORMAT	Causes the date to be shown in short format.
DTS_TIMEFORMAT	Causes the time to be displayed.
DTS_UPDOWN	Causes an up-down control to the right of the date time picker control, which can be used to modify date-time values.

Table 8.9	Date and time picker control notifications.
Notification	**Sent When**
DTN_CLOSEUP	The user closes the drop-down month calendar.
DTN_DATETIMECHANGE	A change occurs.
DTN_DROPDOWN	The user activates the drop-down month calendar.
DTN_USERSTRING	The user finishes editing a string in the control.
NM_KILLFOCUS	The control has lost the input focus.
NM_SETFOCUS	The control has received the input focus.

Here's how you might create a date and time control:

```
m_date.Create(WS_CHILD | WS_VISIBLE | DTS_SHORTDATEFORMAT,
  CRect(x1, y1, x2, y2), this, IDC_DATE);
```

If you build an application with a date and time picker control, you will see how easy it is to use. Click the drop-down box next to the short date and a calendar will drop down. Notice that today's date is circled on the month part of the calendar.

This month calendar is a control of its own. Here, the date picker created one; however, let's move on to the next section and look at the actual month calendar.

The Month Calendar Control

The month calendar control provides you with a basic calendar interface, from which users can select a date. The user can change the display by taking the following actions:

➤ Scrolling backward and forward, from month to month.

➤ Clicking the "today" text to display the current day (if the **MCS_ NOTODAY** style isn't used).

➤ Picking a month or a year from a pop-up menu.

A number of styles are available that allow you to customize the month calendar. These styles are shown in Table 8.10.

CMonthCalCtrl encapsulates the functionality of a month calendar control. A number of member functions enable you to customize the control, setting

Table 8.10 Month calendar control styles.	
Style	**Description**
MCS_DAYSTATE	Specifies that the control should request information about which days should be bold. It does this by sending the **MCN_GETDAYSTATE** notification.
MCS_MULTISELECT	Allows the user to select a range of dates.
MCS_NOTODAY	The "today" date at the bottom of the control will not be displayed.
MCS_NOTODAYCIRCLE	The "today" date will not circled.
MCS_WEEKNUMBERS	Week numbers (1 to 52) will be displayed to the left of each row of days.

colors and fonts, and whether weeks start on Sunday or Monday. **CMonth CalCtrl::GetCurSel()** fills a **COleDateTime** or **CTime** object, or a **SYSTEMTIME** structure. The calendar control has a few notification codes it can send its parent. The more interesting ones are shown in Table 8.11.

The Slider Control

There are times when you might need the user to enter a value that lies within a specific range. You can implement this capability a number of ways. For example, you could require the user to type the number in an edit control with out-of-the-range values rejected by the application. Another method you might use is the up-down control that was covered in the preceding section.

Why not use, however, a control that is ideal for this kind of operation? Such a control does exist—it's the slider (also called the *trackbar*). A *slider* is simply a window containing a thumb and tick marks. The thumb moves like the thumb in a scroll bar. After you create a slider, you set the minimum and maximum values representing the extremes of the thumb's travel and optionally set the initial thumb position. The user can then reposition the thumb by dragging it with the left mouse button or clicking the channel in which the thumb slides. When the user repositions the thumb, the control sends a message to its parent to indicate the change. A horizontal slider (the default style) sends a **WM_HSCROLL** message, and a vertical slider sends a **WM_VSCROLL** message.

MFC represents sliders with the **CSliderCtrl** class. Table 8.12 shows most of the slider-specific control styles.

Now let's look at some code:

```
// cpp file
// ...
  m_slider.Create(WS_CHILD | WS_VISIBLE | WS_BORDER |
    TBS_AUTOTICKS | TBS_BOTH | TBS_HORZ,
    CRect(x1, y1, x2, y2), this, IDC_TRACKBAR);
  m_slider.SetRange(0, 100, TRUE);
  m_slider.SetTicFreq(10);
  m_slider.SetLineSize(1);
  m_slider.SetPageSize(10);

// ...
void CMyView::OnHScroll(UINT nSBCode, UINT nPos,
    CScrollBar* pScrollBar)
{
```

```
CSliderCtrl * pSlider = (CSliderCtrl *) pScrollBar;
if(pSlider == &m_slider)
{
  m_sliderPosition = pSlider->GetPos();
  // other processing as needed
  return;
}

// handle other scrolling messages, perhaps by
// call the base class
}
```

Table 8.11 Month calendar control notifications.

Notification	Sent When
MCN_GETDAYSTATE	The control is requesting if individual days should be displayed in bold.
MCN_SELCHANGE	The currently selected date or range of dates changes.
MCN_SELECT	The user makes an explicit date selection within a month calendar control.

Table 8.12 Slider control styles.

Style	Description
TBS_AUTOTICKS	Enables the slider to automatically draw tick mark for each increment in its range of values.
TBS_BOTH	Draws tick marks on both sides of the control.
TBS_BOTTOM	Draws tick marks below the control.
TBS_ENABLESELRANGE	Sets a portion of the channel as a selection range.
TBS_HORZ	Orients the slider horizontally. This is the default orientation.
TBS_LEFT	Draws tick marks to the left of the control; used with **TBS_VERT**.
TBS_NOTHUMB	Removes the thumb from the slider.
TBS_NOTICKS	Removes the tick marks.
TBS_RIGHT	Draws tick marks to the right of the control; used with **TBS_VERT**.
TBS_TOOLTIPS	Enables ToolTip support.
TBS_TOP	Draws tick marks above the control; used with **TBS_HORZ**.
TBS_VERT	Orients the control vertically.

There are two items of importance in the preceding code. First, the tick frequency and the page size are the same. This is done so the user won't be confused. Most people assume that the tick marks indicate the size of a page. Second, **CMyView::OnHScroll()** only executes the slider code if the scroll bar that was clicked is the one kept in **m_slider**.

The Image List Control

An *image list* stores a group of identically sized bitmap images as one object. MFC's **CImageList** class provides functions for creating image lists, adding and deleting images, drawing images on the screen, and more. You can use the images in any number of ways. Several common controls use image lists. These controls include the following:

➤ List controls

➤ Tree controls

➤ Property page controls

➤ Toolbar controls

When you supply images to the preceding controls, you pass a pointer to a **CImageList** object or a handle to a **HIMAGELIST**. Individual images in the list are referenced with a zero-based index.

You can create an image list three ways:

1. Create an empty image list and add images to it with **CImageList::Add()**.

2. Create an initialized image list from an existing bitmap containing an array of images.

3. Create an initialized image list by merging images from existing image lists.

CImageList::Create() is overloaded to support five creation methods. Let's look at one of the most commonly used:

```
CImageList imageList;
imageList.Create(16,16,ILC_COLOR,3,0);

HICON hIcon = ::LoadIcon(AfxGetResourceHandle(),
  MAKEINTRESOURCE(IDI_ICON1));
imageList.Add(hIcon);


hIcon = ::LoadIcon(AfxGetResourceHandle(),
  MAKEINTRESOURCE(IDI_ICON2));
imageList.Add(hIcon);
```

```
hIcon = ::LoadIcon(AfxGetResourceHandle(),
  MAKEINTRESOURCE(IDI_ICON3));
imageList.Add(hIcon);
```

The first argument to **Create()** is the width of the image in pixels, and the second is its height. The third argument specifies the type of image list to create. This parameter can be a combination of the values shown in Table 8.13, but it can include only one of the **ILC_COLOR** values. The fourth argument specifies the number of images the image list initially contains, and the fifth specifies the number of images by which the image list can grow.

After you create the image list, the images are added to it. Here, the program first gets a handle to the icon. Then it adds the icon to the image list by calling **CImageList::Add()**.

As stated previously, a number of the common controls use image lists. Here's how you can set the image list created in the preceding code to a **CTreeCtrl** object:

```
CTreeCtrl tree;
tree.Create(WS_CHILD | WS_VISIBLE | WS_BORDER |
  TVS_HASLINES | TVS_LINESATROOT | TVS_HASBUTTONS |
      TVS_EDITLABELS,
  CRect(x1, y1, x2, y2), this, IDC_TREE);

tree.SetImageList(&imageList, TVSIL_NORMAL);
```

Of course, you would then add the items to the tree.

To add images to a **CListCtrl**, you might do the following:

```
// Create the image lists
CImageList smallImages, largeImages;
smallImages.Create(16,16,ILC_COLOR,1,0);
largeImages.Create(32,32,ILC_COLOR,1,0);

HICON hIcon = ::LoadIcon(AfxGetResourceHandle(),
  MAKEINTRESOURCE(IDI_SMALL_ICON));
smallImages.Add(hIcon);

hIcon = ::LoadIcon(AfxGetResourceHandle(),
  MAKEINTRESOURCE(IDI_LARGE_ICON));
largeImages.Add(hIcon);
```

```
// Create the list view and add the images to it
CListCtrl list;
list.Create(WS_VISIBLE | WS_CHILD | WS_BORDER | LVS_EDITLABELS,
    CRect(x1, y1, x2, y2), this, IDC_LIST);
list.SetImageList(&smallImages, LVSIL_SMALL);
list.SetImageList(&largeImages, LVSIL_NORMAL);
```

Table 8.13   CImageList::Create() flags.

Value	Meaning
ILC_COLOR	Specifies that the default behavior is to be used if none of the other **ILC_COLOR** flags is specified.
ILC_COLOR4	Specifies that a 4-bit DIB section is to be used as the bitmap for the image list.
ILC_COLOR8	Specifies that an 8-bit DIB section is to be used.
ILC_COLOR16	Specifies that a 16-bit DIB section is to be used.
ILC_COLOR24	Specifies that a 24-bit DIB section is to be used.
ILC_COLOR32	Specifies that a 32-bit DIB section is to be used.
ILC_COLORDDB	Specifies that a device-dependent bitmap is to be used.
ILC_MASK	Specifies that the image list contains two bitmaps, the image and a mask. The mask is a monochrome bitmap.

Practice Questions

Question 1

Which style flag must be included when creating a common control?

○ a. WS_POPUP

○ b. WS_CHILD

○ c. WS_VISIBLE

○ d. WS_CONTROL

The correct answer is b. Like other controls, common controls are owned and dependent upon a parent window. A child window is always positioned relative to the upper left corner of its parent window's client area. No part of a child window ever appears outside the borders of its parents. The parent window can be an overlapped window, a pop-up window, or another child window. Answer a is incorrect because a pop-up window is a special type of overlapped window used for dialog boxes, message boxes, and other temporary windows that appear outside an application's main window. Answer c is incorrect because a control, like any other window, can be hidden. Answer d is incorrect because **WS_CONTROL** is not a legal style.

Question 2

Which of the following statements are true? [Check all the correct answers]

❏ a. The IP address control is similar to an edit control. It allows the user to enter three 4-digit fields, with a range from 0 to 260.

❏ b. The date and time picker control implements a calendar-like user interface.

❏ c. The IP address control is similar to an edit control. It allows the user to enter four 3-digit fields, with a range from 0 to 255.

❏ d. The default range for the spin button has the maximum set to 0 and the minimum set to 100, thereby causing the position to decrease when the up arrow button is clicked.

The correct answers are c and d. Answer b is incorrect because it is the month calendar control that implements a calendar-like user interface. The date and time picker control's interface is similar in functionality to a combo box. When the user expands the control, a month calendar control appears (by default), allowing the user to specify a particular date. Answer a is incorrect because the range is incorrect.

Question 3

> Which message does a Win32 common control send to its parent when events, such as input from the user, occur in the control?
>
> ○ a. WM_NOTIFY
>
> ○ b. WM_MESSAGE
>
> ○ c. WM_COMMAND
>
> ○ d. WM_EVENT

The correct answer is a. In Windows 3.x, controls notify their parents of events by sending special **WM_COMMAND** messages, with the notification code and control ID packed into **wParam** and the control's handle in **lParam**. When Windows 3.x notification messages need to include additional data, a variety of special-purpose messages, such as **WM_CTLCOLOR** and **WM_VSCROLL** are used. Win32 added a number of sophisticated, complex controls to those supported in Windows 3.x. These controls need to send additional data with their notification messages. Rather than using a new **WM_*** message for each new notification, the Win32 API uses just one message, **WM_NOTIFY**, which can pass any amount of additional data in a standardized fashion. Therefore, answer c is incorrect. **WM_NOTIFY** messages contain the ID of the sending control in **wParam** and a pointer to an **NMHDR** structure (or some larger structure that contains an **NMHDR** structure) in **lParam**.

WM_MESSAGE and **WM_EVENT** are not legal Win32 messages. Therefore, answers b and d are incorrect.

Question 4

Which snippet of code modifies the behavior of the date and time picker control so that the "today" date at the bottom of the control is not displayed and the "today" date will not be circled?

○ a.
```
void CMyDlg::OnDropdownDatetimepicker
               (NMHDR* pNMHDR, LRESULT* pResult)

    {
       CDateTimeCtrl * pDTC = (CDateTimeCtrl*)pNMHDR;
       pDTC->ModifyStyle(0,
                  MCS_NOTODAY | MCS_NOTODAYCIRCLE);
       *pResult = 0;
    }
```

○ b.
```
void CMyDlg::OnDropdownDatetimepicker
               (NMHDR* pNMHDR, LRESULT* pResult)

    {
       CDateTimeCtrl * pDTC
       =(CDateTimeCtrl*)FromHandle(pNMHDR->hwndFrom);
       CMonthCalCtrl * pMonthCal
        = pDTC->GetMonthCalCtrl();
       pMonthCal->ModifyStyle(0,
                  MCS_NOTODAY | MCS_NOTODAYCIRCLE);
       *pResult = 0;
    }
```

○ c.
```
void CMyDlg::OnDropdownDatetimepicker
               (NMHDR* pNMHDR, LRESULT* pResult)

    {
       pNMHDR->ModifyStyle(0,
                  MCS_NOTODAY | MCS_NOTODAYCIRCLE);
       *pResult = 0;
    }
```

(continued)

Question 4 *(continued)*

```
O d. void CMyDlg::OnDropdownDatetimepicker
          (NMHDR* pNMHDR, LRESULT* pResult)
  {
    CMonthCalCtrl * pMonthCal
      = pNMHDR->GetMonthCalCtrl();
    pMonthCal->ModifyStyle(0,
              MCS_NOTODAY | MCS_NOTODAYCIRCLE);
    *pResult = 0;
  }
```

The correct answer is b. The **NMHDR** structure contains a handle to the **CDateTimeCtrl** control that generated the **DTN_DROPDOWN** notification. By passing this handle to **CWnd::FromHandle()** and casting the returned pointer to a **CDateTimeCtrl***, you can call **CDateTimeCtrl::GetMonthCalCtrl()**, which returns a pointer to the child month calendar control created when the user clicked the drop-down arrow. You can then use the returned pointer to call the functions provided by **CMonthCalCtrl**. The **ModifyStyle()** function, inherited from **CWnd**, allows you to modify the control's window style. **ModifyStyle()** takes three parameters. The first parameter specifies the window styles to be removed, and the second specifies the styles to be added. The third, if specified, indicates how the window position is to be modified.

Answer a is incorrect because it doesn't obtain a pointer to the child month calendar control, but instead calls the **ModifyStyle()** member function of **CDateTimeCtrl**. Answer c is incorrect because **ModifyStyle()** is not a member of **NMHDR**. Answer d is incorrect because **GetMonthCalCtrl()** is not a member of **NMHDR**.

Need To Know More?

 Bates, Jon and Tim Tompkins. *Using Visual C++ 6*. Que Corporation, Indianapolis, IN, 1998. ISBN 0-7897-1635-6. This book is aimed at the beginning-to-intermediate programmer, and in typical Que style, its focus is on "how-to." Chapter 6 covers **CListCtrl** and **CTreeCtrl**. Chapter 7 covers **CProgressCtrl**, **CScrollBar**, **CSliderCtrl**, **CDateTimeCtrl**, and **CMonthCalCtrl**. This book provides a good introduction to the controls it covers.

 Prosise, Jeff. *Programming Windows with MFC*. Microsoft Press, Redmond, WA, 1999. ISBN 1-57231-695-0. This is the updated version of the author's popular book, *Programming Windows 95 with MFC*. Chapter 16, "The Common Controls," provides an excellent overview of common controls, followed by detailed descriptions for many of the common controls. There are two example programs in Chapter 16. The first is a demonstration of how slider controls, spin button controls, and ToolTip controls can be put to work in a dialog box. The second is a dialog-based application that uses the **CComboBoxEx** control.

 MSDN Library, Platform SDK\User Interface Services\Shell and Common Controls\Windows Common Controls

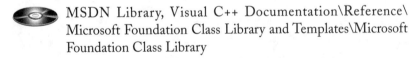 MSDN Library, Visual C++ Documentation\Reference\ Microsoft Foundation Class Library and Templates\Microsoft Foundation Class Library

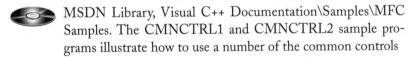 MSDN Library, Visual C++ Documentation\Samples\MFC Samples. The CMNCTRL1 and CMNCTRL2 sample programs illustrate how to use a number of the common controls

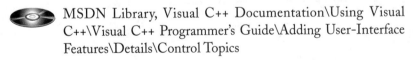 MSDN Library, Visual C++ Documentation\Using Visual C++\Visual C++ Programmer's Guide\Adding User-Interface Features\Details\Control Topics

Using ActiveX Controls

Terms you'll need to understand:

√ Interface

√ Properties

√ Methods

√ ActiveX control containers

√ Events

√ Type library

√ **coclass**

Techniques you'll need to master:

√ Implementing an MFC ActiveX control container

√ Adding an ActiveX control to your application

√ Accessing the control's methods and properties

√ Adding event handlers for the control

√ Dynamically creating an ActiveX control

ActiveX Controls technology is one of the basic categories of what Microsoft is now calling *Active technology*. Active technologies (formerly called ActiveX and before that OLE) use the Component Object Model (COM) to enable software components to interact with one another in a networked environment. ActiveX controls are designed for use both in ordinary ActiveX control containers and on the Internet, in World Wide Web pages. ActiveX controls, unlike Java applets and Netscape plug-ins, are language-neutral and can be used in applications written in programming languages different than the one used to create the ActiveX control.

ActiveX controls are 32-bit controls that can be used in any container that can support the control's interfaces. This interface provides a collection of related attributes (called properties) and functions (called methods) and is the mechanism through which the control exposes its functionality. *Properties* are values that are maintained by the control and that change the appearance or behavior of the control. Properties have symbolic names that are matched to integer indexes. Each property has a name, such as **BackColor** or **TitleFont**, and a type, such as **int** or **BSTR**. A typical ActiveX control consists of a user interface representation both at design time and runtime. The design time interface allows the application developer to specify a property's initial value. The runtime interface, of course, allows a client program to change a property at runtime. A client program retrieves and sets a control's property by specifying the property's index.

Methods define the actions the control is capable of performing. A method has a symbolic name, a set of parameters, and a return value. You call a method by calling a C++ member function of the class representing the control.

When an ActiveX control is used within an ActiveX *control container*, the container communicates with the control through the control's properties and methods. However, for the control to communicate with the container, a second mechanism is used. When the control wishes to notify the container that something has happened to the control, the control "fires" an *event*. Common examples of events include clicks on the control, data entered using the keyboard, and changes in the control's state. When these actions occur, the control fires an event to alert the container. An event has a symbolic filename and can have an arbitrary sequence of parameters.

ActiveX controls are implemented as in-process servers and are essentially simple COM objects that support the **IUnknown** interface. However, if **IUnknown** were the only interface supported, the control wouldn't do much more than take up disk space. It, therefore, usually supports many more interfaces in order to offer functionality, but all additional interfaces can be viewed as optional, and as such, a container should not rely on any additional interfaces being supported. By not specifying additional interfaces that a control must support, a control can efficiently target a particular area of functionality without having to support particular interfaces to qualify as a control. As always with COM, whether in a control or a container, it should never be assumed that an interface is available, and standard return-checking conventions should always be followed. It is important for a control or container to degrade gracefully and offer alternative functionality if a required interface is not available.

As COM servers, ActiveX controls have *type libraries*. A type library contains information about the control's properties, methods, and events. Type libraries can exist as separate files (usually with a .tlb extension, but occasionally .olb is used) or can be included in the same file as the control. Type libraries also contain the control's **coclass** (COM class) information. A **coclass** contains one or more interfaces that are defined by the control.

Selecting And Adding ActiveX Controls To Your Project

Literally thousands of ActiveX controls are available today, with functionality ranging from a timer control (which simply notifies its container at a particular time) to full-featured spreadsheets and word processors. Very sophisticated third-party ActiveX controls are readily available that quickly and easily integrate into your application. This can save you hours, weeks, or even months of programming effort. ActiveX controls are freely distributed or available as shareware on the Internet. Keep in mind, however, that you usually get want you pay for and with shareware controls, the documentation is often lacking in quality or nonexistent.

Assume, however, that you have found a neat ActiveX control that you want to use. First, you need to copy it to your hard disk. You probably want to put it in the \Windows\System or \Winnt\System32 directory. If there are accompanying help (HLP) files and license (LIC) files, copy them into the same directory.

Next, you need to register the control in the Windows Registry. Because all ActiveX Controls must support self-registration by implementing **DllRegisterServer()** and **DllUnregisterServer()**, this step is quite simple. You merely run the Windows utility RegSvr32, passing it the control filename on the command line.

After you register your ActiveX control, you need to add it to your project using the Components and Controls Gallery. Go to the Project menu, choose Add To Project, then select Components And Controls. Select Registered ActiveX Controls, as shown in Figure 9.1.

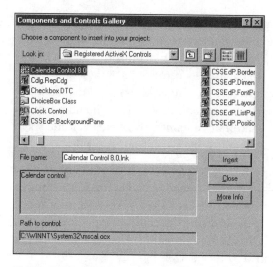

Figure 9.1 The Components And Controls Gallery dialog box.

This shows you all the ActiveX controls registered on your system. Notice that the controls are shown as normal Windows Explorer shortcuts. The code-holding file for each control is shown in the Path To Control box at the bottom of the window.

The calendar control is supplied with Office 97, so it's probably installed and registered on your system. If you select and click Insert, you'll be prompted with an Insert This Component? dialog box; click OK to insert the control.

The Confirm Classes dialog box (shown in Figure 9.2) is displayed to let you know which files will be added to your project and to give you an opportunity

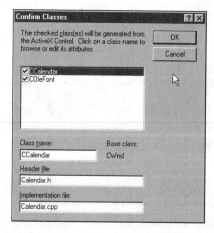

Figure 9.2 The Confirm Classes dialog box.

to change the class and file names. These files implement the interface classes (also known as *dispatch classes*) needed for the control.

Whenever you insert an ActiveX control, ClassWizard uses the information in the control's type library to generate a wrapper class for each of the control's internal coclasses. These wrapper classes provide an easy programmatic interface for a control. In the case here, with the calendar control, two classes, **CCalendar** and **COleFont**, are added to your project. Each class has member functions for all properties and methods, and each has constructors that you can use to dynamically create an instance of the control. The following code shows the member functions ClassWizard generated for the Calendar control's **Year** property and **NextYear** method:

```
short CCalendar::GetYear()
{
  short result;
  InvokeHelper(0xf, DISPATCH_PROPERTYGET, VT_I2,
               (void*)&result, NULL);
  return result;
}

void CCalendar::SetYear(short nNewValue)
{
  static BYTE parms[] =
    VTS_I2;
  InvokeHelper(0xf, DISPATCH_PROPERTYPUT, VT_EMPTY, NULL, parms,
               nNewValue);
}

void CCalendar::NextYear()
{
  InvokeHelper(0x19, DISPATCH_METHOD, VT_EMPTY, NULL, NULL);
}
```

These functions are known as *dispatch functions*. Each dispatch function calls the **CWnd::InvokeHelper()** function. Properties always have separate *Set* and *Get* functions. As shown in the preceding code, the Year property has a **GetYear()** function and a **SetYear()** function. To call a method, you simply call the corresponding function.

InvokeHelper() converts the parameters to **VARIANTARG** values, then invokes the **IDispatch::Invoke()** method. The first parameter passed to **InvokeHelper()** specifies the dispatch ID for the corresponding property or method in the control. The second parameter is a flag describing the context of the **Invoke** call. As you can see, these two parameters provide the needed information to determine the specific implementation code. The fourth parameter is the address of the variable that will receive the property value or return value. It must match the type specified by the third parameter. Table 9.1 shows the possible value that can be used for the third parameter.

Adding An ActiveX Control To A Dialog Box

Not only have the wrapper classes for the new control been added to your project, a new icon representing the ActiveX control has been added to the Resource Editor's Control toolbar. You place this control on the dialog box just like any other control.

After the control has been added to the dialog box, you can change the properties. Like regular controls, there are several properties that you can set for the ActiveX controls, arranged as pages in a property sheet. Property sheets for ActiveX controls have one General tab, which—like normal controls—allows you to assign an ID and set the standard enabling and visible flags. The other property pages are specific to the control itself.

Table 9.1	VARENUM enumeration values.
Symbol	Return Type
VT_BOOL	BOOL
VT_BSTR	BSTR
VT_CY	CY
VT_DATE	DATE
VT_DISPATCH	LPDISPATCH
VT_EMPTY	void
VT_ERROR	SCODE
VT_I2	short
VT_I4	long
VT_R4	float
VT_R8	double
VT_UNKNOWN	LPUNKNOWN
VT_VARIANT	VARIANT

Using the ClassWizard, you can add a member variable for the ActiveX control. However, you can only map an ActiveX control against its dispatch or interface class. Therefore, the Category combo box only allows the Control category, and the Variable type can only be the wrapper class. After the control variable is defined, you can invoke methods and get and set properties by calling the appropriate wrapper class member functions. For example:

```
short theYear = m_calendar.GetYear();
m_calendar.NextYear();
```

You can add event handlers for ActiveX controls in the normal fashion by adding an event handler with ClassWizard or by the New Windows Message And Event Handlers dialog box, as shown in Figure 9.3. The first time you add an event handler, an event sink map is declared and defined in your project. For each handler, an event map entry (**ON_EVENT**) is added to the event sink map and an event handler function is added to the container's CPP file.

Notice that the calendar control has nine events that it can fire. Here is the code the ClassWizard added to the CPP file when the NewYear event was added to the container:

```
BEGIN_EVENTSINK_MAP(CCalendarDlg, CDialog)
  //{{AFX_EVENTSINK_MAP(CCalendarDlg)
    ON_EVENT(CCalendarDlg, IDC_CALENDAR1, 4 /* NewYear */,
      OnNewYearCalendar1, VTS_NONE)
  //}}AFX_EVENTSINK_MAP
END_EVENTSINK_MAP()

void CCalendarDlg::OnNewYearCalendar1()
{
    // TODO: Add your control notification handler code here
}
```

Creating ActiveX Controls At Runtime

In this section, you'll learn how to build a small dialog-based application that will create and exercise the Multimedia control. This application allows the user to select and play WAV files. When completed, it will look the application shown in Figure 9.4.

Here are the programming steps to follow when you create an ActiveX control at runtime without a resource entry:

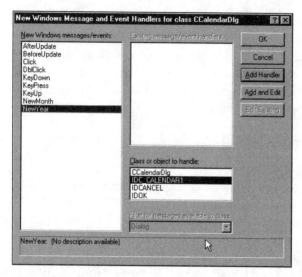

Figure 9.3   The New Windows Message And Event Handlers For Class **CCalendarDlg** dialog box.

Figure 9.4   The application in its initial state.

1. Insert the component into the project.

2. Add an embedded ActiveX control wrapper class member to the appropriate window class.

3. Add an ID for the control.

4. Add code to call the control's **Create()** function.

5. Add the event sink declaration and definition macros.

6. Add the necessary event message handlers and prototypes.

Create a dialog-based application. Because the application is going to create and use the Microsoft Multimedia control, I named the project "Player". At AppWizard Step 2, be sure that the ActiveX control option is selected (this is the default). When the AppWizard ActiveX control option is checked, AppWizard inserts the following line of code to **InitInstance()** of your application class:

```
AfxEnableControlContainer();
```

It also inserts the following to the project's **StdAfx.h** file:

```
#include <afxdisp.h>
```

If you build an application without this option checked and you later decide to use ActiveX controls, you can simply add the preceding lines of code.

Inserting The Component Into The Project

Bring up the Components And Controls Gallery dialog box. Select the Microsoft Multimedia Control. (Mine is version 6.0; you might have a different version.)

Click on the More Info button. This opens Help, where you can learn about the control's properties and events. The control doesn't have very many methods, but for some reason, information on even the few that it does have is not provided. Notice how all the code examples are written in Visual Basic.

Insert the control into your project. When the Confirm Classes dialog displays, click the CPicture option to deselect it. Generally, unless you are familiar with the structure of the **coclasses**, you would leave everything checked so that all of the wrapper classes are generated. Accept the default **Cmci** class name, and click OK. Close the Components And Controls Gallery dialog box.

Adding An Embedded ActiveX Control Wrapper Class Member

In PlayerDlg.h, add the following lines of code immediately after the DECLARE_MESSAGE_MAP() macro:

```
private:
  Cmci m_mci;
```

Because **m_mci** is an embedded C++ object, it will be constructed and destructed along with the **CPlayer** object.

Adding An ID For The Control

Choose Resource Symbols from Visual C++'s View menu. Add a resource constant and name it **IDC_MCI_CONTROL**.

Adding Code To Call Create()

The MCI control has a total of nine buttons. Figure 9.5 shows the property settings for buttons.

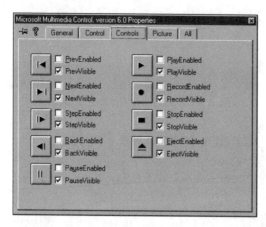

Figure 9.5 Microsoft Multimedia Control properties tab.

You will only be using four of the buttons. So, when you create the control, you will also set the appropriate **Visible** properties to **FALSE**. Here is the code to create and initialize the control:

```
BOOL CPlayerDlg::OnInitDialog()
{
// ...
  // TODO: Add extra initialization here

  // Adjust the window
  CRect rect(0,0, 125, 40);
  CalcWindowRect(&rect);
  SetWindowPos(0,0,0,rect.Width(),rect.Height(),
      SWP_NOZORDER | SWP_NOMOVE | SWP_NOREDRAW);

  // Create Media control
  rect = CRect(10,10, CW_USEDEFAULT, CW_USEDEFAULT);
  m_mci.Create("MediaControl", WS_VISIBLE, rect, this,
             IDC_MCI_CONTROL);
  m_mci.SetEjectVisible(FALSE);
  m_mci.SetRecordVisible(FALSE);
  m_mci.SetPauseVisible(FALSE);
  m_mci.SetBackVisible(FALSE);
  m_mci.SetStepVisible(FALSE);
  m_mci.SetAutoEnable(FALSE);
  m_mci.SetNotify(TRUE);
  m_mci.SetWait(TRUE);
  m_mci.SetShareable(FALSE);
  m_mci.SetDeviceType("waveaudio");
```

```
return TRUE; //return TRUE unless you set the focus to a control
}
```

First, the window is adjusted to a small size, just slightly larger than the default size of the control. Then the control is created. Then the **Eject, Record, Pause, Back,** and **Step** properties are set to nonvisible. After that, the **AutoEnable, Notify, Wait,** and **Shareable** properties are set to the proper states that will allow the program to manipulate the control. Last, the **DeviceType** is set to play WAV files.

Adding The Event Sink Macros

In PlayerDlg.h, add the following lines of code immediately after the **DECLARE_MESSAGE_MAP()** macro:

```
DECLARE_EVENTSINK_MAP()
```

Then in PlayerDlg.cpp, add the following lines of code immediately after the **END_MESSAGE_MAP()** macro:

```
BEGIN_EVENTSINK_MAP(CPlayerDlg, CDialog)
ON_EVENT(CPlayerDlg, IDC_MCI_CONTROL, 10,
        OnPrevGotFocus, VTS_NONE)
ON_EVENT(CPlayerDlg, IDC_MCI_CONTROL, 12,
        OnNextGotFocus, VTS_NONE)
ON_EVENT(CPlayerDlg, IDC_MCI_CONTROL, 14,
        OnPlayGotFocus, VTS_NONE)
ON_EVENT(CPlayerDlg, IDC_MCI_CONTROL, 23,
        OnStopGotFocus, VTS_NONE)
ON_EVENT(CPlayerDlg, IDC_MCI_CONTROL, 38,
        OnDone,         VTS_PI2)
END_EVENTSINK_MAP()
```

Adding The Event Message Handlers And Prototypes

Here are the prototypes for the event handlers and one helper function:

```
void OnPrevGotFocus();
void OnPlayGotFocus();
void OnNextGotFocus();
void OnStopGotFocus();
void OnDone(short * NotifyCode);
void EnableButtons (BOOL prev, BOOL next, BOOL play, BOOL stop);
```

Add member functions to **CPlayerDlg**. That takes care of the six steps required in creating the control. Now you'll add code to get everything to work.

Implementing the Event Handlers And The Helper Function

Add the following code to PlayerDlg.cpp:

```
void CPlayerDlg::OnPlayGotFocus()
{
  m_mci.SetCommand("Play");
  EnableButtons(FALSE, FALSE, FALSE, TRUE);
}
void CPlayerDlg::OnNextGotFocus()
{
  m_mci.SetCommand("Next");
  EnableButtons(TRUE, FALSE, FALSE, FALSE);
}
void CPlayerDlg::OnPrevGotFocus()
{
  m_mci.SetCommand("Prev");
  EnableButtons(FALSE, TRUE, TRUE, FALSE);
}
void CPlayerDlg::OnStopGotFocus()
{
  m_mci.SetCommand("Stop");
}
void CPlayerDlg::OnDone(short *NotifyCode)
{
  switch(*NotifyCode)
  {
  case eNotifySuccessful:
    EnableButtons(TRUE, FALSE, FALSE, FALSE);
    break;
  case eAborted:
    EnableButtons(TRUE, TRUE, TRUE, FALSE);
    break;
  default:
    break;
  }
}
void CPlayerDlg::EnableButtons(BOOL prev, BOOL next,
                               BOOL play, BOOL stop)
{
  m_mci.SetPrevEnabled(prev);
```

```
  m_mci.SetNextEnabled(next);
  m_mci.SetPlayEnabled(play);
  m_mci.SetStopEnabled(stop);
}
```

The **OnPlayGotFocus()**, **OnNextGotFocus()**, **OnPrevGotFocus()**, and **OnStopGotFocus()** handlers simply call the control's **SetCommand()** member passing a string that contains the command to execute. The first three then call the helper function to enable and disable the control's buttons accordingly.

The Done event fires when the WAV file completes playing or when a **Stop** command is issued. **OnDone()** checks the **NotifyCode** to determine which condition caused the Done event to fire and then sets the control's button configuration appropriately.

The various notify codes need to be defined, so place the following code near the top of PlayerDlg.cpp:

```
enum
{
  eNotifySuccessful = 1,
  eNotifySuperceded = 2,
  eAborted          = 4,
  eFailure          = 8
};
```

You might be wondering why I used the GotFocus events rather than the Click events. I thought the Click would be the right event, but it didn't work reliably. However, it works just fine with Visual Basic.

Adding Code To Open A File

In this section, you'll add a menu item to the system menu that allows the user to select a WAV file to play. Figure 9.6 shows what the menu will look like.

First, choose Resource Symbols from Visual C++'s View menu and add a resource constant. Name it **IDM_OPEN_FILE**, and set its value to 0×0020. Then add the following shaded lines of code to PlayerDlg.h:

Figure 9.6   The Player application's system menu.

```
   DECLARE_MESSAGE_MAP()
   DECLARE_EVENTSINK_MAP()
private:
   Cmci m_mci;
   void OnPrevGotFocus();
   void OnPlayGotFocus();
   void OnNextGotFocus();
   void OnStopGotFocus();
   void OnDone(short * NotifyCode);
   void EnableButtons(BOOL prev, BOOL next, BOOL play, BOOL stop);
   CFileDialog m_fileDlg;
   void OpenNewFile();
   OSVERSIONINFO m_osv;
};
```

In PlayerDlg.cpp, modify the constructor to initialize the **CFileDialog** object.
Here's the code:

```
////////////////////////////////////////////////////////////////////
// CPlayerDlg dialog
CPlayerDlg::CPlayerDlg(CWnd* pParent /*=NULL*/)
   : CDialog(CPlayerDlg::IDD, pParent)
   , m_fileDlg(TRUE,        // use Open dialog
               "*.WAV",     // default extension
               "*.WAV",     // current file name
               OFN_FILEMUSTEXIST | OFN_PATHMUSTEXIST |
               OFN_LONGNAMES,
               "Wave Files (*.Wav)||",
               NULL)        // no parent pointer
{
   //{{AFX_DATA_INIT(CPlayerDlg)
      // NOTE: the ClassWizard will add member initialization here
   //}}AFX_DATA_INIT
   // Note that LoadIcon does not require a subsequent DestroyIcon
   m_hIcon = AfxGetApp()->LoadIcon(IDR_MAINFRAME);
}
```

The embedded **CFileDialog** object is initialized as an Open dialog box with
default file settings for a WAV file. Then a determination is made as to the
system type, and the initial directory is set appropriately.

With the constructor taken care of, let's move on to **OnInitDialog()**. I've included the complete function, but you need only take note of the shaded lines:

```
BOOL CPlayerDlg::OnInitDialog()
{
```

```
CDialog::OnInitDialog();

// Add "Open..." menu item to system menu.
// IDM_OPEN_FILE must be in the system command range.
ASSERT((IDM_OPEN_FILE & 0xFFF0) == IDM_OPEN_FILE);
ASSERT(IDM_OPEN_FILE < 0xF000);

CMenu* pSysMenu = GetSystemMenu(FALSE);
pSysMenu->AppendMenu(MF_SEPARATOR);
pSysMenu->AppendMenu(MF_STRING, IDM_OPEN_FILE, "Open...");

// Set the icon for this dialog.  The framework does this
// automatically when the application's main window isn't a dialog
SetIcon(m_hIcon, TRUE);            // Set big icon
SetIcon(m_hIcon, FALSE);           // Set small icon

// Adjust the window
CRect rect(0,0, 125, 40);
CalcWindowRect(&rect);
SetWindowPos(0,0,0,rect.Width(),rect.Height(),
    SWP_NOZORDER | SWP_NOMOVE | SWP_NOREDRAW);

// Create Media control
rect = CRect(10,10, CW_USEDEFAULT, CW_USEDEFAULT);
m_mci.Create("MediaControl", WS_VISIBLE, rect, this,
            IDC_MCI_CONTROL);
m_mci.SetEjectVisible(FALSE);
m_mci.SetRecordVisible(FALSE);
m_mci.SetPauseVisible(FALSE);
m_mci.SetBackVisible(FALSE);
m_mci.SetStepVisible(FALSE);
m_mci.SetAutoEnable(FALSE);
m_mci.SetNotify(TRUE);
m_mci.SetWait(TRUE);
m_mci.SetShareable(FALSE);
m_mci.SetDeviceType("waveaudio");

return TRUE; // return TRUE unless you set the focus to a control
}
```

As you can see, everything to do with the AboutBox menu item has been removed and replaced with an Open File menu item. Two ASSERT statements are ensuring that **IDM_OPEN_FILE** has a value between 0x0010 and 0x0FF0 and that it is a multiple of sixteen. All the predefined window menu items have IDs greater than 0xF000, and Windows uses the lower four bits for special purposes.

Next, the **OnSysCommand()** function needs to be modified for the removal of the AboutBox menu item and the addition of the Open menu item. Here's the code:

```
void CPlayerDlg::OnSysCommand(UINT nID, LPARAM lParam)
{
  if ((nID & 0xFFF0) == IDM_OPEN_FILE)
  {
    OpenNewFile();
  }
  else
  {
    CDialog::OnSysCommand(nID, lParam);
  }
}
```

The only thing left is the function that actually opens the file:

```
void CPlayerDlg::OpenNewFile()
{
// set the default directory
  char dir[MAX_PATH];
  ExpandEnvironmentStrings("%SystemRoot%", dir, MAX_PATH);
  strcat(dir, "\\Media");
  m_fileDlg.m_ofn.lpstrInitialDir = dir;
  // set the initial file name
  strcpy(m_fileDlg.m_ofn.lpstrFile,"*.wav");
  if(m_fileDlg.DoModal() == IDOK)
  {
    m_mci.SetCommand("Close");
    m_mci.SetFileName(m_fileDlg.GetPathName ());
    EnableButtons(FALSE, TRUE, TRUE, FALSE);
    m_mci.SetCommand("Open");
  }
}
```

Practice Questions

Question 1

Which statements are true? [Check all the correct answers]

❑ a. Type libraries contain coclass information.

❑ b. Type libraries always exist as separate TLB files.

❑ c. Type libraries contain information about a control's properties, methods, and events.

❑ d. A coclass can only expose a single interface.

Answers a and c are correct. A type library is a file or component within another file that contains type information about COM objects. A control container uses the type information to learn about a control's methods, properties, and events. A type library also contains a control's **coclass** information. Because most controls will support a number of interfaces, the control's **coclass** will expose each of these interfaces for use by the control container.

Question 2

Which statement is correct?

○ a. An ActiveX control must support at least the IDispatch interface.

○ b. An ActiveX control must support at least all of the interfaces that an OLE control must support.

○ c. An ActiveX control must support at least the IUnknown interface and be self-registering.

○ d. An ActiveX control must support at least the IDispatch::Invoke() method.

Answer c is correct. Technically, the only interface an ActiveX control is required to support is **IUnknown**. The idea here is that an ActiveX control only needs to support the interfaces it needs—unlike an OLE control, which is required to support a minimum set of interfaces. Obviously, for an ActiveX control to be useful—one that can be used in a Web page, an MFC dialog, or a Visual Basic form—it needs to expose some number of methods and properties. It does this by implementing **IDispatch**. Additionally, it will usually have the capability to fire one or more events.

Unfortunately, there is confusion about what constitutes an ActiveX control. Terms such as OLE, COM, and ActiveX have been defined differently at different points in time. Microsoft's documentation doesn't help the situation either. For instance, if you look up ActiveX controls in the MSDN, there will nearly always be a statement like "...ActiveX controls, formerly called OLE controls ...".

You should be aware that although answer c is technically correct, when people talk about ActiveX controls, they are almost always talking about *full-blown* controls.

Question 3

Assume that you've built an application using AppWizard, and in Step 2, you deselected the ActiveX control option. Now you have decided that you do want to use an ActiveX control. Which of the following is correct?

○ a. You must add a call to EnableControlContainer() in the dialog box object's OnInitDialog() function.

○ b. You must add a call to AfxEnableControlContainer() in your application object's InitInstance() function and add #include <afxdisp.h> to your project's stdafx.h file.

○ c. You must add a call to AfxEnableControlContainer() in your application object's OnInitialUpdate() function and add #include <afxdisp.h> to your project's stdafx.h file.

○ d. You must add a call to EnableControlContainer() in your application object's InitInstance() function and add #include <Afxdisp.h> to your project's Stdafx.h file.

Answer b is correct. Answers a, c, and d will not allow you to use an ActiveX control.

Question 4

Which function do the dispatch functions call to invoke an ActiveX control's methods?

○ a. CWnd::InvokeMethod()

○ b. COleDispatchDriver::Invoke()

○ c. CWnd::Dispatch()

○ d. CWnd::InvokeHelper()

Answer d is correct. The dispatch functions generated by the ClassWizard wrap the **InvokeHelper()** function. To invoke an ActiveX control's method, you simply call the appropriate dispatch function. The dispatch function, in turn, calls **InvokeHelper()**, passing it five arguments. The first two, **dwDispID** and **wFlags**, identify the method or property to be invoked and the context of the call.

Need To Know More?

 Bates, Jon and Tim Tompkins. *Using Visual C++ 6*. Que Corporation, Indianapolis, IN, 1998. ISBN 0-7897-1635-6. This book is aimed at the beginning-to-intermediate programmer, and in typical Que style, its focus is on "how-to." Chapter 9 covers the use of ActiveX controls.

 Kruglinski, David J., George Shepherd, and Scot Wingo. *Programming Microsoft Visual C++*, 5th ed. Microsoft Press, Redmond, WA, 1998. ISBN 1-57231-857-0. This book strikes a good balance between theory and practical application. It is divided into six parts and covers nearly every aspect of MFC programming, from the basics to database management and the Internet. Chapter 8 is all about using ActiveX controls. One of the examples shows how to use the Web Browser ActiveX control.

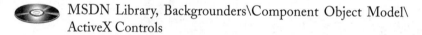 MSDN Library, Backgrounders\Component Object Model\ ActiveX Controls

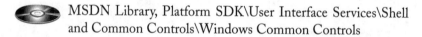 MSDN Library, Platform SDK\User Interface Services\Shell and Common Controls\Windows Common Controls

 MSDN Library, Technical Articles\Component Object Model\OLE Controls\OLE Controls and Control Containers Guidelines, Version 1.1

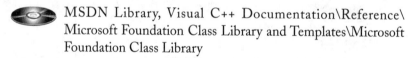 MSDN Library, Visual C++ Documentation\Reference\ Microsoft Foundation Class Library and Templates\Microsoft Foundation Class Library

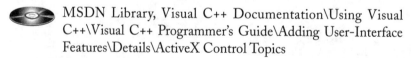 MSDN Library, Visual C++ Documentation\Using Visual C++\Visual C++ Programmer's Guide\Adding User-Interface Features\Details\ActiveX Control Topics

Adding Help

Terms you'll need to understand:

√ Rich Text Format (RTF)

√ Hypertext Markup Language (HTML)

√ WinHelp

√ HTML Help

√ Microsoft Help Workshop

√ Context-sensitive help

√ Hypertext

√ Hypergraphics

√ Hot spot

√ Context reference ID

√ MakeHm

√ Microsoft HTML Help Workshop

Techniques you'll need to master:

√ Authoring help using the Microsoft Help Workshop

√ Authoring help using the Microsoft HTML Workshop

√ Invoking WinHelp from an application

√ Invoking HTML Help from an application

195

Most commercial applications provide some form of online help. Most applications today use Rich Text Format (RTF), but the trend is toward the Hypertext Markup Language (HTML) format. The first is commonly known as WinHelp and the latter as HTML Help. This chapter covers both formats.

Using WinHelp

The Microsoft Help Workshop allows you to create HLP files that can be attached to your application. Once the HLP file is in place, it is a simple matter of calling **WinHelp()** or **CWinApp::WinHelp()** to invoke the WinHelp application. The MFC AppWizard can also add code that makes it easy for you to provide context-sensitive help.

The WinHelp application provides a consistent interface to the user that allows the user to select an item from the Help Contents, then view, search, and navigate the various help screens by jumping from one topic to another.

 The Microsoft Help Workshop's online help, usually referred to as the Help Author's Guide, is a graphical help (Hcw.HLP) file that is an excellent source of information. It will provide you with much of the information needed to author and create a robust help system.

Building Simple Help Files

The process of building your own help files consists of four distinct steps:

1. Create the Help Text file using Microsoft Word or another RTF-compatible word processor.

2. Create the Help Project file using Visual C++ or another text editor.

3. Compile the Help file using the Help Compiler and Project file.

4. Attach the Help file to your application.

Creating The Help Text

The Help Text or Topic file contains topics that are linked together via *hypertext* or *hypergraphics*. Hypertext is text composed of blocks of words that contains links to other text. Hypergraphics are images with hot spots that, like hypertext, link to text. This linking is what enables a user to move from one topic to another or display a pop-up window.

The hypertext jumps are double-underlined blocks of text followed immediately by a "tag" phrase that is formatted as hidden text. In the help window, hypertext jumps are underlined and colored green. For example, a double-underlined phrase "Application Object" appears as single underlined, in green text to the user.

You can place a jump phrase in your Help Text file by following these steps:

➤ Select the double-underline feature of your editor. In Word, you can press Ctrl+Shift+D or select Format|Font|Font|Underline|Double.

➤ Type the double-underlined phrase.

➤ Turn off double underlining, and select the editor's hidden-text feature. In Word, you turn on hidden text by pressing Ctrl+Shift+H or by selecting Format|Font|Font|Hidden.

➤ Type the jump tag assigned to the topic; this is the target of the jump. Each jump tag must be unique.

➤ Turn off hidden text.

 Be careful that there are no spaces between the double-underlined text and the hidden text. If the hidden text occurs at the end of a paragraph, make sure that the paragraph mark is not formatted as part of the hidden text.

 While creating your Help Text file, you might find it helpful to turn on the viewing of all nonprinting characters. In Word you can do this by selecting Tools|Options|View|All.

Each jump page must be a separate word process page. In Word, press Ctrl+Enter or select Insert|Break|Page Break. You use a custom footnote symbol (#) to connect the jump page text to the jump phrase.

Two other custom footnote symbols can be used. The $ symbol is used to place a reference to the jump page in the Help system's Search list box. A single uppercase K is used to specify a keyword with which a user may search for a topic. You can specify multiple keywords for the same jump page; simply separate them by semicolons. Figure 10.1 shows two jump pages and associated

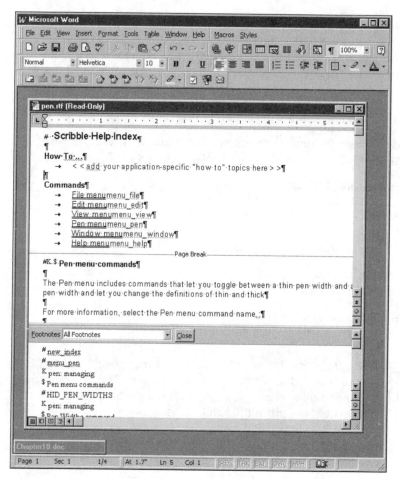

Figure 10.1 The PEN.RTF file.

footnote symbols contained in PEN.RTF. This is one of the files that make up the SCRIBBLE tutorial.

When you create a jump to another topic, the default is to display the topic in the main help window. You can cause the topic to display in a secondary window by placing, immediately after the jump tag, a greater than (>) symbol followed by the name of the window, like so:

```
JumpTag>WindowName
```

When you format a jump phrase as single-underlined rather than double-underlined, the text in the help window will appear in green with a light dotted underline. Then, when the user clicks on the jump phrase, rather than jumping to a topic page, a small pop-up window appears. These small pop-up windows are usually used to display a definition or provide additional information.

Creating The Help Project File

The Help Project file is a simple ASCII text file that you create with your favorite text editor. It is formatted like a INI file. The most commonly used sections are presented in Table 10.1. Refer to Microsoft Help Workshop's online help for detailed information about the Help Project file.

Here's what the initial version of a simple Help Project file might look like:

```
[OPTIONS]
ERRORLOG = MyApp.err
CONTENTS = HID_CONTENTS
TITLE = MyApp Help

[FILES]
MyApp.rtf

[WINDOWS]
Main = "MyApp Help",(190,100,560,630),,,(192,192,192)
```

 You can also use Microsoft Help Workshop to create and maintain your HPJ file.

Compiling And Viewing The Help File

This step is the easiest. First, from Windows, run the Microsoft Help Workshop utility. Open the HPJ file, and then click on the Save And Compile button.

Table 10.1	Frequently used Help Project file sections.
Section	**Description**
OPTIONS	Specifies how the Help file is to be compiled.
FILES	Specifies the RTF files to be used to create the HLP file.
WINDOWS	Defines the primary help window. Required when implementing context help.
ALIAS	Equates one context ID with another.

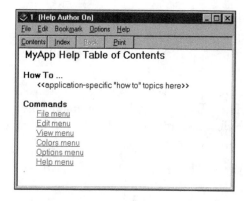

Figure 10.2 An example help screen.

Then, from Windows Explorer, double-click on the new HLP file. The main screen might look something like Figure 10.2.

Using The Tree-View Table Of Contents

To add the tree-view table of contents, you need to create a text file with a .CNT extension. Here's a partial example:

```
:Base MyApp.hlp
1 File Menu
2 New = HID_FILE_NEW
2 Open = HID_FILE_OPEN
2 Close = HID_FILE_CLOSE
... additional topics go here
1 Edit Menu
2 Undo = HID_EDIT_UNDO
2 Cut = HID_EDIT_CUT
2 Copy = HID_EDIT_COPY
2 Paste = HID_EDIT_PASTE
1 View Menu
... View menu topics go here
1 Colors Menu
2 Black = HID_COLORS_BLACK
2 Blue = HID_COLORS_BLUE
2 Green = HID_COLORS_GREEN
2 Red = HID_COLORS_RED
1 Options Menu
... Options menu topics go here
1 Help Menu
... Help menu topics go here
```

Refer to Microsoft Help Workshop's online help for detailed information about the contents (CNT) file.

After creating and saving your contents file, when you run WinHelp with the HLP file, you'll see a new contents screen similar to Figure 10.3.

Adding Help To Your Program

Adding help to a Win32 program is a simple matter of adding a menu item and handler. In the handler, you need to call the API **WinHelp()** function to activate the WinHelp application. The code might look something like the following:

```
case ID_HELP:
{
  WinHelp(hWnd, "MyApp.hlp", HELP_FINDER, 0);
  break;
}
```

The first argument is the handle of the requesting window. The second argument is the path to the help file, which, in this example, is in the same directory as the application. The third argument indicates that the Help Topics dialog

Figure 10.3   The tree-view table of contents.

box is to be displayed. The fourth argument is used to provide additional information depending on the value of the third argument. Here's the prototype for **WinHelp()**:

```
BOOL WinHelp(HWND hWndMain,    // requesting window
             LPCTSTR lpszHelp, // path to help file
             UINT uCommand,    // type of request
             DWORD dwData);    // additional info for uCommand
```

Refer to Visual C++ online help for a complete list of values for **uCommand** and the corresponding values to use for **dwData**. For a partial list, see Table 10.2.

CWinApp::WinHelp() is used to invoke the WinHelp application from within an MFC program. Here is its prototype:

```
virtual void WinHelp(DWORD dwData, UINT nCmd = HELP_CONTEXT);
```

The parameters map to the fourth and third parameters in the API call. The name of the help file used matches the name of the application. Assuming that the name of your application is MyApp.exe and the help file is MyApp.hlp, you would invoke the WinHelp application and display the contents screen using one of the following:

```
AfxGetApp->WinHelp(0, HELP_INDEX); // old style
```

```
AfxGetApp->WinHelp(0, HELP_FINDER); // new style, .CNT required
```

 You can use a name different than the name of the application by setting CWinApp::m_pszHelpFilePath.

Creating Context-Sensitive Help

Most Windows applications allow the user to press F1 to find out context information. When the user presses F1, the application is smart enough to determine which object (window, control, menu item, and so on) has the focus, read the object's context reference, and send it to WinHelp, which in turn displays the appropriate help topic. The **[MAP]** section of your HPJ file is where you define your context reference IDs. You can use **#define**, **#include**, and assignment statements in the **[MAP]** section. Many times it is convenient

Table 10.2	**A partial list of values for uCommand.**
uCommand	**Description**
HELP_CONTEXT	Display topic identified by number in **dwData**
HELP_QUIT	Terminate help
HELP_INDEX	Display index
HELP_FINDER	Display table of contents (.CNT required)
HELP_HELPONHELP	Display help on Help
HELP_ KEY	Display topic for keyword in **dwData**

to use your program's resource IDs as the context reference IDs, which means you can simply place a single **#include** statement in the [**MAP**] section, like so:

```
#include MyApp.h
```

The problem with this approach is that the jump tag names in your RTF file must be the same as your resource ID names. Another approach is to use the [**ALIAS**] section to associate your program resource IDs with the jump tags used in the RTF file. Here's an abbreviated example:

```
[ALIAS]
ID_COLORS_BLACK=HID_COLORS_BLACK
ID_COLORS_BLUE=HID_COLORS_BLUE
ID_COLORS_GREEN=HID_COLORS_GREEN
ID_COLORS_RED=HID_COLORS_RED
ID_HELP=HID_COLORS_MENU
IDM_ABOUT=HID_MAIN_INDEX
IDM_EXIT=HID_APP_EXIT

[MAP]
ID_COLORS_BLACK=0x9000
ID_COLORS_BLUE=0x9001
ID_COLORS_GREEN=0x9002
ID_COLORS_RED=0x9003
ID_HELP=32771
IDM_ABOUT=104
IDM_EXIT=105
```

Using Context-Sensitive Help With The SDK

When the user presses F1, a **WM_HELP** message is sent to the window that has the keyboard focus. If the window is a child window, however, the message goes to the child window's parent. If the user presses F1 while a menu is active, the **WM_HELP** message is sent to the window associated with the menu. When the window receives the **WM_HELP** message, **lParam** will contain a pointer to a **HELPINFO** structure. This structure contains detailed information about the item for which help is requested. Refer to Visual C++ online help for a description of **HELPINFO**. Here's a snippet of code that shows how you might provide context-sensitive help for your menu items:

```
case WM_HELP:
{
  HELPINFO & helpInfo = * reinterpret_cast<LPHELPINFO>(lParam);
  if(helpInfo.iContextType == HELPINFO_MENUITEM)
  {
    WinHelp(hWnd, "MyApp.hlp", HELP_CONTEXT, helpInfo.iCtrlId);
  }
  break;
}
```

Using Context-Sensitive Help With MFC

You can add help to an application by hand if you so desire. However, it is simpler to have AppWizard add the basic support when you initially create your project. You do this by selecting the Context-sensitive Help option at MFC AppWizard - Step 4 of 6 for MDI and SDI projects, and at MFC AppWizard - Step 2 of 4 for Dialog-Based Projects.

For SDI and MDI projects, AppWizard adds the necessary message-map entries, a menu item to the Help menu, and a button to the toolbar. For Dialog projects, a message-map entry and Help button are added.

AppWizard also provides a Help starter kit. It creates a Help Project (HPJ) file, a Help Contents (CNT) file, a number of bitmap (BMP) files, and depending on the type of project, one or more starter topic (RTF) files. All of these files are placed in an HLP directory that AppWizard creates in your project directory. The HPJ file is added to your project so that you can build the HLP file from the Build menu.

As you add new resources to your project, you should add topic information to your RTF file. Visual C++ automatically provides you with context reference IDs to use as your jump tags. The context reference ID names are simply the resource ID names with an H added as the first letter. The values assigned are the sum of your resource ID value and a base value. Each resource type has its own base value. These base values are defined in afxpriv.h and explained in the online help article "TN028: Context-Sensitive Help Support." The context reference IDs are kept in a help mapping (HM) file that is maintained by Visual C++. When you do a build and your resource.h file has changed, Visual

C++ runs the MakeHm application. MakeHm reads your resource.h file and creates an HM file, which is included in the **[MAP]** section of the HPJ file. Assume that resource.h contains the following resource IDs:

```
#define IDD_ABOUTBOX         100
#define IDR_MAINFRAME        128
#define IDR_WITHCOTYPE       129
#define IDM_COLORS_BLACK     0X9000
#define IDM_COLORS_BLUE      0X9001
#define IDM_COLORS_GREEN     0X9002
#define IDM_COLORS_RED       0X9003
```

The HM file would look like this:

```
// Commands (ID_* and IDM_*)
HIDM_COLORS_BLACK            0x19000
HIDM_COLORS_BLUE             0x19001
HIDM_COLORS_GREEN            0x19002
HIDM_COLORS_RED              0x19003

// Prompts (IDP_*)

// Resources (IDR_*)
HIDR_MAINFRAME               0x20080
HIDR_WITHCOTYPE              0x20081

// Dialogs (IDD_*)
HIDD_ABOUTBOX                0x20064

// Frame Controls (IDW_*)
```

Using Graphics And Hypergraphics

When adding a graphic or hypergraphic image to the RTF file, you can either paste it directly into the file or you can include it by reference. Placing the bitmap image directly into the help file is the easiest method, but it is very restrictive. Inserting the bitmap image by reference provides many advantages and is not too difficult to do. Simply place special "embraced" text in the file. Then when you compile the help file, the compiler will include the image as part of the HLP file. Here's the syntax for creating a reference to a bitmap file:

```
{Command FileName}
```

FileName is the name of the bitmap file without a path. The path is defined by the **BMROOT** entry in the **[OPTION]** section of the HPJ file. **Command** instructs the compiler on the placement of the image. Refer to Table 10.3.

Table 10.3	Graphic reference commands.
Command	Description
bmc	Align bitmap image as characters.
bml	Align bitmap image at the left margin. Text is allowed to wrap along the right edge of the image.
bmr	Align image at the right margin. Text is allowed to wrap along the left edge of the image.

You create hypergraphics with the Hotspot Editor (SHED.EXE), normally located in C:\Program Files\Microsoft Visual Studio\Common\Tools. You can use the Hotspot Editor to open a BMP, a DIB, or a WMF, and add hot spots to the existing graphic image. You then save the file as a hypergraphic (SHG) file. After you have defined the hot spots, the file can be included by reference into your RTF file, and then compiled into your help (HLP) file.

A hot spot can be any rectangular area within the image. After drawing a hot spot, you will need to specify its context ID and its type. Its type can be a jump, pop-up, or macro.

Using Help Macros

Help macros are routines built into the WinHelp application that allow you to further customize your help system. More than 50 macros are available to use to customize the way the WinHelp application works with your help files. These macros can be grouped into four major categories:

➤ Button manipulation

➤ Menu manipulation

➤ Hypertext link

➤ WinHelp auxiliary

Macros can be placed in the HPJ file, the RTF file, or your application. If you place a macro in the **[CONFIG]** section, the macro will run when WinHelp first opens your help file. If you place a macro in a topic footnote, the macro runs whenever the user jumps to the topic. When placing a macro in a topic footnote, always use the special footnote symbol, an exclamation mark (!). You can also use macros with hypertext and hypergraphics rather than jump tags. To run a macro for your application, do it like so:

```
char macroName[] = "HelpOn()";
WinHelp(hWnd, "MyApp.hlp",
        HELP_COMMAND, reinterpret_cast<DWORD>(macroName));
```

Make sure that you know the various file types and the purpose of each type. Don't forget, AppWizard and Visual C++ generate some help-related files that you don't directly maintain.

Using HTML Help

By using HTML-based Help, you will be able to provide a wide range of new and better types of help. HTML Help can include such features as hyperlinks, ActiveX controls, scripting, and Dynamic HTML (DHTML). Microsoft touts HTML Help as their next-generation online authoring system. Like WinHelp, HTML Help uses a project file to combine topic, content, index, and other source files into one compiled help file. Which types of files you use in your Help project will depend on your design and how you plan to distribute it. After you have your HTML Help system complete, you can mount it on disk, on the Internet, or on an intranet. Table 10.4 lists some of the most commonly used files.

Refer to the online help article "Installing HTML Help" if HTML Help is not installed on your system.

Creating Help

As with WinHelp, HTML Help uses a project file to bring together all the various help components. You use the HTML Help Workshop to create your project file, and most other files as well. One very useful feature of the HTML Help Workshop is the ability to convert existing WinHelp projects. You simply select File|New, choose Project and click OK, then select the Convert WinHelp project checkbox. The wizard does the rest.

After converting a WinHelp project or when creating a new HTML Help project, you can add or remove HTML topic files, and specify the location of index, contents, image, and multimedia files. When creating a new HTML topic file, the HTML Help Workshop provides a skeleton to which you add text; pointers to graphics, sounds, and animated images; and links or jumps within the same file, to another file, or to a Web site. Each topic requires its own HTM file. You can design your table of contents so that the user will be able to click on a topic and the HTML topic file will open. The topic file itself can be part of the CHM file stored locally or a file located on some remote

Table 10.4 Commonly used HTML Help files.

Name	Type	Description
Project	HHP	To manage your topics, art, contents, index, and other source files. Also defines the on-screen appearance of your help system.
Topic	HTM, HTML	Contains the text that appears on screen and formatting codes (tags) that tell a browser how to display each page.
Image	JPEG, GIF, PNG	HTML image files.
Contents	HHC	Contains the topic titles for your table of contents.
Index	HHK	Contains the index entries (keywords) for your index.
Alias	ALI	Maps IDs to help topics. Used for context-sensitive help support.
Compiled	CHM	A single file that contains all the elements of your help system. This file is distributed with your application and can be viewed using Internet Explorer.

system or Web site. The index file behaves in the same manner as the topic file, but it uses keywords rather than topics. There are two types of indexes that you can use depending on your requirements. The binary index is used with a CHM file, whereas the site map index works on a Web site.

Compiling Help By Using Visual C++

By adding your HTML Help Project file to your Visual C++ project, you ensure that any time one of your help source files change, a new version of your CHM file will be built. For this to occur, you must use the Visual C++ custom build rules. After adding your HHP file to your project, in the Workspace pane, select the HHP file, then select Project|Settings|Custom Build, and make the necessary entries. The Command entry is as follows:

```
pathname\hhc.exe $(InputDir)\$(InputName).hhp
@echo off
```

The Output entry is as follows:

```
$(InputDir)\$(InputName).chm
```

Calling HTML Help From Your Application

As with WinHelp, only one API is used with HTML Help. This function is **HtmlHelp()**, which is prototyped as follows:

```
HWND HtmlHelp( HWND hwndCaller,
               LPCSTR pszFile,
               UINT uCommand,
               DWORD_PTR dwData
             );
```

As you can see, this function is modeled after **WinHelp()**. This makes it simple to update existing programs from WinHelp to HTML Help. Be aware, however, that the command names and parameters are different.

Now for a closer look at **HtmlHelp()**. The first parameter is the handle of the window making the call and the window that will receive the focus when the help window exits. The *pszFile* parameter is the name of your compiled help file, a URL, or a window definition. The *uCommand* parameter specifies the action to be performed. These actions are grouped into seven major categories: window types, context-sensitive help, keyword lookups, navigation pane, error messages, contents synchronization, and single threading. The last parameter, *dwWord*, as with **WinHelp()**, is dependent on *uCommand*. Here's an example of how you would open a help topic in a specified help window:

```
HWND hwnd = AfxGetApp()->m_pMainWnd->GetSafeHwnd();

HWND hRtn = HtmlHelp(
                hwnd,
                "E:\\MyHelp.chm::/colors_black.htm>mainwin",
                HH_DISPLAY_TOPIC,
                NULL);
```

This example causes the topic **colors_black.htm**, located in file MyHelp.chm, to be displayed in a mainwin type of help window.

To use **HtmlHelp()** in your program, you need modify your project settings to include the paths to the HTML Help support files:

➤ Use Project|Settings|Link|Category: Input|Additional Library Path to specify the directory location of HtmlHelp.lib.

➤ Use Project|Settings|Link|Category: Input|Object/Library Modules to specify HtmlHelp.lib.

➤ Use Project|Settings|C/C++|Category: Preprocessor|Additional Include Directories to specify the directory location of HtmlHelp.h.

➤ Place **#include <HtmlHelp.h>** in your Stdafx.h file.

HTML Help comes with an authoring guide with sections on how to design a help system and how to use the HTML Help Workshop. This is currently the best source of information.

Practice Questions

Question 1

You are implementing an MFC application (MyApp.EXE) that supports printing and persistence. You used AppWizard to generate an SDI application, and in Step 4 of 6, you selected Context-sensitive Help and accepted all of the defaults, including Printing and Print Preview. You want your online help to cover all aspects of your application. When you distribute your application, which of the following files will you need to include as part of the installation? [Check all the correct answers]

❑ a. MyApp.EXE

❑ b. afxprint.rtf

❑ c. MyApp.HLP

❑ d. MyApp.CNT

The correct answers are a, c, and d. This question tries to trick you by referring to printing and then providing an answer that has *print* in its name. Answer b is incorrect because the afxprint.rtf file is used in the creation of MyApp.HLP during development, but it doesn't need to be installed on the user's machine. Answer a is the application itself, so naturally it must be installed. Answer c is the help file, so it too must be installed. Answer d is the contents file and must be installed in order for WinHelp to provide a tree-view table of contents.

Question 2

You used AppWizard to generate an MDI application, and in Step 4 of 6, you selected Context-sensitive Help. The user will be able to access context-sensitive help with which of the following methods?

○ a. By pressing F1 only

○ b. By pressing F1 or by pressing Shift+F1

○ c. By pressing F1 or by clicking the Context Help toolbar button

○ d. By pressing F1 or by pressing Shift+F1 or by clicking the Context Help toolbar button

The correct answer is d. Context-sensitive help can be accessed by pressing F1 or by pressing Shift+F1 or by clicking the Context Help toolbar button. When the user presses F1, the program makes a best guess about the help context and calls WinHelp. In this mode, help is invoked for the currently active GUI object. Shift+F1 is more powerful than F1. When the user presses Shift+F1, the cursor changes to an arrow with a question box. While in this mode, the program can identify help context for a selected menu item, a toolbar button, a window, the status bar, and other client and non-client elements. When the user clicks the Context Help toolbar button, it is the same as pressing Shift+F1.

Question 3

What special task does the MakeHm utility carry out?

○ a. It creates a CNT file.

○ b. It produces a help mapping file that defines the help context IDs.

○ c. It compiles the HPJ file and produces the HLP file.

○ d. It updates the resource.h file with the current help context IDs.

The correct answer is b. MakeHm is a console application that reads resource.h, maps the resource IDs to help context IDs, and generates an HM file. Answer a is incorrect because the CNT file is a text file that is created by the AppWizard or by you, the developer. Answer c is incorrect because the Help Workshop (hcrtf.exe) produces the HLP file. Answer d is incorrect because MakeHm doesn't update resource.h; instead, it reads resource.h and generates an HM file.

Question 4

HTML Help provides which of the following features? [Check all the correct answers]

❑ a. Support for HTML

❑ b. Capability to jump from a help topic to a site on the Internet

❑ c. Support for BMP images

❑ d. Support for ActiveX, Java, and Visual Basic Script

The correct answers are a, b, and d. Answer a is correct because the help topics in HTML Help are written in HTML. Answer b is correct because the hyperlinks in HTML Help provide the capability to jump within the same file, to another file, or to a Web site. Answer d is correct because HTML Help supports ActiveX, Java, and scripting, including JavaScript and Visual Basic Script. Answer c is incorrect because HTML Help supports HTML image formats (JPEG, GIF, and PNG), and not BMP images, although HTML Help Image Editor can convert BMP and other images to one of the supported types.

Need To Know More?

 Kruglinski, David J., George Shepherd, and Scot Wingo. *Programming Microsoft Visual C++*, 5th ed. Microsoft Press, Redmond, WA, 1998. ISBN 1-57231-857-0. Chapter 21 covers MFC and the WinHelp system of context-sensitive help.

MSDN Library, Visual Studio 6.0 Documentation\Visual C++ Documentation\Using Visual C++\Visual C++ Programmer's Guide \Adding User Interface Features\Details\Help Topics (WinHelp): Context-Sensitive Help for Your Programs

MSDN Library, Visual Studio 6.0 Documentation\Visual C++ Documentation\Using Visual C++\Visual C++ Programmer's Guide \Adding User Interface Features\Details\Help Topics (HTML Help): Context-Sensitive Help for Your Programs

MSDN Library, Visual Studio 6.0 Documentation\Visual C++ Documentation\References\Microsoft Foundation Class Library and Templates\Microsoft Foundation Class Library\MFC Technical Notes\TN028: Context-Sensitive Help Support

MSDN Library, Visual Studio 6.0 Documentation\Platform SDK\Tools and Languages\Tools\Resource Files\Creating Segmented Hypergraphics

MSDN Library, Visual Studio 6.0 Documentation\Platform SDK\Tools and Languages\Tools\Resource Files\Creating Help Files

MSDN Library, Visual Studio 6.0 Documentation\Platform SDK\User Interface Services\Windows Shell\Shell Programmers Guide\Handling Online Help

Storing And Printing

Terms you'll need to understand:

√ Serialization

√ **CFile**

√ **CArchive**

√ **DECLARE_SERIAL()**

√ **IMPLEMENT_SERIAL()**

Techniques you'll need to master:

√ Describing what serialization is and how it works

√ Implementing serialization in an application

√ Describing how MFC responds to the Save, Save As, and Open commands

√ Describing how printing works with MFC

√ Implementing multipage printing in an application

Serialization

The MFC framework provides the means whereby an application's objects can persist on disk after the program exits. Then, upon restart, the application's objects can be restored. This process of writing and reading an object to and from persistent storage used by MFC is known as *serialization*. Two classes, a **CObject** virtual function, and a couple of macros are the key ingredients to the framework's built-in support for serialization.

A **CFile** object is created and used to encapsulate a binary file handle. This provides unbuffered binary disk input/output operations. The **CFile** object is then attached to a **CArchive** object, which is used to serialize the data to and from a file.

The **CArchive** object is what directs the serialization process. It provides the mechanism for streaming the objects to and from disk. The **CArchive** object maintains a flag that indicates whether it is writing to disk or reading from disk. **CArchive::IsStoring()** and **CArchive::IsLoading()** are used to test this flag. **CArchive** overloads **operator<<()** and **operator>>()** for the primitive data types shown in Table 11.1. Also, **::operator<<()** and **::operator>>()** are overloaded for the types shown in Table 11.2.

Writing A Serializable Class

For a class to be serializable, you must follow these five steps:

Table 11.1 Primitive data types supported by CArchive::operator<<() and CArchive::operator>>().	
Type	**Description**
BYTE	8-bit unsigned integer
WORD	16-bit unsigned integer
LONG	32-bit signed integer
DWORD	32-bit unsigned integer
float	32-bit single-precision floating point
double	64-bit double-precision floating point
int	32-bit signed integer
short	16-bit signed integer
char	8-bit signed char
unsigned	32-bit unsigned integer

Table 11.2	User data types supported by ::operator<<() and ::operator>>() for the CArchive class.
Type	**Description**
CObject	Pointer to a **CObject** object
CString	A **CString** object
SIZE and **CSize**	An object defining a size as a cx, cy pair
POINT and **CPoint**	An object defining a point as an x, y pair
RECT and **CRect**	An object defining a rectangle by its upper left and lower right corners
CTime	An object that represents an absolute time and date
CTimeSpan	An object that represents a relative time span
COleCurrency	An object that encapsulates the **CURRENCY** data type
COleDateTime	An object that encapsulates the **DATE** data type
COleDateTimeSpan	An object that represents a relative time span
COleVariant	An object that encapsulates the **VARIANT** data type

1. Derive your class from **CObject** or a **CObject**-derived class.

2. Provide a default constructor.

3. Include the **DECLARE_SERIAL()** macro in the class declaration using the name of your class as its one argument. This macro takes one argument: the name of your class.

4. Include the **IMPLEMENT_SERIAL()** macro in the class implementation file. This macro takes three parameters: the name of your class, its base class, and a schema (version) number.

5. Override the base class's **Serialize()** function.

Here's what a **COrder** class definition might look like:

```
class COrder : public CObject                      // step 1
{
public:
  COrder(){}                                       // step 2
  COrder(CString orderNumber,
         CString customerName,
         COleDateTime orderDate);
  void Serialize(CArchive&);
  . . .
```

```
private:
  CString m_strOrderNumber;
  CString m_strCustomerName;
  COleDateTime m_dtOrderDate;

  DECLARE_SERIAL(COrder)                              // step 3
};
```

Somewhere in the class's implementation file you would add the following:

```
IMPLEMENT_SERIAL(COrder, CObject, 1)                 // step 4
```

The class's **Serialize()** function would look like this:

```
// step 5
void COrder::Serialize(CArchive & ar)
{
  CObject::Serialize(ar);
  if(ar.IsStoring())
  {
    ar << m_strOrderNumber
       << m_strCustomerName
       << m_dtOrderDate;
  }
  else
  {
    ar >> m_strOrderNumber
       >> m_strCustomerName
       >> m_dtOrderDate;
  }
}
```

Your serialization function will almost always call the **Serialize()** function of its base class before it archives its own data members. If **CEmployee** is derived from **CPerson**, then **CEmployee::Serialize()** might look like this:

```
 void CEmployee::Serialize(CArchive & ar)
{
  CPerson::Serialize(ar);
  if(ar.IsStoring())
  {
    ar << m_nDept;
  }
  else
  {
```

```
  ar >> m_nDept;
  }
}
```

Serializing An Object

If your application employs the document/view architecture, everything is keyed to the document. When the user selects the Save or Open option from the File menu, the framework creates a **CFile** object. It then creates a **CArchive** object, passing it the **CFile** object. Next, it calls your document class's **Serialize()** function, passing a reference to the **CArchive** object. Your document's **Serialize()** function then serializes each of its data members.

Outside the document/view architecture, you will need to provide the code to do what the framework does when using the document/view architecture. Follow this three-step process to serialize your objects:

1. Create a **CFile** object and open the file.

2. Create a **CArchive** object, passing it the **CFile** object.

3. Call the object's **Serialize()** function, and pass it a reference to the **CArchive** object.

The following program statements open MyFile.dat for reading and serialize a **CManager** object named **m_manager**:

```
CFile fIn;
if(fIn.Open("MyFile.dat", CFile::modeRead))
{
  CArchive ar(&fIn, CArchive::load);
  m_manager.Serialize(ar);
}
```

Serializing the object to disk isn't much different:

```
CFile fOut;
if(fOut.Open("MyFile.dat", CFile::modeCreate | CFile::modeWrite))
{
  CArchive ar(&fOut, CArchive::store);
  m_manager.Serialize(ar);
}
```

After you have serialized all of your objects, you can then close the archive file by calling **CArchive::Close()** and **CFile::Close()**. Or, you can let the **CArchive** and **CFile** destructors close the archive and file when the objects go out of scope.

Embedded Object Vs. Pointers

If you look at Table 11.2 closely, you will notice that **::operator<<()** and **::op-erator>>()** have been overloaded for **CObject** pointers but not for embedded **CObject** objects. This means that the following will not work:

```
COrder order ("012345678", "Jon Johnson", ::time(NULL));
ar << order;
```

But this will:

```
COrder * pOrder = new COrder("012345678",
                             "Jon Johnson",
                             ::time(NULL));
ar << pOrder;
```

Different authors suggest different ways around this problem. You can provide overloads of the insertion and extraction operators for your class in the same manner that you would provide overloads for **cin** and **cout**. Here are the proto-types for **COrder**:

```
friend CArchive & operator<<(CArchive & ar, COrder & order);
friend CArchive & operator>>(CArchive & ar, COrder & order);
```

The more common approach is to ignore the problem and call the **Serialize()** function directly. However, the downside to both of these approaches is that version checking is bypassed. To include the versioning capability when serial-izing embedded **CObjects**, you can use code like this:

```
// Serialize
COrder order("012345678", "Jon Johnson", ::time(NULL));
ar << & order;
```

The code to deserialize can use a copy constructor or an overload of the **operator=()** function:

```
// Deserialize — using a copy constructor
COrder * pOrder;
ar >> pOrder;

COrder order = * pOrder; // copy constructor
delete pOrder;

// Deserialize — using an operator=() overload
COrder * pOrder;
```

```
ar >> pOrder;
COrder order;
order = * pOrder;      // operator=()
delete pOrder;
```

CFile And Its Derivatives

All programs maintain and manipulate data in one way or another. Many programs also store and retrieve their data to and from a disk or other medium. MFC makes this task easier for the programmer by providing a family of classes that abstract the medium being used. All of these classes are derived directly or indirectly from **CFile**. Figure 11.1 shows the hierarchy of these classes.

CFile

CFile doesn't have to be used with **CArchive**. You can use it by itself to perform basic disk I/O in an object-oriented manner. **CFile** has over 25 functions

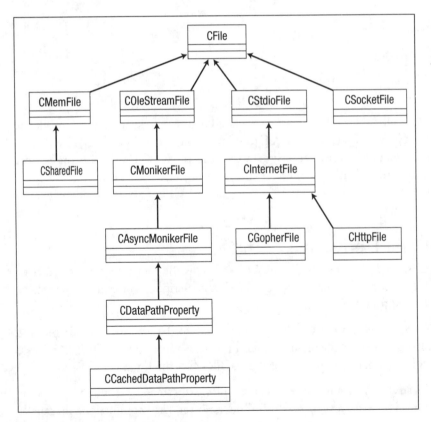

Figure 11.1 **CFile** and its derivatives.

that allow you to do such things as read, write, position, and extract status. Many of these functions throw a **CFileException** object when an error occurs. Here's a small snippet of code that shows how **CFile** might be used to copy one file to another:

```
try
{
  CFile inFile("TheInputFile.dat", CFile::modeRead);
  CFile outFile("TheOutputFile.dat",
              CFile::modeWrite | CFile::modeCreate);
  BYTE buf[0x1000];
  DWORD dwBytesRemaining = inFile.GetLength();
  while(dwBytesRemaining > 0)
  {
    UINT nBytesRead = inFile.Read(&buf, sizeof(buf));
    outFile.Write(&buf, nBytesRead);
    dwBytesRemaining -= nBytesRead;
  }
}
catch(CFileException * e)
{
  e->ReportError();
  e->Delete();
}
```

Here, all the **CFile** code has been placed in a **try** block, and a **catch** block has been provided to catch a **CFileException** object thrown by any of **CFile**'s member functions. Notice the signature of the **catch**. You must use the correct signature, and unless the code rethrows the object, it must be deleted. But don't use the C++ **delete** operator; instead, call the **CFileException** member function **Delete()**.

CFile Derivatives

As shown previously in Figure 11.1, **CFile** is the root class for a number of MFC classes. Table 11.3 provides a short description for each of the classes derived from **CFile**.

As you can see from the descriptions, some of these classes provide file-like interfaces to non-file media. Others provide wrappers around OLE interfaces, and still others simplify the reading of files over the Internet.

Because **CFile** reads and writes binary files, extra steps are required if you want to read or write text files. **CStdioFile**, however, has two functions that make

Table 11.3   A short description for classes derived from CFile.

Class Name	Description
CMemFile	A **CMemFile** object behaves like a **CFile** object, except that the file is stored in RAM rather than on disk. **CMemFile** allocates, reallocates, and deallocates memory using the runtime library functions **malloc**, **realloc**, and **free**.
CSharedFile	The class is like **CMemFile**, except that **GlobalAlloc** is used to allocate memory, which returns an **HGLOBAL** handle instead of a pointer.
COleStreamFile	This class represents an **IStream** in a compound file as part of OLE Structured Storage.
CMonikerFile	This class binds a moniker to a stream, giving you **CFile** functionality. By using **CMonikerFile**, you do not have to bind to a stream yourself.
CAsyncMonikerFile	This class allows you to Internet-enable your application and ActiveX controls. It uses the **IMoniker** interface to access a data stream asynchronously.
CDataPathProperty	Implements an OLE control property that can be loaded asynchronously.
CCachedDataPath Property	Like **CDataPathProperty**, but cached in a memory file.
CSocketFile	Used for sending and receiving data across a network via Windows Sockets.
CStdioFile	Represents a C runtime stream file.
CGopherFile	Used to find and read files on a Gopher server.
CHttpFile	Used to find and read files on an HTTP server.
CInternetFile	Base class for **CGopherFile** and **CHttpFile**.

this task much simpler: **ReadString()** and **WriteString()**. The following code shows how **ReadString()** can be used:

```
// header file
  CStringArray m_objFileData;

// implementation file
m_objFileData.RemoveAll();
try
{
  CString string;
```

```
CStdioFile file(theFileName, CFile::modeRead);
while(file.ReadString(string))
{
   m_objFileData.Add (string);
}
}
catch(CFileException *e)
{
  m_objFileData.RemoveAll();
  e->ReportError();
  e->Delete();
}
```

Here, a **CStringArray** container is used to hold the contents of the file. Before using it, all the elements it contained are removed and its initialize size is set. Then the **try** block is entered where the file is opened by the constructor. A **while** loop is used to read the file one line of text at a time, placing it in the container.

Printing

Printing is one of the harder parts of writing a Windows program. MFC, with its document/view architecture, makes this task easier, but there are still a lot of details that need to be attended to. An item of major importance is correctly setting the size of the document and figuring out where the page breaks go.

Printing In Windows

Although printing in Windows is much easier than printing in DOS, it still involves a number of steps:

1. Obtain a device context for the printer.

2. Call **::StartDoc()**.

3. Call **::StartPage()**.

4. Output to the page.

5. Call **::EndPage()**. For a multipage document, loop back to Step 3, repeating Steps 3 through 5 until all pages are printed.

6. If printing was successful, call **::EndDoc()**; otherwise, call **::AbortDoc()**.

7. Delete the device context.

Because a long job could take minutes or even hours to finish, you need to provide a way for the user the terminate the print job before it is finished. This is just one of the complications you need to deal with.

Printing With MFC

MFC provides a set of wrappers that takes care of most of the details of printing. And when you add printing capabilities to a document/view application, things become even simpler. Printing from a document/view application, like drawing on the screen, is managed by a **CView**-derived class.

Roles And Responsibilities—Yours And MFC's

The MFC wrapper classes take on much of the responsibilities that otherwise would be yours. Nevertheless, it is still your responsibility to ensure that your view class performs the following tasks:

➤ Inform the framework of the number of pages.

➤ Print each page as required, including headers and footers.

➤ Allocate and deallocate the necessary resources.

It is the framework's responsibility to:

➤ Display the Print dialog box.

➤ Create a CDC object.

➤ Inform the printer driver when a new print job is to start or end.

➤ Inform the printer driver when a new page is to be started, inform the view class which page should be printed, and inform the printer driver when the page is finished. This step is repeated for each page.

➤ Call the view overrideable functions at the appropriate times.

Understanding The Printing Sequence

Key to printing from a document/view application is a set of virtual functions of the view class. The framework calls these functions at various stages of the printing process. By overriding these functions, you can tailor the printing process as you see fit. Which of these functions you override and what you do in the override depends on the type of document you are printing. The beauty of these functions is that you can put almost all, if not all, of your printing code in them. These functions are listed in Table 11.4.

Table 11.4 Key CView print overrideables.	
Function	**Description**
OnBeginPrinting	Override to allocate fonts and other resources needed for the print job. You can also set the maximum page count here. This function is called just before printing starts.
OnEndPrinting	Override to deallocate resources allocated in **OnBeginPrinting**. This function is called when printing ends.
OnPrepareDC	Override to modify the device context. This function is called before each page is printed.
OnPreparePrinting	Override to call **DoPreparePrinting()**, which is responsible for displaying the Print dialog box and creating the printer DC. This function is called at the beginning of the print job.
OnPrint	Override to print headers, footers, and other page elements that are not drawn by **OnDraw** or to do all printing here instead of in **OnDraw**. This function is called to print (or preview) one page.

Many applications draw on the printer just as they draw on the screen—in OnDraw(). However, trying to manage both drawing on the screen and drawing on the printer in **OnDraw()** can become quite complicated. Even when you are able to manage drawing on both from **OnDraw()**, more times than not, you will need to override **OnPrint()** to handle such things as page numbers, headers, and footers. Therefore, it is sometimes more practical to just go ahead and put the entire printer output logic in **OnPrint()**.

When printing a document, MFC calls the functions in Table 11.4 in a specific order. Each of these functions, along with sample code, is presented below in the sequence in which MFC calls them.

1. **OnPreparePrinting()**

```
BOOL CExampleView::OnPreparePrinting(CPrintInfo* pInfo)
  {
  // default preparation
    return DoPreparePrinting(pInfo);
  }
```

This is how AppWizard implements **OnPreparePrinting()**. As you can see, it receives a pointer to a **CPrintInfo** object and then calls **DoPreparePrinting()**, passing it the **CPrintInfo** object. **DoPrepare**

Printing() presents the Print dialog box and creates a printer device context.

The **CPrintInfo** object has a number of functions that allow you to do things such as set the document's minimum and maximum page numbers and find out the number of the last page the user selected for printing. **CPrintInfo**'s data members also provide information like the current number of the page being printed and whether the document is in print preview.

If you know the maximum number of pages in your document, you should call **CPrintInfo::SetMaxPage()** before calling **DoPreparePrinting()**. This will allow the Print dialog box to present the page count to the user.

2. **OnBeginPrinting()**

```
void CExampleView::OnBeginPrinting(CDC * pDC,
                                   CPrintInfo * pInfo)
{
  m_font.CreatePointFont(100, _T("Courier New"), pDC);

  TEXTMETRIC tm;
  CFont * pOldFont = pDC->SelectObject(&m_font);
  pDC->GetTextMetrics(&tm);
  m_cyLineHeight = tm.tmHeight + tm.tmExternalLeading;
  CString str(SAMPLESTRING);
  CSize size = pDC->GetTextExtent(str, 81);
  pDC->SelectObject(pOldFont);
  m_cxLineWidth = size.cx;
  m_cxLeftMargin = (pDC->GetDeviceCaps(HORZRES) - size.cx) / 2;

  m_nLinesPerPage = (pDC->GetDeviceCaps(VERTRES) -
  (m_cyLineHeight * (3 + (2 * PRINTMARGIN)))) / m_cyLineHeight;

  m_nMaxPage = max(1, (m_nTotalLines + (m_nLinesPerPage - 1)) /
  m_nLinesPerPage);
  pInfo->SetMaxPage(m_nMaxPage);

}
```

OnBeginPrinting() receives two parameters: a pointer to a device context and a pointer to the same **CPrintInfo** object that was passed to **OnPreparePrinting()**. In this example the font that will be used for printing is created. Next, a number of calculations are performed to determine the line width based on an example string of text, the position of the left margin, the number of lines per page, and the maximum number of pages to print. Then, because the maximum number of pages is known, **CPrintInfo::SetMaxPage()** is called to set the number of the last page of the document.

3. **OnPrepareDC()**

This function is called once for each page of the document. Here is where you should control print-time pagination and set the document's viewpoint origin.

4. **OnPrint()**

```
void CExampleView::OnPrint(CDC *pDC, CPrintInfo *pInfo)
{
PrintPageHeader(pDC, pInfo->m_nCurPage);
  PrintPage(pDC, pInfo->m_nCurPage);
}

  void CExampleView::PrintPageHeader(CDC *pDC,
        UINT nPageNumber)
  {
    CString strPageNumber;
      strPageNumber.Format("Page %d of %d", nPageNumber,
          m_nMaxPage);

    int nMaxHdr = sizeof(SAMPLESTRING) -
                            (strPageNumber.GetLength() + 2);
    CString strHeader = GetDocument()->GetPathName();
    if(strHeader.GetLength() > nMaxHdr)
    strHeader = GetDocument()->GetTitle();

    UINT nSpaces = sizeof(SAMPLESTRING) -
                      strPageNumber.GetLength() -
                      strHeader.GetLength() - 1;
    for(UINT i = 0; i < nSpaces; i++)
      strHeader += SPACE;
    strHeader += strPageNumber;

    UINT y = m_cyLineHeight * PRINTMARGIN;
    CFont *pOldFont = pDC->SelectObject(&m_font);
    pDC->TextOut(m_cxLeftMargin, y, strHeader);

    y += (m_cyLineHeight * 3) / 2;
    pDC->MoveTo(m_cxLeftMargin, y);
    pDC->LineTo(m_cxLeftMargin + m_cxLineWidth, y);
```

```
      pDC->SelectObject(pOldFont);
}

void CExampleView::PrintPage(CDC *pDC, UINT nPageNumber)
{
  if(m_nTotalLines != 0)
  {
    UINT nStart = ((nPageNumber - 1) * m_nLinesPerPage) + 1;
    UINT nEnd = min(m_nTotalLines + 1,
                        nStart + m_nLinesPerPage);

    CFont * pOldFont = pDC->SelectObject(&m_font);
    for(UINT i = nStart; i < nEnd; i++)
    {
      CString str = FormatLine(i);
      UINT y = ((i - nStart) + PRINTMARGIN + 3) *
                  m_cyLineHeight;
      pDC->TextOut(m_cxLeftMargin, y, str);
    }
    pDC->SelectObject(pOldFont);
  }
}

CString CExampleView::FormatLine(UINT index)
{
  int size = 1;
  for(int n = m_nTotalLines/10; n > 0; n /= 10)
    size++;
  CString format;
  format.Format("%%%dd  %%s", size);
  CString string;
  string.Format(format, index,
                  GetDocument()->GetLine(index));
  return string;
}
```

MFC calls **OnPrint()** to print the actual page. If you are using **OnDraw()** to do printing, after printing the header and footer, you would call the base class's **OnPrint()**, which, in turn, would call **OnDraw()**. Here, everything is being printed from **OnPrint()**, or more accurately, from a couple of helper functions that **OnPrint()** calls.

PrintPageHeader() first creates the text for the page number. Next, based on the size of the line, it determines whether the complete path will fit in front of the page number text. If it will, it is used; otherwise, just the document's title is used. It then outputs the line of text and draws a line across the page immediately following the text.

PrintPage() outputs one line of text at a time until the page is full. It calls **FormatLine()** for the line of text that is to be printed. **FormatLine()** gets the line of text from the document object, prepends the line number, and returns the formatted line of text.

5. As long as there are more lines to print, MFC continues to call **OnPrepareDC()** and **OnPrint()** for each page in the document. After the last page has been printed, MFC calls **OnEndPrinting()**. **OnEndPrinting()** is used to destroy any resources that were created in **OnBeginPrinting()**.

```
void CFormatPrinterView::OnEndPrinting(CDC*, CPrintInfo*)
{
  m_font.DeleteObject();
}
```

Practice Questions

Question 1

> Which function invokes the Print dialog box and creates a printer device context?
>
> ○ a. CView::OnPrepareDC()
>
> ○ b. CView::DoPreparePrinting()
>
> ○ c. CView::OnPreparePrinting()
>
> ○ d. CPrintInfo::DoPreparePrinting()

The correct answer is b. The question asks which function *invokes* the Print dialog box, not which function do you *override*. **CView::OnPreparePrinting()** is called by the framework before a document is printed. **CView::OnPreparePrinting()** is where **CView::DoPreparePrinting()** is called. **CView::OnPrepareDC** is used to adjust device-context attributes, perform print-time pagination, and send escape codes to the printer. There is no function **CPrintInfo::DoPreparePrinting()**. **CPrintInfo** is used to hold information about the print job. All of **CPrintInfo**'s member functions are used to either *get* or *set* its attributes.

Question 2

> Your application is printing a four-page document. Consider the below statements. Which are true? [Check all correct answers]
>
> ❏ a. The framework calls OnBeginPrinting() exactly four times.
>
> ❏ b. The framework calls OnPrepareDC() exactly one time.
>
> ❏ c. The framework calls OnPrint() exactly four times.
>
> ❏ d. The framework calls OnEndPrintPreview() exactly one time.

The correct answer is c. When printing a multipage document, the framework calls **OnPrint()** for each page that is to be printed. It calls **OnPreparePrinting()**, **OnBeginPrinting()**, and **OnEndPrinting()** only one time whether the document is a single page or many pages. Strangely, the framework calls **On PrepareDC()** two times for each page. Answer d is incorrect because the **OnEnd PrintPreview()** function is only called when preview mode is exited.

Question 3

Which statements are true? [Check all the correct answers]

☐ a. A CFile object provides an actual connection to a physical file.

☐ b. MFC always provides version checking on embedded objects derived from CObject.

☐ c. MFC provides the CArchive class to facilitate transferring a document's data to a storage medium.

☐ d. CFile provides buffered file I/O.

The correct answers are a and c. **CFile** and **CArchive** objects work together to provide serialization of MFC objects. The **CFile** object provides unbuffered, binary disk I/O to and from a physical file. The **CArchive** object provides a type-safe buffering mechanism for writing or reading serializable objects to or from a **CFile** object. The insertion and extraction operators are overloaded both as member functions of **CArchive** and as global functions for a number of different data types. These overloads provide version checking. However, MFC does not provide an overload for **CObject** embedded objects.

Question 4

Your SDI application does multipage printing. You want to print the page number at the bottom of each page. Which function should you override to print the footer?

○ a. CView::OnDraw()

○ b. CView::OnPreparePrinting()

○ c. CView::OnPrint()

○ d. CView::OnBeginPrinting()

The correct answer is c. Although **OnDraw()** is often used to draw to both the screen and printer, the **OnPrint()** member function is the appropriate place to print headers and footers. **OnPrint()** is used because it is called for each page that is to print, and it is only used for printing.

Need To Know More?

 Kruglinski, David J., George Shepherd, and Scot Wingo. *Programming Microsoft Visual C++*, 5th ed. Microsoft Press, Redmond, WA, 1998. ISBN 1-57231-857-0. Chapters 17 and 18 include information on serialization. Chapter 19 covers printing and print preview.

 Prosise, Jeff. *Programming Windows with MFC*. Microsoft Press, Redmond, WA, 1999. ISBN 1-57231-695-0. This is the updated version of the author's popular book, *Programming Windows 95 with MFC*. Chapters 6 and 9 address serialization. Chapter 13 covers printing and print previewing.

 Sphar, Chuck. *Learn Microsoft Visual C++ 6.0 Now*. Microsoft Press, Redmond, WA, 1999. ISBN 1-57231-965-8. Chapter 16 covers serialization, and Chapter 17 covers printing. This is a basic Visual C++ book, but it provides a through and clear description for both serialization and printing.

 MSDN Library, Visual C++ Documentation\Using Visual C++\ Visual C++ Programmer's Guide\Adding User-Interface Features\ Details\Serialization Topics

Multithreading
In MFC

12

. . . .

Terms you'll need to understand:

√ Multitasking

√ Process

√ Thread

√ Multithreading

√ Symmetric multiprocessing

√ Scheduler

√ Thread priority

√ User interface (UI) thread

√ Worker thread

√ Primary thread

√ Event object

√ Signaled state

√ Unsignaled state

√ Critical section

√ Blocked thread

√ Mutex

√ Semaphore

Techniques you'll need to master:

√ Creating a secondary thread

√ Communicating between threads

√ Synchronizing thread execution

√ Correctly identifying which type of thread—UI or worker—to implement

√ Choosing the most appropriate method to communicate between threads in your application

√ Selecting the best synchronization object to use in your application

Most modern operating systems allow you to run several programs at the same time. This capability is called *multitasking*. Each running task, in the Win32 environment, constitutes a *process*, and each process consists of one or more threads. A *thread*, simply stated, is a path or flow of execution through a process's code. As a programmer, threads give you the ability to execute different parts of your program at the same time. In essence, they allow you to have multitasking within multitasking. This chapter covers how to create and manage threads in your MFC program.

Threads

All of the true 32-bit Windows operating systems are preemptive. This means that they control how long a thread executes. At the end of its allocated time, the executing thread is stopped and a different thread starts executing. The amount of time a thread is allowed to execute is very small; so to a human, all of the threads appear to be executing at the same time. If you are running Windows NT on a system with more than one processor, it may indeed mean that multiple threads are executing at the same time. Windows NT is a *symmetric multiprocessing*, or *SMP*, operating system, which means it is capable of assigning different threads, including threads belonging to the operating system, to different processors.

The CPU knows nothing about threads; it simply executes one instruction after another. As each instruction executes, it changes one or more of the CPU registers, or some part of memory, or maybe the instruction counter. It is the operating system that switches the flow of execution from one thread to another. To do this, the operating system maintains information about each thread. This information is collected into a thread context, or context record. This collection of data is used to restore the CPU so that a thread can pick up execution in the same state it was in before losing control. Switching from one thread to another is done in such a manner that a thread never knows about it.

Thread Priorities

The *scheduler* is the component of the operating system that decides which threads run when and for how long. The scheduler uses a variety of techniques to improve multitasking performance and to try to ensure that each thread in the system gets an adequate amount of CPU time. The amount of time a thread gets is based on its own needs and the needs of the process it serves. Ultimately, the decision about which thread should execute next boils down to the thread with the highest current priority value. At any given moment, each thread is assigned a value from 1 to 31, which is a combination of the process's priority class, the thread's priority level, and the dynamic boost currently being applied by the operating system. The higher the number, the higher the base priority level.

The system uses the current priority value of all executable threads to determine which thread gets the next slice of CPU time. Threads are scheduled in a round-robin fashion at each priority level, and only when there are no executable threads at a higher level does scheduling of threads at a lower level take place. Table 12.1 shows the possible process priority classes.

The priority level is used to adjust the priority class of the process. Without knowing the importance of the process you can change the relative importance of a thread. The priority levels are shown in Table 12.2.

Table 12.1   Process priority classes.

Priority	Meaning
IDLE_PRIORITY_CLASS	Assign to tasks that should run only when the system is idle. Base value is 4.
NORMAL_PRIORITY_CLASS	Assign to tasks with no special scheduling needs. Base value is 7 for background tasks and 9 for foreground tasks.
HIGH_PRIORITY_CLASS	Assign to time-critical tasks that must be executed immediately. Apply caution when using this priority class. Base value is 13.
REALTIME_PRIORITY_CLASS	Assign to tasks that are extremely time-sensitive. Base value is 24.

Table 12.2   Thread priority levels.

Priority	Adjustment Value
THREAD_PRIORITY_IDLE	16 for **REALTIME_PRIORITY_CLASS**, 1 for all others
THREAD_PRIORITY_LOWEST	−2
THREAD_PRIORITY_BELOW_NORMAL	−1
THREAD_PRIORITY_NORMAL	0
THREAD_PRIORITY_ABOVE_NORMAL	+1
THREAD_PRIORITY_HIGHEST	+2
THREAD_PRIORITY_TIME_CRITICAL	31 for **REALTIME_PRIORITY_CLASS**, 15 for all others

Most processes start life with the priority class of **NORMAL_PRIORITY_ CLASS**. However, after it is started, if it needs to, a process can call **::SetPriorityClass()** to change its priority class. Exercise caution when changing the priority class to **HIGH_PRIORITY_CLASS**. If a thread runs at the highest priority level for extended periods, other threads in the system won't get processor time. You should almost never use **REALTIME_ PRIORITY_ CLASS,** because this interrupts system threads that manage mouse input, keyboard input, and background disk flushing. This class can be appropriate for applications that "talk" directly to hardware or that perform brief tasks that should have limited interruptions.

All threads are created using **THREAD_PRIORITY_NORMAL.** This means that the thread priority is the same as the process priority class. After it's created, you can use **::SetThreadPriority()** or **CWinThread::SetThreadPriority()** to adjust the thread's priority relative to other threads in the process.

Thread Types

All threads are the same as far as Windows is concerned. However, MFC distinguishes between *user interface (UI) threads*, which have a message pump and typically, as you would expect, perform user interface tasks, and *worker threads*, which do not. Creating a UI thread is particularly appropriate when you need to have a thread running to service a particular window and the processing associated with it. On the other hand, you usually create a worker thread when you need to perform background tasks that receive no direct input from the user.

Every process has at least one thread: the *primary thread*, sometimes called the *main thread.* This thread is created by the system when the process is loaded into memory and begins executing and runs as long as the program is active. For an MFC program, the **CWinThread portion of** your **CWinApp** object represents the primary thread. It, like any thread, can dynamically create and destroy other threads. It is also possible for a thread to decide for itself to terminate.

There are two ways to create threads in MFC applications. The first is very much the same as creating any other Windows object: Create an instance of the **CWinThread** class, and then call that object's **CreateThread()** function to create the thread. The second method is to call the **AfxBeginThread()** function. MFC defines two versions of this function: one for UI threads and another for worker threads.

The first version takes a pointer to a **RUNTIME_CLASS** information object, which identifies the **CWinThread**-derived class you will be using to control the thread. It looks like this:

```
CWinThread * AfxBeginThread(
            CRuntimeClass  * pThreadClass,
            int              nPriority = THREAD_PRIORITY_NORMAL,
            UINT             nStackSize = 0,
            DWORD            dwCreateFlags = 0,
            LPSECURITY_ATTRIBUTES lpSecurityAttrs = NULL );
```

The other version, the one that creates a worker thread, takes a pointer to a function that will control the thread:

```
CWinThread * AfxBeginThread(
            AFX_THREADPROC   pfnThreadProc,
            LPVOID           pParam,
            int              nPriority = THREAD_PRIORITY_NORMAL,
            UINT             nStackSize = 0,
            DWORD            dwCreateFlags = 0,
            LPSECURITY_ATTRIBUTES lpSecurityAttrs = NULL );
```

The worker thread's control function can be a static class member function or a function declared outside a class. It is prototyped this way:

```
UINT ThreadFunc(LPVOID pParam);
```

The **pParam** argument is a 32-bit value whose value equals the **pParam** passed to **AfxBeginThread()**. This parameter is usually the address of an application-defined data structure containing information passed to the worker thread by the thread that created it.

Both **AfxBeginThread()** overloads do more than simply create a thread. They also initialize internal variables used by the framework, perform sanity checks at various points during the creation process, establish the thread's priority, and take measures to ensure that the runtime library is accessed in a thread-safe manner.

 Don't use the Win32 API functions in a MFC application. When using the Win32 API, always link with the multithreaded C runtime library; then use **_beginthreadex()** to create a thread and **_endthreadex()** to terminate a thread.

Creating A Worker Thread

To create a worker thread using MFC, all you need to do is write a function that you want to run parallel with the rest of your application. Then call **AfxBeginThread()** to start a thread that will execute your function. The thread remains active as long as the thread's function is executing; when the thread function exits, the thread is destroyed.

Creating A User Interface Thread

Creating a user interface thread is entirely different than creating a worker thread. You must derive a class from **CWinThread** and override some functions to make sure you gain the functionality you need. **CWinThread::InitInstance()** is similar to **CWinApp::InitInstance()** in that it is called each time you create the thread that is wrapped by the instance of the thread. You must override **InitInstance()**. This is where you should perform any initialization your thread needs. **CWinThread** has a corresponding **ExitInstance()** function that is called when your thread terminates. This is where you would place any destruction code required by your thread.

A Simple Thread In Action

To see a simple thread in action, build the SimpleWorker application as detailed in the following steps:

1. Start a new AppWizard project workspace called SimpleWorker (see Figure 12.1).

2. Give the new project the following settings in the AppWizard dialog boxes: Step 1: Single Document; Step 2: Default Settings; Step 3: Default Settings; Step 4: Turn off all options; Step 5: Default Settings; and Step 6: Default Settings.

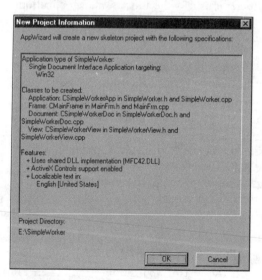

Figure 12.1 New Project Information dialog box.

3. Use the Resource Editor to add a Thread menu to the application's **IDR_MAINFRAME** menu. Give the menu two commands—Start Thread and Stop Thread. Assign them command IDs of **ID_START_THREAD** and **ID_STOP_THREAD**. Enter a prompt and tooltip that makes sense. Refer to Figure 12.2.

4. Use ClassWizard to generate the message handlers. Select the **CSimpleWorkerView** class, and then add the messages as shown in Table 12.3. Accept the default names.

5. Add two member variables to **CSimpleWorkerView**. The code is shown here:

```
// Implementation
public:
  BOOL m_bRunning;
  BOOL m_bQuit;
  virtual ~CSimpleWorkerView();
```

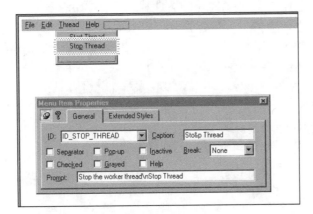

Figure 12.2 Thread menu.

Table 12.3 Message handlers for CSimpleWorkerView.		
ID	**Message**	**Member Function**
ID_START_THREAD	COMMAND	OnStartThread
ID_START_THREAD	UPATE_COMMAND_UI	OnUpdateStartThread
ID_STOP_THREAD	COMMAND	OnStopThread
ID_STOP_THREAD	UPATE_COMMAND_UI	OnUpdateStopThread

6. Add code to initialize both variables:

```
// CSimpleWorkerView construction/destruction

CSimpleWorkerView::CSimpleWorkerView()
  : m_bQuit(FALSE)
  , m_bRunning(FALSE)
{
```

7. Near the top of SimpleWorkerView.CPP, add the following code:

```
static char THIS_FILE[] = __FILE__;
#endif

UINT ThreadProc(LPVOID param)
{
  TRACE("\nThread activated.\n");

  LPBOOL pQuit = static_cast<LPBOOL>(param);

  SYSTEMTIME tm;

  while( ! *pQuit )
  {
    ::GetLocalTime(&tm);

    TRACE( "Current Time: %d:%d:%d\n",
              tm.wHour, tm.wMinute, tm.wSecond );

    ::Sleep(1000);
  }

  *pQuit = FALSE;
  return 0;
}

/////////////////////////////////////////////////////////////
///
// CSimpleWorkerView
```

8. Now edit the handlers as shown here:

```
void CSimpleWorkerView::OnStartThread()
{
  AfxBeginThread(ThreadProc, &m_bQuit);
  m_bRunning = TRUE;
}
```

```
void CSimpleWorkerView::OnUpdateStartThread(CCmdUI* pCmdUI)
{
  pCmdUI->Enable(!m_bRunning & !m_bQuit);
}
void CSimpleWorkerView::OnStopThread()
{
  m_bQuit = TRUE;
m_bRunning = FALSE;
}
void CSimpleWorkerView::OnUpdateStopThread(CCmdUI* pCmdUI)
{
  pCmdUI->Enable(m_bRunning);
}
```

9. Use the ClassWizard to override the **PostNcDestroy** function, and then add the following code:

```
void CSimpleWorkerView::PostNcDestroy()
{
  if(m_bRunning)
    m_bQuit = TRUE;

  if(m_bQuit)
    while(m_bQuit)
      ;
CView::PostNcDestroy();
}
```

10. Build and test the application. Press F5 to start the application under the debugger. Use the Thread menu to start and stop the thread. While the thread is running, observe the Output window. It should look like the following:

```
Thread activated.
Current Time: 14:23:14
Current Time: 14:23:15
Current Time: 14:23:16
Current Time: 14:23:17
The thread 0xFFF6F58B has exited with code 0 (0x0).

Thread activated.
Current Time: 14:23:24
Current Time: 14:23:25
Current Time: 14:23:26
The thread 0xFFF6FB5F has exited with code 0 (0x0).
The thread 0xFFF76523 has exited with code 0 (0x0).
```

```
The program 'E:\SimpleWorker\Debug\SimpleWorker.exe' has exited
with code 0 (0x0)
```

Each time you choose Start Thread from the Thread menu, **OnStartThread()** calls **AfxBeginThread()**. The first parameter is the name of the thread control function. The second parameter is a pointer that the main thread and the worker thread will use to communicate. Here, a single **BOOL** is being used for communication. A global could also have been used in this simple example. In general, however, global variables are an unsophisticated approach to thread communication and can be a dangerous technique. The most common technique used is to pass a pointer to a structure of information to the controlling function.

ThreadProc() obviously doesn't do very much. It loops until the main thread tells it to stop. Each time through the loop, it displays a message of the local time in the output window and then goes to sleep for one second.

There are two ways that a worker thread can safely terminate: executing a **return** statement or calling **AfxEndThread()**.

Thread Communication And Synchronization

In the above section, you saw a simple method for communicating between the main thread and the worker thread. What if there were multiple worker threads that the main thread needed to communicate with, or the reverse—when one of the worker threads needs to communicate with the main thread? Or what about the case in which two threads require access to the same resource and they need to ensure that they are not trying to modify it at the same time? In the follow sections, you'll look at how these situations, as well as others, can be managed.

User-Defined Windows Messages

User-defined Windows messages are probably the easiest method there is for a worker thread to communicate with a user interface thread. The first step is to define a user message:

```
const int WM_THREADEND = WM_APP + 100;
```

After defining the message, you can call **::PostMessage()** from the worker thread to post the message in the message queue connected with the user interface thread. A typical call to **::PostMessage()** might look like this:

```
::PostMessage((HWND)param, WM_THREADEND, 0, 0);
```

The **param** parameter is the window's handle, which is passed to the worker thread through the second parameter of the **AfxBeginThread()** function:

```
AfxBeginThread(ThreadProc, m_hWnd);
```

In the header file for the window, you need a prototype for the message handler:

```
afx_msg LONG OnThreadEnd(WPARAM wParam, LPARAM lParam);
```

Switch to the implementation file for the window, and add a line to the class's message map:

```
ON_MESSAGE(WM_THREADEND, OnThreadEnd)
```

Now add a handler to your implementation file to process the **WM_THREAD END** message. That's all there is to it. Your worker thread can now communicate with the user interface thread.

In cases where you want to retain the ability for the main thread to communicate with the worker thread and you also want the worker thread to send messages to the main thread, you can use an application-defined data structure that contains the necessary information. A typical one might look like this:

```
struct THREAD_INFO
{
  HWND hWnd;
  LPBOOL lpKillThread;
};
```

::**PostThreadMessage()** can be used to post messages to a thread. ::**PostThreadMessage()** takes a thread ID instead of a window handle. The receiving thread must have a message queue.

Events

A somewhat more sophisticated method of signaling between threads is to use *event objects*. An event object can be in one of two states: *signaled* or *unsignaled*. You can create an event and leave it in its unsignaled state. Then, when the condition you wish to signal occurs, you can signal the event. Any other thread watching will know the event is signaled and so perform the appropriate action. Creating an event object is as easy as declaring a global variable and is done as follows:

```
CEvent g_PrintingDone;
```

The **CEvent** constructor has four optional arguments, but you can normally take the defaults as shown in the previous line of code. On creation, the event is in the unsignaled state. To signal the event, you call the object's **SetEvent()** member function:

```
g_PrintingDone.SetEvent();
```

Any thread watching for the signal might do so by calling ::**WaitForSingleObject()**. Here's its prototype:

```
DWORD WaitForSingleObject(
    HANDLE hHandle,            // Handle to the object.
    DWORD dwMilliseconds );  // Time-out interval, in milliseconds
```

The function returns if the interval elapses, even if the object's state is nonsignaled. If **dwMilliseconds** is zero, the function tests the object's state and returns immediately. If **dwMilliseconds** is **INFINITE**, the function's time-out interval never elapses. The return value can be tested for **WAIT_OBJECT_0** or **WAIT_TIMEOUT**. **WAIT_OBJECT_0** indicates that the state of the specified object is signaled. **WAIT_TIMEOUT** means that the time-out interval elapsed, and the object's state is nonsignaled.

Critical Sections

Critical sections are an easy way to ensure that only one thread at a time can access a resource. When you use a critical section, you give your threads a **CCriticalSection** object that they share. When each thread requires exclusive access to the resource, it locks the critical section before accessing the resource. If another thread, running in the same process, tries to lock the same critical section while it's locked by the first thread, the second thread blocks until the first thread unlocks the critical section. MFC encapsulates critical-section objects in the **CCriticalSection** class. To create a critical-section object, you simply create an instance of the **CCriticalSection** class. The following snippet of code shows how you might use a critical section to manage a linked list:

```
// Global data
CCriticalSection g_CriticalSection;
    .
    .
    .
// Thread 1
g_CriticalSection.Lock();
// Add an entry to the linked list
```

```
g_CriticalSection.Unlock();

   .

   .

   .

// Thread 2
g_CriticalSection.Lock();
// Read an entry from the linked list
g_CriticalSection.Unlock();
```

An even better approach might be to build the data you want to protect into a thread-safe class:

```
class CMyList
{
  public:
    CMyList();
    ~CMyList();
    void AddItem(ListItem * theItem);
    void GetFirstItem(ListItem * theItem);
    void GetNextItem(ListItem * theItem);
  private:
    ListItem * pHead;
    ListItem * pTail;
    ListItem * pCurrent;
    CCriticalSection theCriticalSection;
};

   .

   .

   .

void CMyList::AddItem(ListItem * theItem)
{
    theCriticalSection.Lock();
   // Add an entry to the linked list
    theCriticalSection.Unlock();
}

void CMyList:: GetNextItem(ListItem * theItem)
{
    theCriticalSection.Lock();
   // Read the entry from the linked list
    theCriticalSection.Unlock();
}
```

Mutexes

Critical sections are almost all you need to write good multithreaded applications. They are easy to use and impose little overhead. However, they are only visible in one process, and there are occasions when you might need to protect data accessed by two different threads in two different processes. To address this situation, Windows implements a larger variety of critical sections called *mutexes*. "Mutex" is a contraction of the words "mutually" and "exclusive." The **CMutex** class wraps access to mutexes for MFC applications. Here's the **CMutex** constructor:

```
CMutex::CMutex(BOOL bInitiallyOwn = FALSE,
               LPCTSTR lpszName = NULL,
               LPSECURITY_ATTRIBUTES lpsaAttribute = NULL );
```

When you create a **CMutex** object, you can request immediate ownership of the object and can also specify a name for the object. If you create a mutex with the default constructor, you will create a new mutex object that cannot be shared across processes. If you create a mutex and use a name that doesn't exist anywhere on the system, you'll get a new unique handle. Threads in other processes can open the same mutex by creating a **CMutex** object using the same name that the creating thread used.

Let's look at a few snippets of pseudocode to see how this might work for two instances of the same application where both need to access the same file:

```
// Globl Data
CMutex g_FileMutex(FALSE, "MyFileMutex");
    .
    .
    .
if(g_FileMutex.Lock(15000)
{
  // access the file
  g_FileMutex.UnLock();
}
else
{
  // Object did not become signaled, take appropriate action
}
```

MFC provides a couple of classes—**CSingleLock** and **CMultiLock**—that provides an access-control mechanism that can be used to wrap **CMutex**, **CEvent**, and **CSemaphore**. Here's how you might use **CSingleLock** with a **CMutex** object:

```
// Globl Data
```

```
CMutex g_FileMutex(FALSE, "MyFileMutex");
   .
   .
   .
CSingleLock access(&g_FileMutex);
if(access.Lock(15000)
{
  // access the file
  access.UnLock();
}
else
{
  // Object did not become signaled, take appropriate action
}
```

CSingleLock lets you gain access to a single object at a time. In situations where you need to acquire more than one resource, you can use **CMultiLock**. **CMultiLock** requires an array of **CSyncObject** pointers and a count of them. Here's a code fragment that locks on three **CMutex** objects:

```
CSyncObject * pSyncObjs[3];
pSyncObjs[0] = &g_mutex01;
pSyncObjs[1] = &g_mutex02;
pSyncObjs[2] = &g_mutex03;
CMultiLock theLocker(pSyncObjs, 3);
   .
   .
   .
DWORD rtnValue = theLocker.Lock();
```

The **CMultiLock::Lock()** function takes three optional parameters. Here's its prototype:

```
DWORD Lock( DWORD dwTimeOut   = INFINITE,
            BOOL  bWaitForAll = TRUE,
            DWORD dwWakeMask  = 0 );
```

The first parameter is the time-out in milliseconds. Like **CSingleLock**, this value can be the constant **INFINITE**. The second parameter specifies whether or not you want to wait for all of the objects to signal. The third parameter, **dwWakeMask**, is a flag that specifies other conditions that will wake up the thread. Descriptions of the various conditions are provided in the documentation for **::WaitForMultipleObjects()**.

The return value from **CMultiLock::Lock()** indicates what situation caused the function to return. If **Lock** fails, it returns −1. If successful, it returns a value that must be compared against **WAIT_OBJECT_0, WAIT_ABANDONED_0,** and **WAIT_TIMEOUT**. Consult the documentation for **CMultiLock::Lock()** to see how these comparisons should be done.

Semaphores

Events, critical sections, and mutexes are binary in the sense that **Lock()** blocks on them if any other thread has them locked. Semaphores are different. They maintain a resource count. The *semaphore* decreases its count whenever **CSemaphore::Lock()** is called. When the resource count goes to zero, any future calls to **CSemaphore::Lock()** will block the thread making the call. This thread will remain blocked until another thread unlocks the semaphore and thereby raises the resource count, or a specified time-out period has elapsed. A semaphore's count never goes negative.

The maximum number of users who can access the controlled resource at one time is specified during construction of the **CSemaphore** object. To use a **CSemaphore** object, construct the **CSemaphore** object when it is needed. Specify the name of the semaphore you wish to create, and that your application should initially own it. You can then access the semaphore when the constructor returns. The **CSemaphore** constructor takes four parameters and looks like this:

```
CSemaphore::CSemaphore
      ( LONG lInitialCount = 1,          // The initial count
        LONG lMaxCount = 1,              // The maximum count
        LPCTSTR pstrName = NULL,         // Name of the semaphore,
                                         //   must be named in order
                                         //   to be accessed across
                                         //   process boundaries
        LPSECURITY_ATTRIBUTES lpsaAttributes = NULL ); // Security
                                         // attributes
                                         //   of the semaphore
                                         //   object
```

Practice Questions

Question 1

Which statements are true?

❏ a. A user interface thread can only be terminated by calling AfxEndThread().

❏ b. All Win32 operating systems use a scheme called symmetric processing.

❏ c. A suspended thread can call ResumeThread() on itself.

❏ d. A thread can call SuspendThread() on itself.

Answer d is the only correct answer. Answer a is incorrect because a user interface can terminate in two ways: when the thread itself calls **AfxEndThread()** and when a **WM_QUIT** message is posted to its message queue. Answer b is incorrect because Windows 95 and Windows 98 are not SMP operating systems. Answer c is incorrect because when a thread is suspended, it is not running, and if it is not running, it is not possible to call **ResumeThread()** or any other function.

Question 2

Which statement is true?

❏ a. Using multiple threads in your application will make it run faster.

❏ b. User interface threads are normally derived from CWinThread.

❏ c. A worker thread's thread function must be a global function.

❏ d. An easy way for the main thread to communicate with a worker thread is to use PostMessage().

Answer b is the only correct answer. Although user interface threads are sometimes derived from **CWinApp**, they are normally derived from **CWinThread**. Answer a is incorrect because multiple threads can make your application more responsive, not faster. Answer c is incorrect because a worker thread's function can be a static class member function or a function declared outside a class. Answer d is incorrect because a worker thread does not have a message loop.

Question 3

> Which statement is correct? [Check all the correct answers]
>
> ❑ a. Mutexes and semaphores maintain a resource count.
>
> ❑ b. Events and critical sections are binary in nature.
>
> ❑ c. Semaphores can be used to synchronize threads that belong to different processes.
>
> ❑ d. The base class for all MFC synchronization classes is CSyncObject.

Answers b, c, and d are correct. Answer a is incorrect because only semaphores maintain a resource count. Answer b is correct because events, critical sections, and mutexes do not maintain a reference count. Answer c is correct because both mutexes and semaphores allow you to control access to data across different processes. They are both (as are events) shareable by name. Answer d is correct because **CEvent, CCriticalSection, CMutex,** and **CSemaphore** are all derived from the abstract class **CSyncObject**.

Question 4

> Which function or functions must you override when creating a user interface thread?
>
> ○ a. CWinThread::Run() only.
>
> ○ b. CWinThread::ProcessMessageFilter() and CWinThread::InitInstance() only.
>
> ○ c. CWinThread::InitInstance() and CWinThread::ExitInstance() only.
>
> ○ d. CWinThread::InitInstance() only.

Answer d is correct. You must override **InitInstance()** to initialize each new instance of a user interface thread. Answer a is incorrect because you only override **Run()** when you need to customize the default message loop. Answer b is incorrect because you only override **ProcessMessageFilter()** when you want to intercept certain messages before they are sent to your application's normal message processing. Answer c is incorrect because you only override **ExitInstance()** when cleanup needs to be performed when your thread terminates.

Need To Know More?

 Kruglinski, David J., George Shepherd, and Scot Wingo. *Programming Microsoft Visual C++*, 5th ed. Microsoft Press, Redmond, WA, 1998. ISBN 1-57231-857-0.

 Pham, Thuan Q. and Pankaj K. Garg. *Multithreaded Programming with Win32*. Prentice Hall, PTR, Upper Saddle River, NJ:,1998. ISBN 0-13-010912-6.

 Prosise, Jeff. *Programming Windows with MFC*. Microsoft Press, Redmond, WA. 1999. ISBN 1-57231-695-0.

 Richter, Jeffrey. *Advanced Windows*, 3rd Ed. Microsoft Press, Redmond, WA, 1997. ISBN 1-57231-548-2.

 MSDN Library, Platform SDK\Base Services\Processes and Threads

 MSDN Library, Partial Books\Windows 98 Developer's Handbook\Chapter Fourteen Multiple Threading Applications

 MSDN Library, Visual C++ Programmer's Guide\Adding Program Functionality\Details\Multithreading Topics

Dynamic Link
Libraries

Terms you'll need to understand:

√ Dynamic link library (DLL)

√ Implicit linking

√ Explicit linking

√ Exports table

√ Dynamic libraries

√ Static libraries

√ Regular MFC DLL

√ MFC extension DLL

Techniques you'll need to master:

√ Choosing the most appropriate type of DLL to build

√ Building a regular DLL that statically links MFC

√ Building a regular DLL that dynamically links MFC

√ Building an MFC extension DLL

A *dynamic link library (DLL)* is a binary file that contains functions and, sometimes, data and resources that can be used by an application (or another DLL). Before a process can use a DLL, the DLL's file image must first be loaded into memory and mapped to the process's address space. This can be done in one of two ways: implicit load-time linking or explicit runtime linking. DLLs are used for a number of reasons, primarily for either of the following:

➤ Modularizing an application so that functionality can be updated and reused more easily

➤ Sharing common functionality across a number of executing applications at the same time

There are two categories of DLLs in Visual C++—those that use MFC and those that don't. Each category has its own AppWizard. The support provided by AppWizard and MFC in Visual C++ 6 has made the development of DLLs much easier than it was in the past.

Basic DLL Theory

Before you look at MFC's support for DLLs, it is important to understand how Win32 integrates DLLs into a process. As stated above, in order for a process to call a function contained within a DLL, the DLL must be mapped to the virtual address space of the process. The DLL's functions are then available to all the threads running within the process. To the threads in the process, the DLL functions simply look like any other function in the process's address space. Whenever a thread calls a DLL function, the thread's stack is used for the passing of parameters and local variables. Also, the calling thread or process owns any objects created by the DLL function.

DllMain()

When a DLL loads, it will usually need to do some initialization. By default, the linker assigns the main entry point _DllMainCRTStartup() to your DLL. When Windows loads the DLL, it calls this function, which does several things, including initializing the C/C++ runtime library and invoking C++ constructors on static, nonlocal variables. In addition to initializing the C/C++ runtime library, _DllMainCRTStartup() calls a function called DllMain(). Depending on the type of DLL, Visual C++ provides DllMain(), and it gets linked in so that _DllMainCRTStartup() has something to call. Here's one example of code provided by AppWizard:

```
BOOL APIENTRY DllMain( HANDLE hModule,
                       DWORD  ul_reason_for_call,
                       LPVOID lpReserved )
```

```
{
  switch (ul_reason_for_call)
  {
    case DLL_PROCESS_ATTACH:
    case DLL_THREAD_ATTACH:
    case DLL_THREAD_DETACH:
    case DLL_PROCESS_DETACH:
            break;
  }
  return TRUE;
}
```

The first parameter, **hModule**, is a module handle for the dynamic link library instance that is just being loaded. Because the DLL is a separate module, it can have its own resources. If this is the case, **hModule**'s value should be saved in nonvolatile memory for later use.

The second parameter, **ul_reason_for_call**, indicates why **DllMain()** is being called. In addition to being the entry point during loading, **DllMain()** is also called when the DLL is terminating. During load, **ul_reason_for_call** is set to **DLL_PROCESS_ATTACH**, and during termination, it is set to **DLL_PROCESS_ DETACH**. You should also be aware that **DllMain()** is called when a thread in the process creates or destroys a secondary thread. For the creation of a thread, **ul_reason_for_call** will be set to **DLL_ THREAD_ATTACH**, and when a thread terminates, it will be set to **DLL_THREAD_DETACH**.

The third parameter, **lpReserved**, provides addition information concerning initialization and cleanup.

Exporting And Importing Functions

Dynamic linking provides a way for a process to call a function that is not part of its executable code. The executable code for the function, located in a DLL, is linked to the process in one of two ways: implicitly at load-time or explicitly at runtime. Dynamic linking depends on a table contained in the DLL. This table, commonly referred to as the *exports table* or *name table*, holds the symbolic names and ordinal numbers of every function and global data variable the DLL exposes to the outside world. The address for each exposed function is also in the name table. When the process first loads the DLL, it doesn't know the address of the functions it needs to call, but it does know the symbols or ordinals. The dynamic linking process connects the client's calls to the function addresses in the DLL.

The exports table is included in the DLL by the linker. But how does the linker know which symbols (functions and variables) to put in the exports table?

Well, there are two ways of letting the linker know. One way is to list the exported symbols in a module-definition (DEF) file. A module-definition file is a text file that contains statements for defining an EXE file or DLL. The descriptions of the module-definition statements provided in the online *Visual C++ Programmer's Guide* give the command-line equivalent for each statement. The second way to let the linker know which symbols to include is to explicitly declare in the DLL code each function that should be exported. Here's an example:

```
__declspec(dllexport) int DoSomething(int n);
```

In the client code, you need to explicitly declare each of the functions that need to be imported. You do it like this:

```
__declspec(dllimport) int DoSomething(int n);
```

By convention, a header file and a preprocessor macro are used to make the inclusion of DLL declarations much simpler. The technique might look like this:

```
// MYDLL.H
#if !defined(_MYDLL_H_)
#define _MYDLL_H_

#if !defined(_MYDLL_)
#define MYDLL_LIB  __declspec(dllimport)
#else
#define MYDLL_LIB  __declspec(dllimport)
#endif // !defined(_MYDLL_)

MYDLL_LIB int DoSomething(int n);

#endif // !defined(_MYDLL_H_)
```

By including the header file, you let the preprocessor decide whether to export or import the **DoSomething()** function. Now you can share the header file between the DLL developer and the DLL user. The only difference is that the DLL developer needs to define **_MYDLL_H_** in the implementation file prior to the **include** statement:

```
// MYDLL.CPP
#define _MYDLL_H_
#include "mydll.h"
```

Many shops are finding that without a DEF file, there's no centralized interface definition, and they lose control of the interface. DEF files can help you keep your interfaces concise and cohesive, and control dependencies.

While building the DLL, the linker produces a companion import (LIB) file, which contains the symbolic name and ordinal value of all of the exported symbols. The LIB file is a surrogate for the DLL that must be added to the client program's project to enabling implicit linking.

Implicit Linking

As you learned above, there are two ways to link to a DLL: implicitly and explicitly. Implicitly linking your application to a dynamic link library is by far the most common method, for the simple reason that it requires little extra work. The application programmer simply includes the necessary header file, makes the desired function calls, and links with the DLL's static LIB file. During linking, the imported symbols (or ordinals) are matched to the exported symbols in the LIB file, and those symbols are bound into the EXE file.

Now everything is in place so that when the application gets loaded, Windows finds and loads the DLL and then dynamically links it by symbol or by ordinal. When attempting to load a DLL, Windows uses the following order:

1. The directory containing the EXE

2. The current directory for the process

3. The Windows system directory

4. The Windows directory

5. The directories in the system PATH environment variable

Clearly, implicit linking usually is the way to go. However, there are two drawbacks to be aware of:

➤ Load time will be increased if a lot of dynamic link libraries are being used.

➤ A dynamic link library will be loaded even if no function in the DLL is ever called.

To use an extension other than .dll with implicit linking, you must override the default output file name passed to linker (/OUT). This option allows you to change the location and file name of your dynamic link library. It also puts the file name in the LIB file.

Explicit Linking

Explicit linking involves specifically telling Windows which file to load and when to load it. For an application programmer, using explicit linking requires more work than implicit linking. Here's the process:

1. The client calls ::**LoadLibrary()**, passing it the name of the DLL to load. If successful, the specified DLL is mapped into the address space of the calling process and a handle to the DLL is returned to the client. **LoadLibrary()** attempts to locate the DLL, using the same search sequence used for implicit linking. If the function fails, it returns **NULL**.

2. The client calls ::**GetProcAddress()**, passing it the handle returned by ::**LoadLibrary()** and the symbolic name or ordinal value of the desired function. If successful, it returns the address of the DLL's exported function. This address can be used like a normal function pointer. If ::**GetProcAddress()** fails, it returns **NULL**. To get extended error information, call ::**GetLastError()**.

3. Step 2 must be repeated for each function the client wishes to use.

4. When the client is finished with the DLL, it should call ::**FreeLibrary()** to unload the library.

The preceding series of steps is tedious and prone to error, but it allows the application programmer to avoid the drawbacks intrinsic to implicit linking.

MFC DLLs

When you build a DLL with MFC, you must first decide if you want a regular DLL or an extension DLL. This decision can be made, in part, by answering the following questions:

1. Will the DLL use MFC but not expose MFC-derived classes to applications that use the DLL?

2. Will the DLL let applications referencing the DLL use MFC-derived classes from the DLL?

3. Will the DLL be called from other front-end development tools, such as Visual Basic or PowerBuilder?

4. Should the DLL statically or dynamically link to the MFC library?

Regular MFC DLLs

A *regular MFC DLL* is a DLL that uses MFC internally and can export C-style functions. This, of course, means that you need to be mindful of name mangling and use **extern "C"** appropriately. If you need to write a DLL that can be used by Visual Basic, Delphi, or another language that can call C-style functions, then this is the DLL to build.

When you build a regular MFC DLL, you can choose whether to statically or dynamically link it to MFC. The method you choose will determine whether or not you will need to distribute the MFC DLLs with your application.

The easiest method of creating a regular MFC DLL is with the aid of AppWizard. After invoking AppWizard, simply choose the MFC AppWizard (DLL) project type. The first dialog box is where you specify the type of DLL and, for a regular DLL, whether you want it linked statically or dynamically. Refer to Figure 13.1.

Only the Standard Edition of Visual C++ allows dynamic linking to the MFC libraries.

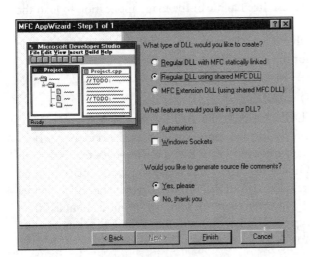

Figure 13.1   MFC AppWizard - Step 1 of 1.

If you look at the code AppWizard generates, you won't find **DllMain()**. You know there must be one, so where is it? Well, as it turns out, it's inside the framework, and you end up with a class derived from **CWinApp** (and a global object of that class), just as you would with an EXE program. The advantage of having a **CWinApp** class is that you can program your DLL as you would any other **CWinApp**-derived class. For example, you can override **CWinApp::InitInstance()** and **CWinApp::ExitInstance()** to initialize and deinitialize your DLL. **DllMain()** calls **InitInstance()** whenever a process attaches to the DLL and calls **ExitInstance()** whenever a process detaches from the DLL.

Once loaded, any C or C++ program that doesn't use MFC can call your DLL. No extra initialization or protection is needed. If your program does, however, use MFC and you want to pass MFC objects between the program and the DLL, some extra work is required in coding the DLL.

MFC keeps some internal global state information regarding the application or DLL. So, if your DLL dynamically links to MFC, you must use the **AFX_MANAGE_STATE()** macro to maintain the proper global state. Here's an example:

```
extern "C" int ShowDlg(HWND hwParent)
{
  AFX_MANAGE_STATE(AfxGetStaticModuleState());
  CWnd * pParent = CWnd::FromHandle(hwParent);
  CDialog dlg(IDD_DIALOG1, pParent);
  return dlg.DoModal();
}
```

By default, MFC uses the resource handle of the main application to load the resource template. Because the exported function, **ShowDlg()**, launches a dialog box using a template that is actually stored in the DLL module, the module state must be switched for the correct handle to be used.

MFC Extension DLLs

Whereas regular MFC DLLs are typically used by non-MFC clients, *MFC extension DLLs* are used to export functions and classes that enhance MFC. For example, let's say you have created a class called **CEmployee** that is derived from the MFC class **CObject**. To export this class, you would place it in an extension DLL. Like a regular MFC DLL, an MFC extension DLL can be created with AppWizard. However, there are a number of fundamental differences between the two types of DLLs. To understand these differences, start by looking at the code AppWizard generates:

```
// MyExt.cpp for the DLL.
//

#include "stdafx.h"
#include <afxdllx.h>

#ifdef _DEBUG
#define new DEBUG_NEW
#undef THIS_FILE
static char THIS_FILE[] = __FILE__;
#endif

static AFX_EXTENSION_MODULE MyExtDLL = { NULL, NULL };

extern "C" int APIENTRY
DllMain(HINSTANCE hInstance, DWORD dwReason, LPVOID lpReserved)
{
  // Remove this if you use lpReserved
  UNREFERENCED_PARAMETER(lpReserved);

  if (dwReason == DLL_PROCESS_ATTACH)
  {
    TRACE0("MYEXT.DLL Initializing!\n");
nkLibrary(MyExtDLL);
    }
    else if (dwReason == DLL_PROCESS_DETACH)
    {
      TRACE0("MYEXT.DLL Terminating!\n");
      / Terminate the library before destructors are called
      AfxTermExtensionModule(MyExtDLL);
    }
    return 1;   // ok
}
```

You'll notice that unlike a regular MFC DLL, an MFC extension DLL does not have a **CWinApp**-derived object. It does, however, have a **DllMain()** function.

DllMain()
The first thing you see in **DllMain()** is the **UNREFERENCED_ PARAM-ETER()** macro. This macro is used to eliminate compiler warnings; however, it's no longer needed with VC++ 6.

Next is an **if** statement that determines whether a process is attaching to or detaching from the DLL. When a process is attaching, the DLL module state needs to be initialized. That is what **AfxInitExtensionModule()** does for you.

AfxInitExtensionModule() takes two parameters: a reference to an **AFX_ EXTENSION_MODULE** structure and a handle to the instance of the DLL. After initialization, the **AFX_EXTENSION_MODULE** structure contains the state of the DLL, which allows the DLL to work with MFC properly. If **AfxInitExtensionModule()** returns **FALSE**, something is terribly wrong, so **0** is returned from **DllMain()**. If **AfxInitExtensionModule()** returns **TRUE**, a **CDynLinkLibrary** object is created. **CDynLinkLibrary** allows the extension DLL to export **CRuntimeClass** objects or resources to the client application. The framework maintains a linked list of **CDyn LinkLibrary** objects.

The last thing to look at is the situation where the process is detaching from the DLL. Here, the only thing to be done is to delete any local storage attached to the module and remove any entries from the message map cache, which is exactly what **AfxTermExtensionModule()** does.

There might, of course, be some other work that you will need to do in DllMain(). While attaching, be sure to do that work after your call to **AfxInitExtensionModule()**, and while detaching, do it before your call to **AfxTermExtensionModule()**.

Exporting Classes And Functions

You normally implement an MFC extension DLL when you need to export classes that are based on MFC. To expose a class, you simply add the C++ class to your project and add the **AFX_EXT_CLASS** macro to the class declaration, as shown here:

```
class AFX_EXT_CLASS CEmployee : public CObject
```

This modification goes into the H file for the class. Both the DLL project and any client project then use this same H file. The **AFX_EXT_CLASS** macro generates different code depending on the situation—it exports the class in the DLL and imports the class in the client.

On occasion, you might not need to export an entire class. In these situations, you still use **AFX_EXT_CLASS**, but instead of placing it in front of the class name, you simply place it in front of the function you wish to export:

```
class CEmployee : public CObject
{
public:
  AFX_EXT_CLASS CEmployee(LPCTSTR name, UINT id, double salary);
  CEmployee();
```

```
CEmployee(CEmployee & theEmp);
. . .
```

Note that the first constructor is exported, whereas the second and third aren't. This means that the client can construct a **CEmployee** object when the employee's name, ID, and salary are known. However, the client can use neither the default constructor nor the copy constructor to build **CEmployee** objects.

Resources

As mentioned previously, resources can be stored in DLLs. Retrieving these resources is easy, provided you have the handle to the module that contains the resource. MFC makes things even easier by providing the **AfxGetResource Handle()** function. This function returns the handle that should be used to retrieve resources. If you're executing in the context of your DLL, MFC will return the handle of your DLL's module; otherwise, it will return the handle of the executing application. Once obtained, the handle can then be used as a parameter to the **LoadResource()** and **FindResource()** functions.

Another situation in which you might use the **AfxGetResourceHandle()** function is when you need to set the default module that MFC uses to first locate requested resources. There are two circumstances where this might be the case: faster resource availability and two similar resources in different modules with the same ID.

If your application code requests that MFC load a resource, MFC first attempts to load the requested resource from the current module. If the requested resource cannot be located in the current module, MFC "walks" the application's linked list of **CDynLinkLibrary** objects in an attempt to locate the resource. Walking the list means that resources at the beginning will be found faster than those at the end. It also means that resources that have the same ID as those earlier will be hidden. Fortunately, you can change the search sequence. Suppose you want your application to search the MFC extension DLL first. Here's how you might do it:

```
// get the EXE's resource handle
HINSTANCE hInstance = AfxGetResourceHandle();

// use the Dll's handle instead
AfxSetResourceHandle(::GetModuleHandle("Employee.dll"));
CString strRes;
strRes.LoadString(IDS_NAME);
```

```
// restore EXE's resource handle
AfxSetResourceHandle(::GetModuleHandle(hInstance));
```

 Be sure to keep in mind that an MFC extension DLL can move pointers to MFC-based objects across the DLL-application boundary and a regular MFC DLL can't.

Practice Questions

Question 1

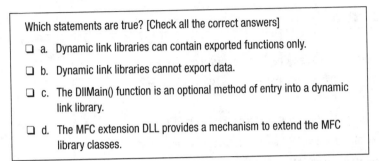

Which statements are true? [Check all the correct answers]

- ❑ a. Dynamic link libraries can contain exported functions only.
- ❑ b. Dynamic link libraries cannot export data.
- ❑ c. The DllMain() function is an optional method of entry into a dynamic link library.
- ❑ d. The MFC extension DLL provides a mechanism to extend the MFC library classes.

The correct answers are c and d. Dynamic link libraries can contain functions, data, and resources. Although each of these items can be defined as exported and internal, data is usually not exported. The name **DllMain()** is an optional placeholder for a user-defined function that provides a single entry/exit point for the DLL. You can extend the MFC library classes by deriving new classes from the existing MFC classes and placing them in an MFC extension DLL for use by MFC applications.

Question 2

Which statements are true? [Check all the correct answers]

- ❑ a. The C++ decorated names in a DEF file are compiler-specific.
- ❑ b. Functions in a DLL to be exported must be listed in a DEF file.
- ❑ c. C++ functions can be exported with undecorated names by using extern "C".
- ❑ d. Ordinal values may be exported from a DLL by using the __declspec() statement.

The correct answers are a and c. The simplest way to export functions is by using the **__declspec(dllexport)** directive in your DLL, which exports a function by name. Alternately, you can place the function names and (optionally) ordinal values in the **EXPORTS** section of a DEF file. All C++ compilers decorate (or mangle) the names of functions. To turn off name mangling for a specific function, you need to specify standard C linkage by using **extern "C"**. Because vendors decorate C++ function names differently, most vendors provide tools that allow you to obtain the decorated names generated by their compiler.

For Visual C++, you can use the linker switch /MAP or the DUMPBIN utility. Answer d is trying to trick you by using the word "exported" in the same sentence with the key word __declspec(). However, __declspec(dllexport) exports symbol names, not ordinal values.

Question 3

Which statements are true? [Check all the correct answers]

☐ a. A regular MFC DLL is a DLL that uses MFC internally and can export C-style functions.

☐ b. A regular MFC DLL must be statically linked to MFC.

☐ c. Both MFC and non-MFC applications can use a regular MFC DLL.

☐ d. Both MFC and non-MFC applications can use an extension DLL.

The correct answers are a and c. A regular MFC DLL can be either statically or dynamically linked to MFC. The advantage of a regular DLL that dynamically links to MFC is that the file size is much smaller than one that statically links to MFC. One disadvantage to dynamically linking to MFC is that you must distribute the appropriate shared MFC DLLs along with your DLL.

Question 4

Which statement is true?

○ a. The AFX_MANAGE_STATE() macro must be placed in an extension MFC DLL that dynamically links to MFC.

○ b. The AFX_MANAGE_STATE() macro must be placed at the beginning of all the exported functions in all MFC DLLs.

○ c. The AFX_MANAGE_STATE() macro is used to maintain the proper global state in regular MFC DLLs that dynamically link to MFC.

○ d. A regular MFC DLL that is statically linked to MFC must be compiled with _AFXDLL defined.

The correct answer is c. When a regular MFC DLL is dynamically linked to MFC, all exported functions that use MFC resources must switch the module's state so that the correct resource handle is used. You can do this by placing the **AFX_MANAGE_STATE()** macro at the beginning of function. The preprocessor symbol **_AFXDLL** must be defined for extension DLLs, and regular DLLs dynamically linked to the MFC library.

Need To Know More?

 Kruglinski, David J., George Shepherd, and Scot Wingo. *Programming Microsoft Visual C++*. 5th Ed. Microsoft Press, Redmond, WA, 1998. ISBN 1-57231-857-0. Chapter 22 covers dynamic link libraries.

 Richter, Jeffrey. *Advanced Windows*. 3rd Ed. Microsoft Press, Redmond, WA, 1997. ISBN 1-57231-548-2. Chapter 12 covers dynamic link libraries.

 MSDN Library, Platform SDK\Base Services\DLLs, Processes, and Threads\Dynamic Link Libraries

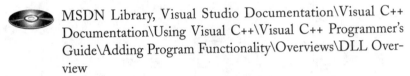 MSDN Library, Visual Studio Documentation\Visual C++ Documentation\Using Visual C++\Visual C++ Programmer's Guide\Adding Program Functionality\Overviews\DLL Overview

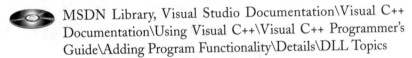 MSDN Library, Visual Studio Documentation\Visual C++ Documentation\Using Visual C++\Visual C++ Programmer's Guide\Adding Program Functionality\Details\DLL Topics

Component Object Model

Terms you'll need to understand:

- ✓ Interface
- ✓ IUnknown
- ✓ QueryInterface(), AddRef(), Release()
- ✓ HRESULT
- ✓ SUCCEEDED() and FAILED()
- ✓ Reference counting
- ✓ GUID, IID, and CLSID
- ✓ IClassFactory
- ✓ CreateInstance()
- ✓ CoGetClassObject()
- ✓ CoCreateInstance()
- ✓ STDMETHOD and STDMETHOD_
- ✓ STDMETHODIMP and STDMETHODIMP_
- ✓ DECLARE_INTERFACE() and DECLARE_INTERFACE_()
- ✓ PURE
- ✓ DllGetClassObject()
- ✓ DllCanUnloadNow()
- ✓ CoInitialize()
- ✓ CoUninitialize()

Techniques you'll need to master:

- ✓ Understanding the purpose of and use of (COM)
- ✓ Describing what a class factory object is and how it is used
- ✓ Writing code that implements the IClassFactory and the IUnknown interfaces
- ✓ Writing code that implements a COM component
- ✓ Creating a COM component by using the SDK
- ✓ Instantiating and invoking a COM component

271

COM is the foundation on which ActiveX, OLE, OLE DB, ADO, and DirectX are built. It is a language- and platform-independent standard that defines how different objects can communicate with each other using a common protocol. It provides a way in which large and small applications can be decomposed into a number of small standalone components. Because COM is language-neutral, developers can write these components in the language of their choice. However, some languages are better than others. Those languages that support arrays of function pointers, and can call functions through those pointers, can be used directly. These include C, C++, and Pascal. Languages that do not support arrays of functions can be extended so that they can create and call COM objects. The most obvious example of such a language is Visual Basic.

Key to COM is the idea of interfaces. An *interface* is a logical grouping of behaviors. It consists of function prototypes and a protocol for their use. Each interface is a contract between the client program and the COM object that specifies the passing of parameters and return values. Microsoft has predefined a number of *standard interfaces* that any COM object can support. Interfaces that are user-defined are called *custom interfaces*.

Interfaces

Every COM object supports one or more interfaces. There is, however, one interface that every COM object must support: the **IUnknown** interface. All COM interfaces are derived from **IUnknown**, directly or indirectly. In C++, the **IUnknown** interface is an abstract class that has three pure virtual functions: **QueryInterface()**, **AddRef()**, and **Release()**.

> Don't confuse COM inheritance with C++ inheritance. Although you can model COM inheritance using C++ inheritance, it isn't a requirement. Lots of COM objects have been written in C.

It is important to realize that the definition of an interface does not include the implementation. The component has the responsibility of providing the implementation that is appropriate to that component. Realize also that an interface can be reused in different situations. One component can be swapped with another component that supports the same set of interfaces.

Pure abstract base classes provide little more than a table of function entry points, and the entry points are allocated by the compiler. This table is commonly known as a *vtable*. Any language or tool that can use pointers or references can construct this table. However, C++ compilers use vtables, so using the vtable as the standard COM interface structure was a logical choice. This standard also makes defining and implementing COM interfaces easy for C++ programmers.

QueryInterface()

As mentioned above, the **IUnknown** interface declares three pure virtual functions, and it is up to the component to provide the implementation. The first of these functions, **QueryInterface()**, is used by the client to request an interface of the component. If successful, the client can then, through indirection, call the functions of the interface. Here's the prototype for **QueryInterface()**:

```
HRESULT QueryInterface(REFIID iid, void ** ppvObject);
```

As you can see, **QueryInterface()** has two parameters. The first is an interface identifier, which will be discussed in detail later. The second is a pointer to an interface pointer. The return value is of type **HRESULT**, which is the COM return type. **HRESULT** is simply a 32-bit number containing an error code. **HRESULT** consists of four parts: severity (bit 31), reserved (bits 29 and 30), facility code (bits 16 to 28), and return code (bits 0 to 15). The predefined severity constants are **SEVERITY_SUCCESS** (zero) and **SEVERITY_ERROR** (one). You should use the **SUCCEEDED()** or **FAILED()** macros to test an **HRESULT** for simple success or failure. Use **if(SUCCEEDED(hr))** or **if(FAILED(hr))**; don't use **if(S_OK == hr)**. Many of the predefined **HRESULT** codes can be found in winerror.h; however, Table 14.1 provides a list of the key ones.

You can use the **MAKE_HRESULT**(*sev, fac, code*) macro to construct an **HRESULT**.

There are five rules that every implementation of **QueryInterface()** must follow:

1. *Identity*—Comparing **IUnknown** pointers is the only way of determining object identity. If the **IUnknown** pointers match, the interfaces are from the same component.

2. *Predictability*—If a call to **QueryInterface()** for a pointer to a specified interface succeeds the first time, it must succeed again; if it fails the first time, it must fail on all subsequent queries.

3. *Reflexivity*—Querying an interface for itself always succeeds.

Table 14.1	Key HRESULT error codes.
Name	**Meaning**
S_OK	Success
S_FALSE	Success, but function returned Boolean **FALSE**, in contrast to **S_OK**
E_ABORT	Operation aborted
E_ACCESSDENIED	General access-denied error
E_FAIL	Unspecified failure
E_HANDLE	Function has been given an invalid handle
E_INVALIDARG	One or more arguments are invalid
E_NOINTERFACE	No such interface supported
E_NOTIMPL	Not implemented
E_OUTOFMEMORY	Failed to allocate necessary memory
E_POINTER	Invalid pointer
E_UNEXPECTED	Catastrophic failure

4. *Symmetry*—If you can successfully query an interface for a second interface, you can also successfully query the first interface from the second interface.

5. *Transitivity*—If you can query an interface for a second interface and you can successfully query the second interface for a third interface, then you can successfully query the first interface for the third interface.

Reference Counting

COM interfaces do not have virtual destructors; instead, COM has a strict protocol that is followed for deleting objects. All objects that implement **IUnknown,** or any interface based upon it, must maintain an internal reference count on that interface. When a client gains a pointer to an interface, the internal reference count must be incremented. When a client releases a pointer to an interface, the internal reference count is decremented. And if the internal reference count goes to zero, the object destroys itself. **AddRef()** and **Release()** are the functions used to increment and decrement the reference count.

To ensure that reference counts are maintained correctly, remember the following:

➤ If the call to **QueryInterface()** is successful, the reference count is incremented.

➤ If you make a copy of an interface pointer, you must call **AddRef()**.

➤ If you are finished with an interface, you must call **Release()**.

Identifiers And The Registry

You saw in the preceding example where **QueryInterface()**'s first parameter is of type **REFIID**, which is a reference to an **IID**. IIDs are just **GUIDs** used to identify interfaces. **GUID** stands for Globally Unique Identifier. A GUID is a 128-bit number created mainly from a combination of the Ethernet card in the machine it's generated on and the current time in 100-nanosecond intervals since 1582.

 You can generate your own **GUIDs** using the **GUID** generator (guidgen.exe) supplied with Visual C++. If you should ever need to generate a **GUID** programmatically, you can call **CoCreateGuid()**.

Every interface must be identified by an **IID** so that there is a unique way of referring to it with no possibility of name clashes between it and all the other interfaces in the world. Using **QueryInterface()**, the client asks an activated object if it supports a particular interface by passing it an **IID**. But how does the client locate the component? Well, it simply asks COM, and COM looks in the Registry. Each COM object class is identified by a **CLSID**, which, like an **IID**, is a **GUID**. All the COM classes registered on your system have entries under **HKEY_CLASS_ROOT\CLSID\{***clsid***}**, where {*clsid*} represents the 128-bit number. Under the **CLSID\{***clsid***}** is a key that associates the **CLSID GUID** with a server that will create and manage the COM object when requested. These keys are usually **InprocServer32** or **LocalServer32**. Under each of these keys is the path and file name of the DLL or EXE that creates and manages the COM object.

For example, Figure 14.1 shows the Registry Editor, sized to show the Excel object's **CLSID,** along with its local server, which is excel.exe.

Using COM

You now know how the client specifies which object it wants and how COM can use that information to determine which module to load. However, still to be answered is how the component actually gets created. Well, a specific type of COM component, known as a *class factory object*, is used to create the requested object. A class factory object is responsible for instantiating other components.

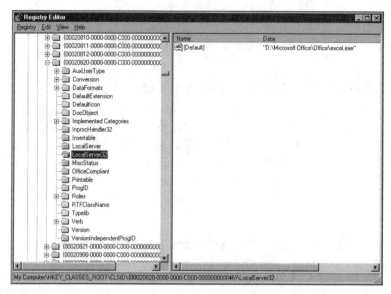

Figure 14.1 Registry Editor displaying a **CLSID** registration entry.

Class factory objects implement **IClassFactory,** which is derived from **IUnknown.** In addition to the functions inherited from **IUnknown,** class factory objects must implement the two functions declared in **IClassFactory:** **CreateInstance()** and **LockServer().** Here are their prototypes:

```
HRESULT IClassFactory::CreateInstance(IUnknown * pUnkOuter,
             REFIID riid, void ** ppvObject);
HRESULT IClassFactory::LockServer(BOOL fLock);
```

CreateInstance() creates an instance of the object and returns an interface pointer to the client through **ppvObject.** So, now you know that the class factory object creates the requested object, but how does the class factory object get created? You call **CoGetClassObject()** to create a class factory object. You can then use the returned **IClassFactory** pointer to call **CreateInstance()** to create one or more instances of the requested object. If you only need to create one instance of an object, you can use **CoCreateInstance().** It combines the two steps of obtaining a class factory and then calling **CreateInstance(). CoCreateInstance()** creates a single uninitialized object of the class associated with a specified **CLSID.** If you call **CoCreateInstance()** several times, the class factory may be created and destroyed between each call. Here are the prototypes for these two functions:

```
STDAPI CoGetClassObject(
    REFCLSID rclsid,      //CLSID associated with the class object
```

```
    DWORD dwClsContext,  //Context for running executable code
    COSERVERINFO * pServerInfo, // Machine info
    REFIID riid, // Reference to the identifier of the interface
    LPVOID * ppv // Indirect pointer interface requested in riid
);

STDAPI CoCreateInstance(
    REFCLSID rclsid, // Class identifier (CLSID) of the object
    LPUNKNOWN pUnkOuter, // Pointer to whether object is or isn't
                         // part of an aggregate
    DWORD dwClsContext, // Context for running executable code
    REFIID riid, // Reference to the identifier of the interface
    LPVOID * ppv // Indirect pointer interface requested in riid
);
```

The **rclsid** and **riid** parameters are both references to **GUID**s.

 Make sure that you understand the difference between **CoGetClassObject()** and **CoCreateInstance()**. Also, be careful that you don't confuse **CreateInstance()** with **CoCreateInstance()**. You should also be aware that there is a **CoCreateInstanceEx()** function.

The **dwClsContext** parameter specifies the server application type:

➤ **CLSCTX_INPROC_SERVER**—The class factory runs in the same process as the client. The full path of the host DLL is provided as the default value of the **InprocServer32** subkey in the Registry.

➤ **CLSCTX_INPROC_HANDLER**—A special in-process server that implements client-side proxies for remote method invocations. The DLL is specified in the **InprocHandler32** subkey.

➤ **CLSCTX_LOCAL_SERVER**—The class factory runs on the same machine but in a different process. The EXE is specified in the **LocalServer32** subkey.

➤ **CLSCTX_REMOTE_SERVER**—The class factory runs on a totally different machine. The remote process is specified in the **Remote ServerName** subkey.

➤ **CLSCTX_SERVER**—The class factory will support in-process, local, or remote activation requests. This definition is the "bitwise OR" of **CLSCTX_INPROC_SERVER, CLSCTX_LOCAL_SERVER,** and **CLSCTX_REMOTE_SERVER.**

➤ **CLSCTX_ALL**—Indicates all class contexts. This definition is the "bitwise OR" of **CLSCTX_INPROC_HANDLER** and **CLSCTX_SERVER**.

The **pServerInfo** parameter is a pointer to a machine on which the class object is instantiated (NULL if the machine is local). The **ppv** parameter is where the interface pointer goes. **STDAPI** indicates that the function returns a value of type **HRESULT**.

Implementing A COM Client And Server

This section shows how to build a simple in-process COM component using the SDK. In order to place the emphasis on the steps involved in building a COM component, the component itself will be simple. This component will have only one interface and two methods. As you will see, most of the source code, of which there will be more than you might expect, will be concerned with supporting the mechanics of interacting with the COM subsystem. Be forewarned, however: To do this exercise, every line of code must be typed by hand. All of the code is provided in the text.

This component implements the business rules regarding shipping for a mail-order catalog business. To simplify things, the business only ships within the continental U.S.

Building The Server

The server will implement two classes. **CComShipping** will implement a custom interface called **IShipping**, which will provide two methods: **Basic()** and **Overnight()**. Each of these methods takes two parameters. One parameter specifies the total weight of the items to be shipped, and the other returns the dollar amount the customer will be charged for shipping and handling. (Remember, the return value for most COM methods is **HRESULT**.) CShipping ClassFactory is a class factory for the **CComShipping** class. For each call to IClassFactory::CreateInstance(), a new instance of **CComShipping** will be created on the heap by the **CShippingClassFactory** class object, using C++'s **new** operator.

Start up Visual C++ and create a new Win32 dynamic link library project named "ShippingProject". Make sure that you select An Empty DLL Project.

Building The Interface

The first thing you need to do is uniquely identify the component and its interface. Create a new header file named "guids.h". Then use the GUIDGEN utility to create two **GUID**s, and place them in guids.h. The first **GUID** names the component **CLSID_Shipping**, and the second identifies the interface as **IID_IShipping**. The guids.h file will also bring in the necessary operating system **include** files, windows.h and ole2.h. Here's what guids.h should look like (of course, your **GUID** values will be different):

```
#if !defined(GUIDS_H_INCLUDED)
#define GUIDS_H_INCLUDED

#include <windows.h>
#include <ole2.h>

// {D0C10AB4-CA5B-11d2-A46F-00C04F688CFA}
DEFINE_GUID(CLSID_Shipping,
0xd0c10ab4, 0xca5b, 0x11d2, 0xa4, 0x6f, 0x0, 0xc0, 0x4f, 0x68,
 0x8c, 0xfa);

// {DDE05C0E-CA5B-11d2-A46F-00C04F688CFA}
DEFINE_GUID(IID_IShipping,
0xdde05c0e, 0xca5b, 0x11d2, 0xa4, 0x6f, 0x0, 0xc0, 0x4f, 0x68,
 0x8c, 0xfa);

#endif  // !defined(GUIDS_H_INCLUDED)
```

The next step is to declare the component's interface as an abstract class. Create another header file, and name it "IShipping.h". This file contains the information needed by a client in order to use the component's functionality. It provides the correct vtable layout and parameter types so clients can access the component. Here's IShipping.h:

```
#if !defined(ISHIPPING_H_INCLUDED)
#define ISHIPPING_H_INCLUDED

#include "guids.h"

DECLARE_INTERFACE_(IShipping, IUnknown)
{
  STDMETHOD(Basic)( /* in */  double dWeight,
                    /* out */ double * dCost) PURE;

  STDMETHOD(Overnight)( /* in */  double dWeight,
                        /* out */ double * dCost) PURE;
};

#endif  // !defined(ISHIPPING_H_INCLUDED)
```

Notice the first thing that happens is that the guids.h header file is included. Immediately after that is where the definition of the interface actually starts. The **DECLARE_INTERFACE_()** macro is used when the new interface inherits from another interface. There is a variation to this macro that doesn't have the trailing underscore. This second form is used when creating a new interface that doesn't inherit from another interface. The **DECLARE_INTERFACE_()** above expands to this:

```
interface IShipping : public IUnknown
```

This might not be quite what you would expect. However, the token **interface** is simply a redefinition of the C++ keyword **struct**.

The next item of interest is the **STDMETHOD()** macro, which is used to declare the **Basic()** and **Overnight()** methods. Like **DECLARE_INTERFACE()**, there are two flavors of **STDMETHOD()**. The first version, **STDMETHOD()**, is used when the method returns a standard COM **HRESULT**. The other version, **STDMETHOD_()** (again, note the trailing underscore), allows you to specify your own return type. You should normally use the first form, which is in compliance with Microsoft's interface design rule that interface methods should return an **HRESULT**. This rule provides a logical, consistent way of handling errors. Because error information is handled through a method's return value, an output parameter is used to return method output. Like the **Basic()** and **Overnight()** methods, the output parameter is always returned via a pointer.

The last item to look at is the **PURE** macro that is placed at the end of a method declaration. This macro evaluates to = **0**, which designates the method as a C++ pure virtual function.

After expansion of all the macros, the declaration of the **IShipping** interface would look like the following:

```
interface IShipping : IUnknown
{
virtual HRESULT __stdcall Basic( /* in */  double dWeight,
                                 /* out */ double * dCost) = 0;
virtual HRESULT __stdcall Overnight(/* in */  double dWeight,
                                    /* out */ double * dCost) = 0;
};
```

Implementing The Component

Because the interface is an abstract class, it simply provides a contract between the COM component and the outside world. Before the component can be used, there must be an actual class that can be instantiated. So, the next step in the process implements such a class. Use the Insert|New Class... menu to create a new class, and name it "CComShipping". Here's what ComShipping.h should look like:

```
// ComShipping.h: interface for the CComShipping class.
//
//////////////////////////////////////////////////////////////////////

#if !defined(AFX_COMSHIPPING_H_INCLUDED_)
#define AFX_COMSHIPPING_H_INCLUDED_

#if _MSC_VER > 1000
#pragma once
#endif // _MSC_VER > 1000

#include "IShipping.h"

class CComShipping  : public IShipping
{
public:
  CComShipping();
  ~CComShipping();

  // IUnknown
  STDMETHOD(QueryInterface)(REFIID, void**);
  STDMETHOD_(ULONG, AddRef)();
  STDMETHOD_(ULONG, Release)();

  // IShipping
  STDMETHOD(Basic)( /* in */  double dWeight,
                    /* out */ double * dCost);

  STDMETHOD(Overnight)( /* in */  double dWeight,
                        /* out */ double * dCost);
private:
  long m_lRef; // reference count
};

#endif // !defined(AFX_COMSHIPPING_H_INCLUDED_)
```

Everything here should be familiar. **CComShipping** inherits from the **IShipping** interface, which, in turn, inherits from **IUnknown**. This means there are five pure virtual functions for which **CComShipping** has to provide implementations. There is one private data member, **m_lRef**, which is used to hold the reference count.

Next comes the implementation file. Here's ComShipping.cpp:

```cpp
// ComShipping.cpp: implementation of the CComShipping class.
//
//////////////////////////////////////////////////////////////////////
#include "ComShipping.h"
#include "Counters.h"

struct ShippingCost
{
  double weight;
  double cost;
};
static const ShippingCost g_CostTable[] =
{
  { 5.0,  8.75},
  {10.0, 13.95},
  {20.0, 22.50},
  {30.0, 33.50},
  {50.0, 44.25}
};
static const long g_NumCost =
                  sizeof(g_CostTable) / sizeof(ShippingCost);
//////////////////////////////////////////////////////////////////////
// Construction/Destruction
//////////////////////////////////////////////////////////////////////

CComShipping::CComShipping()
  : m_lRef(0)
{
  CCounters::IncObjectCount();
}


CComShipping::~CComShipping()
{
  CCounters::DecObjectCount();
}


//////////////////////////////////////////////////////////////////////
// IUnknown
//////////////////////////////////////////////////////////////////////
STDMETHODIMP CComShipping::QueryInterface(REFIID rIID,
                                          void ** ppv)
{
 if(!ppv)
    return E_POINTER;
```

```
  *ppv = 0;
  if(rIID==IID_IUnknown || rIID == IID_IShipping)
    *ppv = static_cast<IShipping*>(this);
  else
    return E_NOINTERFACE;

  reinterpret_cast<IUnknown*>(*ppv)->AddRef();
  return S_OK;
}

STDMETHODIMP_(ULONG) CComShipping::AddRef()
{
  return InterlockedIncrement(&m_lRef);
}

STDMETHODIMP_(ULONG) CComShipping::Release()
{
  if(InterlockedDecrement(&m_lRef) == 0)
  {
    delete this;
    return 0;
  }
  return m_lRef;
}

//////////////////////////////////////////////////////////////
// IShipping
//////////////////////////////////////////////////////////////
STDMETHODIMP CComShipping::Basic(double dWeight, double * dCost)
{
  static const double theRatePerPound = 1.05;
  int i = 0;
  do
  {
    *dCost = g_CostTable[i].cost;
    if(dWeight <= g_CostTable[i].weight)
      break;
    i++;
  } while(i < g_NumCost);

  if(i == g_NumCost)
    *dCost = dWeight * theRatePerPound;

  return S_OK;
}
```

```
STDMETHODIMP CComShipping::Overnight(double dWeight,
                                         double * dCost)
{
   static const double theOverNightAdder = 7.75;

   Basic(dWeight, dCost);
   *dCost += theOverNightAdder;

   return S_OK;
}
```

The constructor initializes the internal reference count and then calls a function that increments the instance count for the DLL. Rather than using global data, the object count is wrapped in a simple class. Its data member, as well as its functions to increment, decrement, and read the count, is static, meaning that an object never needs to be instantiated. Next is the destructor, which simply decrements the instance count for the DLL by calling **CCounters::DecObjectCount()**. You'll see the **CCounters** class later.

Following the destructor is the implementation of the **IUnknown** interface. First is the **QueryInterface()** method, which in addition to returning a pointer back to the method's caller does two other things. It verifies that the caller is asking for a supported interface and calls **AddRef()** to increment the reference count.

AddRef() and **Release()** are concerned with reference counting. They use the Win32 API thread-safe functions **InterlockedIncrement()** and **Inter lockedDecrement()**. Take a look at **Release()**. Notice how it deletes itself when the reference count goes to zero.

The remaining two member functions provide the implementation of the **IShipping** interface. Although they are what make the component unique, they couldn't be much simpler.

The Class Factory

Now that you have the component implemented, you need to provide a way for it to be instantiated. Remember that every COM object is instantiated by a class factory. This implies that you need to write a class factory for **CComShipping**. As previously discussed, the class factory will inherit from the standard **IClassFactory** interface, which, in turn, inherits from **IUnknown**. **IClassFactory** is composed of two methods. These two methods plus the three for **IUnknown** mean a total of five functions must be implemented.

Start by creating a new class, and name it **CShippingClassFactory**. Here's what the header should look like:

```
// ShippingClassFactory.h: interface for the CShippingClassFactory.
//
//////////////////////////////////////////////////////////////////
#if !defined(AFX_SHIPPINGCLASSFACTORY_H_INCLUDED_)
#define AFX_SHIPPINGCLASSFACTORY_H_INCLUDED_

#if _MSC_VER > 1000
#pragma once
#endif // _MSC_VER > 1000

#include "IShipping.h"

class CShippingClassFactory : public IClassFactory
{
public:
  CShippingClassFactory();

    // IUnknown
  STDMETHOD(QueryInterface)(REFIID, void**);
  STDMETHOD_(ULONG, AddRef)();
  STDMETHOD_(ULONG, Release)();

  // IClassFactory
  STDMETHOD(CreateInstance)(LPUNKNOWN, REFIID, void **);
  STDMETHOD(LockServer)(BOOL);

private:
  long m_lRef; // reference count
};

#endif // !defined(AFX_SHIPPINGCLASSFACTORY_H_INCLUDED_)
```

Nothing new here, so let's move on to ShippingClassFactory.cpp:

```
// ShippingClassFactory.cpp: implementation of the
// CShippingClassFactory class.
//
//////////////////////////////////////////////////////////////////
#define INITGUID
#include "ShippingClassFactory.h"
#include "ComShipping.h"
#include "Counters.h"


//////////////////////////////////////////////////////////////////
// Construction/Destruction
//////////////////////////////////////////////////////////////////
```

```
CShippingClassFactory::CShippingClassFactory()
  : m_lRef(0)
{
}


/////////////////////////////////////////////////////////////////
// IUnknown
/////////////////////////////////////////////////////////////////
STDMETHODIMP CShippingClassFactory::QueryInterface(REFIID rIID,
                                                   void ** ppv)
{
  if(!ppv)
    return E_POINTER;

  *ppv = 0;
  if(rIID==IID_IUnknown || rIID == IID_IClassFactory)
    *ppv = static_cast<IClassFactory*>(this);
  else
    return E_NOINTERFACE;

  reinterpret_cast<IUnknown*>(*ppv)->AddRef();
  return S_OK;
}
STDMETHODIMP_(ULONG) CShippingClassFactory::AddRef()
{
  return InterlockedIncrement(&m_lRef);
}
STDMETHODIMP_(ULONG) CShippingClassFactory::Release()
{
  if(InterlockedDecrement(&m_lRef) == 0)
  {
    delete this;
    return 0;
  }
  return m_lRef;
}
/////////////////////////////////////////////////////////////////
// IClassFactory
/////////////////////////////////////////////////////////////////
STDMETHODIMP CShippingClassFactory::CreateInstance(
                                    LPUNKNOWN pUnkOuter,
                                    REFIID rIID,
                                    void ** ppvInterface)
{
  if(!ppvInterface)
    return E_POINTER;
  *ppvInterface = 0;
```

```
// Check for a controlling unknown
if(pUnkOuter)
  return CLASS_E_NOAGGREGATION;

CComShipping *pObj = new CComShipping;
if(!pObj)
  return E_OUTOFMEMORY;

HRESULT hr = pObj->QueryInterface(rIID, ppvInterface);
if(FAILED(hr))
{
  delete pObj;
  return hr;
}
  return S_OK;
}
STDMETHODIMP CShippingClassFactory::LockServer(BOOL bLock)
{
  if(bLock)
    CCounters::IncLockCount();
  else
    CCounters::DecLockCount();
  return S_OK;
}
```

The first thing to look at is the **#define INITGUID** statement. Earlier you created a guids.h file and placed two **GUID**s in it using the **DEFINE_GUID** macro. If you recall, the **DEFINE_GUID** macro takes the name of the variable that you want to declare and then the components of the **GUID**. The beauty of using this macro is that you don't need to worry about declaring global, static constant, class, and interface IDs that are accessible from anywhere within the application, and at the same time, you ensure that they are only defined once.

Normally, **DEFINE_GUID** ignores all the **GUID** pieces and just expands to a declaration. For example:

```
DEFINE_GUID(CLSID_Shipping,
0xd0c10ab4, 0xca5b, 0x11d2, 0xa4, 0x6f, 0x0, 0xc0, 0x4f, 0x68,
0x8c, 0xfa);
```

expands into

```
extern "C" const GUID CLSID_Shipping;
```

However, by declaring **INITGUID** before including the standard OLE header files, the **DEFINE_GUID** macro will expand to the following:

```
extern "C" const CLSID_Shipping = \
{ 0xd0c10ab4, 0xca5b, 0x11d2, 0xa4, 0x6f, 0x0, 0xc0, 0x4f, 0x68,
  0x8c, 0xfa)};
```

Remember that a given **GUID** must be included in your source code with **INITGUID** defined exactly one time.

Because **IUnknown** is familiar, move to the implementation of the **IClassFactory** methods. Most of the action is in **CreateInstance()**, so let's start there.

The first thing **CreateInstance()** does is check to see whether another object is trying to use the component as part of an aggregate relationship. This component doesn't support aggregation. Therefore, if another object tries to use it in this way, **CreateInstance()** returns the **CLASS_E_NOAGGREGATION** error.

Next, **CreateInstance()** creates the new **CComShipping** object. If **new** failed, the **E_OUTOFMEMORY** error is returned. Otherwise, the object was created, and **CreateInstance()** calls **QueryInterface()** to obtain an interface pointer to return back to the client. The interface pointer is passed back to the client through the pointer the client provided when calling **CreateInstance()**. If the new object doesn't support the requested interface, **QueryInterface()** returns the **E_NOINTERFACE** error, causing **CreateInstance()** to delete the object and pass the error code back to the client.

The only thing left is the **LockServer()** function, which is trivial. It either calls **CCounters::IncLockCount()** or **CCounters::DecLockCount()**, depending on the value of the input parameter.

The CCounters Class

In a multithreaded environment, you can never be certain that global data hasn't been modified without your knowledge, unless you use some external means to ensure otherwise. There are a number of ways that this might be managed. In the following code, a class is used to wrap the variables that would normally have global scope. This restricts their scope to a specific class. Additionally, the **InterlockedIncrement()** and **InterlockedDecrement()** functions are being used to prevent more than one thread from using the same variable simultaneously. This might be viewed as overkill, but it's trivial to implement, and **CCounter** can easily be moved from one project to the next. Here's the code for Counters.h followed by Counters.cpp:

```
// Counters.h: interface for the CCounters class.
//
//////////////////////////////////////////////////////////////////////
```

```
#if !defined(AFX_COUNTERS_H_INCLUDED_)
#define AFX_COUNTERS_H_INCLUDED_
#if _MSC_VER > 1000
#pragma once
#endif // _MSC_VER > 1000
#include <windows.h>
class CCounters
{
public:
  // Locks
  static long GetLockCount()
              { return m_nLocks; }
  static long IncLockCount()
              { return InterlockedIncrement(&m_nLocks); }
  static long DecLockCount()
              { return InterlockedDecrement(&m_nLocks); }
  // Objects
  static long GetObjectCount()
              { return m_nObjects; }
  static long IncObjectCount()
              { return InterlockedIncrement(&m_nObjects); }
  static long DecObjectCount()
              { return InterlockedDecrement(&m_nObjects); }
private:
  static long m_nLocks;
  static long m_nObjects;
};
#endif // !defined(AFX_COUNTERS_H_INCLUDED_)


// Counters.cpp: implementation of the CCounters class.
//
////////////////////////////////////////////////////////////////////
#include "Counters.h"

// Initialize the static variables
long CCounters::m_nLocks   = 0UL;
long CCounters::m_nObjects = 0UL;
```

Creating The Component's Housing

Everything is starting to come together. You now have a complete implementation of a COM object and a class factory to create it. The only thing left is the code needed to make the component an in-process server. There are a number of issues related to how COM obtains class factories from servers and how servers communicate to COM that they are ready to be unloaded. This is one area where in-process servers and local servers are very different. We'll look at a local server later. For an in-process server, both of these problems involve two functions that are exposed from the DLL, **DllGetClassObject()** and **DllCanUnloadNow()**. These functions are shown in the following code in this section.

Create a new file and call it "InProcServer.cpp". This provides the housing for the component and contains the implementation of the **DllGetClassObject()** and **DllCanUnloadNow()** functions. Here's the code:

```cpp
// InprocServer.cpp: implementation of initialization routines.
//
////////////////////////////////////////////////////////////////////////
#include "guids.h"
#include "ShippingClassFactory.h"
#include "Counters.h"

// This function is called by COM to obtain an interface pointer
// to the housing's class factory
STDAPI DllGetClassObject( REFCLSID rClsID,
                          REFIID rIID,
                          void ** ppvInterface )
{
  if(rClsID != CLSID_Shipping)
    return CLASS_E_CLASSNOTAVAILABLE;

  CShippingClassFactory * pFactory = new CShippingClassFactory;
  if(!pFactory)
    return E_OUTOFMEMORY;

  HRESULT hr = pFactory->QueryInterface(rIID, ppvInterface);
  if(FAILED(hr))
  {
    delete pFactory;
    return hr;
  }

  return S_OK;
}
// This function is called by COM to determine whether the
// server can be unloaded from memory.
STDAPI DllCanUnloadNow()
{
  return ( CCounters::GetLockCount()   == 0   &&
           CCounters::GetObjectCount() == 0 ) ?  S_OK : S_FALSE;
}
```

The **DllGetClassObject()** function is called by COM whenever it needs to obtain a class factory for a given component. It takes three parameters: the class ID that identifies which class factory COM is looking for, an interface ID that identifies which interface within the factory is being requested, and the address of where to put the interface pointer.

DllGetClassObject() checks the class ID to ensure that COM is requesting the class factory for the Shipping component. If anything other than the Shipping class factory is being requested, **E_FAIL** is returned. Otherwise, the class factory is instantiated and its **QueryInterface()** method is called. As you can see, this is looking a lot like **CShippingClassFactory()::CreateInstance()**. Because you understand how **CShippingClassFactory::CreateInstance()** works, the remaining code in **DllGetClassObject()** should be evident.

DllCanUnloadNow() is even easier; it simply communicates to the COM subsystem when it is acceptable to unload the in-process server from memory. Thanks to the **CCounters** class, the implementation of **DllCanUnloadNow()** is trivial. As long as either count is nonzero, **DllCanUnloadNow()** returns an **S_FALSE**, indicating that it cannot be unloaded.

The Module Definition File

You need to explicitly export the **DllGetClassObject()** and **DllCanUnloadNow()** functions. Create a text file, name it "ShippingProject.def", and add it to your project. Here's what you need to type in:

```
LIBRARY         ShippingProject
EXPORTS
        DllGetClassObject       PRIVATE
        DllCanUnloadNow         PRIVATE
```

Registering The Server

When a client wants to use the server, it makes a request to the COM subsystem. The client does this by passing COM the server's **CLSID**. COM then looks for a match in the Registry and, if found, uses the information stored under the key to locate the server. COM then loads the server into memory, calls **DllGetClassObject()**, and returns a pointer to the class factory's interface back to the client. This process will be covered in more detail later, when you build the client, but first you need to register your server.

Normally, the housing will contain four functions instead of just the two you have implemented. The two that you have not implemented are **DllRegisterServer()** and **DllUnregisterServer()**. As their names indicate, they provide a component with the ability to register and unregister itself. These functions will be covered later. For now, you will need to register the server by hand.

Create a text file and name it "InProcServer.reg". Type in the below information. There's a lot of typing involved, and you need to be careful that you get it right. It has been spaced out to make it easier to read, but you need to be sure that all the text following an **HKEY_CLASSES_ROOT** is placed on one line. In other words, except for the first line, all other lines should start with **HKEY_CLASSES_ROOT**.

```
REGEDIT
HKEY_CLASSES_ROOT\MailOrder.Shipping.1 =
   MailOrder Shipping Component

HKEY_CLASSES_ROOT\MailOrder.Shipping.1\CLSID =
   {D0C10AB4-CA5B-11d2-A46F-00C04F688CFA}

HKEY_CLASSES_ROOT\MailOrder.Shipping =
   MailOrder Shipping Component

HKEY_CLASSES_ROOT\MailOrder.Shipping\CurVer =
   MailOrder.Shipping.1

HKEY_CLASSES_ROOT\MailOrder.Shipping.1\CLSID =
   {D0C10AB4-CA5B-11d2-A46F-00C04F688CFA}

HKEY_CLASSES_ROOT\CLSID\{D0C10AB4-CA5B-11d2-A46F-00C04F688CFA} =
   MailOrder Shipping Component

HKEY_CLASSES_ROOT\CLSID\{D0C10AB4-CA5B-11d2-A46F-00C04F688CFA}
\ProgID = MailOrder.Shipping.1

HKEY_CLASSES_ROOT\CLSID\{D0C10AB4-CA5B-11d2-A46F-00C04F688CFA}
\VersionIndependentProgID = MailOrder.Shipping

HKEY_CLASSES_ROOT\CLSID\{D0C10AB4-CA5B-11d2-A46F-00C04F688CFA}
\InprocServer32 =
   E:\MailOrder\ShippingProject\Debug\ShippingProject.dll

HKEY_CLASSES_ROOT\CLSID\{D0C10AB4-CA5B-11d2-A46F-00C04F688CFA}
\NotInsertable
```

You'll need to use the **CLSID GUID** from guids.h. Be sure that the line that specifies the location of the DLL is the proper path on your machine.

After you have everything typed in, you can merge it into the Registry using RegEdit or by double-clicking on the file in Explorer. Figures 14.2 and 14.3 show the entries using RegEdit.

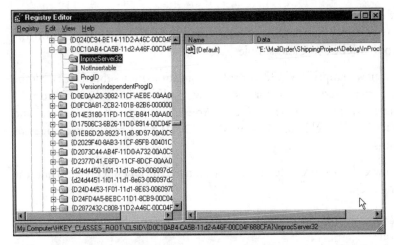

Figure 14.2   Registry Editor displaying the CLSID information for shipping.

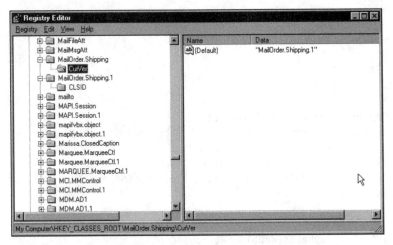

Figure 14.3   Registry Editor displaying the MailOrder.Shipping entry.

Building The Client

The client will be composed of four logical sections or phases:

1. *Initialization*—This section will call the necessary APIs needed to initialize the COM subsystem and prepare it for use.

2. *Acquisition*—This section obtains the class factory and then uses it to create a new instance of the COM component.

3. *Usage*—This section uses the object obtained in the acquisition phase to do some work.

4. *Termination*—This section uninitializes the COM subsystem.

These four sections will exercise each portion of the component. Because the goal is to gain an understanding of how to build a COM client application, the client code will be short and simple.

Create a new "empty" Win32 console application in a subdirectory of the ShippingProject server's directory, so relative paths to the server's files can be used. Name the project "Client". Go to Project|Settings|C/C++|General and add **WIN32_WINNT=0x0400** or **WIN32_DCOM** to the Preprocessor definitions.

Add a new C/C++ source file to the project, name it "Client.cpp", and add the following code:

```cpp
// Client.cpp: implementation of the client for the "shipping"
// server.
//
/////////////////////////////////////////////////////////////////////
#include <iostream>
#include <string>
using namespace std;

#define INITGUID
#include "..\IShipping.h"

// Display error message and HRESULT
inline void DisplayError(const string & theErrorText, HRESULT hr)
{
  cout << "Error: " << theErrorText << '\n';
  cout << "HRESULT: 0x" << hex << static_cast<ULONG>(hr)
       << endl;
}

inline void DisplayBasic(double dW, double dC)
{
  cout << "Weight: " << dW << "  Basic cost: " << dC << endl;
}

inline void DisplayOvernight(double dW, double dC)
{
  cout << "Weight: " << dW << "  Overnight cost: " << dC << endl;
}


int main()
{
  cout << "Initializing section" << endl;
  HRESULT hr = CoInitializeEx(0, COINIT_APARTMENTTHREADED);
```

```
  if(FAILED(hr))
  {
    DisplayError("Unable to initialize COM", hr);
    return -1;
  }

  cout << "Acquisition section" << endl;

#define USEPROGID
#if !defined(USEPROGID)
  IClassFactory *pICF;
  hr = CoGetClassObject( CLSID_Shipping,
                         CLSCTX_INPROC_SERVER,
                         0,
                         IID_IClassFactory,
                         (void**) &pICF );
#else
  CLSID clsid;
  hr = CLSIDFromProgID(L"MailOrder.Shipping.1", &clsid);
  if(FAILED(hr))
  {
    DisplayError("Could not obtain CLSID from ProgID", hr);
    CoUninitialize();
    return -1;
  }

  IClassFactory *pICF;
  hr = CoGetClassObject( clsid,
                         CLSCTX_INPROC_SERVER,
                         0,
                         IID_IClassFactory,
                         (void**) &pICF );
#endif
  if(FAILED(hr))
  {
    DisplayError("Could not obtain Shipping class factory", hr);
    CoUninitialize();
    return -1;
  }

  IShipping *pIShip;
  hr = pICF->CreateInstance(0, IID_IShipping, (void**) &pIShip);
  if(FAILED(hr))
  {
    DisplayError("Could not create a new Shipping object", hr);
    pICF->Release();
    CoUninitialize();
```

```
        return -1;
    }

    pICF->Release();
    pICF = 0;

    cout << "Usage section" << endl;
    double dWeight, dCost;

    dWeight = 4.99;
    pIShip->Basic(dWeight, &dCost);
    DisplayBasic(dWeight, dCost);

    dWeight = 5.00;
    pIShip->Basic(dWeight, &dCost);
    DisplayBasic(dWeight, dCost);

    dWeight = 50.00;
    pIShip->Basic(dWeight, &dCost);
    DisplayBasic(dWeight, dCost);

    dWeight = 51.00;
    pIShip->Basic(dWeight, &dCost);
    DisplayBasic(dWeight, dCost);

    dWeight = 5.00;
    pIShip->Overnight(dWeight, &dCost);
    DisplayOvernight(dWeight, dCost);

    dWeight = 49.99;
    pIShip->Overnight(dWeight, &dCost);
    DisplayOvernight(dWeight, dCost);

    pIShip->Release();
    pIShip = 0;

    cout << "Termination section" << endl;
    CoUninitialize();

    return 0;
}
```

Initialization

The **CoInitializeEx()** function prepares the COM library for use by the current process. This function returns an error for invalid arguments, out of memory, and others. It returns **S_OK** if the COM library was initialized successfully. If the COM library is already initialized and ready for use, **CoInitializeEx()** returns **S_FALSE**.

Acquisition

After initializing the COM library, the next step is to actually create an instance of a COM component. **CoGetClassObject()** creates and provides a pointer to an interface on a class associated with a specified **CLSID**. Notice that the client code shows two ways in which the **IClassFactory** pointer can be obtained. If **USEPROGID** is defined, **CLSIDFromProgID()** is used to obtain the **CLSID**, which is then passed to **CoGetClassObject()**. If **USEPROGID** isn't defined, the **CLSID_Shipping** constant is used. After the pointer to the class factory object is obtained, it is used to call **CreateInstance()**, which creates a new uninitialized object.

Because in this example only one object is needed, the code could be simplified by using **CoCreateInstance()** instead of **CoGetClassObject()** and **CreateInstance()**. Remember, **CoCreateInstance()** connects to the class factory object associated with the specified **CLSID**, creates a single uninitialized object, and then releases the class factory object.

Usage

After obtaining an interface pointer for the new object, the object's methods can be called. When you are finished with the object, you simply call **Release()**.

Termination

When all of the interface pointers have been properly released, the program terminates the COM subsystem by calling **CoUninitialize()**.

Practice Questions

Question 1

You are implementing an in-process COM component that has a ProgID of "MathComponent". In which subkey of HKEY_CLASSES_ROOT is the fully qualified path and DLL name of your server located?

○ a. CLSID\InprocServer32

○ b. CLSID\{*clsid*}\InprocServer32

○ c. InprocServer32

○ d. ProgID\InprocServer32

The correct answer is b. COM classes are registered under the **HKEY_CLASSES_ROOT\CLSID** key. Each class is a subkey of **HKEY_CLASSES_ROOT\CLSID**, where the name of the class subkey corresponds to the class **GUID**. The class subkey has several critical subkeys hanging off it, which vary depending on the server type. Here, the COM component is an inprocess server, so the path and DLL name are located in the **InProcServer32** subkey. The complete entry would look like: HKEY_CLASSES_ROOT\CLSID\{*clsid*}Inproc Server32 = "C:\My Components\MathComponent.dll".

Question 2

If you only want to create a single instance of a COM component, which function should you call?

○ a. CreateInstance()

○ b. CoGetClassObject()

○ c. CoCreateInstance()

○ d. CoGetInstance()

The correct answer is c. Although you can create a single instance of an object by calling **CoGetClassObject()** and then calling **CreateInstance()**, it is less complicated to simply call **CoCreateInstance()**. Therefore, answers a and b are incorrect. **CoCreateInstance()** combines the two steps of obtaining a class factory and creating a single instance of the component. **CoGetInstance()** is not a legal function. Therefore, answer d is incorrect.

Question 3

Which one of the following statements is true regarding reference counting?

- ○ a. The client should call AddRef() whenever it makes a copy of a non-null interface pointer.
- ○ b. QueryInterface() always initializes the reference count by setting it to one.
- ○ c. After calling Release(), the client can continue to safely use the interface pointer until the pointer goes out of scope.
- ○ d. If the client deletes a non-null interface pointer, the object's destructor must call Release().

The correct answer is a. Answer b is incorrect because successful calls to **QueryInterface()** causes the object's reference count to be increased by one, not set to one. Answer c is incorrect because when the client calls **Release()** it is telling the object that it is no longer needed. The client must then assume that the interface pointer is invalid. From a practical standpoint, when **Release()** is called an object's reference count can theoretically fall to zero after any call to **Release()**, and therefore, an interface pointer should never be used after calling **Release()**. Answer d is incorrect because the client should not delete a COM object; instead, the client calls **Release()**, and if the reference count goes to zero, the object can self-destruct by performing **delete this**.

Question 4

Which of the following statements are true? [Check all the correct answers]

- ❑ a. When an interface is returned by a call to QueryInterface(), the client can assume that the reference count has been incremented.
- ❑ b. COM methods should indicate error conditions by returning HRESULT, a 32-bit code.
- ❑ c. Given any interface pointer to an object, you can get the pointer to any other interface implemented by the object.
- ❑ d. In addition to CoGetClassObject() and CoCreateInstance(), the client can call CoCreateInstanceEx() to obtain a COM object.

The correct answers are a, b, c, and d. This is a trick question because all answers are correct.

Need To Know More?

 Box, Don. *Essential COM*. Addison-Wesley, Reading, MA, 1998. ISBN 0-201-63446-5. This is not a book for beginners. However, if you have been working with COM for a while and want to gain real insight into how COM actually works, this is the book for you. The author addresses the spirit of COM as much as he does the technology. He knows the subject well and covers the material thoroughly.

 Chappell, David. *Understanding ActiveX and OLE: A Guide for Developers and Managers*. Microsoft Press, Redmond, WA, 1996. ISBN 1-57231-216-5. This book is very well written and easy to understand. It isn't a programming book and contains little code. However, if you don't know COM and want to establish a good foundation, this is the book to use. The author covers the basic theory and concepts with the least clutter.

 Rogerson, Dale. *Inside COM: Microsoft's Component Object Model*. Microsoft Press, Redmond, WA, 1997. ISBN 1-57231-349-8. This book does a good job of explaining the theory and implementation of COM objects. It covers basically the same territory as Chappell's book but includes a fair amount of code to illustrate key points. It has clear explanations on each of the key areas.

 MSDN Library, Platform SDK\Component Services\COM

 MSDN Library, Technical Articles\Component Object Model

 www.microsoft.com/com is Microsoft's Web page for COM. This Web site contains white papers, presentations, resources, technologies, and so on. Under Resources, you'll find the COM Spec and a number of sample programs. Explore this Web page; it provides a wealth of information.

MFC And COM

Terms you'll need to understand:

- √ ExternalQueryInterface()
- √ ExternalAddRef()
- √ ExternalRelease()
- √ InternalAddRef()
- √ InternalRelease()
- √ InternalQueryInterface()
- √ METHOD_PROLOGUE()
- √ Interface map
- √ DECLARE_INTERFACE_MAP()
- √ BEGIN_INTERFACE_PART()
- √ END_INTERFACE_PART()
- √ BEGIN_INTERFACE_MAP()
- √ END_INTERFACE_MAP()
- √ INTERFACE_PART()
- √ COleObjectFactory
- √ IClassFactory2
- √ DECLARE_OLECREATE()
- √ IMPLEMENT_OLECREATE()

Techniques you'll need to master:

- √ Using the AppWizard to generate an MFC in-process server
- √ Creating a COM component by using MFC

301

As it does for the Win32 (API), MFC abstracts much of COM to allow developers to concentrate on the business problem they are solving. This chapter looks at the support MFC provides for the development of COM components.

COM Components

Within the MFC framework, **CCmdTarget** provides the implementation for the **IUnknown** interface. The three **IUnknown** methods—**QueryInterface()**, **AddRef()**, and **Release()**—are implemented in two sets. The first set—**ExternalQueryInterface()**, **ExternalAddRef()**, and **ExternalRelease()**—is used the most. The other set has an **Internal** prefix.

MFC COM interfaces are implemented as nested classes. To simplify the coding required, MFC includes an implementation of *interface maps* and a number of macros similar to MFC's implementation of message maps and dispatch maps. The surrounding class is the component, which is derived from **CCmdTarget**. The nested classes form the interfaces. Used within the interface methods, the macro **METHOD_PROLOGUE()** creates access to the outer class by defining a variable **pThis**. With this variable, access is granted to the **IUnknown** methods and data members of the component. The **METHOD_PROLOGUE()** macro uses the C runtime function **offsetof()** to calculate a back pointer.

METHOD_PROLOGUE() takes two parameters: The first is the component class name, and the second is the current interface. The naming convention for interfaces used by the MFC COM macros is **m_xInterfaceName**, where InterfaceName is the second parameter and **m_x** is a prefix attached by the macro.

 See "TN038: MFC/OLE IUnknown Implementation" for a detailed description of MFC's implementation of **IUnknown**.

The Interface Maps

The following macros declare and define the interface maps:

Header file:

➤ DECLARE_INTERFACE_MAP()

➤ BEGIN_INTERFACE_PART()

➤ END_INTERFACE_PART()

Source file:

➤ BEGIN_INTERFACE_MAP()

➤ END_INTERFACE_MAP()

➤ INTERFACE_PART()

DECLARE_INTERFACE_MAP() declares the map and lookup table used by **InternalQueryInterface()**. BEGIN_INTERFACE_PART() and END_INTERFACE_PART() together create an interface as a nested class, create an instance of the interface, and generate function prototypes for **QueryInterface()**, **AddRef()**, and **Release()**. The STDMETHOD() and STDMETHOD_() macros are placed between BEGIN_INTERFACE_PART() and END_INTERFACE_PART() to declare additional members of the interface.

The BEGIN_INTERFACE_MAP() and END_INTERFACE_MAP() macros are used in the implementation file to actually define the interface map. For each interface implemented, there is one or more INTERFACE_PART() macro invocations.

The MFC COleObjectFactory Class

The **COleObjectFactory** class is used to create objects at runtime. This class is a wrapper around **IClassFactory2**. All you need to do is use macros like these in the class declaration:

```
DECLARE_DYNCREATE(CShipping)
DECLARE_OLECREATE(CShipping)
```

And use macros like these in the implementation file:

```
IMPLEMENT_DYNCREATE(CShipping, CCmdTarget)
// {FF62987B-AA1B-11d2-A46A-00C04F688CFA}
IMPLEMENT_OLECREATE(CShipping, "CShipping", 0xff62987b, 0xaa1b,
    0x11d2, 0xa4, 0x6a, 0x0, 0xc0, 0x4f, 0x68, 0x8c, 0xfa);
```

DECLARE_DYNCREATE() and IMPLEMENT_DYNCREATE() enable **CShipping** to be created dynamically at runtime. DECLARE_OLECREATE() and IMPLEMENT_OLECREATE() declare and define a global object of class **COleObjectFactory** with the specified **CLSID**.

IClassFactory2 is an extension of **IClassFactory**. **IClassFactory2** enables a class factory executing on a licensed machine to provide a license key that can be used later to create an object instance on an unlicensed machine. The license key gives only the one client application the right to instantiate objects through **IClassFactory2** when a full machine license does not exist.

Implementing An MFC COM Server

Unlike the SDK server, which only had one interface, this server will have two interfaces. The first interface will be an enhanced version of the interface used in the last chapter. However, to postpone the matter of versioning, just assume that no relation exists between the component in this chapter and the one in the last chapter. The second interface will implement the business rules regarding sales tax.

Start up Visual C++, create a new MFC AppWizard (dll) project, and name it "DomesticProject". At MFC AppWizard - Step 1 of 1, select the Regular DLL Using Shared MFC DLL option, make sure that Automation is checked, and then click on Finish.

The wizard creates a source, resource, module definition, object description language, and a variety of header files. The object description language (ODL) is not required for the **DomesticProject** component. It was provided to support ActiveX Automation, which you will not be using. To remove the ActiveX Automation support, you need to do the following:

➤ Comment out or delete all references to messages maps (leave the wizard-generated comments) in both DomesticProject.h and DomesticProject.cpp.

➤ Delete the ODL file from the project.

➤ Comment out or delete the line **1 TYPELIB "DomesticProject.tlb"** from **DomesticProject.rc** (you'll need to open it as a text file).

➤ Comment out or delete the lines #include <afxodlgs.h> // MFC OLE dialog classes and #include <afxdisp.h> // MFC Automation classes from StdAfx.h.

Building The Interface

First, you'll need to declare the **IDomesticShipping** and **IStateSalesTax** interfaces. Add the following header file to your project:

```
// interface.h : header file
//
#if !defined(IDomesticShipping_INTERFACE_H_INCLUDED)
#define IDomesticShipping_INTERFACE_H_INCLUDED

#include "guids.h"

DECLARE_INTERFACE_(IDomesticShipping, IUnknown)
{
  STDMETHOD(Basic)(double dWeight, double * dCost) PURE;
  // Three business days or less
  STDMETHOD(Express)(double dWeight, double * dCost) PURE;
  // Two business days or less
  STDMETHOD(Expedited)(double dWeight, double * dCost) PURE;
  STDMETHOD(Overnight)(double dWeight, double * dCost) PURE;
};

DECLARE_INTERFACE_(IStateSalesTax, IUnknown)
{
  STDMETHOD(GetStateTax)(BSTR bstrState, double * dTax) PURE;
};

#endif  // !defined(IDomesticShipping_INTERFACE_H_INCLUDED)
```

The **GetStateTax()** method's first parameter is a **BSTR**. Make sure that you understand what a **BSTR** is and know the rules for creating and deleting them.

Notice the **#include "guids.h"** statement. You need to create the file and provide **DEFINE_GUID**s for **IID_IDomesticShipping** and **IID_IStateSalesTax** like you did in the last chapter. However, don't include a **GUID** for the **CLSID**; the ClassWizard will automatically define it and place it in your component's implementation file. You won't distribute the **CLSID** to clients; instead, clients will use the program identifier to load the component module. Your guids.h file should look like this:

```
#if !defined(IDomesticShipping_GUIDS_H_INCLUDED)
#define IDomesticShipping_GUIDS_H_INCLUDED

// {4ED5EEA6-CCD7-11d2-A46F-00C04F688CFA}
DEFINE_GUID(IID_IDomesticShipping,
0x4ed5eea6, 0xccd7, 0x11d2,
0xa4, 0x6f, 0x0, 0xc0, 0x4f, 0x68, 0x8c, 0xfa);
```

```
// {561E5D9F-CCD7-11d2-A46F-00C04F688CFA}
DEFINE_GUID(IID_IStateSalesTax,
0x561e5d9f, 0xccd7, 0x11d2,
0xa4, 0x6f, 0x0, 0xc0, 0x4f, 0x68, 0x8c, 0xfa);

#endif  // !defined(IDomesticShipping_GUIDS_H_INCLUDED)
```

Implementing The Component

When implementing your component, you now have a couple of approaches. One approach is to not use the wizards, which means you must type everything, as you did for the SDK version. The other approach, which is shown here, is to use the wizards and delete or change the code appropriately.

Using ClassWizard, create a new class derived from **CCmdTarget**. Name it "**CDomestic**" and select the Createable By Type ID radio button within the Automation group box. In the adjunct edit box, enter **MailOrder.Domestic** (see Figure 15.1).

In Domestic.h and Domestic.cpp, remove all references to the message map. Because the component won't be using the **IDispatch** interface, also remove all references from the header and source. In Domestic.h, comment out or delete **DECLARE_DISPATCH_MAP()**. In Domestic.cpp, comment out or delete the following:

➤ **BEGIN_DISPATCH_MAP(CDomestic, CCmdTarget)**

➤ **END_DISPATCH_MAP()**

➤ **INTERFACE_PART(CDomestic, IID_IDomestic, Dispatch)**

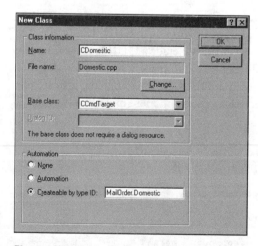

Figure 15.1   New Class dialog box for **CDomestic**.

Next, comment out or delete references to Automation:

➤ EnableAutomation()

➤ AfxOleLockApp()

➤ AfxOleUnlockApp()

You now have a basic COM component you can use as a foundation for your Domestic component. Add the following shaded code to Domestic.h:

. . .

```
// Attributes
public:

// Operations
public:
  // IDomesticShipping members
  BEGIN_INTERFACE_PART(Shipping, IDomesticShipping)
     STDMETHOD(Basic)(double dWeight, double * dCost);
     // Three business days or less
     STDMETHOD(Express)(double dWeight, double * dCost);
     // Two business days or less
     STDMETHOD(Expedited)(double dWeight, double * dCost);
     STDMETHOD(Overnight)(double dWeight, double * dCost);
  END_INTERFACE_PART(Shipping)

  // IStateSalesTax members
  BEGIN_INTERFACE_PART(SalesTax, IStateSalesTax)
     STDMETHOD(GetStateTax)(BSTR bstrState, double * dTax);
  END_INTERFACE_PART(SalesTax)

// Overrides
```

. . .

MFC COM components consist of an outer wrapper class that maintains a nested class for each interface that it supports. The **DECLARE_INTERFACE_MAP()** macro tells the framework that this class will have a custom interface map. Recall that it provides various methods and data members required to support the interface mapping process. The **BEGIN_INTERFACE_PART()** declares the beginning of a new nested class and includes the standard methods to support the **IUnknown** interface. Here, two nested classes—**XShipping** and **XSalesTax**—are declared; the "X" is prefixed to the name to differentiate the nested classes from global classes, which start with "C", and interfaces, which start with "I".

END_INTERFACE_PART() finishes the class declaration and then declares an instance of the class with a variable name of m_*xnested-class-name*. In this case, the two nested members are named **m_xShipping** and **m_xSalesTax**. **END_ INTERFACE_PART()** also makes the nested class a *friend* of the outer class so that the nested class is able to access the outer class's member data and functions. Between the **BEGIN_INTERFACE_PART()** and **END_INTERFACE_ PART()** macros, each of the methods the interface will expose are declared using the **STDMETHOD** and **STDMETHOD_()** macros. These macros are used so that the **_stdcall** and **virtual** keywords are provided as appropriate for the target platform.

Remember that, in addition to these macros, two other important macros exist that must always be included in the class definition of an MFC COM component. Jointly, these two macros are key in the instrumentation to allow for automatic class-factory support. The first macro, **DECLARE_DYNCREATE()**, declares that the class allows dynamic creation. The second, **DECLARE_OLECREATE()**, actually declares the class factory.

At this point, the **CDomestic** class has been declared, and by a variety of MFC macros, the class has been instrumented to include support for the two nested interface classes, an interface map, and a class factory. You now need to turn your attention to Domestic.cpp and do the following:

➤ Remove the definition of **IID_IDomestic**.

➤ Add an entry for each interface to the interface map.

➤ Implement **IUnknown** for the nested classes.

➤ Implement the **IDomesticShipping** and **IStateSalesTax** interface.

Following is the implementation of the **CDomestic** class; non-germane code is not shown and changes from what the ClassWizard generated are shaded:

```
// Domestic.cpp : implementation file
//
#include "stdafx.h"
#include "DomesticProject.h"
#include <initguid.h>
#include "interface.h"
#include "Domestic.h"

...

BEGIN_INTERFACE_MAP(CDomestic, CCmdTarget)
  INTERFACE_PART(CDomestic, IID_IDomesticShipping, Shipping)
```

```
  INTERFACE_PART(CDomestic, IID_IStateSalesTax, SalesTax)
END_INTERFACE_MAP()

// {8CC2B79F-CCBB-11D2-A46F-00C04F688CFA}
IMPLEMENT_OLECREATE(CDomestic, "MailOrder.Domestic", 0x8cc2b79f,
0xccbb, 0x11d2, 0xa4, 0x6f, 0x0, 0xc0, 0x4f, 0x68, 0x8c, 0xfa)

/////////////////////////////////////////////////////////////////////
// CDomestic message handlers

// IDomesticShipping
STDMETHODIMP_(ULONG)
CDomestic::XShipping::AddRef()
{
  METHOD_PROLOGUE(CDomestic, Shipping);
  return pThis->ExternalAddRef();
}

STDMETHODIMP_(ULONG)
CDomestic::XShipping::Release()
{
  METHOD_PROLOGUE(CDomestic, Shipping);
  return pThis->ExternalRelease();
}
STDMETHODIMP
CDomestic::XShipping::QueryInterface(REFIID riid, void ** ppv)
{
  METHOD_PROLOGUE(CDomestic, Shipping);
  return pThis->ExternalQueryInterface(&riid, ppv);
}

STDMETHODIMP
CDomestic::XShipping::Basic(double dWeight, double * dCost)
{
  *dCost = dWeight * theBasicRatePerPound;
  return S_OK;
}

...

// IStateSalesTax

...

STDMETHODIMP
CDomestic::XSalesTax::GetStateTax(BSTR bstrState, double * dTax)
```

```
{
    // look up tax rate and return it in *dTax

    return S_OK;
}
```

The first thing to look at is the **#include <initguid.h>** statement. This file brings in the version of **DEFINE_GUID** that defines your **IID**s.

In the header file (Domestic.h), **DECLARE_INTERFACE_MAP()** is used to tell the framework that **CDomestic** has a custom interface map. In the implementation file (Domestic.cpp), **BEGIN_INTERFACE_MAP()** and **END_INTERFACE_MAP()** are used to actually define the interface map. Between the **BEGIN_INTERFACE_MAP()** and **END_INTERFACE_MAP()** macros, there is an **INTERFACE_PART()** macro for each **IID** supported. The **INTERFACE_PART()** macro maps the **IID** to a specific part of the **CDomestic** class. In this case, the **INTERFACE_PART()** macros connect **IID_IDomesticShipping** with **m_xDomesticShipping** and **IID_IStateSalesTax** with **m_xSalesTax**, respectively. **CCmdTarget::External QueryInterface()** uses this map to return pointers to the embedded objects when requested. You don't need to include an entry for **IID_IUnknown**; the framework will use the first interface in the map (in this case, **m_ xDomestic Shipping**) when **IID_IUnknown** is requested.

The **BEGIN_INTERFACE_PART()** macro is used in the header file to declare **QueryInterface()**, **AddRef()**, and **Release()** for each of the nested classes. The actual implementation for each of these functions is provided in the implementation file. As shown above for **CDomestic::XShipping**, the implementations for each of these functions all work the same way and couldn't be much simpler. First, the **METHOD_PROLOGUE()** macro is used to define the **pThis** variable and to switch to the correct module state. Then, the **IUnknown** method inherited from **CCmdTarget** is called on the **pThis** pointer. The implementation for **CDomestic::XSalesTax** would be similar to the definitions for **CDomestic::XShipping**. Although it's possible to create a macro that can be used to automatically generate these functions (earlier in MFC/OLE development, this was indeed the case), it's difficult to set break points when a macro generates more than one line of code. For this reason, this code is expanded manually.

Like many other macros in MFC, the **DECLARE_DYNCREATE()** and **DECLARE_OLECREATE()** macros have their **IMPLEMENT** counterparts. The **IMPLEMENT_DYNCREATE()** macro expands to provide **CDomestic** with a method named **CreateObject()**. **CreateObject()** is used by the MFC-provided class factory to create new instances of **CDomestic**. The **IMPLEMENT_OLECREATE()** macro initializes the class factory object (**COleObjectFactory**) and provides it with the information it will need to create new instances of **CDomestic**.

All of these macros can be confusing. Be sure that you know which ones go in the header file and which ones go in the implementation file. Also, make sure that you know the purpose of each one and which ones work together.

The Component's Housing

So far, the fact that the in-process server is a dynamic link library (DLL) has been ignored. It's now time to turn your attention to the component's housing.

AppWizard Generated Code

When requesting a regular DLL with Automation support, AppWizard generates the following code:

```
// DomesticProject.cpp : Defines the initialization routines

...


/////////////////////////////////////////////////////////////////////////
// CDomesticProjectApp initialization
BOOL CDomesticProjectApp::InitInstance()
{
   // Register all OLE server (factories) as running.  This enables
   // the OLE libraries to create objects from other applications.
   COleObjectFactory::RegisterAll();
   return TRUE;
}


/////////////////////////////////////////////////////////////////////////
// Special entry points required for in-proc servers
STDAPI DllGetClassObject(REFCLSID rclsid, REFIID riid,
LPVOID* ppv)
{
   AFX_MANAGE_STATE(AfxGetStaticModuleState());
   return AfxDllGetClassObject(rclsid, riid, ppv);
}


STDAPI DllCanUnloadNow(void)
{
```

```
  AFX_MANAGE_STATE(AfxGetStaticModuleState());
  return AfxDllCanUnloadNow();
}

// by exporting DllRegisterServer, you can use regsvr.exe
STDAPI DllRegisterServer(void)
{
  AFX_MANAGE_STATE(AfxGetStaticModuleState());
  COleObjectFactory::UpdateRegistryAll();
  return S_OK;
}
```

The server contains an application instance that is derived from **CWinApp**. For an in-process server, the application class is extremely simple. However, it must possess an override of **InitInstance()** that calls the **COleObjectFactory::RegisterAll()** static function to register all object factories of the DLL.

AppWizard has provided three special entry points for the in-process server. The names of two of these functions are familiar. Notice that both **DllGetClassObject()** and **DllCanUnloadNow()** simply turn around and call an MFC global function, neither of which are documented in the MSDN Library.

AfxDllGetClassObject() iterates through the list of object factories, returning the factory that has a **CLSID** that matches the requested **CLSID**. **AfxDllCanUnloadNow()** checks for instantiated objects and factories with a reference count greater than one. It returns a **TRUE** or **FALSE** based on its findings.

The last function to look at is **DllRegisterServer()**. As you can probably guess, this function registers the component. It does so by calling the **COleObjectFactory::UpdateRegistryAll()** static function. This function iterates over each of the object factories residing in the server, querying the factory's **CLSID** and creating the appropriate Registry entries. There is also a **DllUnregisterServer()** function, which is used to unregister the server.

Finishing The Server

The code AppWizard provides is fine, but incomplete. For completeness, the **DllUnregisterServer()** function needs to be added to the housing. Here's the code that you need to add to DomesticProject.cpp:

```
#include "stdafx.h"
#include "DomesticProject.h"
#include <afxctl.h>    // brings in AfxOleUnregisterClass
```

```
#ifdef _DEBUG

...

STDAPI DllUnregisterServer(void)
{
  AFX_MANAGE_STATE(AfxGetStaticModuleState());

  CLSID clsid;
  HRESULT hr = ::CLSIDFromProgID(L"MailOrder.Domestic", &clsid);
  if(hr != S_OK)
    return FALSE;

  return AfxOleUnregisterClass(clsid, "MailOrder.Domestic");
}
```

Be sure to update **DomesticProject.def** to export **DllUnregisterServer()**.

Registering The Server

Because an in-process server resides in a DLL and doesn't receive command-line arguments, a helper application is required to load the in-process server and call the **DllRegisterServer()** method. Visual C++ ships with a utility called RegSvr32, whose sole purpose is to register and unregister in-process servers. To register a server, you need to type a command line from within the server DLL directory. To unregister a server, you need to specify the /u command-line switch. This switch instructs RegSvr32 to invoke the **DllUnregisterServer()** function. Use the following command lines to register and unregister your server:

C:\DomesticProject\Debug>regsvr32 domesticproject.dll

C:\ DomesticProject\Debug>regsvr32 /u domesticproject.dll

Practice Questions

Question 1

Which MFC class implements the IUnknown interface?

○ a. CObject

○ b. CWinApp

○ c. COleObject

○ d. CCmdTarget

The correct answer is d. **CCmdTarget** implements two sets of **IUnknown** functions. One set does all of the work of reference counting and interface lookup. This set of functions has a prefix of **Internal: InternalAddRef(), InternalRelease(), InternalQueryInterface()**. The other set—**External AddRef(), ExternalRelease(), ExternalQueryInterface()**—is used to aid in COM aggregation. Aggregation is covered in Chapter 16. Answer a is incorrect because **CObject** is the root MFC base class. It provides some very basic services but knows nothing about **IUnknown**. Answer b is incorrect because you derive your application class from **CWinApp**. **CWinApp** inherits the **IUnknown** implementation from **CCmdTarget** through **CWinThread**. Answer c is incorrect because COleObject is not an MFC class.

Question 2

You are using MFC to implement an in-process graphics server. This server has a large number of interfaces, one of which is IDraw. Which of the following snippets of code is a proper implementation for QueryInterface()?

○ a.
```
STDMETHODIMP_(ULONG)
   CGrapics::XDraw::QueryInterface(REFIID riid,
                                    void ** ppv)
   {
   METHOD_PROLOGUE(CDomestic, Shipping);
    return
      pThis->ExternalQueryInterface(&riid, ppv);
   }
```

(continued)

Question 2 *(continued)*

```
○ b.  STDMETHODIMP
       CGrapics::XDraw::QueryInterface(REFIID riid,
                                        void ** ppv)
       {
        METHOD_PROLOGUE(CDomestic, Shipping);
        return
         pThis->InternalQueryInterface(&riid, ppv);
       }


○ c.  STDMETHODIMP
       CGrapics::XDraw::QueryInterface(REFIID riid,
                                         void ** ppv)
       {
         METHOD_PROLOGUE(CDomestic, Shipping);
         return
          pThis->ExternalQueryInterface(&riid, ppv);
       }


○ d.  STDMETHODIMP
       CGrapics::XDraw::QueryInterface(REFIID riid,
                                         void ** ppv)
       {
         METHOD_PROLOGUE(CDomestic, Shipping);
         return
          this->ExternalQueryInterface(&riid, ppv);
       }
```

The correct answer is c. Answer a is incorrect because **QueryInterface()** returns an **HRESULT**, not a **ULONG**. Answer b is incorrect because it calls **InternalQueryInterface()**, not **ExternalQueryInterface()**. Answer d is incorrect because it uses the **this** pointer instead of the **pThis** pointer.

Question 3

Which statements are correct? [Check all the correct answers.]

❑ a. The END_INTERFACE_PART macro creates a stack variable named pThis.

❑ b. Both BEGIN_INTERFACE_PART and BEGIN_INTERFACE_MAP prepend an X to the nested class name.

❑ c. The BEGIN_INTERFACE_PART macro defines a nested class that implements one COM interface.

❑ d. END_INTERFACE_PART declares a member variable that's an instance of the nested class.

Answers c and d are correct. The **BEGIN_INTERFACE_PART** and **END_INTERFACE_PART** are placed in the header file. **BEGIN_INTERFACE_PART** defines the nested class and prepends an X to the class name. It also declares **QueryInterface()**, **AddRef()**, and **Release()**, which you must implement. **END_INTERFACE_PART** ends the class definition and declares a member variable of the nested class. It names the variable **m_x** plus the class name. Each nested class requires its own pair of **BEGIN_INTERFACE_PART** and **END_INTERFACE_PART** macros.

Answer a is incorrect because **METHOD_PROLOGUE()** defines **pThis**. Answer b is incorrect because only **BEGIN_INTERFACE_PART** prepends an X to the nested class name.

Question 4

Most MFC applications don't explicitly declare an instance of COleObjectFactory. Which pair of MFC macros is used to declare and implement the class factory?

○ a. DECLARE_OLEFACTORY() and IMPLEMENT_OLEFACTORY()

○ b. DECLARE_OLECREATE() and IMPLEMENT_OLECREATE()

○ c. DECLARE_CLASSFACTORY() and IMPLEMENT_CLASSFACTORY()

○ d. DECLARY_DYNCREATE() and IMPLEMENT_DYNCREATE()

The correct answer is b. **DECLARE_OLECREATE()** defines two static variables. One is the class factory object and the other holds the **CLSID** of the object the factory creates. **IMPLEMENT_OLECREATE()** initializes both of the variables. Answer a is incorrect because these two macros are not legal MFC macros. Answer c is incorrect because **DECLARE_CLASSFACTORY()** is used with the Active Template Library (ATL) and **IMPLEMENT_CLASS FACTORY()** does not exist. Answer d is incorrect because these macros provide the framework with the capability to create **CObject**-derived class objects dynamically at runtime.

Need To Know More?

 Kruglinski, David J., George Shepherd, and Scot Wingo. *Programming Microsoft Visual C++*. 5th ed. Microsoft Press, Redmond, WA, 1998. ISBN 1-57231-857-0. This book doesn't provide nearly as much theory or detail about COM as *MFC Internals*. However, unlike *MFC Internals*, it shows how to gain the benefits of COM from within MFC.

 Prosise, Jeff. *Programming Windows with MFC*. Microsoft Press, Redmond, WA, 1999. ISBN 1-57231-695-0. This is the updated version of the author's popular book, *Programming Windows 95 with MFC*. Chapter 18 covers MFC and the Component Object Model.

 Shepherd, George, and Scott Wingo. *MFC Internals: Inside the Microsoft Foundation Class Architecture*. Addison-Wesley, Inc., Reading, MA, 1996. ISBN 0-201-40721-3. If you want to learn how MFC does its magic when it comes to COM, this is the book for you. The authors have done an admirable job of taking a complex topic and presenting it in a straightforward and understandable manner. To aid comprehension, they show what the code looks like after all of the macros are expanded. Although this book is over three years old (a lifetime in the computer field), it is still the best source of information about the inner workings of MFC.

 MSDN Library, Platform SDK\Component Services

 MSDN Library, Technical Articles\Component Object Model

 MSDN Library, Visual Studio 6.0 Documentation\Visual C++ Documentation\References\Microsoft Foundation Classes and Templates\Microsoft Foundation Class Library\MFC Technical Notes

 MSDN Library, Visual Studio 6.0 Documentation\Visual C++ Documentation\Samples\MFC Samples\MFC OLE Samples

Reusing Existing COM Components

Terms you'll need to understand:

√ Containment

√ Aggregation

√ Outer object

√ Inner object

√ Delegation

√ **CLASS_E_NOAGGREGATION**

√ **EnableAggregation()**

√ **OnCreateAggregates()**

√ **GetControllingUnknown()**

√ **INTERFACE_AGGREGATE()**

Techniques you'll need to master:

√ Explaining the difference between aggregation and containment

√ With the SDK, creating a COM component that reuses existing components

√ With MFC, creating a COM component that reuses existing components

Central to Component Object Model (COM) is the idea of code reuse. The ability to use and reuse components dynamically allows developers to build robust, reliable applications. Using an existing, proven component that encapsulates a business rule, a logic entity, or a concept means less time spent coding, debugging, and testing. It can also mean greater functionality. Leveraging the work of others—especially those with more expertise—allows developers to focus on the problem at hand rather than retracing the steps of a hundred programmers before them. Given that this works so well for application development, why not apply this same technique when implementing your own COM classes?

The idea of code reuse has been around for quite some time. Languages such as C++ rely on implementation inheritance as a primary mechanism for reusing existing code. Because COM objects are language-neutral, implementation inheritance is not a viable approach. Instead, COM provides reuse through two other mechanisms: *containment* and *aggregation*.

The concepts behind both containment and aggregation are quite simple. Both rely on a relationship between objects where one object, known as the *outer object*, uses the services of another object, known at the *inner object*.

Containment

With containment, the outer object acts as a client of the inner (or contained) object. The outer object simply creates the inner object and then calls the inner object's functions to carry out its own. The outer object can provide simple wrappers that merely pass method calls through to the inner object. This action is called *delegation*, because the work is being delegated from the outer object to the inner object.

Containment can be more involved than simply wrapping the inner object's methods. The outer object might want to inspect and appropriately modify method parameters before passing them to the inner object. It also might modify the inner object's return value. Additionally, the outer object might provide a higher-level set of methods than that provided by the inner object. Each outer object method would invoke some number of inner object methods in order to carry out its function.

Containment is relatively easy to implement. The inner object doesn't require any special functionality to support containment, and in fact, it can't differentiate between containment and direct use by a client. Any object that can stand alone can be used as an inner object.

There are two basic strategies the outer object can apply concerning the construction of the inner object. As the outer object is being constructed, it can create the inner object via **CoCreateInstance()**. Alternately, the outer object can wait and create the inner object on demand. The outer object releases the inner object in its destructor. For example:

```
// Outer object's constructor with containment
COuter::COuter()
{
  m_lRefCount = 1;
  g_ObjectCount++;

  CLSID clsid;
  CLSIDFromProgID(L"Inner.Object", &clsid);
  CoCreateInstance(clsid, 0, CLSCTX_LOCAL_SERVER, IID_IInner,
        (void**) &m_pInnerObj);
}
// Outer object's distructor
COuter::~COuter()
{
  g_ObjectCount-;
  if(m_pInnerObj)
  {
    m_pInnerObj->Release();
    m_pInnerObj = 0;
  }
}
```

Aggregation

Aggregation differs from containment in two ways. First, the outer object exposes the inner object's interface directly to the client as its own. Second, if an object is to be used via aggregation, the object must be written to support it.

Here's a short description of how aggregation works. When the client queries the outer object for an interface that belongs to the inner object, the outer object simply queries the inner object and returns the interface pointer back to the client. From then on, the outer object is out of the picture. The client uses the interface to directly call methods implemented by the inner object.

Writing an object that can be aggregated is more difficult than writing one that isn't. The two issues that must be managed are getting reference counts right and making sure that **QueryInterface()** works correctly. You do this by implementing two sets of **IUnknown** functions: delegating and nondelegating.

To make aggregation work, the following rules must be followed:

➤ When the outer object is creating the inner object, the outer object must pass its own **IUnknown** to the inner object through the **pUnkOuter** parameter of **IClassFactory::CreateInstance()**.

➤ In **CreateInstance()**, the inner object must check the **pUnkOuter** parameter. If it is non-NULL and the inner object supports aggregation, **pUnkOuter** is stored for later use. **AddRef()** is not called. If the inner object does not support aggregation, it must fail with **CLASS_E_ NOAGGREGATION**.

➤ If the **pUnkOuter** parameter in **CreateInstance()** is non-NULL, the inner object returns its nondelegating **IUnknown**.

➤ When the client queries for the interface that is supported by the inner object, the outer one delegates that call to the inner.

➤ When **QueryInterface()**, **AddRef()**, or **Release()** is called on any inner object interface (except for **IUnknown**), the inner object must delegate to **pUnkOuter**.

Look at the following code snippets. Lines of particular interest are highlighted with a comment explaining the point of interest. The inner object is **IShipping**. First, the outer object's constructor and **QueryInterface()**:

```
// Outer object's constructor and destructor
CComOuter::CComOuter()
  : m_lRef(0)
  , m_pShipping(0)
{
  CCounters::IncObjectCount();

  CLSID clsid;
  HRESULT hr = CLSIDFromProgID(L"MailOrder.Shipping.1", &clsid);
  if(FAILED(hr))
    return;

  CoCreateInstance(
        clsid,
        this,                 // outer IUnknown for aggregation
        CLSCTX_INPROC_SERVER,
        // in aggregation, must always be IUnknown
        IID_IUnknown,
        // pointer to the aggregate object
        reinterpret_cast<void**>(&m_pShipping));

}

// Outer object's QueryInterface
STDMETHODIMP CComOuter::QueryInterface(REFIID rIID, void ** ppv)
{
  if(!ppv) return E_POINTER;
```

```
*ppv = 0;
if(rIID == IID_IUnknown || rIID == IID_IOuter)
  *ppv = static_cast<IOuter *>(this);

if(*ppv)
{
  reinterpret_cast<IUnknown*>(*ppv)->AddRef();
  return S_OK;
}

// If the client queried for the interface that's supported
// by the inner object, then delegate the query
if(m_pShipping && rIID == IID_IShipping)
  return m_pShipping->QueryInterface(rIID, ppv);

  return E_NOINTERFACE;
}
```

Next is an example of how the class factory for the inner object is modified to support aggregation:

```
STDMETHODIMP CShippingClassFactory::CreateInstance(
                                LPUNKNOWN pUnkOuter,
                                REFIID rIID,
                                void ** ppvInterface)
{
  *ppvInterface = 0;

  // Check for a controlling unknown
  if(pUnkOuter && rIID != IID_IUnknown)
    return CLASS_E_NOAGGREGATION;

  CAgg *pObj = new CAgg(pUnkOuter); // pass the outer object's
                                    // IUnknown

  if(!pObj)
    return E_OUTOFMEMORY;

  HRESULT hr = pObj->QueryInterface(rIID, ppvInterface);
  if(FAILED(hr))
  {
    delete pObj;
    return hr;
  }
  return S_OK;
}
```

The **CreateInstance() pUnkOuter** parameter is **NULL** unless the object is being created as part of an aggregate. If **pUnkOuter** is not **NULL**, then it must be a pointer to the controlling (outer) **IUnknown** interface of the aggregate. After checking **pUnkOuter**, it is passed to the **CAgg** constructor. You'll see what the constructor does with **pUnkOuter** shortly.

Next, look at the aggregate object. Remember, an aggregate object needs two **IUnknown** implementations: delegating and nondelegating. Here is what the class definition might look like with everything stripped away except the declarations for the two **IUnknown**s:

```
class CAgg : public IUnknown
{
private:
  class CComShipping  : public IShipping
  {
  public:
    IUnknown * m_pDelegateTo;

    // Delegating IUnknown
    STDMETHOD(QueryInterface)(REFIID, void**);
    STDMETHOD_(ULONG, AddRef)();
    STDMETHOD_(ULONG, Release)();

    // IShipping
    STDMETHOD(Basic)( /* in */  double dWeight,
                     /* out */ double * dCost);

    STDMETHOD(Overnight)( /* in */  double dWeight,
                         /* out */ double * dCost);
  } m_Delegating;  // nested object

  // Data members
  IUnknown * m_pUnkOuter;
  long       m_lRef;

public:
  // ctor and dtor
  CAgg(IUnknown *); // takes a pointer to IUnknown
  ~CAgg();

  // Nondelegating IUnknown
  STDMETHOD(QueryInterface)(REFIID, void**);
  STDMETHOD_(ULONG, AddRef)();
  STDMETHOD_(ULONG, Release)();
};
```

CAgg derives directly from **IUnknown**, and its **IUnknown** methods will be the nondelegating **IUnknown**. **CAgg** contains a nested class, **CComShipping**, which derives from **IShipping**. **CComShipping** delegates all its **IUnknown** method calls to the outer (nondelegating) **IUnknown**. Notice that both the outer (**CAgg**) class and the inner (**CComShipping**) class contain **IUnknown** pointers. The inner class's **IUnknown** will hold a pointer to the outer object's **IUnknown** or to its own internal nondelegating **IUnknown**, depending on whether or not the object is part of an aggregate.

The constructor takes a pointer to **IUnknown**. If this parameter is not **NULL**, it indicates that the object is being created as part of an aggregate. In this case, the pointer must point to the outer **IUnknown**.

Now for some of the implementation:

```
CAgg::CAgg(IUnknown * pUnkOuter)
  : m_lRef(0)
  , m_pUnkOuter(pUnkOuter)
{
  CCounters::IncObjectCount();
  m_Delegating.m_pDelegateTo = m_pUnkOuter ? m_pUnkOuter : this;
}
```

The constructor tells the delegating **IUnknown** class who to delegate to. If **pUnkOuter** is **NULL**, then a pointer to the object is stored in **m_pDelegateTo**. Otherwise, **pUnkOuter** contains a pointer to the outer **IUnknown**, and that is stored in **m_pDelegateTo**.

Next is the implementation of the nondelegating **IUnknown**:

```
// Nondelegating IUnknown
STDMETHODIMP CAgg::QueryInterface(REFIID rIID, void ** ppv)
{
  *ppv = 0;
  if(rIID == IID_IUnknown)
  {
    *ppv = this;
    AddRef();
    return S_OK;
  }
  if(rIID == IID_IShipping)
  {
    *ppv = &m_Delegating;
    m_Delegating.AddRef();
    return S_OK;
  }
```

```
        return E_NOINTERFACE;
    }


    // Delegating IUnknown
    STDMETHODIMP CAgg::CDelegate::QueryInterface(REFIID rIID,
                                                  void ** ppv)
    {
        return m_pDelegateTo->QueryInterface(rIID, ppv);
    }


    STDMETHODIMP_(ULONG) CAgg::CDelegate::AddRef()
    {
        return m_pDelegateTo->AddRef();
    }


    STDMETHODIMP_(ULONG) CAgg::CDelegate::Release()
    {
        return m_pDelegateTo->Release();
    }
```

When the client calls **QueryInterface()** requesting **IUnknown**, a pointer to the nondelegating **IUnknown** is returned.

If the client is requesting **IShipping**, a pointer to the **IShipping** that derives from the delegating **IUnknown** is returned and the delegating **IUnknown** AddRef() is called. When **CAgg::CDelegate ::AddRef()** is called, it delegates its call to the appropriate **AddRef()**, either to the outer **IUnknown** when aggregated or to its own internal nondelegating **IUnknown** when it is running standalone.

Well, I said it was tricky. As it turns out, there is an easier way. Both MFC and ActiveX Template Library (ATL) make supporting aggregation almost trivial. In the next section, you'll look at MFC. ATL will be covered later in the book.

Containment And Aggregation With MFC

As with the SDK, MFC doesn't provide any direct support for containment. You simply create other COM objects during your own operations, use them as needed, and release them when you are finished with them.

The support MFC provides makes aggregation almost as simple as containment. To allow your component to be part of an aggregate, you simply call **CCmdTarget::EnableAggregation()** in your object's constructor. That's all there is to it. This one line replaces all the tricky code you looked at above. Because this is so trivial and adds little overhead, it's a good idea to always add this method call to your class's constructor.

Creating a component that is an outer object requires more effort, but it's pretty straightforward and isn't much different than what is needed for containment.

Building An MFC Server That Uses Containment And Aggregation

In the next few sections, you will build an in-process server that employs both containment and aggregation. You'll use the **MailOrder.Domestic** component from Chapter 15 as the contained component, but you'll need to create another component to use as the inner object.

Create a new folder and name it "CanadaProject". Start up Visual C++, create a new MFC AppWizard (DLL) project, place it in the CanadaProject folder, and name it "CanadaProject". At MFC AppWizard - Step 1 of 1, select Regular DLL Using Shared MFC DLL, along with Automation, and then click on Finish.

The wizard creates a source, resource, module definition, object description language, and some header files. The object description language (ODL) isn't needed for the **CanadaProject** component. It was provided to support ActiveX Automation, which you will not use. To remove the ActiveX Automation support, you need to do the following:

1. Comment out or delete all references to messages maps (leave the wizard-generated comments) in both CanadaProject.h and Canada Project.cpp.

2. Delete the ODL file from the project.

3. Comment out or delete the line **1 TYPELIB "CanadaProject.tlb"** from **CanadaProject.rc** (you need to open it as a text file).

4. Comment out or delete the lines **#include <afxodlgs.h>** // MFC **OLE dialog classes** and **#include <afxdisp.h>** // MFC Automation **classes** from **StdAfx.h**.

Building An MFC Aggregatable Component

This component is a stripped-down version of **MailOrder.Domestic**. Because the mail-order business is going to start shipping to Canada in the near future, you need a **MailOrder.Canada** component that encapsulates these business rules (of course, this will be an oversimplification). You'll need to add two header files and a class to your project. Follow the steps you used when building **DomesticProject** in Chapter 15. All code, edited for readability, is provided below. Here's the first header file:

```
// guids.h
//
#if !defined(IID_ICanadaShipping_GUIDS_H_INCLUDED)
#define IID_ICanadaShipping_GUIDS_H_INCLUDED

// {22853480-CF64-11d2-A46F-00C04F688CFA}
DEFINE_GUID(IID_ICanadaShipping,
            0x22853480, 0xcf64, 0x11d2,
            0xa4, 0x6f, 0x0, 0xc0, 0x4f, 0x68, 0x8c, 0xfa);

#endif  // !defined(IID_ICanadaShipping_GUIDS_H_INCLUDED)
```

Here's the interface:

```
// interface.h : header file
//
#if !defined(ICanadaShipping_INTERFACE_H_INCLUDED)
#define ICanadaShipping_INTERFACE_H_INCLUDED

#include "guids.h"

DECLARE_INTERFACE_(ICanadaShipping, IUnknown)
{
  STDMETHOD(Basic)(double dWeight, double * dCost) PURE;
  // Three business days or less
  STDMETHOD(Express)(double dWeight, double * dCost) PURE;
};
#endif  // !defined(ICanadaShipping_INTERFACE_H_INCLUDED)
```

The interface is simple and to the point. The client calls one of two methods to find what it costs to ship to Canada. The mail-order business can only ship via Basic or Express; Overnight and Expedited shipments to Canada are not possible.

Use ClassWizard to create **CCanada** derived from **CCmdTarget**. Be sure to select the Creatable by Type ID radio button within the Automation group box. In the adjunct edit box, enter **MailOrder.Canada**. Here's the Canada.h file:

```
#if !defined(AFX_CANADA_H_INCLUDED_)
#define AFX_CANADA_H_INCLUDED_
// Canada.h : header file
//////////////////////////////////////////////////////////////////
```

```
class CCanada : public CCmdTarget
{
  DECLARE_DYNCREATE(CCanada)
  CCanada();//  protected constructor used by dynamic creation
// Operations
public:
  // ICanadaShipping members
  BEGIN_INTERFACE_PART(Shipping, ICanadaShipping)
    STDMETHOD(Basic)(double dWeight, double * dCost);
    // Three business days or less
    STDMETHOD(Express)(double dWeight, double * dCost);
  END_INTERFACE_PART(Shipping)

  //{{AFX_VIRTUAL(CCanada)
  public:
  virtual void OnFinalRelease();
  //}}AFX_VIRTUAL
  // Implementation
protected:
  virtual ~CCanada();

  DECLARE_OLECREATE(CCanada)
  DECLARE_INTERFACE_MAP()
};
#endif // !defined(AFX_CANADA_H_INCLUDED_)
```

There's nothing here that you wouldn't expect. On to the implementation file:

```
// Canada.cpp : implementation file
//
#include "stdafx.h"
#include "CanadaProject.h"
#include <initguid.h>
#include "interface.h"
#include "Canada.h"
#ifdef _DEBUG
#define new DEBUG_NEW
#undef THIS_FILE
static char THIS_FILE[] = __FILE__;
#endif

static const double theBasicRatePerPound = 2.55;
static const double theExpressAdder      = 3.75;
/////////////////////////////////////////////////////////////////
// CCanada
IMPLEMENT_DYNCREATE(CCanada, CCmdTarget)
CCanada::CCanada()
```

```
  {
    EnableAggregation();
  }
  CCanada::~CCanada()
  {
  }
  void CCanada::OnFinalRelease()
  {
    CCmdTarget::OnFinalRelease();
  }
  BEGIN_INTERFACE_MAP(CCanada, CCmdTarget)
    INTERFACE_PART(CCanada, IID_ICanadaShipping, Shipping)
  END_INTERFACE_MAP()
  // {8BD1F9F6-CF2D-11D2-A46F-00C04F688CFA}
  IMPLEMENT_OLECREATE(CCanada, "MailOrder.Canada", 0x8bd1f9f6,
  0xcf2d, 0x11d2, 0xa4, 0x6f, 0x0, 0xc0, 0x4f, 0x68, 0x8c, 0xfa)
  /////////////////////////////////////////////////////////////////
  // CCanada message handlers
  // ICanadaShipping
  STDMETHODIMP_(ULONG)
  CCanada::XShipping::AddRef()
  {
    METHOD_PROLOGUE(CCanada, Shipping);
    return pThis->ExternalAddRef();
  }
  STDMETHODIMP_(ULONG)
  CCanada::XShipping::Release()
  {
    METHOD_PROLOGUE(CCanada, Shipping);
    return pThis->ExternalRelease();
  }
  STDMETHODIMP
  CCanada::XShipping::QueryInterface(REFIID riid, void ** ppv)
  {
    METHOD_PROLOGUE(CCanada, Shipping);
    return pThis->ExternalQueryInterface(&riid, ppv);
  }
  STDMETHODIMP
  CCanada::XShipping::Basic(double dWeight, double * dCost)
  {
    *dCost = dWeight * theBasicRatePerPound;
    return S_OK;
  }
  STDMETHODIMP
  CCanada::XShipping::Express(double dWeight, double * dCost)
  {
```

```
Basic(dWeight, dCost);
*dCost += theExpressAdder;
return S_OK;
}
```

Note that the constructor calls **EnableAggregation()**. All else should look familiar. However, something not addressed in Chapter 15 now needs to be covered. In Chapter 15 you saw how **CCmdTarget** provides two varieties of **IUnknown** methods. These sets of **IUnknown** methods provide the same basic functionality as the methods you saw previously in the SDK version.

In your **CCmdTarget**-derived class, you call the set of **IUnknown** methods with the **External** prefix. These external **IUnknown** methods call the internal **IUnknown** methods unless the object is part of an aggregate. If the object is part of an aggregate, then the external **IUnknown** methods call the outer **IUnknown** methods. This should all sound very familiar. If you are interested, **CCmdTarget::ExternalQueryInterface()** looks like this:

```
// QueryInterface that is exported to normal clients
DWORD CCmdTarget::ExternalQueryInterface(const void* iid,
    LPVOID* ppvObj)
{
    // delegate to controlling unknown if aggregated
    if (m_pOuterUnknown != NULL)
        return m_pOuterUnknown->QueryInterface(*(IID*)iid, ppvObj);

    return InternalQueryInterface(iid, ppvObj);
}
```

Now update the component's housing by adding **DllUnregisterServer()** to CanadaProject.cpp. Don't forget the **#include <afxctl.h>**:

```
STDAPI DllUnregisterServer(void)
{
  AFX_MANAGE_STATE(AfxGetStaticModuleState());

  CLSID clsid;
  HRESULT hr;
  if(hr = ::CLSIDFromProgID(L"MailOrder.Canada", &clsid) !=NOERROR)
    return FALSE;

  return AfxOleUnregisterClass(clsid, "MailOrder.Canada");
}
```

Next, update **CanadaProject.def** to export **DllUnregisterServer()**. After compiling and linking, be sure to register the server by running RegSvr32. Be sure to build a client and test the server. Before using it as an inner object you want to make sure it works correctly. Use the client in Chapter 15 as a model.

Building The Main Server: MailOrder.Object

Start by creating a project named MailOrder. Use the same steps you followed for the CanadaProject project. This server will contain the **MailOrder.Domestic** component and aggregate the **MailOrder.Canada** component. To keep it simple and perhaps more interesting, all **MailOrder.Domestic** functionality will not be provided to the client. Domestic shipping will be restricted to the same methods that are available for Canada. Here's the interface for **MailOrder. Object**:

```
// interface.h : header file
//
#if !defined(IUSShipping_INTERFACE_H_INCLUDED)
#define IUSShipping_INTERFACE_H_INCLUDED

#include "guids.h"

DECLARE_INTERFACE_(IUSShipping, IUnknown)
{
  STDMETHOD(Basic)(double dWeight, double * dCost) PURE;
  // Three business days or less
  STDMETHOD(Express)(double dWeight, double * dCost) PURE;
};

#endif  // !defined(IUSShipping_INTERFACE_H_INCLUDED)
```

The important thing to note here is that the interface is named **IUSShipping** and that it inherits from **IUnknown**, not **IDomesticShipping**. This interface will be exposed to clients, and they will have no knowledge that the component is using a preexisting component to provide the basic functionality.

```
#if !defined(AFX_COMMAILORDER_H_INCLUDED_)
#define AFX_COMMAILORDER_H_INCLUDED_
// ComMailOrder.h : header file
////////////////////////////////////////////////////////////////////
// CComMailOrder command target
class CComMailOrder : public CCmdTarget
{
  DECLARE_DYNCREATE(CComMailOrder)
  CComMailOrder(); // protected constructor used b/dynamic creation
```

```
// Operations
public:
  // IUSShipping members
  BEGIN_INTERFACE_PART(Shipping, IUSShipping)
    STDMETHOD(Basic)(double dWeight, double * dCost);
    // Three business days or less
    STDMETHOD(Express)(double dWeight, double * dCost);
  END_INTERFACE_PART(Shipping)

// Overrides
  // ClassWizard generated virtual function overrides
  //{{AFX_VIRTUAL(CComMailOrder)
  public:
  virtual void OnFinalRelease();
  //}}AFX_VIRTUAL
// Implementation
protected:
  virtual BOOL OnCreateAggregates();
  virtual ~CComMailOrder();
  // Generated message map functions
  //{{AFX_MSG(CComMailOrder)
  // NOTE - the ClassWizard will add and remove member...
  //}}AFX_MSG

  DECLARE_OLECREATE(CComMailOrder)
  DECLARE_INTERFACE_MAP()
private:
  IUnknown         * m_pUnkCanadaShipping;
  IUnknown         * m_pUnkDomesticShipping;
  IDomesticShipping * m_pDomesticShipping;
};
#endif // !defined(AFX_COMMAILORDER_H_INCLUDED_)
```

Highlighted are two important things that should be noted about the **CComMailOrder** class declaration. First is the declaration that overrides the virtual method **OnCreateAggregates()**. As part of the construction process, the class factory calls this method so that the component can create the aggregate object.

The second item to note is the declaration of the pointers **m_pUnk CanadaShipping, m_pUnkDomesticShipping**, and **m_pDomestic Shipping**. At the first pointer, the **CComMailOrder** class will hold on to the **IUnknown** interface belonging to the aggregated component. The second and third pointers are used to hold on to the interfaces belonging to the contained component.

Now look at the implementation of **CComMailOrder**:

```
// ComMailOrder.cpp : implementation file
//
#include "stdafx.h"
#include "MailOrder.h"
#include <initguid.h>
#include "..\DomesticProject\interface.h"
#include "..\CanadaProject\interface.h"
#include "interface.h"
#include "ComMailOrder.h"

#ifdef _DEBUG
#define new DEBUG_NEW
#undef THIS_FILE
static char THIS_FILE[] = __FILE__;
#endif
/////////////////////////////////////////////////////////////////////
// CComMailOrder
IMPLEMENT_DYNCREATE(CComMailOrder, CCmdTarget)

CComMailOrder::CComMailOrder()
  : m_pUnkCanadaShipping(0)
  , m_pUnkDomesticShipping(0)
  , m_pDomesticShipping(0)
{
  CLSID clsid;
  HRESULT hr = CLSIDFromProgID(L"MailOrder.Domestic", &clsid);
  if(FAILED(hr))
    return;
  hr = CoCreateInstance( clsid,
                         0,
                         CLSCTX_INPROC_SERVER,
                         IID_IUnknown,
                         (void **) &m_pUnkDomesticShipping );
  if(FAILED(hr))
  {
    m_pDomesticShipping = 0;
    return;
  }
  hr = m_pUnkDomesticShipping->QueryInterface(IID_IDomesticShipping,
                                (void**) &m_pDomesticShipping );
  if(FAILED(hr))
  {
    m_pUnkDomesticShipping->Release();
    m_pUnkDomesticShipping = 0;
    m_pDomesticShipping = 0;
    return;
  }
```

```
   EnableAggregation();
}


CComMailOrder::~CComMailOrder()
{
  // Release the contained object
  if(m_pDomesticShipping)
  {
    m_pDomesticShipping->Release();
    m_pDomesticShipping = 0;
  }
  if(m_pUnkDomesticShipping)
  {
    m_pUnkDomesticShipping->Release();
    m_pUnkDomesticShipping = 0;
  }

  // Release the aggregated object
  if(m_pUnkCanadaShipping)
  {
    m_pUnkCanadaShipping->Release();
    m_pUnkCanadaShipping = 0;
  }
}


BOOL CComMailOrder::OnCreateAggregates()
{
  CLSID clsid;
  HRESULT hr;

  hr = CLSIDFromProgID(L"MailOrder.Canada", &clsid);
  if(FAILED(hr))
    return FALSE;

  hr = CoCreateInstance( clsid,
                         GetControllingUnknown(),
                         CLSCTX_INPROC_SERVER,
                         IID_IUnknown,
                         (void **) &m_pUnkCanadaShipping );
  if(FAILED(hr))
    return FALSE;

  return TRUE;
}
void CComMailOrder::OnFinalRelease()
{
  CCmdTarget::OnFinalRelease();
}
```

```
BEGIN_INTERFACE_MAP(CComMailOrder, CCmdTarget)
  INTERFACE_PART(CComMailOrder, IID_IUSShipping, Shipping)
  INTERFACE_AGGREGATE(CComMailOrder, m_pUnkCanadaShipping)
END_INTERFACE_MAP()


// {667F0BB2-CFD6-11D2-A46F-00C04F688CFA}
IMPLEMENT_OLECREATE(CComMailOrder, "MailOrder.Object", 0x667f0bb2,
 0xcfd6, 0x11d2, 0xa4, 0x6f, 0x0, 0xc0, 0x4f, 0x68, 0x8c, 0xfa)


/////////////////////////////////////////////////////////////////
// CComMailOrder message handlers
// IUSShipping
STDMETHODIMP_(ULONG)
CComMailOrder::XShipping::AddRef()
{
  METHOD_PROLOGUE(CComMailOrder, Shipping);
  return pThis->ExternalAddRef();
}
STDMETHODIMP_(ULONG)
CComMailOrder::XShipping::Release()
{
  METHOD_PROLOGUE(CComMailOrder, Shipping);
  return pThis->ExternalRelease();
}
STDMETHODIMP
CComMailOrder::XShipping::QueryInterface(REFIID riid, void ** ppv)
{
  METHOD_PROLOGUE(CComMailOrder, Shipping);
  if(riid == IID_IUSShipping && !pThis->m_pDomesticShipping)
    return E_FAIL;
  return pThis->ExternalQueryInterface(&riid, ppv);
}
STDMETHODIMP
CComMailOrder::XShipping::Basic(double dWeight, double * dCost)
{
  METHOD_PROLOGUE(CComMailOrder, Shipping);
  HRESULT hr;
  hr = pThis->m_pDomesticShipping->Basic(dWeight, dCost);
  return hr;
}
STDMETHODIMP
CComMailOrder::XShipping::Express(double dWeight, double * dCost)
{
  METHOD_PROLOGUE(CComMailOrder, Shipping);
  HRESULT hr;
  hr = pThis->m_pDomesticShipping->Basic(dWeight, dCost);
  if(FAILED(hr))
```

```
   return hr;
 *dCost += 4.50;
   return S_OK;
}
```

We'll discuss only the new stuff, which is highlighted. Starting at the top of the code and moving down, the first highlighted area is the constructor. The contained component is created in the constructor. This code isn't really any different from what you would see in a client. In fact, this component is a client of the **MailOrder.Domestic** component. Notice the second argument being passed to **CoCreateInstance()**. This parameter is the **pUnkOuter** pointer. Here, a null is being passed, indicating the component will not be a part of an aggregate. If you actually passed a pointer, the **CLASS_E_NOAGGREGATION** error code would be returned. Remember, the **MailOrder.Domestic** component doesn't call **EnableAggregation()**. In a final move, the constructor calls **EnableAggregation()** so that this component can be created as part of an aggregate.

Next is the destructor, which simply releases both the contained and the aggregated components.

Moving on to **OnCreateAggregates()** where the inner object is created, the class factory calls **OnCreateAggregates()** after instantiating the outer object. In **OnCreateAggregates()**, you should instantiate all the aggregated objects. Notice how much **OnCreateAggregates()** looks like the constructor. Only three differences are worthy of discussion. First note the second argument being passed to **CoCreateInstance()**. **GetControllingUnknown()** returns the controlling unknown. This value isn't valid during the constructor, so aggregated objects must be created later in the construction process. Second, note that **QueryInterface()** isn't called. Remember, the inner object's interface is exposed directly to the client as if it belongs to the outer component and it is the client that will call **QueryInterface()**.

The last thing to note: **OnCreateAggregates()** returns a **BOOL** indicating whether the component was successfully created; if **TRUE**, the class factory returns **S_OK** to the client. If **OnCreateAggregates()** returns a **FALSE**, the class factory returns **E_OUTOFMEMORY**.

The next highlighted area is the **INTERFACE_AGGREGATE()** macro, which is used to add a nondelegating **IUnknown** pointer to the interface map. **INTERFACE_AGGREGATE()** takes two parameters: the name of the component class and the name of a member variable that will contain an **IUnknown** (or **IUnknown**-derived) pointer to the inner object. There should be an **INTERFACE_AGGREGATE()** macro and an **IUnknown** attribute for each aggregated component.

Next, look at the highlighted lines in **CComMailOrder::XShipping::QueryInterface()**. Because the contained component is being created in the constructor, no way exists to let the client know when something goes wrong during the creation process. Therefore, code has been added to **QueryInterface()** for reporting an error that occurred earlier. This is clearly an undesirable situation, which can be avoided by simply moving the creation of the contained component into **OnCreateAggregates()**.

Last, look at the implementation of the **Express()** method for this component. A couple of items should be pointed out. First, unlike **CComMailOrder::XShipping::Basic()**, which is a simple wrapper around **IDomesticShipping::Basic()**, **CComMailOrder::XShipping::Express()** provides an implementation that has nothing to do with **IDomesticShipping::Express()**. Rather than calling **IDomesticShipping::Express()**, the **CComMailOrder::XShipping::Express()** method calls **IDomesticShipping::Basic()** and adjusts the output value. Note the **pThis** pointer use. Remember that MFC uses nested classes to provide interface implementation, and through the **pThis** pointer, nested classes have access to data members of the component.

Building The Client

The client program that tests the server is also an MFC-based application. It's probably among the simplest-minded MFC programs ever written; it doesn't even have a window. Here's the one and only file:

```
// Client.cpp
//
#include <afxwin.h>          // MFC core and standard components
#include <objbase.h>
#include <initguid.h>
#include "..\CanadaProject\interface.h"
#include "..\MailOrder\interface.h"

class CClientApp : public CWinApp
{
public:
  virtual BOOL InitInstance();
};

CClientApp theApp; // The one and only CClientApp object

BOOL CClientApp::InitInstance()
{
  CString msg;
  // Initialize COM
```

```
HRESULT hr = CoInitialize(0);
if(FAILED(hr))
{
  msg.Format("Couldn't initialize COM.\n HRESULT = 0x%x", hr);
  ::AfxMessageBox(msg, MB_ICONINFORMATION | MB_OK);
  return FALSE;
}

// Create the component
CLSID clsid;
IUnknown *pIUnknown;

hr = CLSIDFromProgID(L"MailOrder.Object", &clsid);
if(FAILED(hr))
{
  msg.Format( "Couldn't create the component.\n HRESULT = 0x%x",
              hr);
  ::AfxMessageBox(msg, MB_ICONINFORMATION | MB_OK);
  return FALSE;
}

hr = CoCreateInstance( clsid,
                       0,
                       CLSCTX_INPROC_SERVER,
                       IID_IUnknown,
                       (void**) &pIUnknown );
if(FAILED(hr))
{
  msg.Format("Couldn't create a new component.\n"
             "HRESULT = 0x%x", hr);
  ::AfxMessageBox(msg, MB_ICONINFORMATION | MB_OK);
  return FALSE;
}

//////////////////////////////////////////////////
// Get the interface for the aggregrated object
ICanadaShipping * pICanadaShipping;
hr = pIUnknown->QueryInterface(IID_ICanadaShipping,
                               (void**) &pICanadaShipping);
if(FAILED(hr))
{
  msg.Format( "Couldn't obtain CanadaShipping interface.\n"
              " HRESULT = 0x%x", hr);
  ::AfxMessageBox(msg, MB_ICONINFORMATION | MB_OK);
  pIUnknown->Release();
  return FALSE;
}
```

```
      // Use the aggregated object
      double weight = 3.5;
      double rate;
      pICanadaShipping->Basic(weight, &rate);
      msg.Format( "ICanadaShipping::Basic\n weight = %f\n rate = %f",
                  weight, rate);
      ::AfxMessageBox(msg, MB_ICONINFORMATION | MB_OK);

      // Release the aggregated object
      pICanadaShipping->Release();
      pICanadaShipping = 0;

      ///////////////////////////////////////////////////
      // Get the interface for the contained object
      IUSShipping * pIUSShipping;
      hr = pIUnknown->QueryInterface( IID_IUSShipping,
                                      (void**) &pIUSShipping );
      if(FAILED(hr))
      {
        msg.Format( "Couldn't obtain USShipping interface.\n"
                    " HRESULT = 0x%x", hr);
        ::AfxMessageBox(msg, MB_ICONINFORMATION | MB_OK);
        pIUnknown->Release();
        return FALSE;
      }

      // Use the contained object
      pIUSShipping->Basic(weight, &rate);
      msg.Format( "IUSShipping::Basic\n weight = %f\n rate = %f",
                  weight, rate);
      ::AfxMessageBox(msg, MB_ICONINFORMATION | MB_OK);

      // Release the contained object
      pIUSShipping->Release();
      pIUSShipping = 0;

      // Release the component
      pIUnknown->Release();
      pIUnknown = 0;

   CoUninitialize();

   return FALSE;
}
```

Everything happens in **InitInstance()**. After initializing COM and creating the component, each of the interfaces are exercised—first the aggregated object and then the contained object. If an error occurs at any time, a message box displays the error information. After displaying the message box, minimal cleanup is performed and **FALSE** is returned to the framework.

A normal MFC program creates and registers the application's main window in **InitInstance()**. However, this doesn't happen here. Because a window is never created and only a **FALSE** value is returned to the framework, MFC aborts the program.

Practice Questions

Question 1

Which one of the statements is correct concerning aggregation?

○ a. The inner object will cache a pointer to the outer object's IUnknown interface.

○ b. The inner object must maintain a reference count to ensure that it is not destroyed prematurely.

○ c. The outer object must provide two sets of implementations for IUnknown.

○ d. The outer object might specialize the interface by adding code before and after the code for the inner object.

The correct answer is a. At creation, the outer object passes its **IUnknown** interface pointer to the inner object. The inner object caches this pointer and uses it to forward any **IUnknown** method calls on to the outer object. Answer b is incorrect because the inner object does not maintain a reference count. Because the inner object and the outer object must appear to the client as one object, only one reference count should be maintained. As the controlling object, it is the outer object's responsibility to maintain the reference count. Answer c is incorrect because it is the inner object that provides two sets of implementations for **IUnknown,** not the other way around. The first implementation is called the delegating unknown and the other is called the nondelegating or implicit unknown. Answer d is incorrect because the inner object's interface is exposed directly to the client. Specialization of an interface can occur with containment, not with aggregation.

Question 2

Which of the following actions must you take in order to make an MFC class aggregatable?

- ○ a. Include an INTERFACE_AGGREGATE() macro entry in your interface map.

- ○ b. Declare an IUnknown * member variable and initialize it during OnCreateAggregates().

- ○ c. In the object's constructor, call EnableAggregation().

- ○ d. Declare an IUnknown * member variable and initialize it by calling GetControllingUnknown().

The correct answer is c. This question tries to trick you by providing two answers, a and b, that would be correct if you were implementing an MFC class that employed aggregation. Enabling an MFC component to be aggregated is trivial. By calling **EnableAggregation()** in your component's constructor, MFC initializes object's inner unknown pointer with an **IUnknown** vtable. This is all you need to do to enable your component to operate smoothly as an inner object.

Question 3

Which two of the following statements are true?

- ❏ a. Given a class that can be aggregated, when created as a nonaggregated component, the constructor must ensure that the IUnknown * member variable is NULL.

- ❏ b. When the outer object queries an interface belonging to the inner object, the reference count belonging to the outer object is incremented.

- ❏ c. One of the advantages of containment over aggregation is that when using containment the interface can be extended by adding code to an existing interface.

- ❏ d. A client can determine if a component is using aggregation.

The correct answers are b and c. When queried, the inner object delegates the **AddRef()** call to the outer unknown. The result is that the outer object component's reference count is incremented and not the inner object component's reference count. One of the major uses of containment is to extend an interface by adding your own code, which you can't do when you use aggregation. Answer a is incorrect because the inner object's **IUnknown*** member variable must be initialized to point to the outer unknown or the inner unknown. At no time should it be **NULL**. Answer d is incorrect because the inner component's **IUnknown** is hidden from the client. When client queries for **IUnknown**, it is always presented with the outer component's **IUnknown**.

Need To Know More?

 Chappell, David. *Understanding ActiveX and OLE: A Guide for Developers & Managers.* Microsoft Press, Redmond, WA, 1996. ISBN 1-57231-216-5. This book is well written and is easy to understand. It isn't a programming book and contains little code. However, if you don't want to establish a good COM foundation, use this book. The author covers basic theory and concepts with minimal clutter. This may the best introductory book on COM available.

 Rogerson, Dale. *Inside COM: Microsoft's Component Object Model.* Microsoft Press, Redmond, WA, 1997. ISBN 1-57231-349-8. This book explains theory and implementation of COM objects well. It covers basically the same territory as Chappell's book but includes a fair amount of code to illustrate key points. It has clear explanations on each of the key areas. Chapter 8 is devoted to containment and aggregation using the SDK.

 Shepherd, George and Scott Wingo. *MFC Internals, Inside the Microsoft Foundation Class Architecture.* Addison-Wesley, Reading, MA, 1996. ISBN 0-201-40721-3. To learn how MFC does its magic when it comes to COM, read this book. The authors have done an admirable job of presenting a complex topic in a straightforward and understandable manner. To aid comprehension, they show what the code looks like after all the macros are expanded. Although this book is over three years old, which in the computer field is a lifetime, it's still the best source of information about the innerworkings of MFC.

 MSDN Library, Visual Studio 6.0 Documentation\MFC technical notes\MFC OLE category

 MSDN Library, Visual Studio 6.0 Documentation\Platform SDK, COM and ActiveX Object Services

 MSDN Library, Visual Studio 6.0 Documentation\Technical articles\Component Object Model

 Microsoft's Web page for COM is **www.microsoft.com/com**. It contains white papers, presentations, resources, technologies, and so on. Under Resources, you will find the COM Spec and a number of sample programs. Explore this Web page; it provides a wealth of information.

Local Servers

Terms you'll need to understand:

- √ In-process server and out-of-process server
- √ Execution context
- √ Apartment
- √ Local server and remote server
- √ Location transparency
- √ Marshaling
- √ Proxy and Stub
- √ Interface Description Language
- √ Type library marshaling
- √ Universal Marshaler
- √ Standard and custom marshaling
- √ **IMarshal**
- √ **import**, **typedef**, and **coclass**
- √ **AfxOleLockApp()**
- √ **AfxOleUnlockApp()**
- √ **AfxOleInit()**
- √ **UpdateRegisterAll()**
- √ **AfxOleUnregisterClass()**
- √ **CoAddRefServerProcess()**
- √ **CoReleaseServerProcess()**
- √ **CoRegisterClassObject()**
- √ **GetProxyDllInfo()**
- √ **nmake**

Techniques you'll need to master:

- √ Understanding the role of local servers
- √ Understanding the necessities of marshaling
- √ Understanding and describing how marshaling works
- √ Building and registering a proxy-stub server
- √ Building an MFC local server
- √ Building an SDK local server

Chapters 14 through 16 covered in-process servers because in-process server is one of the two general categories of servers in the COM world. The other category is out-of-process servers. *Out-of-process servers* are housed in EXE files, run in their own address space, and have their own execution context. An *execution context* is an encapsulated execution scope that can be a single thread or a collection of threads. In the world of COM, an execution context is known as an *apartment*. Whenever COM calls span apartment or process boundaries, parameters must be marshaled between the processes. There are two types of out-of-process servers. One resides and executes on a client's machine. This type of out-of-process server is a *local server*. The other out-of-process server executes on a remote machine and is a *remote server*. This chapter is about local servers.

Because the housing for a local server is constructed and registered different than an in-process server, the development of local servers requires some additional effort. Fortunately, all the extra work concerns the housing itself and doesn't impact the code used to implement a component's functionality, which can be placed either in an in-process server or in a local server

Local servers provide benefits unavailable with in-process servers. First, local servers offer more protection to the client application. Because a local server is loaded into its own address space, a fatal error in the server will not crash the client application. Instead, an error will be returned. The second advantage local servers have over in-process servers is that local servers have more control over their threading model, which allows them to build in their own scalability features.

Whether a server is in-process, local, or even remote is usually not important and is unknown to the client. This is called *location transparency*. When a client requests COM to load a component, COM looks in the Registry for the component's location and activation information.

Marshaling

When a client holds a pointer to an in-process server interface, the pointer points directly to the object's interface. However, when the object is a local server, the pointer will point to a *proxy* object within the client's address space. Then when the client invokes a method using the interface pointer, the proxy takes the parameters passed by the client, packages them for transfer, and sends an interprocess request to the server transferring the package of parameters.

When the request arrives at the local server, another piece of special code known as a *stub* unpackages the parameters and invokes the appropriate server method.

The method executes, and any results are packaged by the stub and send back to the proxy. The proxy unpackages and returns to the client.

The process of packaging and sending data across process and machine boundaries is known as *marshaling*. As you might well imagine, the marshaling code can be rather involved. Luckily, COM hides all the details of marshaling from both the client and the server.

You don't need to know a lot about marshaling in order to use it. For standard COM interfaces, such as **IUnknown** and **IClassFactory**, Microsoft provides proxy and stub implementations that COM uses automatically. However, for custom interfaces—those you develop—you must also provide the necessary proxies and stubs.

You can code the proxy and stub code manually, but a much easier way is to write and compile an IDL file. IDL stands for *Interface Description Language*. In general, the IDL file is used to describe remote procedures named *interfaces*, but Microsoft extended it to include support for COM-based interfaces. It defines, in a language-independent way, a component's interface, which can then be used by clients of the component.

You compile an IDL file by using the MIDL (*Microsoft Interface Description Language)* tool. The MIDL tool creates a series of files (shown in Table 17.1) that produces a standard proxy-stub DLL. Although the MIDL tool produces all the necessary files, it's up to you to actually build the proxy-stub DLL. To build a proxy-stub DLL, simply compile and link the files produced by the MIDL tool. By building and then registering the proxy-stub DLL, you provide standard marshaling for your component.

If you don't want to ship a proxy-stub DLL for each component, you can use *type library marshaling* instead. COM provides a proxy-stub DLL, *Universal Marshaler*, which is implemented in oleaut32.dll. The marshaler can be used to marshal any interface described in a type library. When using the Universal Marshaler, make sure that you use only automation types (covered later) and add the **oleautomation** attribute to your interface declaration.

Table 17.1	MIDL generated proxy-stub files for MailOrder1.
File	**Description**
MailOrder1.h	A header file with the C/C++ compatible interface declarations
MailOrder1_p.c	The code that implements the proxy/stub
MailOrder1_i.c	A C file that contains the interface GUIDs
DllData.c	A C file that implements a DLL for the proxy-stub code

Both MIDL-produced marshaling and type library marshaling are forms of what is known as *standard marshaling*. Occasionally, standard marshaling might not meet your needs. In this case, you can use your own *custom marshaling*. Custom marshaling requires that your component implement the **IMarshal** interface. You'll still need to provide a proxy object for a client to communicate with your component.

Don't make the mistake of thinking that your custom interfaces require custom marshaling. Typically, you will only choose to implement custom marshaling when COM does not support the desired behavior or you have detailed knowledge that can be used to increase performance.

Using MIDL

MIDL is IDL-extended to support COM. As you have seen in previous chapters, you don't need to specify your interfaces in MIDL. However, specifying your interfaces in MIDL can make life easier. The MIDL compiler will generate the files listed previously in Table 17.1. These files are then used in the building and distribution of your objects. The MIDL syntax is C-like. The only real difference is that attributes are specified for all data, methods, interfaces, classes, and libraries. Attributes always prefix what they modify and are enclosed in brackets.

Creating A Custom Interface

Once again, the mail-order catalog business will be used, and to keep it interesting, the interface will again be changed. The following code shows what an IDL file for the mail-order catalog business might look like. To build your own IDL file, create a text file and save it as mailorder1.idl.

```
// Bring in needed system IDL files
import "wtypes.idl";
import "unknwn.idl";

typedef enum
{
  Basic,
  Express,   // Three business days or less
  Expedited, // Two business days or less
  Overnight
```

```
} Method;

typedef enum
{
  Alabama,
  Alaska,
     // other states go here
  Wisconsin,
  Wyoming,
  MAXSTATE
} State;
//
// Interface information for IMailOrder1
//
[
  object,
  uuid(754F2088-D313-11d2-A470-00C04F688CFA)
]
interface IMailOrder1 : IUnknown
{
  HRESULT GetShippingCost( [in] Method eMethod,
                           [in] double weight,
                           [out, retval] double *rate );
  HRESULT GetTaxRate( [in] State eState,
                      [out, retval] double *rate );
}

//
// Class information for MailOrder1
//
[
  uuid(DE5DAF86-D2FD-11D2-A470-00C04F688CFA)
]
coclass MailOrder1
{
  interface IMailOrder1;
};
```

The MailOrder component provides a means by which a client can obtain the following:

1. The shipping cost, based on the method of shipment

2. The tax rate for a specific state

Keep in mind that **IMailOrder1** is simply a description of protocol. Following is a cursory look at mailorder1.idl.

The import Directive

The **import** directive is similar to **#include** in C++. Here it is used to bring in two standard IDL files provided with Visual C++. The wtypes.idl file provides the declaration of many common Windows and OLE types. The unknwn.idl file contains the declarations for the **IUnknown** and **IClassFactory** interfaces.

The typedef Statement

The **typedef** statement can be used like you would in C. However, unlike C and C++, the **typedef** keyword has an optional syntax that lets you associate special attributes with the new type being declared. A total of nine different attributes are available that can legally be used in a **typedef** attribute list. The syntax for a **typedef** statement looks like this:

```
typedef [ the-attribute-list ] type-specifier declarator-list;
```

The interface Keyword

The **interface** keyword is followed by the name of the interface being declared. As you already know, the **interface** keyword, like **typedef**, can be preceded by a list of optional attributes. The **interface** keyword always requires that you specify the **object** and **uuid** attributes when declaring a custom COM interface. The **object** keyword specifies that this is a custom interface, and it ensures that the COM library will provide the standard marshaling code. The **uuid** attribute, as you can see, contains the interface's IID.

Method Prototypes

Method prototypes are like C/C++ function prototypes, except that each method argument will have one or more attributes associated with it. The most important of these attributes is an input parameter, output parameter, or both. The **in** and **out** attributes specify the semantics of data transfer. An in attribute specifies that the parameter is an input *to* the method. An **out** attribute specifies that the parameter is an output *from* the method. These attributes are important because they tell the MIDL compiler how to generate the code needed to marshal the data between client and server. These attributes indicate which entity is responsible for allocating and freeing memory. The following rules apply:

➤ [in]—The client is responsible for allocating and freeing memory.

➤ [out]—The server is responsible for allocating the memory, and the client is responsible for freeing the memory.

➤ [in,out]—The client is responsible for allocating and freeing the memory. However, the server can reallocate memory if it needs to.

Input parameters are passed by value, and output parameters are always passed via a pointer. Another frequently used attribute is **retval**. This attribute designates the parameter that receives the logical return value of the method (**retval** indicates the parameter that should look like a return value in languages such as Visual Basic, which mask the actual **HRESULT** return value). The parameter must also have the **out** attribute and, of course, must be a pointer.

Two other commonly used attributes are **size_is()** and **string**. You use the **size_is()** attribute to specify the size in bytes of the data that a pointer is pointing to. For example, in the following method prototype, **pbData** points to a block of memory that is **lSize** bytes in length.

```
HRESULT PutBinaryData( [in] long lSize,
                       [in, size_is(lSize)] byte * pbData);
```

The **string** attribute is used to inform the marshaler that the data is a null-terminated array of char, **wchar_t**, or **byte** data. Here's an example of how it might be used:

```
HRESULT GetStateName( [out, string] wchar_t ** pwszStateName);
```

COM manipulates all strings as Unicode strings. This means that if you use **char ***, it will be converted to a **wchar_t ***. This is true for Windows NT 4.0 and above as well.

Recall that all of your methods should return an **HRESULT** value. By using **HRESULT** return values even with methods that you think can never fail, you are providing a means whereby COM can step in and relay error information to the client. COM also places a restriction on the data types that can be used as arguments. Because the marshaling layer must know the size of all data, the data types that can be used are restricted to the base types shown in Table 17.2.

You can declare arrays of the basic types, and you can specify your own user data type by creating an **enum** or a **struct**. A **struct** can include one or more of the base types or user types. Of course, **IUnknown *** and derivatives may also be used as method arguments.

Now back to the **IMailOrder1** interface. The interface has two methods. The first method, **GetShippingCost()**, has two input parameters and a single output parameter that is also the return value. The *eMethod* parameter is of type **Method**, which is a user-defined type. This parameter specifies the mode of

Table 17.2	Base data types that can be used for method arguments.		
MIDL Data Type	Number Of Bits	VC++ Data Type	Comment
boolean	8	unsigned char	-
byte	8	unsigned char	-
char	8	unsigned char	-
double	64	double	-
float	32	float	-
hyper	64	__int64	Can be signed or unsigned; default is signed
int	32	int	Can be signed or unsigned; default is signed
long	32	long	Can be signed or unsigned; default is signed
short	16	short	Can be signed or unsigned; default is signed
small	8	char	Can be signed or unsigned; default is signed
wchar_t	16	wchar_t	Unsigned short

shipment. The second parameter specifies the weight in pounds, and the third parameter returns the shipping cost in dollars.

The second method, **GetTaxRate()**, has one input parameter and one output/ return value. A user-defined data type, **State**, is being used to specify the state for which the tax rate is desired, and the second parameter returns the tax rate as a percent.

The coclass Keyword

The last section uses the **coclass** keyword to indicate the declaration of a new COM class type. Immediately following the **coclass** keyword is the name of the new component. The **coclass** keyword has an attribute list associated with it, which requires that the **uuid** attribute always be specified.

There will undoubtedly be one or more questions on the exam about IDL files. So, make sure that you are familiar with the keywords and basic structure of the language.

Using The MIDL Compiler

To compile your custom interface, you have at least two choices. First, you can run the compiler from a DOS prompt. For example, you would use the following command:

```
midl /Oicf mailorder1.idl
```

Use the **/Oicf** switch with Windows NT 4 or above to improve performance.

You can also compile your custom interface from the VC++ IDE. Create a Utility Project and then add the mailorder1.idl file to the project. Next, right-click on the IDL file project entry, and select Settings from the pop-up menu. When the Build Settings dialog box opens, make sure that the settings are the same as shown in Figure 17.1. Now compile the mailorder1.idl file.

Implementing The Component Functionality

At this point, you can implement the component's functionality by using the SDK or MFC. When deciding which method to use when building a compo-

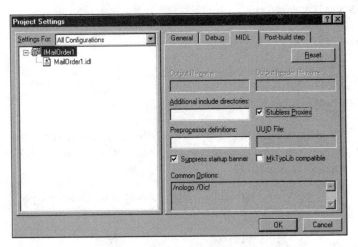

Figure 17.1 Project settings for the IDL file.

nent, you need to make tradeoffs. For example, do you need to build the component quickly, or can you take longer to issue it for the best performance and smallest footprint?

Using MFC

Recall that MFC provides a number of macros and classes that enable you to deal with COM in a more abstract manner than with the SDK. This allows you to focus on the uniqueness of your component. This section shows how you might implement the **IMailOrder1** object by using MFC. Here's what the header file might look like:

```
#if !defined(MAILORDER_H_INCLUDED_)
#define MAILORDER_H_INCLUDED_
// MailOrder.h : header file
//
class CMailOrder : public CCmdTarget
{
public:
  CMailOrder();
virtual ~CMailOrder();
protected:
  // IMailOrder1 members
  BEGIN_INTERFACE_PART(InnerMailOrder, IMailOrder1)
    STDMETHOD(GetShippingCost) ( Method eMethod,
                                 double weight,
                                 double *rate );
    STDMETHOD(GetTaxRate) ( State eState,
                            double *rate );
  END_INTERFACE_PART(InnerMailOrder)
  DECLARE_DYNCREATE(CMailOrder)
  DECLARE_OLECREATE(CMailOrder)
  DECLARE_INTERFACE_MAP()
private:
  void Init();
};
#endif // !defined(AFX_MAILORDER_H_INCLUDED_)
```

The header file is straightforward. The **CMailOrder** class is derived from **CCmdTarget**, and the class has a constructor, a destructor, the necessary MFC macros, and a function named **Init()**.

The implementation file is also straightforward, so only a few lines are provided:

```
// MailOrder.cpp : implementation file
```

```
//
#include "stdafx.h"
#include "..\IMailOrder1\MailOrder1.h"
#include "..\IMailOrder1\MailOrder1_i.c" // IID_IMailOrder1 and
                                        //  CLSID_MailOrder1
#include "MailOrder.h"

    // . . .

static double g_StateTax[MAXSTATE];
////////////////////////////////////////////////////////////////
// CMailOrder
IMPLEMENT_DYNCREATE(CMailOrder, CCmdTarget)
CMailOrder::CMailOrder()
{
    AfxOleLockApp();
   Init();
}
CMailOrder::~CMailOrder()
{
   AfxOleUnlockApp();
}
BEGIN_INTERFACE_MAP(CMailOrder, CCmdTarget)
   INTERFACE_PART(CMailOrder, IID_IMailOrder1, InnerMailOrder)
END_INTERFACE_MAP()

// Support a class factory
// {DE5DAF86-D2FD-11D2-A470-00C04F688CFA}
IMPLEMENT_OLECREATE(CMailOrder, "MailOrder1", 0xde5daf86,
                    0xd2fd, 0x11d2, 0xa4, 0x70, 0x0, 0xc0,
                    0x4f, 0x68, 0x8c, 0xfa);

    //  . . .
```

First, notice the included files. MailOrder1.h is one file generated by the MIDL compiler. It provides C and C++ definitions of the interface that is specified in the IDL file. MailOrder1_i.c contains definitions for all the GUIDs specified in the IDL file.

Next, look at the constructor. It calls two functions. The first, **AfxOleLockApp()**, increments the object count to ensure the object is not destroyed while its server is still being used by a client. The second function called by the constructor simply initializes the tax rates for all of the states. **AfxOleUnlockApp()** is called by the destructor to decrement the object count and causes the server to shut down if the count goes to zero.

Using SDK

Recall that with SDK you must provide both the component's functionality and a class factory to generate objects of your component; much of the code will be boilerplate. You may be able to copy most of the boilerplate code from other projects, or you may need to create it. Either way, it's a tedious and error-prone process. However, when you need high performance and/or smallest footprint, SDK is probably a better tool than MFC.

The COM Object

Because the SDK doesn't provide macros that declare the **IUnknown** methods, you must declare them. You also need to define a member variable to use for reference counting. This section shows how you can implement the **IMailOrder1** object using the SDK. Here's what the header file for the object might look like:

```
// CoMailOrder.h: interface for the CCoMailOrder class.
//
////////////////////////////////////////////////////////////////

#if !defined(COMAILORDER_H_)
#define COMAILORDER_H_

#if _MSC_VER > 1000
#pragma once
#endif // _MSC_VER > 1000

class CCoMailOrder : public IMailOrder1
{
public:
  CCoMailOrder() : m_lRef(0) { CCounters::IncObjectCount(); }
  ~CCoMailOrder() { CCounters::DecObjectCount(); }

  // IUnknown
  STDMETHOD(QueryInterface)(REFIID, void**);
  STDMETHOD_(ULONG, AddRef)();
  STDMETHOD_(ULONG, Release)();

  // IShipping
  STDMETHOD(GetShippingCost)(Method eMethod,
                             double dWeight,
                             double * dRate);
  STDMETHOD(GetTaxRate)(State eState,
                        double * dRate);
private:
  void Init();
```

```
   long m_lRef;
};
#endif // !defined(COMAILORDER_H_)
```

The differences between this class definition and the one found in MFC is what you would expect. Here, the class is derived from **IMailOrder1** rather than **CCmdTarget**. Note that a data member was provided for storing the reference count. Also of interest are the constructor and destructor. The constructor initializes **m_lRef** and calls **CCounters::IncObjectCount()**. **CCounters::IncObjectCount()** is one of four functions that is used to coordinate the lifetime of the whole COM component. Lifetime management will be addressed later in this chapter.

The implementation file is straightforward and can be modeled after the file ComShipping.cpp in Chapter 14. Be sure to include the MailOrder1.h file that the MIDL compiler generated.

The Class Factory

There are only a couple of differences between this class factory and the one used in Chapter 14. Recall that **CLSID**s and **IID**s are provided by a file (MailOrder1_i.c) generated by the MIDL compiler, which means there is no need to provide the **#define INITGUID** statement at the top of the class factory's implementation file. As in the previous COM object file, you need to include the MailOrder1.h file.

One other item of importance deals with reference counting associated with the class factory. Because the factory is a singleton, the implementation of **AddRef()** and **Release()** has been changed so that both functions simply return a 1. The following code has the old code commented out:

```
STDMETHODIMP_(ULONG) CMailOrderClassFactory::AddRef()
{
   return 1; //InterlockedIncrement(&m_lRef);
}

STDMETHODIMP_(ULONG) CMailOrderClassFactory::Release()
{
//   if(InterlockedDecrement(&m_lRef) == 0)
//   {
//      delete this;
//      return 0;
//   }
   return 1; // m_lRef;
}
```

Building A Local Server

This section looks at two local servers. One uses MFC and the other uses the SDK. Both servers are generic and can be used to implement other COM local servers.

A local server is slightly more complicated than an in-process server in a number of ways. First, RegSvr32.exe is not used to register and unregister a local server. Instead, a local server must determine from command-line arguments whether it should register or unregister itself. So you need to provide code to implement this functionality.

The second thing that makes local servers different than in-process servers is that a local server can also be a full-blown application. Examples of this are Word and Excel.

A Local Server Using MFC

This server will provide minimal user interaction. It simply presents a dialog box that allows the user to register or unregister the server with the system.

The server class inherits from **CWinApp**. You will need to override **InitInstance()** and provide two functions, one to register the component and the other to unregister it. Here's the **CLocalServerApp** class:

```
// LocalServer.h : main header file for the LOCALSERVER application
//
#if !defined(LOCALSERVER_H_INCLUDED_)
#define LOCALSERVER_H_INCLUDED_


#include "resource.h"                        // main symbols
/////////////////////////////////////////////////////////////////////
// CLocalServerApp:
// See LocalServer.cpp for the implementation of this class
//
class CLocalServerApp : public CWinApp
{
public:
  virtual BOOL InitInstance();
private:
  void Register(const CString &strProgID,
                bool bSilentOperation = true);
  void Unregister(const CString &strCLSID,
                  const CString &strProgID,
                  bool bSilentOperation = true);
};
#endif // !defined(AFX_LOCALSERVER_H_INCLUDED_)
```

A local server relies on command-line arguments to determine its mode of operation. Depending on the argument, a local server either starts the class factory or updates the Registry. Here, most of the action occurs in **InitInstance()**. First, **AfxOleInit()** is called to initialize COM. Then the command line is examined. If the command line contains an **Embedding** or **Automation** argument, the class factory is started and a **TRUE** is returned back to the framework. Returning a **TRUE** allows the application's message loop to run. If **Embedding** or **Automation** was not found, the command line is again examined, this time for **RegServer** or **UnregServer**. If the command line contains **RegServer**, the member function **Register()** is called to register the component. **Unregister()** is called to unregister the component if the command line contains **UnregServer**. After the appropriate member function is called, a **FALSE** is returned to the framework, causing the application to terminate. The absence of any of the command-line arguments indicates that the user started the application from the command line or desktop.

When started by the user, the application presents a dialog box that asks the user whether the server should be registered or unregistered. After taking the appropriate action, a **FALSE** is returned to the framework. Here's the implementation of the server:

```
/////////////////////////////////////////////////////////////////
// LocalServer.cpp : Defines the class behaviors.
//
#include "stdafx.h"
#include "LocalServer.h"
#include "LocalServerDlg.h"
#include "ServerCmdLine.h"
/////////////////////////////////////////////////////////////////
// CLocalServerApp
/////////////////////////////////////////////////////////////////
// The one and only CLocalServerApp object
CLocalServerApp theApp;
/////////////////////////////////////////////////////////////////
// CLocalServerApp initialization

BOOL CLocalServerApp::InitInstance()
{
  if(!AfxOleInit())
  {
    AfxMessageBox("Couldn't initialize COM subsystem.",
                MB_ICONSTOP);
    return FALSE;
  }
  CServerCmdLineInfo cmdInfo;
  ParseCommandLine(cmdInfo);
```

```
    if(cmdInfo.m_bRunEmbedded || cmdInfo.m_bRunAutomated)
    {
      COleObjectFactory::RegisterAll();
      return TRUE;
    }
    CString strCLSID, strProgID;
    strCLSID.LoadString(IDS_CLSID);   // This is the CLSID
    strProgID.LoadString(IDS_PROGID); // This is "MailOrder1"
    if(cmdInfo.m_bRegister)
    {
      Register(strProgID);
      return FALSE;
    }
    if(cmdInfo.m_bUnregister)
    {
      Unregister(strCLSID, strProgID);
      return FALSE;
    }

    // Let the user register or unregister the server. Pass the
    // name of the component to the dialog box so that it can be
    // displayed in the title bar.
    CLocalServerDlg dlg(strProgID);
    int nResponse = dlg.DoModal();
    if (nResponse == ID_REGISTER)
    {
      Register(strProgID, false);
    }
    else if (nResponse == ID_UNREGISTER)
    {
      Unregister(strCLSID, strProgID, false);
    }
    return FALSE;
}

void CLocalServerApp::Register(const CString &strProgID,
                               bool bSilentOperation)
{
  COleObjectFactory::UpdateRegistryAll();
  if(bSilentOperation)
    return;
  CString msg = "The " + strProgID +
                " server has been registered.";
  AfxMessageBox(msg, MB_ICONINFORMATION);
}

void CLocalServerApp::Unregister(const CString &strCLSID,
```

```
                              const CString &strProgID,
                              bool bSilentOperation)
{
  BSTR bstrCLSID = strCLSID.AllocSysString();
  CLSID clsid;
  CLSIDFromString(bstrCLSID, &clsid);
  SysFreeString(bstrCLSID);
  AfxOleUnregisterClass(clsid, strProgID);
  if(bSilentOperation)
    return;
  CString msg= "The " + strProgID +
               " server has been unregistered.";
  AfxMessageBox(msg, MB_ICONINFORMATION);
}
```

The **CCommandLineInfo** class handles command-line arguments of embedding and automation but doesn't recognize **register** or **unregister**. So a new class, **CServerCmdLineInfo**, derived from **CCommandLineInfo** will be used to handle this small problem. **CServerCmdLineInfo** provides two data members and one function override. Here's what it looks like:

```
#if !defined(SERVERCMDLINE_H_INCLUDED_)
#define SERVERCMDLINE_H_INCLUDED_
// ServerCmdLine.h : header file
//
class CServerCmdLineInfo : public CCommandLineInfo
{
public:
  CServerCmdLineInfo();
  virtual void ParseParam(LPCTSTR lpszParam,
                     BOOL bFlag, BOOL bLast);
  bool m_bRegister;
  bool m_bUnregister;
};
#endif // !defined(SERVERCMDLINE_H_INCLUDED_)

// ServerCmdLine.cpp : implementation file
//
#include "stdafx.h"
#include "LocalServer.h"
#include "ServerCmdLine.h"
/////////////////////////////////////////////////////////////////////
// CServerCmdLine
CServerCmdLineInfo::CServerCmdLineInfo()
: m_bRegister(false)
, m_bUnregister(false)
```

```
{
}

void CServerCmdLineInfo::ParseParam(LPCTSTR lpszParm,
                                    BOOL bFlag, BOOL bLast)
{
  CCommandLineInfo::ParseParam(lpszParm, bFlag, bLast);
  if(!bFlag)
    return;
  CString strArg(lpszParm);
  strArg.MakeLower();
  m_bRegister   = (strArg == "register");
  m_bUnregister = (strArg == "unregister");
}
```

Processing The Server Command Line

After defining **cmdInfo**, **CWinApp::ParseCommandLine** is called to parse the command line. **ParseCommandLine** calls **ParseParam** once for each parameter or flag on the command line, passing the argument to **lpszParam**. If the first character of the parameter is a "-" or a "/", then it is removed and **bFlag** is set to **TRUE**. Although you don't care about it here, **bLast** will be **FALSE**, except when parsing the final parameter.

Registering The Running Class Factory

If either the embedding flag or the automation flag is set, the server was launched by COM. When this happens, the server simply calls **RegisterAll()** and then returns **TRUE**. **RegisterAll()** registers all OLE servers (factories) as running. This enables the OLE libraries to create objects from other applications. Returning **TRUE** informs the framework that everything is okay and that the application should continue by creating a Windows message queue and entering the standard message loop. Here's the code:

```
if(cmdInfo.m_bRunEmbedded || cmdInfo.m_bRunAutomated)
  {
    COleObjectFactory::RegisterAll();
    return TRUE;
  }
```

Registering And Unregistering The Server

If a user or another program launches the server, passing it the register flag or unregister flag, the server will silently register or unregister itself by calling **Register()** or **Unregister()**. **Register()** simply calls **COleObjectFactory::Update RegisterAll()** to update the Registry. **Unregister()** is slightly more complicated because it must change a **CString** into a **CLSID**. **Unregister()** calls **AfxOle**

UnregisterClass() to remove the entry from the Registry. The prototype for AfxOleUnregisterClass() is in the afxctl.h file.

Presenting The Registration Dialog Box

If the server is launched with none of the previously mentioned flags passed in on the command line, the class presents the user with a registration dialog box. This box, the only user interface that the server shows, informs the user that the program is a local COM server and provides no functionality when run manually. However, it does allow the user to register or unregister the server. Because the code is straightforward, it isn't included, but Figure 17.2 shows what the dialog box might look like.

A Local Server Using SDK

In terms of user interaction, this server does even less than the preceding one. Here, no user interaction is provided. However, unlike the MFC version, where lifetime management is handled by the framework, in the SDK version, you must provide the lifetime management code.

Component Lifetime And The CCounters Class

It's important to keep the server alive as long as outstanding locks exist on the server or any live COM objects exist. As with the in-process server in Chapter 14, the CCounters class in this server is key in the component lifetime management. By using a class such as CCounters, the variables and functions that would normally have global scope are encapsulated within a single class. However, CCounters used in Chapter 14 won't work with a local server. Recall that all in-process servers implement the function DllCanUnloadNow(), which the housing can call to determine whether it can unload the in-process server. Recall also that the CCounters class in calls the InterlockedIncrement() and InterlockedDecrement() Win32 API functions to increment and decrement the lock count and object count, and

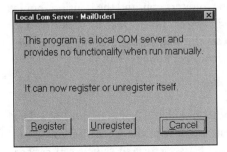

Figure 17.2   The registration dialog box.

that **DllCanUnloadNow()** examines these count values to determine if it is safe to unload. A local server doesn't have a **DllCanUnloadNow()** function so component lifetime must be handled differently.

COM provides two functions, **CoAddRefServerProcess()** and **CoRelease ServerProcess()**, that automatically increment and decrement a per-process reference count, which the COM library maintains for each local server. These two functions are used in **CCounters**. Here's the **CCounters** class:

```
class CCounters
{
public:
  static HANDLE m_hExitEvent;
  // Locks
  static long IncLockCount() { return CoAddRefServerProcess(); }
  static long DecLockCount()
  {
    ULONG ul = CoReleaseServerProcess();
    if(ul == 0)
      SetEvent(m_hExitEvent);
    return ul;
  }
  // Objects
  static long IncObjectCount() { return CoAddRefServerProcess(); }
  static long DecObjectCount()
  {
    ULONG ul = CoReleaseServerProcess();
    if(ul == 0)
      SetEvent(m_hExitEvent);
    return ul;
  }
};
```

Notice that no local lock count or local object count exists. Instead, **CCounters** provides a static variable used to cache the handle to a Win32 event object. This handle should be initialized to 0 in Counters.cpp, and the housing should load it with a valid handle to an event object. Both **DecLockCount()** and **DecObjectCount()** call **SetEvent()** to set the state of the event object to signaled when the COM per-process reference count goes to 0.

The Component's Housing

After initializing the COM library, a local server publishes a component's class factory dynamically at runtime by registering it with the COM Service Control Manager (SCM). This activates the class factory so that it can service object-creating requests. The server uses the **CoRegisterClassObject()** function to register the class factory. It's important that the server revoke the registered class factory before shutting down. The server does this by calling **CoRevokeClassObject()**, which informs the SCM that the class factory is no longer available. Here's an example of a local server:

```
CMailOrderClassFactory g_MailOrderFactory;
int main(int argc, char **argv)
{
  if(argc > 1)
  {
    if(_stricmp(argv[1], "-regserver") == 0 ||
       _stricmp(argv[1], "/regserver") == 0 )
    {
      Register();
      return;
    }
    if(_stricmp(argv[1], "-unregserver") == 0 ||
       _stricmp(argv[1], "/unregserver") == 0 )
    {
      Unregister();
      return;
    }
  }

  CCounters::m_hExitEvent = CreateEvent(NULL, FALSE, FALSE, NULL);
  if(CCounters::m_hExitEvent == NULL)
    assert(false);

  // Initialize COM
  HRESULT hr = CoInitializeEx(NULL, COINIT_MULTITHREADED);

// Error checking left out for brevity

  DWORD dwRegister = 0;
  hr = CoRegisterClassObject(CLSID_MailOrder1,
                             &g_MailOrderFactory,
                             CLSCTX_LOCAL_SERVER,
                             REGCLS_MULTIPLEUSE,
                             &dwRegister);

  WaitForSingleObject(CCounters::m_hExitEvent, INFINITE);

  hr = CoRevokeClassObject(dwRegister);

  // Uninitialize COM
  if(SUCCEEDED(hr))
    CoUninitialize();
```

```
CloseHandle(CCounters::m_hExitEvent);
return 0;
}
```

CoInitializeEx() is declared in objbase.h. Always declare _WIN32_WINNT=0x0400 or _WIN32_DCOM as appropriate for your system.

After checking to see if it should register or unregister the component, the server creates a Win32 event object by calling **CreateEvent()**. The handle to the event object is stored in **CCounters::m_hExitEvent** for use by **CCounters:: DecLockCount()** and **CCounters::DecObjectCount()**. Next, the COM library is initialized and the class factory is registered. Then **WaitFor SingleObject()** is called to wait on the event object to be signaled. The event object becomes signaled when the per-process reference count goes to 0. When **WaitFor SingleObject()** returns, it's time for the server to shut down. So, **Co RevokeClassObject()** is called to unregister the class factory, **CoUninitialize()** is called to shut down COM, and **CloseHandle()** is called to remove the event object.

CoRegisterClassObject's fourth parameter specifies how the class factory is to behave. You should understand the meaning and use of the various flag values that can be specified.

Registering The Component

At a minimum, a local server needs to place two enters in the Registry. The first is a human-readable description for the **CLSID** and the path to the server. For example:

```
[HKEY_CLASSES_ROOT\CLSID\{clsid}]@="MailOrder1"
[HKEY_CLASSES_ROOT\CLSID\{clsid}\LocalServer32]
@="c:\LocalServers\MailOrderSrv.exe"
```

The @ sign indicates the default value for a given key. The **clsid** symbol would be replaced with the actual GUID.

This server uses the function **Register()** to carry out the task of registering the component:

```
void Register()
{
  TCHAR theCLSID[MAX_PATH];
  GetCLSID(theCLSID);

  TCHAR theKey[MAX_PATH];
  TCHAR theValue[MAX_PATH];
  HKEY hKey = 0;
  _tcscpy(theKey, _T("CLSID\\"));
  _tcscat(theKey, theCLSID);
  RegCreateKey(HKEY_CLASSES_ROOT, theKey, &hKey);
  _tcscpy(theValue, _T("MailOrder1"));
  RegSetValueEx(hKey, 0, 0, REG_SZ,
                reinterpret_cast<BYTE*>(theValue),
                ByteLength(theValue));
  RegCloseKey(hKey);

  _tcscat(theKey, TEXT("\\ProgID"));
  RegCreateKey(HKEY_CLASSES_ROOT, theKey, &hKey);
  RegSetValueEx(hKey, 0, 0, REG_SZ,
                reinterpret_cast<BYTE*>(theValue),
                ByteLength(theValue));
  RegCloseKey(hKey);

  _tcscpy(theKey, _T("CLSID\\"));
  _tcscat(theKey, theCLSID);
  _tcscat(theKey, TEXT("\\LocalServer32"));
  RegCreateKey(HKEY_CLASSES_ROOT, theKey, &hKey);
  GetModuleFileName(0, theValue, MAX_PATH);
  RegSetValueEx(hKey, 0, 0, REG_SZ,
                reinterpret_cast<BYTE*>(theValue),
                ByteLength(theValue));
  RegCloseKey(hKey);
}
```

This function is straightforward. After calling **GetCLSID()**, shown later, to get a string that represents the **CLSID**, it then simply uses generic-text routines, and Win32 Registry API functions to create keys and add the necessary named values into the Registry. In addition to the minimum required entries, a **ProgID** entry is provided. Recall that the client can obtain the **CLSID** by calling **CLSIDFromProgID()** and passing the **ProgID**.

Now for the **Unregister()** function. This function simply deletes all the keys created by **Register()**:

```
void Unregister()
{
```

```
    TCHAR theCLSID[MAX_PATH];
    GetCLSID(theCLSID);

    TCHAR theKey[MAX_PATH];
    HKEY hKey = 0;

    _tcscpy(theKey, _T("CLSID\\"));
    _tcscat(theKey, theCLSID);
    _tcscat(theKey, TEXT("\\LocalServer32"));
    RegDeleteKey(HKEY_CLASSES_ROOT, theKey);

    _tcscpy(theKey, _T("CLSID\\"));
    _tcscat(theKey, theCLSID);
    _tcscat(theKey, TEXT("\\ProgID"));
    RegDeleteKey(HKEY_CLASSES_ROOT, theKey);

    _tcscpy(theKey, _T("CLSID\\"));
    _tcscat(theKey, theCLSID);
    RegDeleteKey(HKEY_CLASSES_ROOT, theKey);
}
```

Notice that **Unregister()** removes Registry keys in the opposite order in which they were created. This isn't absolutely required, but that all child keys must be deleted before a parent key can be deleted is required.

 For the exam, you'll need to be prepared to answer both general and specific questions about the Registry. Be sure you are familiar with its structure, the predefined keys, the Registry functions, and the kinds of data the Registry should hold.

Now for the **GetCLSID()** helper function. This function calls **StringFrom CLSID()**, copies the string to the output array, and then frees the memory allocated by **StringFromCLSID()**.

```
void GetCLSID(TCHAR szCLSID[])
{
    LPOLESTR pszOLECLSID;
    StringFromCLSID(CLSID_MailOrder1, &pszOLECLSID);
#ifdef _UNICODE
    wcscpy(szCLSID, pszOLECLSID);
#else
    wcstombs(szCLSID, pszOLECLSID, MAX_PATH);
#endif
    CoTaskMemFree(pszOLECLSID);
}
```

You need to consider a number of questions concerning Unicode and ANSI text and routines. Make sure you understand where each type of text is employed. Also, you should be familiar with the generic-text mappings of data types and routines as defined in TCHAR.H.

Building A Proxy-Stub DLL

You now have a local server built and registered. However, if you had a client program that tried to use it, you would find that any call to **CoCreateInstance()** requesting an **IMailOrder1** interface pointer would return an **E_NOINTER FACE** error. You need the proxy and stub registered to handle the **IMainOrder1** interface. As discussed earlier, the MIDL tool produces the files needed to create the proxy-stub DLL, but it's up to you to build it. First, you need to create **MailOrder1PS.DEF**:

```
LIBRARY      "MailOrder1PS"

EXPORTS
  DllCanUnloadNow        PRIVATE
  DllGetClassObject      PRIVATE
  DllRegisterServer      PRIVATE
  DllUnregisterServer    PRIVATE

  GetProxyDllInfo        PRIVATE
```

 In a module-definition file, be sure to type all of the statements in uppercase and your user-specified identifiers exactly like they are in your program. The online document claims that statements and attribute keywords are not case-sensitive. Statements such as **LIBRARY** and **EXPORTS**, however, must be uppercase, or you will get compiler errors. Be forewarned: The error messages can leave you scratching your head.

The only area that might be unfamiliar in this DEF file is the **GetProxyDllInfo()** entry point. This function is created automatically by a macro expanded in DllData.c. **GetProxyDllInfo()** provides a mechanism for COM to query information about the classes and interfaces supported by the proxy-stub DLL.

You can build your proxy-stub DLL in one of two ways: by using the **nmake** utility or by using the IDE.

Using nmake

The first way to build a proxy-stub DLL is to create a make file and pass it to the **nmake** utility. Here's the make file:

```
MailOrder1ps.dll: dlldata.obj MailOrder1_p.obj MailOrder1_i.obj
  link /dll /out:MailOrder1ps.dll /def:MailOrder1ps.def        \
    /entry:DllMain dlldata.obj MailOrder1_p.obj MailOrder1_i.obj \
    kernel32.lib rpcrt4.lib oleaut32.lib \

.c.obj:
  cl /c /Ox /DWIN32 /D_WIN32_WINNT=0x0400 /DREGISTER_PROXY_DLL $<

clean:
  @del MailOrder1ps.dll
  @del MailOrder1ps.lib
  @del MailOrder1ps.exp
  @del dlldata.obj
  @del MailOrder1_p.obj
  @del MailOrder1_i.obj
```

Here, the make file is named MailOrder1PS.mk. Specified in the first line is that the output file should be named MailOrder1PS.dll. After creating the make file, you can build the proxy-stub DLL by using the following command line:

```
nmake MailOrder1PS.mk
```

In order to use **nmake**, you need to run the **VcVars32.bat** file located in your installation's **\bin** directory. Running **VcVars32.bat** modifies the **PATH, LIB,** and **INCLUDE** environment variables.

You can now register your proxy-stub DLL just as you do any other in-process server:

```
regsvr32 MailOrder1PS.dll
```

Using The IDE

The second way to build a proxy-stub DLL is to use the IDE and create a Win32 Dynamic-Link Library naming it ProxyStub. Make sure that you specify "An empty DLL Project". Then create ProxyStub.def:

```
LIBRARY        "ProxyStub"

EXPORTS
  DllCanUnloadNow      PRIVATE
  DllGetClassObject    PRIVATE
  DllRegisterServer    PRIVATE
  DllUnregisterServer  PRIVATE

  GetProxyDllInfo      PRIVATE
```

Add the DEF file and the MIDL-produced files to your project (see Figure 17.3).

To get everything to compile and link correctly, you need to change some of your project settings. First are the settings for the preprocessor. To use the full IDL syntax supported by MIDL, define either the preprocessor symbol **_WIN32_DCOM** or ensure that **_WIN32_WINNT** is set to a value greater or equal to 0x0400.

DllData.c contains methods and data used by the proxy and stub class factories. For the code to compile properly, the preprocessor symbol **REGISTER_ PROXY_DLL** must be defined. To enter these **_WIN32_WINNT** and **REGISTER_PROXY_DLL** symbols, choose the C/C++|Category and select Preprocessor. Then enter the symbols under Preprocessor Definitions (see Figure 17.4).

Next, you need to change the object/library modules used by the linker. Under Project|Setting, go to the Link tab, and under Category, select General. Then change the Object/Library Modules entry to rpcrt4.lib oleaut32.lib (see Figure 17.5).

After you build the DLL and run RegSvr32.exe, everything is in place for clients to use your local server. You're now ready to build a client and test your

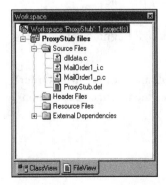

Figure 17.3 Workspace FileView tab.

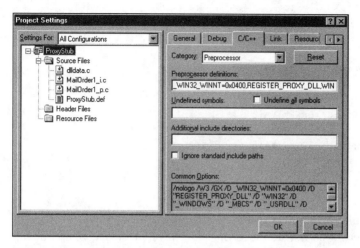

Figure 17.4 The Project Settings dialog box, showing C/C++ preprocessor symbols.

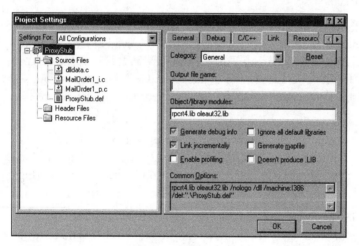

Figure 17.5 Project settings for link object/library modules.

server. If you create a MFC dialog-based application, it might look something like Figure 17.6.

Remember that the definitions of **IID_IMailOrder1** and **CLSID_MailOrder1** are in MailOrder1_i.c, and MailOrder1.h provides the interface declarations.

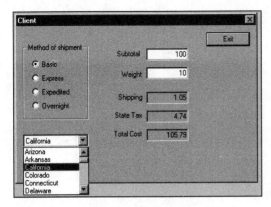

Figure 17.6   The Client dialog box.

Practice Questions

Question 1

> You are implementing a COM local server using MFC. Which function would you use to register your class factory?
>
> ○ a. AfxOleRegisterClass()
>
> ○ b. DllRegisterServer()
>
> ○ c. COleObjectFactory::UpdateRegistryAll()
>
> ○ d. CoRegisterClass()

The correct answer is c. **COleObjectFactory::UpdateRegistryAll()** iterates over each of the object factories residing in the server, querying the factory's **CLSID** and creating the appropriate Registry entries. Other possible correct answers that might be on the exam are **COleObjectFactory::UpdateRegistry()**, **COleTemplateServer::UpdateRegistry()**, and **AfxOleRegisterServerClass()**. Answers a and d are incorrect because **AfxOleRegisterClass()** and **CoRegister Class()** are not valid functions. Answer b is incorrect because **DllRegister Server()** is the function that an application, such as RegSvr32, calls to instruct an in-process server to register itself.

Question 2

> When you register the proxy-stub DLL, which subkeys of HKEY_ CLASSES_ROOT\Interface\{iid} are stored in the Registry? [Choose the two correct answers]
>
> ❑ a. NumMethods
>
> ❑ b. ProgID
>
> ❑ c. ProxyStudClsid32
>
> ❑ d. LocalServer32

Answers a and c are correct. The value entry for **NumMethods** specifies the number of methods the proxy-stub DLL implements. The value entry for **ProxyStubClsid32** maps the interface's IID to the **CLSID** of its proxy and stub objects. Answers b and d are incorrect because these subkeys are created by the server's own registration. The value entry for **ProgID** is the human-readable name of the application and it allows a client to obtain the **CLSID** by calling **CLSIDFromProgID()**. The value entry for LocalServer32 is the full path to the local server.

Question 3

You are using an IDL file to describe your server's COM classes and interfaces. When declaring an interface, which of the following attributes are always required? [Choose all of the correct answers]

❑ a. uuid

❑ b. ptr

❑ c. oleautomation

❑ d. object

Answers a and d are correct. COM requires that an interface must be identified by a 128-bit number, known as an IID. The **uuid** attribute specifies the number. The **object** attribute is what identifies the interface as a COM-style interface. Answer b is incorrect because **ptr** isn't an interface attribute. Answer c is incorrect because the **oleautomation** attribute is needed only when the interface is automation-compatible.

Question 4

You are implementing a COM local server using the SDK. Which function do you use to register your class factory?

○ a. DllGetClassObject()

○ b. CoRegisterClassObject()

○ c. IClassFactory::CreateInstance()

○ d. CoRegisterClassFactory()

The correct answer is b. Answer a is incorrect because **DllGetClassObject()** is a function that returns a class factory object from an in-process server. Answer c is incorrect because **IClassFactory::CreateInstance()** is used to create an object of the class identified with the specified **CLSID**. Answer d is incorrect because **CoRegisterClassFactory()** is not a valid function.

Question 5

Which of the following statements are true? [Check all the correct answers]

❏ a. A method parameter decorated with the [out] attribute indicates that the server will allocate memory for the parameter and that it is the client's responsibility to free the memory.

❏ b. A method parameter decorated with the [in, out] attribute indicates that the client will allocate memory for the parameter and that it is the client's responsibility to free the memory.

❏ c. A method parameter decorated with the [in] attribute indicates that the client must allocate memory for the parameter and that the server must free the memory.

❏ d. A method parameter decorated with the [retval] attribute must also be decorated with the [out] attribute.

❏ e. Method output parameters must always be a pointer type.

Answers a, b, c, d, and e are correct. This question tries to trick you because all the choices are correct. The [**retval**] attribute specifies the parameter that receives a method's return value. [**retval**] cannot be used alone; it must always be accompanied with the [**out**] attribute. The rules concerning memory allocation for method parameters are straightforward:

➤ When a parameter is passed from the client to the server, it is the client's responsibility to both allocate and free the memory.

➤ When a parameter is passed from the server to the client, it is server's responsibility to allocate the memory and the client's responsibility to free it.

➤ When the client passes a parameter to be modified, the client allocates and frees the memory. However, the server, if it chooses, can free and then reallocate memory.

➤ Any parameter that the server allocates memory for must be a pointer type. This includes [**out**], [**out, retval**], and [**in, out**].

If the client passes an interface to the server that the server uses to call the client, then, of course, the roles are reversed.

Need To Know More?

 Box, Don. *Essential COM*. Addison-Wesley, Reading, MA, 1998. ISBN 0-201-63446-5. If you want to gain insight into how COM works, read this book. The author addresses the spirit of COM as much as he does the technology. He knows the subject well and covers the material thoroughly.

 Chappell, David. *Understanding ActiveX and OLE: A Guide for Developers & Managers*. Microsoft Press, Redmond, WA, 1996. ISBN 1-57231-216-5. This book is well written and easy to understand. The author covers basic theory and concepts with little clutter. However, it's not a programming book and contains sparse code.

 Major, Dr. Al. *COM IDL and Interface Design*. Wrox Press Ltd., Acock's Green, Birmingham, U.K., 1999. ISBN 1-861002-25-4. At the time of time writing, this is the only book on the market that is devoted to IDL. This book explains the syntax and usage of IDL in a clear and terse manner.

 Rogerson, Dale. *Inside COM: Microsoft's Component Object Model*. Microsoft Press, Redmond, WA, 1997. ISBN 1-57231-349-8. This book explains theory and implementation of COM objects very well and provides clear explanations on each of the key areas.

 Shepherd, George and Scot Wingo. *MFC Internals: Inside the Microsoft Foundation Class Architecture*. Addison-Wesley, Reading, MA, 1996. ISBN 0-201-40721-3. If you want to learn how MFC does its magic when it comes to COM, this book is for you. The authors did an admirable job of presenting a complex topic and in a straightforward and understandable manner. To aid comprehension, they show what the code looks like after all the macros are expanded. Although this book is over three years old—a lifetime in the computer field—it's still the best source of information about the inner workings of MFC.

 MSDN Library, Platform SDK\Component Services\COM

 MSDN Library, Technical Articles\Component Object Model

MSDN Library, Visual Studio 6.0 Documentation\Visual C++ Documentation\Reference\Microsoft Foundation Class Library and Templates

 Microsoft's Web page for COM is **www.microsoft.com/com**. It contains white papers, presentations, resources, technologies, and so on. Under Resources, you will find the COM spec and a number of sample programs. Explore this Web page; it provides a wealth of information.

Active Template Library

Terms you'll need to understand:

- √ CComModule
- √ import
- √ IDispatch::Invoke()
- √ ATL_NO_VTABLE
- √ DECLARE_REGISTRY_ RESOURCEID()
- √ COM_INTERFACE_ENTRY()
- √ BEGIN_COM_MAP() and END_COM_MAP()
- √ BEGIN_OBJECT_MAP, OBJECT_ ENTRY, and END_OBJECT_MAP
- √ CComObject<>
- √ CComObjectRootBase

- √ CComObjectRootEx<>
- √ CComCoClass<>
- √ [propget], [propput], and [id()]
- √ IDispatch::GetTypeInfo()
- √ IDispatch::GetTypeInfoCount()
- √ COM_SMARTPTR_TYPEDEF()
- √ #import
- √ __com_ptr_t<>
- √ _bstr_t
- √ _com_issue_errorex()
- √ _com_error
- √ IDispatch::GetIDsOfNames()

Techniques you'll need to master:

- √ Describing (the basic features and architecture) of ATL
- √ Implementing a COM component using ATL
- √ Implementing COM clients that use a type library and IDdispatch

The Active Template Library (ATL) makes it easy to develop small, fast, and efficient COM objects. These objects can be implemented so that they do not depend on secondary DLLs, including the standard C runtime DLL. Unlike MFC, where the library is included at link time, ATL works at compile time to configure and control code generation. ATL is basically a set of C++ templates and other kinds of support for writing COM classes. To get at ATL's built-in functionality, you simply **#include** the necessary header and CPP files, then at compile time, the ATL code is included directly into your project. Table 18.1 describes some of these files.

Basic ATL Features

ATL allows you to easily create COM objects, Automation servers, and ActiveX controls. It handles many of the tedious implementation details a developer must deal with when using the SDK. Here's a partial list of benefits you gain by using ATL:

➤ Built-in support for **IUnknown, IClassFactory, IClassFactory2**, and **IDispatch**

➤ Support for the Interface Definition Language (IDL)

➤ Support for dual interfaces and standard COM enumerator interfaces, connection points, tear-off interfaces, and ActiveX controls

➤ Support for OLE DB

➤ Support for Microsoft Management Console Snap-in Objects

➤ Support for dynamic HTML-based Web control

➤ AppWizard, which creates the initial ATL project

➤ Object Wizard, which generates code for basic COM components

➤ Smart pointers for interface pointers, and wrappers for BSTR and VARIANT

ATL Project Structure

The ATL AppWizard creates the initial housing code for your component. After the project is created, you then use the ATL Object Wizard to add components to your project. Both the AppWizard and the Object Wizard create a number of files.

AppWizard-Generated Files

The files that AppWizard generates are listed in Table 18.2.

Table 18.1 ATL files.

File	Description
Atlbase.h	Basic fundamental type and class definitions.
Atlcom.h	Most of ATL's basic functionality.
Atlctl.h, Atlctl.cpp	ActiveX control support.
AtlWin.h, Atlwin.cpp	Basic Windows support.
Statreg.h, Statreg.cpp	Registry update code.
Atliface.idl, Atliface.h	Registrar component support files. Header file is generated by running the IDL file through the MIDL tool.

Table 18.2 AppWizard project files.

File	Description
ProjectName.cpp	The main project file. It contains implementations for all the support functions required by COM to provide a housing for your components. The functions will change depending on whether your housing is a DLL or an EXE.
ProjectName.h	The interface declarations for the components in the housing. This file is initially empty. It is regenerated each time the MIDL compiler is run.
ProjectName.idl	This file contains the specification for the interface. Initially, this file only contains the type library declarations, but as you develop your component, interface, and method, definitions will be added to it.
ProjectName.rc	The resource file for the project.
Resource.h	Resource ID definitions.
StdAfx.h	Includes and definitions used to create the precompiled header. Two key files it includes are atlbase.h and atlcom.h.
StdAfx.cpp	Definitions used to create the precompiled header. It includes atlimp.cpp, which provides implementation for the classes and methods declared in atlbase.h and atlcom.h.
ProjectNamePS.mk	The command-line make file for the project's proxy/stub DLL.
ProjectNamePS.def	Proxy/stub definition file. Windows' definition file, which contains the exposed entry points.
ProjectName.def	DLL projects only.
ProjectName.rgs	EXE projects only. This file is used to register the server. An entry for this file is added to ProjectName.rc.

The AppWizard can create a project for an in-process server, an out-of-process server, or a server that is also a Windows NT service. The focus of this chapter is in-process servers. Assume you create an ATL project, name it ProjectName, and select DLL as the server type. Now let's examine a number of the AppWizard-generated files.

 When you select Service as the server type, AppWizard will generate all the necessary code needed for a Windows NT service. You can take advantage of this feature to develop a Windows NT service, even if you don't want to use COM.

Stdafx.h

The stdafx.h header file contains some interesting **#define**s and pulls in the ATL header files. Here's the stdafx.h header file (adjusted to fit the page):

```
// stdafx.h : include file for standard system include files,
//      or project specific include files that are used frequently,
//      but are changed infrequently

#if !defined(AFX_STDAFX_H__INCLUDED_)
#define AFX_STDAFX_H__INCLUDED_

#if _MSC_VER > 1000
#pragma once
#endif // _MSC_VER > 1000

#define STRICT
#ifndef _WIN32_WINNT
#define _WIN32_WINNT 0x0400
#endif
#define _ATL_APARTMENT_THREADED

#include <atlbase.h>
//You may derive a class from CComModule and use it if you want to
//override something, but do not change the name of _Module
extern CComModule _Module;
#include <atlcom.h>

//{{AFX_INSERT_LOCATION}}
// Microsoft Visual C++ will insert additional declarations
// immediately before the previous line.

#endif // !defined(AFX_STDAFX_H__INCLUDED)
```

Notice first the **#define _WIN32_WINNT** statement. The **_WIN32_WINNT** symbol is used to protect code that is only available for a particular version of Windows NT. If your component is destined to run only on Windows NT 4 or later, you can leave the symbol alone. If you intend to run your component on any system with DCOM installed, you should replace the symbol with **_WIN32_DCOM**. If, by chance, your component is intended for older versions of Windows NT or Windows 95 without DCOM installed, just remove the **#define _WIN32_WINNT** statement altogether.

The next definition in this file is for the symbol **_ATL_APARTMENT_ THREADED**. This symbol defines the default threading model of the DLL to be the apartment model. The various threading models will be covered later.

The other item of interest is the declaration of a **CComModule** object called **_Module**. **CComModule** implements the basic functionality of a COM server and provides basic services such as registering and instantiating the objects supported by the server. This class provides similar functionality to that provided by MFC's **CWinApp** class. Notice the comment that warns you not to change the name of the global **CComModule** instance. Many ATL classes have the **_Module** name hard-coded as part of their implementation and would break if you changed the name.

ProjectName.idl

At this point, the IDL only contains the bare minimum needed for it to compile. As coclasses, interfaces, and their methods and properties are added to the project, the wizards will insert the appropriate code into the IDL file.

```
// ProjectName.idl : IDL source for ProjectName.dll
//

// This file will be processed by the MIDL tool to
// produce the type library (ProjectName.tlb) and marshalling code.

import "oaidl.idl";
import "ocidl.idl";

[
    uuid(AFCF8CC9-C1EF-11D2-A46C-00C04F688CFA),
    version(1.0),
    helpstring("ProjectName 1.0 Type Library")
]
library PROJECTNAMELib
{
    importlib("stdole32.tlb");
```

```
importlib("stdole2.tlb");

};
```

First, two **import** statements bring in definitions of standard types and interfaces used by COM.

Next is the **library** statement, which defines the type library. A *type library* is a binary file that represents the library section of an IDL. The type library (*.TLB) is generated by the MIDL compiler and can be used by clients to determine how to access and use a component. The **library** statement can have attributes associated with it. Attributes always precede the keyword they modify and are enclosed in square brackets. Here, **library** has three attributes: **[uuid]**, **[version]**, and **[helpstring]**.

Within the type library block, you can see the **importlib()** statement has been used to make the standard definitions from the **stdole32.tlb** and **stdole2.tlb** type libraries available in this library. This means that at runtime, clients accessing your type library, **ProjectName.tlb**, will be able to use the information in **stdole32.tlb** and **stdole2.tlb**. This also means that unless they are already on the target machine, both of these type libraries must be distributed with your application.

ProjectName.cpp, ProjectName.h, And ProjectName.def

These files form the basic housing for your component. For DLLs, this support includes the **DllMain()** entry point and the other exports required by COM. For EXEs, it includes **WinMain()** and the primary message loop for the application.

Object Wizard–Generated Files

For each component you add using the Object Wizard, you get the files listed in Table 18.3. Additionally, the wizard adds code to some of the other project files. The actual code generated depends on the category and type of object you select and the attributes you assign.

Assume you create a simple object, name it ObjectName, and accept the defaults for all attributes except for aggregation, which you change to No. The Object Wizard lets you specify whether you want to implement a custom interface or a dual interface. Now, take a moment to understand the interface attribute. Recall that a custom interface is the standard vtable interface, as discussed in Chapter 14. One of the features of a custom interface is that it

Table 18.3   Object Wizard–generated project files.

File	Description
ObjectName.h	The object's header file.
ObjectName.cpp	The object's implementation file.
ObjectName.rgs	The object's Registrar script. This file contains the Registry entries to self-register the component.

requires some form of compile-time binding with the client. In other words, the client must have compile-time knowledge of the interface methods. As you know, this form of binding uses the virtual table of function pointers and is known as "vtable binding." This is fine for C/C++ clients that can include files that contain interface descriptions, CLSIDs, and so on. But what about clients that don't have access to the include files or can't use them, for example, Visual Basic?

One technique is to use the type library. Recall that the type library is a binary representation of what is in the IDL file. So by referencing the type library, Visual Basic is able to statically bind to the methods and properties. However, scripting languages, such as VBScript and JScript, need to be able to bind to methods and properties dynamically at runtime. For this type of client, COM supports the **IDispatch** interface. Each method and property supported by the **IDispatch** interface is assigned a unique ID, known as a *dispid* (dispatch ID). To access a method or property, the client must call **IDispatch::Invoke()**, passing a dispid identifying a given method or property. This type of user-defined interface is commonly referred to as an *Automation interface*. Now that you know what a custom interface is and what an Automation interface is, a dual interface is easy. It's simply a combination of the two. That is, a *dual interface* supports both vtable binding and **IDispatch**.

The **IDispatch** interface consists of the four methods shown in Table 18.4.

Table 18.4   IDispatch methods.

Method	Description
GetTypeInfoCount	Gets the number of type information interfaces. It will return a 1 or a 0.
GetTypeInfo	Gets the type information for an object.
GetIDsOfNames	Gets a list of dispids, given a list of method names.
Invoke	Invokes the target method or property using a dispid.

Interfaces derived from **IDispatch** are restricted to the Automation-compatible types—that is, types listed in the **VARIANT** union. You should be familiar with these types.

Although Object Wizard doesn't support it, you can declare an Automation interface by deriving your interface from **IDispatch**. Alternately, you can use the keyword **dispinterface**, which automatically implies that the actual implementation will be an implementation of the **IDispatch** interface.

Now look at the code that the Object Wizard generated, starting with ObjectName.rgs.

ObjectName.rgs

The RGS file contains script for adding entries to the Registry. This script is compiled into the server as a custom "**REGISTRY**" resource, and is used when the server is told to register itself. The ATL Registrar, which is ultimately responsible for adding the entries to the Registry, understands the Registry script. Your code must have access to the Registrar. There are two ways that this can be achieved. First, you can distribute ATL.DLL with your component. The Registrar lives in the ATL.DLL file. The second method is to choose the Win32 MinDependency target when building your component. This will cause the Registrar code to be statically linked into your component.

Here's an ObjectName.rgs file:

```
HKCR
{
    ProjectName.ObjectName.1 = s 'ObjectName Class'
    {
        CLSID = s '{FF9EF7AC-C052-11D2-A46C-00C04F688CFA}'
    }
    ProjectName.ObjectName = s 'ObjectName Class'
    {
        CLSID = s '{FF9EF7AC-C052-11D2-A46C-00C04F688CFA}'
        CurVer = s 'ProjectName.ObjectName.1'
    }
    NoRemove CLSID
    {
        ForceRemove {FF9EF7AC-C052-11D2-A46C-00C04F688CFA}
                                = s 'ObjectName Class'
```

```
    {
        ProgID = s 'ProjectName.ObjectName.1'
        VersionIndependentProgID = s 'ProjectName.ObjectName'
        ForceRemove 'Programmable'
        InprocServer32 = s '%MODULE%'
        {
            val ThreadingModel = s 'Apartment'
        }
        'TypeLib' = s '{FF9EF792-C052-11D2-A46C-00C04F688CFA}'
    }
  }
}
```

Registry scripts use the keywords described in Table 18.5.

Text that isn't one of the above-listed keywords is either a key or a named value, or the data for that item. Anything to the right of an equal sign is data to be placed in the Registry. If the item to the left of the equal sign has the word **val** in front of it, the data will be added to a named value. If the word **val** is not present the data will be added as the default value of the key. The **%MODULE%** keyword is a replaceable parameter that represents the full pathname of the DLL. The nested braces represent the levels of the keys in the Registry. By default, when registering, all of the keys are added to whatever keys may already be in the Registry. The **ForceRemove** keyword modifies this behavior so that the key to which **ForceRemove** is applied is removed before it is added back in.

The script is also used when unregistering. The default behavior here is to remove every key and subkey of those listed in the script. The **NoRemove** keyword overrides this behavior. Notice in the script above that the **NoRemove** keyword is used with **CLSID**. According to Dr. GUI, this is crucial; otherwise, the unregistering component would remove the entire **CLSID** tree, thereby unregistering every COM object on the system.

Table 18.5	Registry script keywords.
Keyword	**Description**
d	The following value is a **DWORD**
s	The following value is a string
val	The following is a named value, not a key
Delete	Deletes the following key during registration
ForceRemove	Completely removes the following key (if it exists) and then re-creates it
NoRemove	Specifies not to remove the following key during unregistration

If you build the project at this time, the ProjectName will automatically be registered. After building the project, you can run the OLE/COM Object Viewer tool and see that both the type library and object have been registered (refer to Figure 18.1 and Figure 18.2, respectively). You can also run RegEdit and view the entries under the **CLSID** (refer to Figure 18.3).

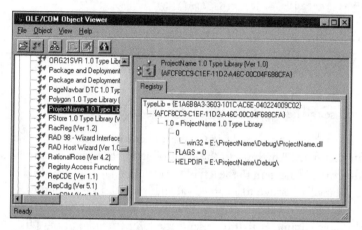

Figure 18.1 OLE/COM object view—Type libraries.

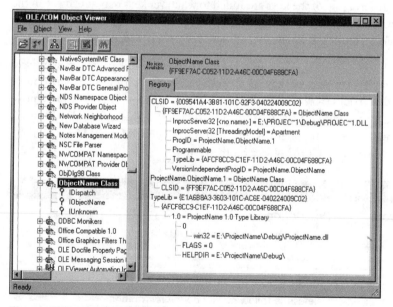

Figure 18.2 OLE/COM object view—Object classes/all objects.

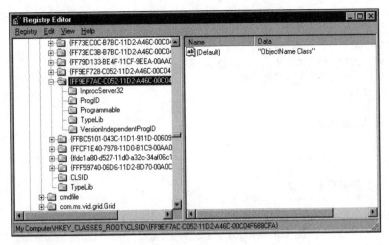

Figure 18.3 RegEdit view of **CLSID**.

ObjectName.h And ObjectName.cpp

These files implement the COM object. At this point, the CPP file is empty
except for a few **#include** statements. The header file looks like this:

```
// ObjectName.h : Declaration of the CObjectName

#ifndef __OBJECTNAME_H_
#define __OBJECTNAME_H_

#include "resource.h"       // main symbols

/////////////////////////////////////////////////////////////////////
// CObjectName
class ATL_NO_VTABLE CObjectName :
  public CComObjectRootEx<CComSingleThreadModel>,
  public CComCoClass<CObjectName, &CLSID_ObjectName>,
  public IDispatchImpl<IObjectName, &IID_IObjectName,
                       &LIBID_PROJECTNAMELib>
{
public:
  CObjectName()
  {
  }

DECLARE_REGISTRY_RESOURCEID(IDR_OBJECTNAME)
DECLARE_NOT_AGGREGATABLE(CObjectName)
```

```
DECLARE_PROTECT_FINAL_CONSTRUCT()

BEGIN_COM_MAP(CObjectName)
  COM_INTERFACE_ENTRY(IObjectName)
  COM_INTERFACE_ENTRY(IDispatch)
END_COM_MAP()

// IObjectName
public:
};

#endif //__OBJECTNAME_H_
```

Even though there isn't much in ObjectName.h, there are several important points to note. First, the component is derived from three template classes. **CComObjectRootEx** takes care of reference counting. **CComCoClass** provides class factory support and basic methods to retrieve its **CLSID**. **IDispatchImpl** provides the implementation of the **IDispatch** portion of the dual interface.

It's possible to implement a COM object with only an **IDispatch** interface, but the Object Wizard doesn't present this as an option. Remember that it allows you to choose either a custom interface or a dual interface. Either way, you only have to implement the methods of your interface once—the custom interface. The ATL **IDispatch** implementation will **Invoke()** the corresponding vtable interface method.

The **ATL_NO_VTABLE** macro expands to _declspec(novtable), which is a special compiler optimization introduced for Visual C++ 5. When _declspec(novtable) is used in a class declaration, it prevents the vtable pointer from being initialized in the class's constructor and destructor. The linker can thus eliminate the vtable and all the functions pointed to by the vtable, reducing the size of your code. It also means that you can't call any virtual functions in the constructor or destructor of such a class. There is more about this later in the chapter.

DECLARE_REGISTRY_RESOURCEID() implements script-based Registry support (as described above) and provides the resource ID for the Registry script information.

The **COM_INTERFACE_ENTRY()** macro adds an entry to a table that provides the interface information ATL needs when performing **QueryInterface()**. When a request for an interface is received, ATL searches the table by executing the code created by the **BEGIN_COM_MAP()** and **END_COM_MAP()** macros.

Changed Files

Because the IDL file is the one with the most changes, take a look at this one first:

```
// ProjectName.idl : IDL source for ProjectName.dll
//

// This file will be processed by the MIDL tool to
// produce the type library (ProjectName.tlb) and marshalling code.

import "oaidl.idl";
import "ocidl.idl";
  [
    object,
    uuid(FF9EF7AB-C052-11D2-A46C-00C04F688CFA),
    dual,
    helpstring("IObjectName Interface"),
    pointer_default(unique)
  ]
  interface IObjectName : IDispatch
  {
  };
[
  uuid(AFCF8CC9-C1EF-11D2-A46C-00C04F688CFA),
  version(1.0),
  helpstring("ProjectName 1.0 Type Library")
]
library PROJECTNAMELib
{
  importlib("stdole32.tlb");
  importlib("stdole2.tlb");

  [
    uuid(FF9EF7AC-C052-11D2-A46C-00C04F688CFA),
    helpstring("ObjectName Class")
  ]
  coclass ObjectName
  {
    [default] interface IObjectName;
  };
};
```

Find where the **IObjectName** interface has been added. Notice that it is derived from **IDispatch**. This is because the dual interface attribute was selected. If you had selected a custom interface, **IObjectName** would be derived from

IUnknown. Next, look at **IObjectName**'s attributes. The **object** attribute specifies that this is a COM custom interface and not a standard Remote Procedure Call-base interface. The IDL can also be used to describe RPC interfaces. The **uuid** keyword specifies the **GUID** for this interface, and the **pointer_default** attribute specifies the default pointer attribute for all non-top-level pointers defined within the interface that are not explicitly qualified. This includes embedded pointers and pointers returned by functions. *Embedded pointers* are member pointers of structures, unions, and arrays. The **unique** attribute specifies that whenever a pointer (except for top-level pointers and other pointers with a **pointer** attribute supplied) is passed through an interface method, the memory associated with the pointer is unique to that pointer. That is, if two pointers are pointing to the same member in the client and both pointers are passed to the server, two unique copies of the data are marshaled.

The other area of change is the entries for the **coclass** (component class). The **coclass** describes the interfaces supported by a given COM object. The **default** attribute indicates that the **IObjectName** interface is the default programmable interface for this **coclass**. That is, it allows Visual Basic and other such languages to use the names **ObjectName** and **IObjectName** interchangeably.

The only other significant change is in the ProjectName.cpp file, where a new header will be included and an entry has been added to the object map. You haven't looked at this file yet, so here it is:

```
// ProjectName.cpp : Implementation of DLL Exports.

// Note: Proxy/Stub Information
//       To build a separate proxy/stub DLL,
//       run nmake -f ProjectNameps.mk in the project directory.

#include "stdafx.h"
#include "resource.h"
#include <initguid.h>
#include "ProjectName.h"

#include "ProjectName_i.c"
#include "ObjectName.h"

CComModule _Module;

BEGIN_OBJECT_MAP(ObjectMap)
OBJECT_ENTRY(CLSID_ObjectName, CObjectName)
END_OBJECT_MAP()

//////////////////////////////////////////////////////////////////
// DLL Entry Point
```

```
extern "C"
BOOL WINAPI DllMain(HINSTANCE hInstance,
                    DWORD dwReason,
                    LPVOID /*lpReserved*/)
{
    if (dwReason == DLL_PROCESS_ATTACH)
    {
        _Module.Init(ObjectMap, hInstance, &LIBID_PROJECTNAMELib);
        DisableThreadLibraryCalls(hInstance);
    }
    else if (dwReason == DLL_PROCESS_DETACH)
        _Module.Term();
    return TRUE;    // ok
}


/////////////////////////////////////////////////////////////////
// Used to determine whether the DLL can be unloaded by OLE

STDAPI DllCanUnloadNow(void)
{
    return (_Module.GetLockCount()==0) ? S_OK : S_FALSE;
}


/////////////////////////////////////////////////////////////////
// Returns a class factory that will create an object of the
// requested type

STDAPI DllGetClassObject(REFCLSID rclsid, REFIID riid,
                         LPVOID* ppv)
{
    return _Module.GetClassObject(rclsid, riid, ppv);
}


/////////////////////////////////////////////////////////////////
// DllRegisterServer - Adds entries to the system registry
STDAPI DllRegisterServer(void)
{
    // registers object, typelib and all interfaces in typelib
    return _Module.RegisterServer(TRUE);
}
/////////////////////////////////////////////////////////////////
// DllUnregisterServer - Removes entries from the system registry

STDAPI DllUnregisterServer(void)
{
    return _Module.UnregisterServer(TRUE);
}
```

Most of what is in this file should be familiar or self-evident. The grayed areas indicate the recent changes. The **BEGIN_OBJECT_MAP()**, **OBJECT_ ENTRY()**, and **END_OBJECT_MAP()** macros set up a table of **CLSID**s and their associated ATL implementation classes. ATL uses this table to update the Registry with information for each component within the housing and to create instances of a component.

There are a few other items worth mentioning. **_Module**, the global instance of **CComModule**, is defined in this file. **DllMain()** on startup calls **CComModule:: Init()** and on shutdown calls **CComModule::Term()**. The four functions every in-process server should implement—**DllCanUnloadNow()**, **DllGetClass Object()**, **DllRegisterServer()**, and **DllUnregisterServer()**—are also provided. They each call the appropriate **CComCoClass** member function.

ATL Architecture

The ATL AppWizard provides the basic housing support that COM components need. After creating the housing, you use the Object Wizard to add COM objects to the housing. All COM objects have several things in common. Each COM object must support the **IUnknown** interface, along with others, such as **IDispatch**, that expose specific functionality. Each COM object must also provide a class factory so that it can be created by client applications. ATL provides built-in support for each of these requirements. This section examines the ATL architecture to determine how the framework satisfies these requirements.

Implementing IUnknown

The implementation and control for **IUnknown** is distributed among several ATL classes to allow for maximal flexibility. This makes it rather difficult to understand, but the most important point to remember is that the implementation of the three **IUnknown** methods isn't determined until your component class is created. Another point to keep in mind is that your class is never instantiated directly. It can't be; it's an abstract class. Two clues to this fact are present in the code reviewed in the previous section.

First, remember the **ATL_NO_VTABLE** macro? In the last section, you saw where the definition of **CObjectName** uses this macro to provide an optimization that eliminates the initialization of the vtable from the class's constructor. You know that there must be a vtable, so where is it?

The second clue isn't quite as apparent as the first. At this point, the **ObjectName.cpp** file doesn't contain any implementation code, but you know

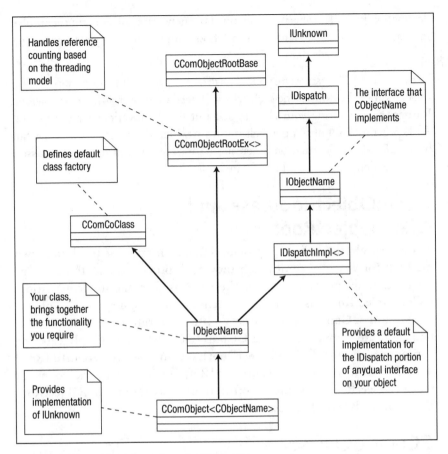

Figure 18.4 Class hierarchy of **CObjectName**.

that the three **IUnknown** methods must be implemented and ATL provides their implementation. So where is the implementation code?

Well, it turns out that both questions have the same answer. Another class is always derived from your class. This other class is always the most-derived class, and it provides the vtable and basic implementation of the three **IUnknown** methods. Figure 18.4 shows the class hierarchy of the COM object based on **CObjectName**.

CComObject<>

This class is one of a number of classes that provide the implementation of the **IUnknown** methods. All of these classes work in a similar manner. They are all template classes that require a **CComObjectRoot**-derived class (your ATL class) parameter. The new class derives from the parameter and is the final destination in ATL's inheritance chain. This new class will contain the implementation of the three **IUnknown** methods and use code in your class to get access to the interface map.

Why doesn't ATL instantiate your class directly? Depending on circumstances, the class at the bottom of the hierarchy will need to exhibit different behaviors. Rather than requiring your class to account for these various circumstances, ATL provides a set of template classes from which the most efficient one can be used for a specific situation. There are 10 of these **CComObject**-like classes, each of which are described briefly in Table 18.6.

CComObjectRootBase And CComObjectRootEx<>

These two classes indirectly provide implementation of the **IUnknown** methods for your class. Although they don't provide the methods themselves, they do provide much of the code used in the implementation. **CComObjectRootBase** provides reference counting for aggregate components, and **CComObjectRootEx<>** provides reference counting for nonaggregate components. The **CComObject**-like class simply calls the appropriate routine: CComObjectRootEx<yourclass>::InternalAddRef() or **CComObjectRootBase::OuterAddRef()** to increment the count, or CComObjectRootEx<yourclass>::InternalRelease() or CComObjectRoot Base::OuterRelease() to decrement the count.

CComCoClass<>

This class provides class factory support, along with basic methods to retrieve the **CLSID** and component-specific error information. It contains very little code and provides most of its support through two macros: DECLARE_ CLASSFACTORY() and **DECLARE_AGGREGATABLE** (*yourclass*). DECLARE_CLASSFACTORY() provides the actual class factory and DECLARE_AGGREGATABLE(*yourclass*) indirectly calls **CreateInstance()**. If you select No or Only as the aggregation attribute in the Object Wizard, one of these two macros will be applied to your class:

```
DECLARE_NOT_AGGREGATABLE(yourclass)

DECLARE_ONLY_AGGREGATABLE(yourclass)
```

Each of these macros will cause a different version of **CreateInstance()** to be used to create your object.

Table 18.6 CComObject<> classes.	
Template Class Name	**Description**
CComObject<>	Most components are created using this class. It doesn't support aggregation.
CComAggObject<>	Like **CComObject<>** except it supports aggregated.
CComPolyObject<>	Supports either aggregated objects or nonaggregated objects.
CComTearOffObject<>	Used by tear-off interfaces. Tear-off interfaces are interfaces that don't exist until requested.
CComCachedTearOffObject<>	Used by tear-off interfaces. Like **CComTearOffObject<>**, except the object can be reused.
CComContainedObject<>	Used by **CComAggObject<>** and **CComPolyObject<>**. It is the embedded member and delegates reference counting calls to the outer methods.
CComObjectCached<>	Implements class factories in a DLL server.
CComObjectGlobal<>	Implements objects at global scope. Its reference count is maintained by the housing global lock count.
CComObjectNoLock<>	Like **CComObject<>** but doesn't change the housing's lock count.
CComObjectStack<>	Designed to be used as an automatic variable. It doesn't do reference counting. **AddRef()** and **Release()** will assert if called in a debug build.

Adding A Property

Properties are attributes of the component that the component user can change, although some may be read-only, hidden, or both. Because COM interfaces follow the OO principle of encapsulation and data hiding, only functions are exported. To allow the client access to a property, the component will provide functions with access to the data member—one to "get" its value and one to "set" its value.

To add a property to your interface, select the ClassView tab in the Project Workspace window, right-click on the **IObjectName** interface name, and select **Add Property** from the context menu. Specify the Property Type as **BSTR** and set the Property Name to **Message**, then click OK. Refer to Figure 18.5.

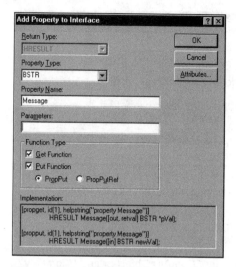

Figure 18.5 Adding a property to the interface.

Now look at the changes the wizard made to ProjectName.idl:

```
// ProjectName.idl : IDL source for ProjectName.dll
//

// This file will be processed by the MIDL tool to
// produce the type library (ProjectName.tlb) and marshalling code.

import "oaidl.idl";
import "ocidl.idl";
  [
    object,
    uuid(AFCF8CD5-C1EF-11D2-A46C-00C04F688CFA),
    dual,
    helpstring("IObjectName Interface"),
    pointer_default(unique)
  ]
  interface IObjectName : IDispatch
  {
    [propget, id(1), helpstring("property Message")]
                HRESULT Message([out, retval] BSTR *pVal);
    [propput, id(1), helpstring("property Message")]
                HRESULT Message([in] BSTR newVal);
  };
[
  uuid(AFCF8CC9-C1EF-11D2-A46C-00C04F688CFA),
  version(1.0),
  helpstring("ProjectName 1.0 Type Library")
]
```

```
library PROJECTNAMELib
{
  importlib("stdole32.tlb");
  importlib("stdole2.tlb");
  [
    uuid(FF9EF7AC-C052-11D2-A46C-00C04F688CFA),
    helpstring("ObjectName Class")
  ]
  coclass ObjectName
  {
    [default] interface IObjectName;
  };
};
```

Notice the shaded lines, which I adjusted so they are easier to read. As you can see, two functions were added. Although both are called **Message** and have the same help string and ID, they are distinguished by their first attribute. The first one has the **[propget]** attribute and therefore is the method used to "get" the value of the property. Because its parameter is used to return a value, the parameter, which is a pointer, has the **[out]** attribute. Conceptually, this is also the return value of the method, and therefore, it additionally has the **[retval]** attribute. The second method has the **[propput]** attribute, indicating that it is used to set the property's value, and its parameter is marked as an input value by the use of the **[in]** attribute.

Add a **CComBSTR** data member named **m_bstrMessage** to **CObjectName**. **CComBSTR** is an ATL-provided wrapper for a **BSTR**. Next, add the shaded lines in the following code to the skeleton functions the Object Wizard added to **CObjectName**.

```
STDMETHODIMP CObjectName::get_Message(BSTR *pVal)
{
  *pVal = SysAllocString(m_bstrMessage.m_str);
  return S_OK;
}

STDMETHODIMP CObjectName::put_Message(BSTR newVal)
{
  m_bstrMessage = newVal;
  return S_OK;
}
```

Now modify the constructor to initialize the property:

```
CObjectName()
  : m_bstrMessage(_T("Hello. How are you?"))
  {
  }
```

Adding A Method

Adding a method to your interface is fairly straightforward. Select the ClassView tab in the Project Workspace window. Then right-click on the **IObjectName** interface name, and select **Add Method** from the context menu. Name the method "Display", and click on OK.

When you press OK, the wizard then generates code and updates the IDL file and the **ObjectName** class files. Now look at change made to the IDL file:

```
[propput, id(1), helpstring("property Message")]
                HRESULT Message([in] BSTR newVal);
  [id(2), helpstring("method Display")] HRESULT Display();
  };
```

Here you see that a method called **Display** has been added to the **IObjectName** interface, and that it has an **[id]** attribute. This attribute specifies its dispatch ID (also called dispid). This is the unique ID used by **IDispatch::Invoke()** to dispatch a call to the appropriate function.

The **Display** function has also been added to the **CObjectName** class. The Object Wizard provided a simple skeleton that does nothing more than return S_OK. Add the following code to **CObjectName::Display()**:

```
STDMETHODIMP CObjectName::Display()
{
  USES_CONVERSION;
  MessageBox(NULL, OLE2CT(m_bstrMessage),
       _T("IObjectName"), MB_OK);
  return S_OK;
}
```

Creating A Client

Because your interface is **dual,** you can access the component using vtable binding or through the **IDispatch** interface. Now use three small C++ programs to test the component. The first one uses the MIDL-generated files, the second uses the type library, and the third uses **IDispatch**.

C++ Client Using MIDL-Generated Files

Create a new Win32 console application in a subdirectory of the ProjectName server's directory, so relative paths to the server's files can be used. Name the project Client.

Add a new source file to the project, name it client.cpp, and add the following code:

```cpp
#include <stdio.h>
#include "..\ProjectName.h"    // Server's interface definitions
#include "..\ProjectName_i.c"  // GUID definitons

int main()
{
  HRESULT hr = CoInitialize(NULL);
  if(FAILED(hr))
    return -1;

  IObjectName * pObj = NULL;
  hr = CoCreateInstance( CLSID_ObjectName,
                         NULL,
                         CLSCTX_ALL,
                         IID_IObjectName,
                         (void**) & pObj );
  if(SUCCEEDED(hr))
  {
    hr = pObj->Display();
    if(FAILED(hr))
    {
      printf("Error: 0x%x\n", hr);
      return hr;
    }

    // Get the message and send it to the console
    BSTR msg;
    hr = pObj->get_Message(&msg);
    if(FAILED(hr))
    {
      printf("Error: 0x%x\n", hr);
      return hr;
    }
    printf("get_Message: %S\n", msg);
    // Change the Message property
    SysReAllocString(&msg, L"Here is the new message");
    hr = pObj->put_Message(msg);
    if(FAILED(hr))
    {
      printf("Error: 0x%x\n", hr);
      SysFreeString(msg);
      return hr;
    }
    printf("put_Message: %S\n", msg);
```

```
    hr = pObj->Display();
    if(FAILED(hr))
    {
        printf("Error: 0x%x\n", hr);
        SysFreeString(msg);
        return hr;
    }

    SysFreeString(msg);
    hr = pObj->Release();
    if(FAILED(hr))
    {
        printf("Error: 0x%x\n", hr);
        return hr;
    }
}
else
{
    // CoCreateInstance() failed, so don't Release() the pointer
    printf("Error: 0x%x\n", hr);
}

CoUninitialize();
return 0;
}
```

The two **#includes** with relative paths bring in two of the files created when the MIDL tool compiles the IDL file. The first **#include** brings in the interface declarations for the components housing, and the second brings in all the **CLSID**s and **IID**s defined for the server.

The first part of the code initializes COM, declares an **IObjectName** pointer, and then calls **CoCreateInstance()** to create an instance of the **ObjectName** coclass, asking for a pointer to the interface.

Next, the return value of **CoCreateInstance()** is checked to determine if the object was successfully created. If not, a simple error message is displayed.

If the object was successfully created, the **Display()** method is called, which displays a message box. After the message box is released, the **Message** property is retrieved from the object and sent to the console. Next, the **Message** property value is changed and the **Display()** method is called.

The last thing to occur is the call to **CoUninitialize()** to shut down COM.

C++ Client Using Type Library

Rather than including the ProjectName.h and ProjectName_i.c files, the type library can be imported using the **#import** directive. The **#import** preprocessor reads the type library and creates two files that it **#includes** in your compilation. These files are stored in your output directory and have the same base name as the type library, with the extensions .TLH and .TLI. The generated files will contain wrapper classes for the interfaces, which have a number of advantages over the MIDL-generated files:

➤ A number of smart pointers are provided, some of which hide the details of reference counting.

➤ Functions return values are specified by **[retval]** instead of **HRESULT**.

➤ Exception handling can be used instead of **HRESULT** testing.

➤ Property methods can be accessed like data members.

Client Implementation

Create another project like the preceding one and add the following code to the CPP file:

```cpp
#import "..\ProjectName.tlb"
using namespace PROJECTNAMELib;
#include <iostream>
#include <comutil.h>

int main()
{
  CoInitialize(NULL);
  BSTR msg;
  try
  {
    IObjectNamePtr pObject(_uuidof(ObjectName));

    msg = pObject->Message;
    std::cout << _com_util::ConvertBSTRToString(msg) << std::endl;

    SysReAllocString(&msg, L"Here is the new message");

    pObject->Message = msg;
    pObject->Display();
    SysFreeString(msg);
  }
```

```
catch(const _com_error & err)
{
    std::cout << err.ErrorMessage() << std::hex << "  0x"
              << err.Error()
<< std::endl;
}
CoUninitialize();
return 0;
}
```

This code is using exception handling, which makes the code a lot easier to follow. A slight disadvantage to exception handling that you should be aware of is that it makes your EXE file larger by 30 KB.

The first statement inside the **try** block is an example of the smart pointers created when you use the **#import** directive to "import" a type library. The TLH file contains a smart pointer definition for each of your interface pointers, using the **COM_SMARTPTR_TYPEDEF()** macro. For example, in **ProjectName.thl**, the **#import** preprocessor has created a smart pointer for the **IObjectName** interface using the following code:

```
_COM_SMARTPTR_TYPEDEF(IObjectName, __uuidof(IObjectName));
```

This macro takes the same parameters as **__com_ptr_t<>**, the interface of the object that the pointer refers to and **IID** of the interface. Here you see the use of the **__uuidof()** operator to obtain the **IID**. After execution of **_COM_SMARTPTR_TYPEDEF()**, there will be a **typedef** of a specialization of **__com_ptr_t<>** with the name of the interface pointer plus a suffix of **Ptr**. When you instantiate this class, it will obtain your class factory, call the class factory to create an object, call **IUnknown::QueryInterface()** to obtain the interface, and create a **__com_ptr_t<>** smart pointer object around this pointer. You then use the indirect member selection operator -> to access its functionality. A major benefit of this smart pointer is that you don't need to worry about reference counting, because the smart pointer will call **AddRef()** and **Release()** automatically.

There are two examples of how the property methods can be accessed like data members. The first one retrieves the value, and the second one changes the value:

```
msg = pObject->Message;
pObject->Message = msg;
```

The TLH File

Now look at the files generated by **#import**, starting with ProjectName.tlh, which I have edited for length.

```
// Created by Microsoft (R) C/C++ Compiler Version ...
//
// e:\projectname\client_tlb\debug\ProjectName.tlh
//
// C++ source equivalent of Win32 type library ..\ProjectName.tlb
// compiler-generated file created ... - DO NOT EDIT!
#pragma once
#pragma pack(push, 8)
#include <comdef.h>
namespace PROJECTNAMELib {
//
// Forward references and typedefs
//
struct /* coclass */ ObjectName;
struct __declspec(uuid("afcf8cd5-c1ef-11d2-a46c-00c04f688cfa"))
/* dual interface */ IObjectName;
//
// Smart pointer typedef declarations
//
_COM_SMARTPTR_TYPEDEF(IObjectName, __uuidof(IObjectName));
//
// Type library items
//
struct __declspec(uuid("ff9ef7ac-c052-11d2-a46c-00c04f688cfa"))
ObjectName;
    // [ default ] interface IObjectName
struct __declspec(uuid("afcf8cd5-c1ef-11d2-a46c-00c04f688cfa"))
IObjectName : IDispatch
{
    //
    // Property data
    //
    __declspec(property(get=GetMessage,put=PutMessage))
    _bstr_t Message;
    //
    // Wrapper methods for error-handling
    //

    _bstr_t GetMessage ( );
    void PutMessage (
        _bstr_t pVal );
    HRESULT Display ( );
    //
    // Raw methods provided by interface
    //
virtual HRESULT __stdcall get_Message ( BSTR * pVal ) = 0;
    virtual HRESULT __stdcall put_Message ( BSTR pVal ) = 0;
```

```
        virtual HRESULT __stdcall raw_Display ( ) = 0;
};
//
// Wrapper method implementations
//
#include "e:\projectname\client_tlb\debug\ProjectName.tli"
} // namespace PROJECTNAMELib
#pragma pack(pop)
```

TLH files consist of sections:

➤ The **#include** statement for COMDEF.H (defines the macros used in header)

➤ Forward references and **typedefs**, structure declarations for interface IDs, and class names

➤ Smart pointer **typedef** declarations, using the **_COM_SMARTPTR_TYPEDEF** macro to create **typedefs** of specialized **_com_ptr_t** template classes

➤ Type library items, class definitions, and other items generated from the specified type library

➤ Named GUID constants' initializations, if the **named_guids** attribute was specified

➤ An **#include** statement for the type library implementation (.TLI) file

Except for the first section and the last line, most of this file is enclosed in a namespace, with its name specified by the **library** statement in the original IDL file. There are a number of attributes that can be applied to the **#import** directive, two of which affect the namespace. One, **no_namespace,** suppresses the namespace altogether; the other, **rename_namespace,** changes the name of the namespace.

Notice how **IObjectName** contains wrapper methods for error handling and how the syntax of these methods has been modified from the interface implementation. For example, **GetMessage()** returns a **_bstr_t.** Notice also that there is a set of virtual methods. These virtual methods provide the vtable through which the smart pointer will call the methods of the actual object.

The TLI File

Here is the ProjectName.tli file (again edited for length):

```
// Created by Microsoft (R) C/C++ Compiler Version ...
//
// e:\projectname\client_tlb\debug\ProjectName.tli
```

```
//
// Wrapper implementations for Win32 type...\ProjectName.tlb
// compiler-generated file created ... - DO NOT EDIT!
#pragma once
//
// interface IObjectName wrapper method implementations
//
inline HRESULT IObjectName::Display ( ) {
    HRESULT _hr = raw_Display();
    if (FAILED(_hr))
        _com_issue_errorex(_hr, this, __uuidof(this));
    return _hr;
}
inline _bstr_t IObjectName::GetMessage ( ) {
    BSTR _result;
    HRESULT _hr = get_Message(&_result);
    if (FAILED(_hr))
        _com_issue_errorex(_hr, this, __uuidof(this));
    return _bstr_t(_result, false);
}
inline void IObjectName::PutMessage ( _bstr_t pVal ) {
    HRESULT _hr = put_Message(pVal);
    if (FAILED(_hr)) _com_issue_errorex(_hr, this, __uuidof(this));
}
```

This file implements *inline* wrappers for the direct COM interface calls. These wrapper functions will *throw* an exception via the **_com_issue_errorex()** call. It throws a **_com_error** object, which your client code is prepared to **catch()**.

C++ Client Using IDispatch

This client will use the Automation interface. Using an Automation interface involves an extensive lookup to resolve **DISPIDS** from given method names, resulting in performance problems. For that reason, C/C++ clients seldom use this approach. However, for clients like VBScript, where dynamic invocation is needed, this approach is great.

Create another project like the preceding one and add the following code to the CPP file.

```
#include "rpc.h"
#include <string>
#include <iostream>
using namespace std;

// Display error message and HRESULT
```

```cpp
inline void DisplayError(const string & theErrorText, HRESULT hr)
{
  cout << "Error: " << theErrorText << '\n';
  cout << "HRESULT: 0x" << hex << (ULONG) hr << endl;
}


int main()
{
  HRESULT hr = CoInitialize(0);
  if(FAILED(hr))
  {
    DisplayError("Unable to initialize COM", hr);
    return 1;
  }


  CLSID clsid;
  hr = CLSIDFromProgID(L"ProjectName.ObjectName", &clsid);
  if(FAILED(hr))
  {
    DisplayError("Could not obtain CLSID from ProgID", hr);
    return 1;
  }


  IDispatch *pDisp = 0;
  hr = CoCreateInstance(clsid,
                        NULL,
                        CLSCTX_ALL,
                        IID_IDispatch,
                        reinterpret_cast<void **>(&pDisp));
  if(FAILED(hr))
  {
    DisplayError("Could not obtain ObjectName object.", hr);
    return 1;
  }


  OLECHAR *method = L"Display";
  DISPPARAMS parms = {NULL, NULL, 0, 0};


  DISPID dispid;
  pDisp->GetIDsOfNames(IID_NULL, &method, 1,
                       LOCALE_SYSTEM_DEFAULT, &dispid);
  pDisp->Invoke(dispid, IID_NULL, LOCALE_SYSTEM_DEFAULT,
                DISPATCH_METHOD, &parms, NULL, NULL, NULL);


  pDisp->Release();
  CoUninitialize();
```

```
  return 0;
}
```

CoCreateInstance() is called to get the dispatch interface pointer. This pointer is then used to get the dispid of the **Display()** method from the object by calling **IDispatch::GetIDsOfNames()** and passing in the methods name. Then **IDispatch::Invoke()** is called, the dispid specifies the method to dynamically invoke.

Visual Basic 6 Client

Because the object is already registered, it is all ready to go. So all you need to do is build a VB project and write some code.

Using Late Binding—IDispatch

Start VB and create a new project, naming both the project and the form Client. Add a button on your form, and set its name and caption to Late. Double-click on the button and type the following code:

```
Private Sub Late_Click()
  Dim obj As Object
  Set obj = CreateObject("ProjectName.ObjectName")
  obj.Display
  Set obj = Nothing
End Sub
```

Here you have dimensioned **obj** as an **Object** and initialized it to your COM object. Visual Basic doesn't know anything about your object until you call **Display**. At that time, it calls **IDispatch::GetIDsOfNames()** to get the ID and then calls **IDispatch::Invoke()**, passing in the ID of **Display**.

Now add two text boxes. Double-click on Text1, and add the following code:

```
Private Sub Text1_Change()
  Dim obj As Object
  Set obj = CreateObject("ProjectName.ObjectName")
  obj.Message = Text1.Text
  Text2.Text = obj.Message
  Set obj = Nothing
End Sub
```

This code is creating an object and then using the object's **Message** property as a conduit to move text from Text1 to Text2. Run the program and type something into Text1. Notice how the property method is being accessed as a data value.

Using Early Binding—Type Library

In early binding, the Visual Basic IDE must know about the object type information at compile time. Select the References option from the Project menu, and find the ProjectName 1.0 Type Library reference (refer to Figure 18.6). Select it and click OK.

Add another button to your form, setting its name and caption to Early. Double-click on the button, and type the following code:

```
Private Sub Early_Click()
Dim obj As New ObjectName
obj.Display
Set obj = Nothing
End Sub
```

Here you dimension **obj** as an **ObjectName** and use the **New** operator to instantiate it. At this point, VB can use vtable binding when calling the **Display** method.

When you typed in the code for using early binding, you should have noticed that VB used auto-completion to guide you while entering the **Display** method of **obj**. Run your program and test it.

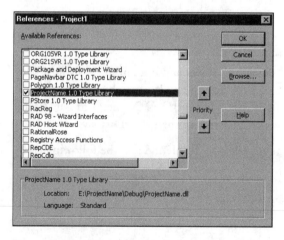

Figure 18.6 Visual Basic's References window.

Practice Questions

Question 1

> Which of the following functions must be implemented by all in-process servers? [Check all the correct answers.]
>
> ❑ a. DllCanUnloadNow()
>
> ❑ b. DllGetClassObject()
>
> ❑ c. DllRegisterServer()
>
> ❑ d. DllUnregisterServer()

Answers a, b, c, and d are correct. This question is trying to trick you by only providing answers that are correct.

Question 2

> Which of the following pairs of macros does ATL use to define the COM interface map?
>
> ○ a. BEGIN_INTERFACE_MAP and END_INTERFACE_MAP
>
> ○ b. BEGIN_OBJECT_MAP and END_OBJECT_MAP
>
> ○ c. BEGIN_INTERFACE_PART and END_INTERFACE_PART
>
> ○ d. BEGIN_COM_MAP and END_COM_MAP

Answer d is correct. Answers a and c are incorrect because these macros are used with MFC. Answer b is incorrect because **BEGIN_OBJECT_MAP** and **END_OBJECT_MAP** are ATL macros that define the map that specifies the servers implemented in the module.

Question 3

Which of the following statements specify that your **ISpell** interface supports dynamic invocation. [Check all the correct answers.]

❑ a.   interface ISpell : IAutomation

❑ b.   dispinterface ISpell

❑ c.   interface ISpell : IDispatch

❑ d.   interface ISpell : IDynamic

Answer b and c are correct. To specify that an interface supports dynamic invocation, you either derive it from **IDispatch** or use the **dispinterface** keyword. Answers a and d are incorrect because **ISpell** is being derived from a nonexistent interface.

Question 4

You are using the Object Wizard to generate a simple object. If you choose the dual option on the Object Wizard's Attribute tab, your ATL class will be derived from which of the follow templates? [Check all the correct answers.]

❑ a.   CComCoClass<>

❑ b.   CComCoGlobal<>

❑ c.   IDispatchImp<>

❑ d.   CComCoDual<>

Answers a and c are correct. Answer a is correct because **CComCoClass<>** is the template that provides class factory support. Answer c is correct because **IDispatchImpl<>** is the implementation for **IDispatch**. Answers b and d are incorrect because both are nonexistent templates.

Need To Know More?

 Armstrong, Tom. *Active Template Library: A Developers Guide.* M&T Books, Foster City, CA, 1998. ISBN 1-5585-1580-1. This book is easy to read and provides a number of good examples. One problem with this book, however, is that it uses Visual C++ 5, and some examples won't work with Visual C++ 6.

 Grimes, Richard. *Professional ATL COM Programming.* Wrox Press Ltd, Birmingham, UK, 1998. ISBN 1-861001-40-1. If you plan on working with ATL a lot, buy this book. Be forewarned, however, that if you are just learning ATL, this is not the first book you should use. Beginners should first become comfortable with C++, VB, HTML, COM, and ATL.

 Grimes, Richard, Alex Stockton, George Reilly, and Julian Templeman. *Beginning ATL COM Programming.* Wrox Press Ltd., Birmingham, UK, 1998. ISBN 1-861000-11-1. A good introduction to ATL, the examples are to the point, accurate, and well explained. Like Armstrong's book, this book uses Visual C++ 5, causing some examples to not work.

 Li, Sing and Panos Economopoulos. *Professional COM Application with ATL.* Wrox Press Ltd., Birmingham, UK, 1998. ISBN 1-861001-70-3. If you have a good COM/ATL foundation, this is the book for you. You start by building an ActiveX control from scratch. Then you use ATL to develop a distributed calendar system. This is a real-world three-tier application that uses flexible, browser-based controls for the client UI, business objects on both the client and server, and UDA to perform queries and updates. One feature I especially like is the authors' use of UML and design patterns.

 MSDN Library, Visual Studio 6.0 Documentation\Visual C++ Documentation\Reference\Microsoft Foundation Class Library and Templates\Active Template Library

 MSDN Library, Platform SDK\Component Services

 MSDN Library, Technical Articles\Component Object Model

www.microsoft.com/com—Microsoft places the most current information online. This Web page contains articles, white papers, presentations, downloadable code, and much more.

 www.worldofatl.com—Alex Stockton maintains The World of ATL Web page. This page provides much useful information and links to many other Web pages.

COM Threading Models

19

Terms you'll need to understand:

√ Single threading model

√ Single-threaded apartment (STA) model

√ Apartment threading model

√ User-interface-style thread

√ Multithreaded apartment (MTA) model

√ Free-threading model

√ Worker thread

√ Main, or primary, STA

√ Reentrancy

√ **CoInitializeEx()**

√ **IMessageFilter**

√ **CoRegisterMessageFilter()**

√ **CoMarshalInterface()**

√ **CoUnmarshalInterface()**

√ **CoMarshalInterThreadInterfaceIn Stream()**

√ **IStream**

√ **CoGetInterfaceAndRelease Stream()**

√ Global Interface Table (GIT)

√ Thread-local storage (TLS)

√ Mixed model

√ Free-Threaded Marshaler (FTM)

Techniques you'll need to master:

√ Understanding the different COM threading models, including their similarities and differences

√ Correctly identifying which type of COM threading model to implement

√ Implementing COM objects that support the STA model

√ Implementing COM objects that support the MTA model

417

Prior to the release of Windows NT 3.51, COM didn't support multithreading, and calls were made only to in-process DLLs. Concurrency and thread safety were not issues developers needed to worry about. Each process had only one thread of execution, and all component access occurred on this thread. This nonthreading model is now referred to as the *single threading model.*

With the introduction of Windows NT 3.51 and Windows 95, developers could take advantage of multithreading. It was now possible for an application to have a number of threads of execution occurring at the same time. To take advantage of multithreading, COM introduced a conceptual entity known as the *single-threaded apartment* (STA) model, sometimes referred to as the *apartment threading model* and occasionally as a *user-interface-style thread.* This model allows multiple threads to be created, where each thread will belong to only one apartment. When instantiated, the COM object is placed in its own apartment and will automatically be thread-safe because the same thread is always used to call its methods. With the release of Windows NT 4.0 and the Windows 95 DCOM upgrade, the *multithreaded apartment* (MTA) model was introduced. This model is sometimes referred to as the *free-threading model* and occasionally as a *worker thread.* The MTA model allows multiple threads to operate within the same thread-safe "box." However, because objects in different threads are able to access one another directly, to maintain thread safety within the box, objects must implement their synchronization.

 Probably the hardest thing to keep straight concerning the COM threading models is the terminology. It is important that you understand each of the models and the different terms used to refer to each of them.

Single-Threaded Apartment

This model allows you to avoid the complexity of interthread communication and synchronization. A single process can have any number of STAs. The first STA created in a process is special and is known as the *main STA* or *primary STA.* All other STAs are simply referred to as STAs. At the heart of each STA is a Windows message pump. A thread enters an STA by calling **CoInitialize(NULL)** or **CoInitializeEx(NULL, COINIT_APARTMENTTHREADED)**, at which point COM creates an invisible window and hooks it to the thread's message queue. Only one thread can ever execute within a particular STA, and it is this thread that pumps the message queue. Whenever a method is called, a request is posted to the message queue, where it stays until it is retrieved and dispatched. If the client and object reside in different apartments, interface pointers and method parameters must be marshaled. Because messages are retrieved and dispatched in order by the apartment thread, the component doesn't need to be thread-safe. That is, global and static data are automatically protected from concurrent access because the same thread can't be doing two things at the same time. You should, however, consider one issue: *reentrancy*. One example of reentrancy occurs when an object inside an STA calls a method in another STA and that method calls back to the first STA. COM also supports reentrancy in STAs by processing certain window messages, such as **WM_PAINT**, while a call is block-waiting for the return of a method invocation.

The **CoInitialize()** function has been deprecated and should no longer be used. All new applications should use **CoInitializeEx()**.

You can also implement an **IMessageFilter** interface to selectively manage outgoing and incoming method calls during the block-wait of an out-of-apartment method call. This lets you add code to improve performance and aid in the prevention of deadlocks. The **IMessageFilter** interface has three methods, shown in Table 19.1, that are called by COM at the appropriate time. The **CoRegisterMessageFilter()** API function must be used to register this interface with COM.

One advantage of using the STA model is that it allows you to develop multithreaded COM applications with minimum effort. Recall that only one thread can enter and thus reside in an STA. So for each additional thread, there must be an additional STA. For example, if the main STA spawns a thread and that thread requests to enter a STA, it will enter into a brand-new STA. The following snippet of code demonstrates this situation:

Table 19.1   The IMessageFilter interface's methods.

Method	Description
HandleIncomingCall()	Allows you to selectively handle or reject an incoming request.
RetryRejectedCall()	Upon detecting that an outgoing request has been rejected, COM calls this function to allow you to handle the problem.
MessagePending()	Allows you to take the appropriate action when a window message is received while your thread is making an outgoing call.

```
#define _WIN32_WINNT 0X0400
#include <windows.h>

DWORD WINAPI STAThread(LPVOID)
{
  // This thread enters its own STA
  CoInitializeEx(NULL, COINIT_APARTMENTTHREADED);
  // code to register class factories goes here
  // To support the STA model, we need a message pump
  MSG msg;
  while(GetMessage(&msg, NULL, 0, 0))
    DispatchMessage(&msg);
  // code to revoke all class factories goes here
  CoUninitialize();
  return 0;
}

int main(int argc, char **argv)
{
  // Enter the main STA
  CoInitializeEx(NULL, COINIT_APARTMENTTHREADED);
  // Now spawn another thread
  DWORD dwThreadId = 0;
  HANDLE hSTA = CreateThread(0, 0, STAThread, 0, 0, &dwThreadId);
  // code to register class factories goes here

  MSG msg;
  while(GetMessage(&msg, NULL, 0, 0))
    DispatchMessage(&msg);
  // code to revoke all class factories goes here
  CoUninitialize();
  return 0;
}
```

As you can see, each STA has an associated thread and its own message pump. Therefore, it's possible for two requests to be processed concurrently. This means that all shared data must be protected using a system synchronization object.

Although the STA model is simple and easy to use, it doesn't scale very well. For example, if you have a large number of objects and create an STA for each one, you will end up with a separate apartment and thread for each object. As the number of apartments and threads increase, so will resource consumption. On the other hand, if you place all of the objects in the same STA, your component can become very sluggish because all the objects will be serialized through the same message queue.

Components written prior to the introduction of the COM threading model are run in the Main STA.

Crossing Apartment Boundaries

Recall that when an interface pointer is passed across an apartment boundary, it must be marshaled. This normally occurs implicitly as part of the normal operation of COM. However, occasionally it is necessary to explicitly marshal an interface from one apartment to another. COM provides two API functions that allow the marshaling and unmarshaling of an interface pointer: **CoMarshalInterface()** and **CoUnmarshalInterface()**. There is nothing especially difficult about these two functions, but they are somewhat low level and require some amount of supporting code. To make things simpler, COM provides two wrapper functions that implement the required support code around **CoMarshalInterface()** and **CoUnmarshalInterface()**. The first one, **CoMarshalInterThreadInterfaceInStream()**, creates a marshaling packet and marshals the given interface. However, unlike **CoMarshalInterface()**, which allows you to marshal an interface pointer from one process to another, **CoMarshalInterThreadInterfaceInStream()** only allows you to marshal an interface pointer from one apartment to another within the same process. **CoMarshalInterThreadInterfaceInStream()** takes an IID, a pointer to the interface to be marshaled, and returns a pointer to an **IStream** interface that contains the necessary information for the marshalling and unmarshaling.

In the other apartment, **CoGetInterfaceAndReleaseStream()** unmarshals the interface pointer and releases the stream. This function takes a pointer to the **IStream** containing the buffer to be unmarshaled, an IID, and returns a pointer to a local interface proxy.

Following is pseudocode that shows how **CoMarshalInterThreadInterface InStream()** and **CoGetInterfaceAndReleaseStream()** can be used to manually share an interface pointer between two apartments within the same process.

```
IStream * g_pStream = 0;
IShipping * g_pShipping = 0;

. . .

DWORD WINAPI STA1(LPVOID)
{
    . . .
```

```
CoMarshalInterThreadInterfaceInStream(IID_IShipping,
                                      g_pShipping,
                                      &g_pStream);
    // create STA2
    . . .
}


DWORD WINAPI STA2(LPVOID)
{
    . . .
    IShipping * pShipping = 0;
    CoGetInterfaceAndReleaseStream(g_pStream,
                                   IID_IShipping,
                                   (void**) &pShipping);
    g_pStream = 0;
    . . .
}
```

In this example, **STA1** has an interface pointer (**g_pShipping**) that **STA2** needs to use. Although **g_pShipping** is visible to **STA2** from a C/C++ standpoint, **STA2** cannot use it. Only the **IStream** pointer holding the buffer for the marshaled interface reference can be accessed by both apartments. **STA1** marshals the interface pointer by calling **CoMarshalInterThreadInterfaceInStream()**. **STA2** then calls **CoGetInterfaceAndReleaseStream()** to unmarshal the stream to get a pointer to an **IShipping** interface proxy.

Notice that after unmarshaling the interface pointer, **STA2** sets the **IStream** pointer to 0. Recall that **CoGetInterfaceAndReleaseStream()** releases the stream, meaning that it can only be used once. Another technique, which uses the *Global Interface Table* (GIT), allows you to write the interface pointer once and read it many times. COM provides one GIT per process. This GIT can be accessed by all apartments in a process and can be used with both objects and proxies.

Multithreaded Apartment

Unlike the STA model, the MTA model doesn't have a hidden window and a message pump is not required. Furthermore, where there can be many STAs, there is at most one MTA per process. However, a single MTA can support any number of threads each with a number of objects. High performance and flexibility are what the MTA model is all about. When you need a component that is I/O-intensive or highly computation-oriented, the MTA model is ideal. A thread enters the only MTA in the process by calling **CoInitializeEx(NULL, COINIT_MULTITHREADED)**. Upon entering an MTA, the thread can directly access any COM object that lives in the MTA and can pass direct pointers to other threads. Thus, all MTA-compatible objects must be thread-safe in every way. This puts the burden on you, the developer, to ensure that all global, static, and instance data and all resources are protected against concurrent access. This means that all class factories and object members must be synchronized using system primitives. For example, you need to implement **AddRef()** and **Release()** like so:

```
STDMETHODIMP_(LONG) AddRef()
{
  return InterlockedIncrement(&m_lRef);
}

STDMETHODIMP_(LONG) Release()
{
  long ref = InterlockedDecrement(&m_lRef);
  if(!ref)
    delete this;
  return ref;
}
```

You will also need to use mutexes, semaphores, critical sections, or events for interthread coordination and communications.

In the MTA model, there is no correlation between objects and threads. That is, each call to a given object can be handled by a different thread. This means that you must not save any kind of object-related state in thread-local storage. *Thread-local storage*, or TLS, is a mechanism whereby each thread has its own unique copy of a local variable.

Mixed Model

It's possible for a process to use what is sometimes referred to as the *mixed model*. This is where one MTA and one or more STAs are supported by the same process. This process has multiple threads. Many threads can enter the MTA, but each STA can only host one thread. The threads within the MTA can use direct interface pointers, but interface pointers that cross apartment boundaries must be marshaled.

Out-Of-Process Server Considerations

When developing an out-of-process server, the possibility of race conditions must be taken into consideration. There are two times in the life of an out-of-process server when a race condition is most like to occur. The first is during activation, and the other is at shutdown.

Activation

Consider the situation where you have an MTA server that registers two or more class factories. After the server registers the first factory, COM will allow it to immediately start servicing incoming activation requests. Before the second factory is registered, it is possible for a client to request an object, use it, and request the server to shut down, thereby causing possible access violations to future calls to use the second factory. To prevent this situation, you need to register all of your factories using the **REGCLS_SUSPENDED** flag. After all of your factories are registered, you would then call **CoResumeClassObjects()**, telling COM to activate the factories. Following is an example of what the code might look like:

```
CDomesticFactory g_DomesticFactory;
CCanadaFactory g_CanadaFactory;

int main(int argc, char **argv)
{
    // code to register and unregister the component

    // Initialize COM
    HRESULT hr = CoInitializeEx(NULL, COINIT_MULTITHREADED);

    // Factory registration
    DWORD dwRegisterDomestic = 0;
    hr = CoRegisterClassObject(CLSID_DomesticFactory,
                               &g_DomesticFactory,
                               CLSCTX_LOCAL_SERVER,
                               REGCLS_MULTIPLEUSE | REGCLS_SUSPENDED,
                               &dwRegisterDomestic);

    DWORD dwRegisterCanada = 0;
    hr = CoRegisterClassObject(CLSID_CanadaFactory,
                               &g_CanadaFactory,
                               CLSCTX_LOCAL_SERVER,
                               REGCLS_MULTIPLEUSE | REGCLS_SUSPENDED,
                               &dwRegisterCanada);

    hr = CoResumeClassObjects();  // let all the factories loose

    // wait for shutdown notification

    hr = CoRevokeClassObject(dwRegisterDomestic);
    hr = CoRevokeClassObject(dwRegisterCanada);

    CoUninitialize();
    return 0;
}
```

Shutdown

Consider the situation where a local server is running an MTA or has multiple STAs registered. There is a small window of opportunity where a new activation request can arrive while the server is shutting down. This race condition would mean that a client would be holding a nonvalid interface pointer. The **CoAddRefServerProcess()** and **CoReleaseServerProcess()** functions introduced in Chapter 17 prevent this potential race condition from occurring. Recall that these two functions increment and decrement a process-wide reference count, and were called by members of the **Counters** class. Following is a modified version of the declaration shown in Chapter 17. In this modified version, instead of having a set of member functions for the lock count and a different set for the object count, a single set of functions is used.

```
class CCounters
{
public:
  static HANDLE m_hExitEvent;
  static long IncCount() { return CoAddRefServerProcess(); }
  static long DecCount()
  {
    ULONG ul = CoReleaseServerProcess();
    if(ul == 0)
      SetEvent(m_hExitEvent);
    return ul;
  }
};
```

The **CoReleaseServerProcess()** function has a built-in feature whereby it automatically calls **CoSuspendClassObjects()** when the reference count goes to 0. **CoSuspendClassObjects()** ensures that any incoming activation requests are refused, so that the component need not worry about a simultaneous activation while unregistering its class factories. An activation request received during shutdown of a component is redirected to the SCM so that a new instance of the component is created.

The preceding code supports component shutdown when the main thread is executing in an MTA. In the case that the main thread is executing in an STA, there is a message pump that waits for the **WM_QUIT** window message. Therefore, rather than setting an exit event, **DecCount()** needs to post the **WM_QUIT** window message to the main thread, causing the component to shut down.

In-Process Server Considerations

In-process components use the Registry to tell COM their concurrency constraints. One of four different threading model types is placed under the HKEY_CLASS_ROOT\CLSID\{*clsid*}\InprocServer32 key. A **Threading Model** value specifies one of four different variations of concurrency.

ThreadingModel=

COM regards in-process components that do not have a **ThreadingModel** value as legacy components. This component and its instantiated objects can only live and execute in the client's main STA. COM assumes that this type of component is totally thread-ignorant and prevents any occurrence of multiple access to the object. Therefore, when implementing a component that doesn't support a threading model, you need not worry about protecting data or resources. These types of objects are the easiest to write, but because there is only one thread of execution, they don't scale.

In-process objects that don't support any **ThreadingModel** are best used with single-threaded clients with only one STA. This is the only case where direct interface pointers will be used. Calls from all other apartments, whether STA or MTA, will not be able to use direct interface pointers. When the client activates an object from an apartment other than the main STA, the apartment will acquire a pointer to an interface proxy.

ThreadingModel=Apartment

In-process objects that support **ThreadingModel=Apartment** can live and execute in any client STA. Unlike objects of a legacy component, which can only be created in the main STA, these objects can be created in multiple STAs of the client process. COM assumes this type of object isn't thread-safe, but that the DLL is. Therefore, you need to protect all global and static data. You also need to ensure that **DllGetClassObject()** and **DllCanUnloadNow()** are thread-safe.

In-process objects that support **ThreadingModel=Apartment** are ideal candidates for use with multithreaded clients with multiple STAs. All STAs that activate an object will receive a direct pointer. However, because the object must be instantiated within an STA, the client MTA will still obtain a pointer to an interface proxy.

ThreadingModel=Free

In-process objects that support **ThreadingModel=Free** live and execute in the client's one and only MTA. Client STAs that wish to access this kind of object must go through a proxy. Recall that COM provides no synchronization whatsoever for this kind of object. Because COM assumes that both the component's objects and the DLL are thread-safe, you must protect all data and resources against concurrent access.

In-process objects that support **ThreadingModel=Free** perform best with clients that have an MTA with many busy worker threads. MTA client threads that activate this type of object will use direct interface pointers. However, when a client STA activates this type of object, the object will be instantiated in the MTA, and calls will be marshaled into and out of it.

ThreadingModel=Both

In-process objects that support **ThreadingModel=Both** can live and execute in any STA or MTA. When an STA thread activates this object, it is created in the STA. Likewise, when an MTA thread activates this object, it is created in the MTA.

In-process objects that support **ThreadingModel=Both** provide the best performance. When the client activates this type of object, the object is instantiated in the same apartment that the client thread is running in, and the client receives a direct pointer to the interface.

Because this kind of object can be created inside an STA or an MTA, it has two special requirements that you need to consider. First, when making a callback, it must use the same thread that passed the callback interface pointer to it. Second, interface pointers must be marshaled between threads.

Interaction Between In-Process Objects

COM allows interoperability using any combination of threading models between clients and components. However, when the threading models do not match, there will be a performance penalty. Often, through a combination of investigation, creative thinking, and careful design, you will be able to avoid this type of problem. Table 19.2 provides a summary on the interaction between in-process objects.

Free-Threaded Marshaler

Recall that in-process components supporting **ThreadingModel=Both** must always marshal interface pointers between threads. Because marshaling is slow, COM provides an object known as the *Free-Threaded Marshaler* (FTM) that can be used to really improve performance. When the FTM is aggregated by an object with **ThreadingModel=Both**, threads in different apartments but in the same process can access the object without going through a proxy. The

Table 19.2 Interaction between in-process objects.

Client Apartment	Threading Model	Object Apartment	Access Method
Main STA		Main STA	Direct
	Apartment	Main STA	Direct
	Free	MTA	Proxy
	Both	Main STA	Direct
Other STA		Main STA	Proxy
	Apartment	STA	Direct
	Free	MTA	Proxy
	Both	STA	Direct
MTA		Main STA	Proxy
	Apartment	STA	Proxy
	Free	MTA	Direct
	Both	MTA	Direct

FTM implements the **IMarshal** interface and performs custom marshaling to marshal 32 bits (a **DWORD**). This **DWORD**, which represents a raw interface pointer, can be passed from one apartment to another. The importing apartment can unmarshal the **DWORD** and convert the 32 bits into a direct interface pointer.

The CoCreateFreeThreadedMarshaler() API function allows objects that support **ThreadingModel=Both** to aggregate the FTM. **CoCreateFree ThreadedMarshaler()** takes two parameters. The first parameter is a pointer to the **IUnknown** of the aggregating object. The second parameter returns a pointer to the **IUnknown** of the FTM. Assume that **CShipping** supports **ThreadingModel=Both** and you want it to provide the best performance for all types of client apartments. The following snippet of code shows how the object's constructor and destructor might look.

```
CShipping::CShipping()
  : m_cRef(1)
  , m_pUnkAggregate(0)
{
  CCounters::IncCount();
  // Aggregate the Free-threaded Marshaler
  CoCreateFreeThreadedMarshaler(this, &m_pUnkAggregate);
}
```

```
CShipping::~CShipping()
{
  if(m_pUnkAggregate)
    m_pUnkAggregate->Release();
  CCounters::DecCount();
}
```

Within **CShipping::QueryInterface()**, the object simply delegates all requests to **IID_IMarshal** into the aggregated object, as shown here:

```
STDMETHODIMP CShipping::QueryInterface(REFIID riid, LPVOID * ppv)
{
  if(ppv == 0)
    return E_INVALIDARG;
  *ppv = 0;
  if(riid == IID_IUNKNOWN || riid == IID_IShipping)
    *ppv = static_cast<IShipping *>(this);
  else if(riid == IID_IMarshal)
    return m_pUnkAggregate->QueryInterface(riid, ppv);
  else
    return E_NOINTERFACE;

  reinterpret_cast<IUnknown *>(*ppv)->AddRef();
  return S_OK;
}
```

If your object aggregates the FTM, it shouldn't cache raw interface pointers as member variables. See Knowledge Base article Q150777 for specific details.

Practice Questions

Question 1

In reference to an STA, which statements are correct? [Check all of the correct answers]

❑ a. A thread exits an apartment by calling CoUninitialize().

❑ b. An STA can execute multiple threads as long as they are executed one at a time.

❑ c. After exiting an apartment, a thread can enter a different apartment if it desires.

❑ d. An STA thread must implement a message pump.

Answers a, c, and d are correct. Answer b is incorrect because only one thread can enter and reside in an STA. If a second thread enters an STA, a second STA is created. Answer a is correct because when a thread is finished with an apartment, it should call **CoUninitialize()** to exit the thread and free up COM-related resources. Answer c is correct because there is no restriction on the number of STAs a thread can enter; it just can't reside in more than one STA at a time. Answer d is correct because COM creates a hidden window and associated message queue for each STA. The STA thread must implement a message pump to get and dispatch messages to the window procedure.

Question 2

Which statement is correct?

○ a. CoMarshalInterThreadInterfaceInStream() allows you to marshal a raw interface pointer from one process to another process.

○ b. By repeatedly calling CoGetInterfaceAndReleaseStream(), you can unmarshal multiple copies of the same interface pointer.

○ c. Threads that execute within an MTA must marshal interface pointers from one thread to another thread.

○ d. Objects that live in an MTA must support both concurrency and reentrancy.

The correct answer is d. COM does not synchronize method invocations to objects in an MTA. Therefore, the objects must support concurrency. When a thread makes an outgoing method invocation to another apartment, the thread will then be blocked until the method invocation returns. During this time, it is possible for a second apartment to make a callback or for a different thread to call a method in the MTA. Therefore, objects in an MTA must support reentrancy. Answer a is incorrect; **CoMarshalInterThreadInterfaceInStream()** only marshals interface pointers from one thread to another thread in the same process. Answer b is incorrect because you can only call **CoGetInterfaceAndReleaseStream()** to unmarshal an interface pointer one time. **CoGetInterfaceAndReleaseStream()** releases the stream, making it impossible to be called more than one time on the same stream. Answer c is incorrect because threads that execute within an MTA can all access a raw interface pointer belonging to the MTA. Marshaling is not required within a single MTA.

Question 3

> You are implementing a multithreaded local server. Which of the following statements are true? [Check all of the correct answers]
>
> ❑ a. You must register your class factories using CoRegisterClassObject().
>
> ❑ b. Your server can support multiple MTAs by specifying COINIT_MULTITHREADED as the second parameter when calling CoInitializeEx().
>
> ❑ c. Your server will manage its lifetime by using the CoAddRefServer Process() and CoReleaseServerProcess() functions.
>
> ❑ d. To avoid race conditions during shutdown, your server must call CoSuspendClassObjects().

The correct answers are a and c. Answer a is correct because a local server must publish a component's class factories dynamically at runtime by registering them with the COM Service Control Manager. It does this using the **CoRegister ClassObject()** function, thereby enabling the class factories to service object-creating requests. Answer c is correct because COM maintains a global per-process reference count for each out-of-process server. Your local server needs to increment and decrement this reference count to correctly manage its lifetime. You use the **CoAddRefServerProcess()** and **CoReleaseServerProcess()** COM API functions for this purpose because they prevent race conditions due to untimely activation requests. Answer b is incorrect because a process can never have more that one MTA. By passing **COINIT_MULTITHREADED** as the second parameter when calling **CoInitializeEx()**, you are specifying that the thread is to enter the only MTA in the process. Answer d is incorrect because your server is not required to call **CoSuspendClassObjects()**. **CoReleaseServerProcess()** calls **CoSuspend**

ClassObjects() automatically when the per-process reference count reaches 0. A local server doesn't normally call **CoSuspendClass Objects()**.

Question 4

> Which statements are correct? [Check all of the correct answers]
>
> ❑ a. A process can have no STAs and no MTAs.
>
> ❑ b. A process can have more than one STA.
>
> ❑ c. A process can have no STAs and one MTA.
>
> ❑ d. A process can have one MTA and more than one STA.
>
> ❑ e. A process can have one STA and no MTAs.

The correct answers are a, b, c, d, and e. Answer a tries to confuse you into thinking about only COM objects. Answer a is correct because it's a process that isn't using COM. Answer b is correct because it's a process that has multiple threads. One thread is the main STA, and the other threads are associated with one and only one apartment. Answer c is correct because it's a process that can have any number of threads using COM. All the threads will belong to the same MTA. Answer d is correct because it's a combination of b and c. This model is commonly referred to as the *mixed model*. Answer e is correct because it has only one thread using COM. This STA is called the *main STA*. COM uses this model to support legacy code.

Need To Know More?

 Box, Don. *Essential COM*. Addison-Wesley, Reading, MA, 1998. ISBN 0-201-63446-5. The author addresses the spirit of COM as much as he does the technology. He knows the subject well and covers the material thoroughly. Chapter 5 provides a good description of the COM threading models.

 Rogerson, Dale. *Inside COM: Microsoft's Component Object Model*. Microsoft Press, Redmond, WA, 1997. ISBN 1-57231-349-8. This book covers the theory and implementation of COM objects well. It has clear explanations on each of the key areas. Chapter 12 covers multiple threads.

 MSDN Library, Platform SDK\Component Services \COM / COM Fundamentals\Guide\Processes, Apartments, and Threads

 support.microsoft.com/servicedesks/msdn/ This is the Knowledge Base of technical support information and self-help tools for Microsoft products. Enter search terms such as "STA" and "MTA". See KB article Q150777, "Descriptions and Workings of OLE Threading Models."

Building ActiveX Controls

Terms you'll need to understand:

- √ Event source (or connectable object) and event sink
- √ Outgoing interface
- √ **IConnectionPointContainer, IConnectionPoint, IEnumConnectionPoints,** and **IEnumConnections, and FindConnectionPoint()**
- √ **Advise()** and **UnAdvise()**
- √ Stock, custom, and ambient properties
- √ **IPropertyPage, IPropertyPage2, ISpecifyPropertyPages,** and **IPropertyPageSite**
- √ **IPersistStreamInit, IPersistStorage** and **IPersistPropertyBag**

- √ Component categories, **CATID, ICatRegister** and **ICatInformation**
- √ **IClassFactory2**
- √ **CComControl, CComComposite Control,** and **CComControlBase**
- √ **CWindowImpl**
- √ **IWebBrowser2**
- √ **ISupportErrorInfo**
- √ **IErrorInfo**
- √ **CAxHostWindow, CAxWindow, CAxWindowT<>,** and **CAx DialogImpl**

Techniques you'll need to master:

- √ Identify which type of library (SDK, MFC, ATL) to use when creating an ActiveX control
- √ Implementing an ActiveX control using the SDK, ATL, and MFC

- √ Creating methods, properties, events, and properties pages
- √ Saving and loading persistent properties

Technically, an ActiveX control is any COM object that exposes the **IUnknown** interface and is self-registering. However, if **IUnknown** were the only interface supported, the control wouldn't do much more than take up disk space. It, therefore, usually supports many more interfaces in order to offer functionality, but all additional interfaces can be viewed as optional, and as such, a container should not rely on any additional interfaces being supported. Because the **IUnknown** interface is the only interface the ActiveX Control Specification (OC96) requires implemented, a control can efficiently target a particular area of functionality without having to support specific interfaces to qualify as a control. As always with COM, whether in a control or a container, it should never be assumed that an interface is available, and standard return-checking conventions should always be followed. It is important for a control or container to degrade gracefully and offer alternative functionality if a required interface is not available.

The SDK can be used to develop ActiveX controls, but this can take weeks or even months. There are far easier ways. One way is with MFC, which developers have been using since 1994. MFC allows a developer to build a sophisticated ActiveX control in a matter of hours. However, a downside to using MFC is that the control is dependent on the MFC library, which can become a problem if the control is used in a Web page. A second way to develop an ActiveX control is to use ATL. Although building an ActiveX control using ATL is not as easy as using MFC, it's a lot easier than using the SDK, and because of the greater flexibility it provides, more and more developers are turning to ATL.

This chapter first covers the basic aspects of ActiveX controls. Then the support that ATL provides is examined, followed by an examination of the support MFC provides. The last section looks at ActiveX control containers. MFC support is touched on, but the primary focus is on the various ways in which a container can be implemented using ATL.

ActiveX Controls

ActiveX controls live inside an in-process component (DLL or OCX) that can be dynamically loaded by a hosting process. This type of server is commonly referred to as an *ActiveX container* or simply as a *container*. Examples of available containers are Visual Basic (VB), MFC dialog boxes, and Internet Explorer (IE). Both the control and the container implement a number of standard, but different, COM interfaces. The control and the container establish and maintain a peer-to-peer relationship by exchanging interface pointers.

Some ActiveX controls are designed to be used with IE. These controls are lightweight components that can readily be downloaded over the Internet and installed on the user's computer automatically by IE. ActiveX controls that are used exclusively by IE are usually referred to as *lite controls*. ActiveX controls that work equally well with VB, MFC dialog boxes, and IE are known as *full-blown controls*.

The Basics

Understanding how controls work can be somewhat confusing. It's quite easy to lose sight of the forest because of the trees. The key is to keep the four areas of functionality in mind: exposing interfaces to the container, providing properties that can be examined and possibly modified, sending events to the container, and presenting a user interface.

Interfaces

Recall that an ActiveX control is a COM object and, therefore, must support as a minimum the **IUnknown** interface. However, to do any meaningful work, an ActiveX control must support a number of interfaces. When building an ActiveX control, you can choose many standard interfaces to implement. Table 20.1 shows a categorized list of some interfaces that you might implement.

A number of the interfaces listed in Table 20.1 have a related interface that the container implements. The container supplies the interface to the control so that the control can call the container's methods. For example, the container uses the **IPersistPropertyBag** interface to supply the control with an **IPropertyBag** interface that the control can use to load or save its properties.

Events

Events always involve two or more COM objects. A COM object that fires an event is called an *event source* or *connectable object*, and a COM object that receives the event notification is called an *event sink*. It's possible for more than one event sink to receive the same event from an event source. ActiveX controls (event source) use this mechanism to make requests and provide notifications to their container (event sink). The control must provide an *outgoing* (or source) interface for its events, and the container must provide a *sink* for that interface. The container reads the control's type library to discover the events the control expects to send. The container then dynamically creates an implementation of **IDispatch::Invoke()** that supports those methods. The ActiveX control standard describes a set of standard events that a control can implement. The events are primarily for user interaction involving the keyboard and mouse.

Table 20.1	ActiveX control interfaces.	
Category	**Interfaces**	**Use**
Automation	IDispatch	To support dynamic invocation. Exposes the control's functionality (methods and properties).
Connection points	IConnection PointContainer, IConnectionPoint, IEnumConnection Points, IEnum Connections	To provide a generic way to establish two-way communication between the object and client.
Drawing the control	IViewObject, IViewObject2, IViewObjectEx	To draw the control's graphical image on the client's DC.
Type information	IProvideClassInfo, IProvideClassInfo2	To access **coclass** type information and provide outgoing interface information.
Error	ISupportErrorInfo	To provide rich error information using the COM error object mechanism.
Persistence	IPersist, IPersist PropertyBag, IPersistStreamInit, IPersistStorage, IPersistMemory	To maintain the state of a control's properties.
Property pages	ISpecifyProperty Pages, IPerProperty Browsing	To indicate that property page objects are supported and allow the container to access property information.
Quick activation	IQuickActivate	To combine all the parameters and handshaking needed for activation into one round-trip, which improves performance.
Runtime control	IRunnableObject	To allow the container to control and monitor the running state of the object.
Presentation date	IOleCache, IOleCache2	To control the presentation data cache.
Specialized actions	IOleControl, IOleObject	To support keyboard activity and ambient properties.
User interface communications	IOleWindow, IOleInPlace Object, IOleIn PlaceActiveObject, IOleInPlaceObject Windowless, IDataObject	To receive window messages, keyboard accelerators, connect to Windows Help, and participate in drag-and-drop operations.

To make events work, the event source must implement the **IConnectionPoint Container**, **IConnectionPoint**, **IEnumConnectionPoints**, and **IEnum Connections** interfaces. On the opposite end, the event sink needs to notify the event source that it wants to receive events. It typically does so by requesting the **IConnectionPointContainer** interface and then calling **FindConnection Point ()** for a specific **IConnectionPoint** interface. If the specific interface exists, the event sink then uses the **IConnectionPoint** interface to call **Advise()**, passing a pointer to its own callback interface. **Advise()** returns a cookie that the sink will pass back to the source when it calls **UnAdvise()**. **UnAdvise()** terminates the flow of events from a specific connection point.

 You can define the callback interface as a custom interface, but if you want scripting environments to receive callbacks, make the callback interface a dispinterface and implement the methods of **IDispatch**.

Properties

ActiveX control properties come in two flavors: stock and custom. *Stock properties* are properties that use names and dispatch IDs specified in the ActiveX control specification and are defined in olectl.h. Examples of stock properties are background color (**BackColor**), border style (**BorderStyle**), and text to be displayed (**Caption**). *Custom properties* are properties that you, the developer, create.

The control container can also have properties. These properties are known as *ambient properties* and are exposed to the control through the default **IDispatch** interface. By reading the ambient properties and taking the appropriate action, a control can smoothly fit into the container's environment. For example, the control might read the container's background color (**AmbientBackColor**) and adjust its own background color to match the container's. An interesting ambient property is **UserMode**. The control can examine this ambient property to determine if the container is in design mode or run mode. Often, a control will need to behave differently in design mode than it behaves in run mode.

Design Time User Interface

Some control containers, such as Visual Basic, provide a properties window, which allows the developer a direct way to examine and change a control's properties. Others, such as Visual C++, do not provide such a mechanism. Therefore, a control must provide another way in which the design time developer can examine and change the control's properties.

Property pages are used to implement this design time interface mechanism. Each property page is a COM object that interacts with the container by exposing an **IPropertyPage** interface or an **IPropertyPage2** interface. A container learns about the property pages a control supports by calling **ISpecify PropertyPages::GetPages()**. GetPages() fills a **CAUUID** structure with a pointer to an array of property page **CLSID**s and a count indicating the number of items in the array. The container can then create a property frame, which instantiates each property page object.

The frame also instantiates a property page frame site object for each property page. Each property frame site object exposes the **IPropertyPageSite** interface and its respective property page; then they communicate with each other. The property page notifies the property frame site object of property value changes by calling **IPropertyPageSite::OnStatusChange()**.

All this requires a lot of code. Fortunately, COM provides functions, **OleCreate PropertyFrame()** and **OleCreatePropertyFrameIndirect()**, that greatly simplify things. These functions create a property sheet dialog box that holds all the property pages that are passed during the call. They also create all necessary property frame site objects and manage interaction between the property pages and the frame.

Property Persistence

A key feature of ActiveX controls is *persistence*, the capability to save the property state between instantiations. An example of persistence is when a control is used in a Visual Basic program. During design time, each control embedded in a form is an instance of that control, and each instance has its own set of property values that make it unique. The developer modifies these values through the Visual Basic properties window or through the control's property pages. Then, when told to do so by the container (form), these values are saved and restored by the control. The container, not the control, determines where the control's property values are stored. Persistence is not restricted to design time. For example, a control that can be hosted in a Word document or a Web page might display different information based on user input. In this case, the control might need to save and reload the user's input.

All this is accomplished through a set of COM interfaces. The three most important are **IPersistStreamInit**, **IPersistStorage**, and **IPersistPropertyBag**. **IPersistStreamInit** lets the container ask the control to load its persistent data from—and save to—a stream. A stream is a simple file structure that provides a stream-oriented structure (a stream of bytes) to the control. By calling **IPersistStreamInit::InitNew()**, the container can let the control know that it's being initialized for the first time. **IPersistStorage** lets the container ask the control to load its persistent data *from and save it to* a storage. A *storage* is an object capable of creating and managing streams and other storages. **IPersistPropertyBag** allows a container to ask the control to load and save its persistence data as text-based properties. This form of persistence is useful in a Web-based environment.

Component Categories

By assigning category identifiers (**CATID**, a **GUID**) to your components, you can group your components into logically related groups or *component categories*. The intent of component categories is to allow components to specify their capabilities and requirements. The **ICatRegister** and **ICatInformation** interfaces provide methods that can be used to write component category information to the Registry, as well as remove and retrieve component category information from it. The defined **CATID**s on an individual are stored under the **HKEY_CLASSES_ROOT\Component Categories** Registry key. Each category has its own unique subkey named by its **CATID**. Figure 20.1 shows some Registry entries under this key. Beneath its subkey, each category has one or more named values that contain the human-readable description of the category. These named values are coded by locale ID; for example, 409 is English. See Figure 20.2.

Under its **CLSID**, each component can have two subkeys that store **CATID**s: Implemented Categories and Required Categories. The *Implemented Categories* entry lists the category capabilities that the component provides, and the *Required Categories* entry lists the categories that require a client or container to implement. Figure 20.3 shows an example of a **CLSID** that has two **CATID** entries under its Implemented Categories subkey.

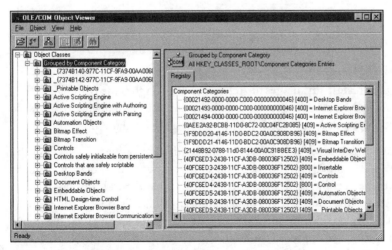

Figure 20.1   The OLE/COM Object Viewer displaying Component Categories entries.

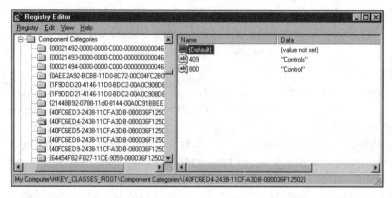

Figure 20.2   The Registry Editor displaying Component Categories entries.

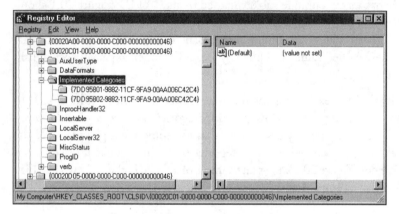

Figure 20.3   The Registry Editor displaying Implemented Categories entries.

Licensing

One of the greatest advantages of ActiveX controls is the ease with which they can be moved from one system to another and reused. However, this wide distribution presents a potential problem—unauthorized use.

Think about a control as it relates to three different parties: the author, the application developer, and the user. The author, for a fee, provides the application developer a copy (DLL or OCX) of the ActiveX control. The application developer uses the control in his or her application and distributes the application and control to the user. The user now has a copy of the control, and without safeguards, the user can reuse the control. The safeguard provided by COM is licensing. Licensing is the feature that allows the author of an ActiveX control to determine how others use the control. In the preceding case, the application developer is a licensed user and possesses a license key. The control container (the application) uses this key to prove it is licensed.

There are two types of license verification. The first type occurs at design time. First, a license file (LIC) must be present in the same directory as the development tool or the control (DLL or OCX). Without this file, the development tool cannot create the control as part of the design time environment. The second type of license verification occurs at runtime, when the application must present the license key when it attempts to instantiate the control.

Licensing relies on the **IClassFactory2** interface. An extension of the **IClass Factory** interface, **IClassFactory2** adds three methods: **CreateInstance Lic()**, **GetLicInfo()**, and **RequestLicKey()**. **CreateInstanceLic()** is used to create an instance of a control. This method is like **IClassFactory::Create Instance()**, but it also requires its caller to pass in a license key. **GetLicInfo()** is called to learn whether a design time license exists on this machine for a control. **RequestLicKey()** is called by obtaining a copy of the license key.

ATL Support

The ATL Object Wizard provides six controls: a full control, a lite control, a composite control, a lite composite control, an HTML control, and a lite HTML control. These controls generally do what you might expect. The *full control* supports the interfaces for all control containers. It implements complete OLE Embedding protocol and complete OLE Control protocol. It can be queried for property pages and persist to streams and storage. Finally, it can provide type information to the client. The *lite control* supports only the subset of interfaces necessary to host the control needed by Internet Explorer. It supports the OLE Control protocol, but not all of the OLE Embedding protocol. A *composite control* is a dialog resource that can host several controls internally. A *lite composite control* is a composite control that supports only the interfaces Internet Explorer needs. An *HTML control* is a full control that contains DHTML functionality and can show Web pages within its frame. A *lite HTML control* is like an HTML control, but it supports only the Internet Explorer interfaces.

When you create a control using the ATL Object Wizard, ATL provides the code needed to implement the basic control. Your control is derived from either **CComControl** or **CComCompositeControl**. You, of course, need to add the necessary code to provide your control's unique functionality.

The full control derives from the **CComControl** template class to provide most of its functionality. **CComControl** supports a number of COM interfaces, stock properties, property persistence, and basic windowing functionality. It is derived from **CComControlBase** and **CWindowImpl**.

The composite control implements the same interfaces as the full control. However, rather than managing a single control, the composite manages a group of other controls. It uses a standard dialog box to host these controls. Instead of deriving from **CComControl**, the composite control derives from **CComCompositeControl**. **CComCompositeControl** is derived from **CComControl** and manages the dialog box.

Like the full control, the HTML control derives from **CComControl**. This control is like the **CComCompositeControl** in that it provides a resource for the layout of its user interface elements. However, rather than using a dialog resource, it uses an HTML resource. That is, it specifies its user interface using HTML. The HTML control programmatically accesses the browser using **IWebBrowser2**.

The lite versions of the controls derive from the same base class as their full-form counterparts. The lite versions are slimmer but support fewer interfaces. Table 20.2 shows which interfaces each control supports. The Full column applies to the full control, the composite control, and the HTML control. The Lite column applies to the lite control, the lite composite control, and the lite HTML control.

Recall that the lite versions of the controls only support the interfaces that Internet Explorer needs. Table 20.2 shows that the Internet Explorer doesn't need **IDataObject**, **IPersistStorage**, **IProvideClassInfo**, **IProvideClassInfo2**, **IQuickActivate**, or **ISpecifyPropertyPages**. **IDataObject** and **IPersistStorage** are part of the complete OLE Embedding protocol. **IDataObject** is used for data transfer between a control and its container, and **IPersistStorage** provides the control with a storage to load or save its properties. **IProvideClassInfo** and **IProvideClassInfo2** are used with dispatch clients. **IProvideClassInfo** gives containers an easy way to get a control's type library information. **IProvideClass Info2** extends **IProvideClassInfo** to supply the **IID** of the control's default outgoing event interface. **IQuickActivate** provides a fast activation mechanism that lets a container load and initialize the control in one round-trip. **ISpecifyPropertyPages** supplies its property pages to a design time container so the container can host them in its property dialog box, thus allowing the developer to change the control's design time properties.

Notice that support for connection points and error reporting isn't shown in Table 20.2. This support is easy to add; simply select the appropriate checkbox on the Attributes tab of the ATL Object Wizard Properties dialog box. Connection points are needed for the control to report events to the container. To handle COM error handling, the **ISupportErrorInfo** interface must be supported.

MFC Support

Visual C++ includes an MFC ActiveX ControlWizard that generates a full ActiveX control. Step 1 of the ControlWizard lets you add from 1 to 99 con-

Table 20.2	The interfaces implemented by the ATL ActiveXcontrols.	
Interface	Full	Lite
IDataObject	Y	N
IDispatch	Y	Y
IOleControl	Y	Y
IOleInPlaceActiveObject	Y	Y
IOleInPlaceObject	Y	Y
IOleInPlaceObjectWindowless	Y	Y
IOleObject	Y	Y
IOleWindow	Y	Y
IPersist	Y	Y
IPersistStorage	Y	N
IPersistStreamInit	Y	Y
IProvideClassInfo	Y	N
IProvideClassInfo2	Y	N
IQuickActivate	Y	N
ISpecifyPropertyPages	Y	N
IViewObject	Y	Y
IViewObject2	Y	Y
IViewObjectEx	Y	Y

trols in the OCX. Step 2 provides several selections that can modify the control's behavior. For each control that the ControlWizard generates, you get a class derived from **COleControl** and a default property page. **COleControl** is a large and complex class that implements basically the same set of interfaces that the ATL full control does. It also handles a large number of Windows messages, implements stock methods, properties, and events, and provides a huge number of virtual functions you can override.

Creating an ActiveX control with MFC is as easy as it gets. Unfortunately, you can create only a full control, and you are dependent on the MFC library, which can be limiting. Another downside to using MFC is that it doesn't support dual interfaces. MFC uses the automation (**IDispatch**) interface, and to support a dual interface, you need to add a lot of extra code.

ActiveX Control Containers

Recall that an ActiveX control container is just a program that can host an ActiveX control. Chapter 9 looked at hosting an ActiveX control in a dialog box and at creating one at runtime. This section will not repeat that, but instead will cover many of the standard COM interfaces that a container might need to support. Unlike a control, a container is required to support certain interfaces.

All ActiveX control containers must support the **IDispatch** interface. This interface is how the container makes ambient properties available to the control. A container also needs to support another **IDispatch** if it traps events fired by the control. For every control that is plugged into a container, the container must provide a control site object that supports the **IOleControlSite** interface. However, not all its methods are mandatory. Nonmandatory methods return **E_NOTIMPL**, **S_FALSE**, or **S_OK** as appropriate.

IOleContainer is a required interface, although like **IOleControlSite**, not every method is mandatory. **IOleContainer** provides the capability to enumerate objects, thus allowing controls to navigate to other controls in the same document or form. For every compound document object a container contains, it must provide one instance of **IOleClientSite**. **IOleClientSite** allows objects to request services from the container. **IOleInPlaceSite** allows the container to participate in in-place activation. This interface allows a control to obtain information about placement-related issues and to send placement notifications to the container. A couple of **IOleInPlaceSite**'s methods are not required.

Like **IOleInPlaceSite**, **IOleInPlaceFrame** is involved with in-place activation. This interface allows an object to merge its top-level user interface (such as menu items and toolbars) with the container's. Nearly all of **IOleInPlaceFrame**'s methods are nonmandatory. **IErrorInfo** is required if the container supports dual interfaces.

Hosting ActiveX Controls Using MFC

MFC makes it easy to use ActiveX controls in an application. Chapter 9 covered this in detail. Recall that by selecting a checkbox in AppWizard, MFC provides the interfaces needed to host an ActiveX control. When AppWizard is done, you can use the Components and Controls Gallery to insert an ActiveX control into your project. Then with the help of the MFC ClassWizard, you can add the desired functionality.

Hosting ActiveX Controls Using ATL

ATL provides four ways in which you can host ActiveX controls: windows, dialog boxes, composite controls, and HTML controls. **CAxHostWindow**, found in ATLHOST.H, implements the required container interfaces. It is both a window and a COM object. You don't create a **CAxHostWindow** directly. Rather, you call **AtlAxWinInit()** to register a Win32 window class named **AtlAxWin**. Next, you create an **AtlAxWin** window instance using the standard Win32 **CreateWindow()** function. Then you use the **IAxWinHost Window** interface to create or load an ActiveX control in the window.

ATL also provides **CAxWindow**, a **typedef** of **CAxWindowT<CWindow>**. **CAxWindow** is easier to use than **CAxHostWindow**; you don't have to deal with **CreateWindow()** or **IAxWinHostWindow**. **CAxWindow** provides methods that allow you to create a window, create and host a control in the window, and attach an existing control to the host.

The ATL Object Wizard can add a dialog resource to your project and generate an associated class, derived from **CAxDialogImpl**. Both Windows controls and ActiveX controls can be added to this **CAxDialogImpl**-derived class.

Hosting ActiveX controls in a composite control is similar to using a dialog box. The ATL composite control uses a dialog resource to lay out its user interface elements, which can be Windows controls or ActiveX controls.

The ATL Object Wizard provides a resource for an HTML control similar to the way it provides a resource for a composite control, except that instead of using a dialog resource, an HTML control uses an HTML resource. The WebBrowser control used by Internet Explorer 4 will parse the HTML resource at runtime. The following code demonstrates an HTML control hosting the Calendar control.

```
<HTML>
<BODY>
<OBJECT
  CLASSID="CLSID:8E27C92B-1264-101C-8A2F-040224009C02"
  WIDTH=400
  HEIGHT=300
  ID="Calendar"
>
<PARAM NAME="BackColor" VALUE=1262256>
</OBJECT>
<BODY>
<SCRIPT LANGUAGE=VBScript>
Sub Calendar_Click()
  dt = Calendar.Day
  mon = Calendar.Month
  yr = Calendar.Year
  MsgBox(CStr (mon) + "/" + CStr(dt) + "/" + CStr(yr))
End Sub
</SCRIPT>
</HTML>
```

Practice Questions

Question 1

Which of the following statements is true regarding connection points? [Check all of the correct answers]

❏ a.   A single connection point can only be connected to one sink at a time.

❏ b.   The IConnectionPointContainer interface lets a container find out about the connection points of a connectable object.

❏ c.   It is the connectable object's responsibility to implement its outgoing interfaces.

❏ d.   IConnectionPoint methods are used to create and terminate connections.

The correct answers are b and d. Answer b is correct because **IConnectionPoint Container::FindConnectionPoint()** allows the client to ask an object if it supports a particular outgoing interface. Also, **IConnectionPointContainer:: EnumConnectionPoints()** allows a client to retrieve a list of the connection points that an object supports. Answer d is correct because **IConnectionPoint:: Advise()** is used by the client to establish a connection with a specific connection point in a connectable object, and **IConnectionPoint::UnAdvise()** is used to break a connection. Answer a is incorrect because it's possible for a single connection point to be connected to many different clients at the same time. This allows the object to send the same event to many clients simultaneously. Answer c is incorrect because the connectable object is responsible for defining, but not implementing, its outgoing interfaces. The sink object implements the connectable object's outgoing interface.

Question 2

The coclass entity is used in an IDL and ODL to describe a COM class in terms of the interfaces and dispinterfaces that it exposes, and the outgoing interfaces that it supports. Which of the following interface definitions specifies that the interface is an outgoing interface?

○ a. [default, events] MyOutGoingInterface;

○ b. [default, source] MyOutGoingInterface;

○ c. [default, sink] MyOutGoingInterface;

○ d. [default, outgoing] MyOutGoingInterface;

The correct answer is b. The **source** attribute is used to declare the outgoing interface of a class—that is, the one that has been implemented using the connectable object protocol. Answers a, c, and d are incorrect because events, sink, and outgoing are not legal attributes.

Question 3

You are using ATL and want to implement a modeless dialog box that supports ActiveX controls. Which of the following classes would you use as the base class?

○ a. CDialogImpl

○ b. CAxDialogImpl

○ c. CSimpleDialog

○ d. CDialog

The correct answer is b. **CAxDialogImpl** can be used as the base class for implementing a modeless or modal dialog box that supports ActiveX controls. Answer a is incorrect; although **CDialogImpl** can be used as the base class for implementing a modeless or modal dialog box, it does not support ActiveX controls. **CSimpleDialog** is a prebuilt modal dialog box that uses standard OK and Cancel buttons and that doesn't support ActiveX controls. Answer d is incorrect because **CDialog** is an MFC class, not an ATL class.

Question 4

The IPropertyBag interface is used to: [Check all of the correct answers]

❑ a. Save the control's ambient properties.

❑ b. Load the control's properties from persistent storage.

❑ c. Load or save the container's properties.

❑ d. Save the control's properties to persistent storage.

The correct answers are b and d. The container calls **IPersistProperty Bag::Load()**, passing an **IPropertyBag** interface to the control. The control then repeatedly calls **IPropertyBag::Read()** to obtain its properties from persistent storage. The control's properties are saved through the use of **IPersistPropertyBag::Save()** and **IPropertyBag::Write()**.

Question 5

The purpose of the IConnectionPoint::UnAdvise() method is to:

○ a. Notify the sink that the connection point has been terminated.

○ b. Inform the client of the IID of the outgoing interface.

○ c. Break a connection between a connection point and a sink.

○ d. Provide the client with the cookie that uniquely identifies the connection.

The correct answer is c. The client calls **IConnectionPoint::UnAdvise()**, passing the cookie that identifies the connection the client wants terminated. Answer a is incorrect because the connection point object doesn't notify the sink that there won't be any more events. This answer could cause you a problem if you spend too much time on it and tried to read something into it, because the connection point object must call **Release()** on the sinks interface to reverse the **AddRef()** that occurred during **IConnectionPoint::Advise()**. Answer b is incorrect because the client obtains the **IID** of the outgoing interface a connect point supports by calling **IConnectionPoint::GetConnectionInterface()**. Answer d is incorrect because **IConnectionPoint::UnAdvise()** is called by the client and it is the client that passes the cookie to the connection point object, not the other way around.

Need To Know More?

 Kruglinski, David J., George Shepherd, and Scot Wingo. *Programming Microsoft Visual C++*, 5th ed. Microsoft Press, Redmond, WA: 1998. ISBN 1-57231-857-0. Chapter 30 covers ActiveX controls. The authors take you through the steps of building an ActiveX control using ATL. They explain the ATL classes, how to respond to window messages, how to create and use property pages, how to add property persistence, and how events work and how to implement them.

 Li, Sing and Panos Economopoulos. *Professional COM Application with ATL*. Wrox Press Ltd., Birmingham, UK: 1998. ISBN 1-861001-70-3. If you have a good COM/ATL foundation, this is the book for you. It starts by having you build an ActiveX control from scratch. Then you use ATL to develop a distributed calendar system. This real-world three-tier application uses flexible, browser-based controls for the client UI, business objects on both the client and server, and UDA to perform queries and updates. One feature I really like is the authors' use of UML and design patterns.

 Prosise, Jeff. *Programming Windows with MFC*. Microsoft Press, Redmond, WA: 1999. ISBN 1-57231-695-0. This is an updated version of the author's popular book. The book has four parts: Fundamentals of Windows and MFC; The Document/View Architecture; Beyond the Basics; and COM, OLE and ActiveX. Chapter 21 first covers ActiveX controls in general and then the specific support MFC provides. Next, the author takes you through the steps of building an ActiveX control using MFC. Then you are shown how to use the control in both an MFC application and a Web page. Last, the author presents an overview of three advanced topics: Windowless Controls, Control Subclassing, and Control Licensing.

 Zaratian, Beck. *Visual C++ 6.0 Programmer's Guide*. Microsoft Press, Redmond, WA: 1998. ISBN 1-57231-866-X. This updated version of the author's book, *Visual C++ Owners Manual* focuses on how to use the Visual C++ tool. However, the section on ActiveX controls has the best explanation I've seen of licensing, what it is, and how it works.

MSDN Library, Technical Articles\Component Object Model

MSDN Library, Visual Studio 6.0 Documentation\Visual C++ Documentation\References\Microsoft Foundation Class Library and Templates\Active Template Library\Articles

MSDN Library, Visual Studio 6.0 Documentation\Visual C++ Documentation\Using Visual C++\Visual C++ Programmer's Guide\Adding User Interface Features\Details\ActiveX Control Topics

MSDN Library, Visual Studio 6.0 Documentation\Visual C++ Documentation\Using Visual C++\Visual C++ Programmer's Guide\Adding Program Functionality\Details\ActiveX Topics

MSDN Library, Platform SDK\Web Services\Component Development\\ActiveX Controls

Data Services

Terms you'll need to understand:

- √ Open database connectivity (ODBC)
- √ Data Access Objects (DAO)
- √ Remote Data Objects (RDO)
- √ Universal Data Access (UDA)
- √ Microsoft Data Access Components (MDAC)
- √ OLE DB
- √ ActiveX Data Objects (ADO)
- √ **CDatabase**

- √ **CRecordset**
- √ **Connection** object
- √ **Command** object
- √ **Recordset** object
- √ **Error** object and **Errors** collection
- √ **Property** object and **Properties** collection
- √ **Parameter** object and **Parameters** collection
- √ **Field** object and **Fields** collection

Techniques you'll need to master:

- √ Determining the appropriate database access model (ODBC, DAO, RDO, or ADO) to use in your application
- √ Describing the role of ADO in applications that require database access
- √ Describing the ADO programming model

- √ Using ADO controls in a C++ program
- √ Implementing an application that uses ODBC
- √ Implementing an application that uses ADO

There are many database management systems (DBMS) that can be used with an application. Each DBMS comes with its own API. The benefit of a native interface is that a developer can take advantage of the special features of a particular DBMS. The shortcoming is that the developer must learn a different API for each DBMS. This means the decision as to which DBMS will be used with an application is driven more by familiarity than by price, performance, and support. Additionally, after a DBMS is selected, it's difficult to change to another one. SQL, which is used in over 100 software products, was an attempt to standardize the database programming interface. However, because the SQL specification is only a guideline, each vendor, in an effort to differentiate its product from the competition, provides its own unique flavor of SQL. To allow standardized access to many difference database systems, Microsoft has, over the years, introduced a number of application layers such as Visual Basic SQL (VBSQL), open database connectivity (ODBC), Data Access Objects (DAO), and Remote Data Objects (RDO).

In the past, organizations used databases and mainframes to store their data. Today, however, in addition to databases and mainframes, an organization's data might be found in file systems, in mail stores, in Web-based text, and more. Universal Data Access (UDA), shown in Figure 21.1, is Microsoft's strategy for providing access to this information no matter where it might be, from the desktop to the enterprise. The Microsoft Data Access Components (MDAC) is a toolkit of the key technologies Microsoft is using to deliver UDA. These components—OLE DB, ActiveX Data Objects (ADO), and ODBC—are described in the following list:

➤ OLE DB is an open specification for a set of COM-based low-level system interfaces designed for both relational and nonrelational information sources. Everything that is specific to a data source is hidden by the OLE DB interface and represented in a general format that an application can always access in the same manner. OLE DB is the foundation of the UDA architecture.

➤ ADO is an open specification for a set of COM-based application-level interfaces designed to support a variety of development needs. ADO uses OLE DB to access the data and presents the developer with an interface that is easy to use and that feels comfortable to developers familiar with DAO or RDO.

➤ ODBC is a proven API that makes it possible for an application to access relational data from a variety of database management systems.

Because Microsoft wants to eventually replace DAO and RDO with ADO, they are encouraging customers and developers to move to OLE DB and ADO.

ODBC is part of MDAC, which provides backward compatibility. This chapter covers ODBC and ADO. OLE DB will be covered in the companion book, *MCSD Visual C++ 6 Distributed Exam Cram.*

In the short term, you will probably need to understand DAO and RDO. Three key points to remember are:

➤ DAO is an object model for accessing local or SQL data through the Microsoft Jet database engine.

➤ RDO is an object model for accessing relational data through ODBC.

➤ Both are COM interfaces.

ODBC

ODBC was Microsoft's first cohesive effort to design an API that could be used by C programmers. ODBC provides its own flavor of SQL. The application passes ODBC SQL to ODBC, which is translated into the flavor of SQL that is appropriate for the DBMS being used. ODBC is a proven interface that makes it possible for an application to access relational data from a variety of database management systems.

The ODBC architecture consists of a top-level driver manager (odbc32.dll) and many DBMS-specific DLLs, known as *drivers*. The driver manager loads and unloads the native drivers, receives requests from the application, and

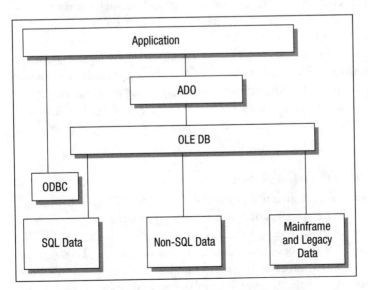

Figure 21.1 The Univeral Data Access architecture.

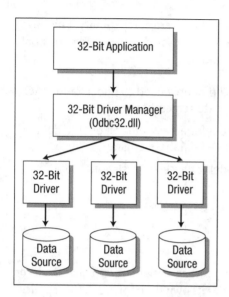

Figure 21.2 The ODBC architecture.

manages the subsequent driver actions. The driver handles the communication between the driver manager and the data source. See Figure 21.2.

ODBC SDK Programming

There are three key ODBC elements that you must know about and manage: the environment, the connection, and the statement. Each of these elements is accessed through *handles*. The environment establishes the link between your application and the ODBC system. The connection provides an association to a specific driver and a data source. The statement can be any legal SQL statement. Using the ODBC SDK consists of connecting to the data source; allocating a statement handle; preparing and executing an SQL statement; processing the data, which can involve database queries and database updates; committing or rolling back the transactions; and disconnecting from the data source.

Connecting To A Data Source

First, you must obtain an environment handle. You do this by calling **SQLAllocHandle()**. An application usually has only one environment handle. Once you have an environment handle, you need to set the **SQL_ATTR_ODBC_VERSION** environment attribute. You can do this by calling **SQLSetEnvAttr()**. Next, you again call **SQLAllocHandle()**, but this time you're allocating a connection handle. Now with all of the preliminaries out of the way, you call **SQLConnect()** to establish a connection. It's possible for an environment to have multiple simultaneous connections. Minus error checking, here's what the code might look like if you want to connect to the SQL Server pubs database:

```
SQLHENV hEnv = SQL_NULL_HENV;
SQLAllocHandle(SQL_HANDLE_ENV, SQL_NULL_HANDLE, &hEnv);
SQLSetEnvAttr(hEnv,
              SQL_ATTR_ODBC_VERSION,
              reinterpret_cast<SQLPOINTER>(SQL_OV_ODBC3),
              SQL_IS_INTEGER);
SQLHDBC hDBC = SQL_NULL_HDBC;
SQLAllocHandle(SQL_HANDLE_DBC, hEnv, &hDBC);
SQLConnect(hDBC,
      reinterpret_cast<SQLCHAR *>("pubs\0"), SQL_NTS,
      reinterpret_cast<SQLCHAR *>("sa\0"), SQL_NTS,
      reinterpret_cast<SQLCHAR *>("\0"), SQL_NTS);
```

SQLAllocHandle() is an ODBC 3.0 generic function that replaces the ODBC 2.0 functions **SQLAllocEnv()**, **SQLAllocConnect()**, and **SQLAllocStmt()**.

All three of the preceding functions can take an assortment of parameters. Use the "Platform SDK, Data Access Services" subset of the MSDN to familiarize yourself with these functions.

Allocating A Statement Handle

Think of a statement in ODBC as being a SQL statement with attributes. These attributes are stored in a structure that is pointed to by a statement handle. Each statement requires its own handle and is associated with a single connection. The generic **SQLAllocHandle()** is used to allocate a statement handle, as shown here:

```
SQLHSTMT hSTMT = SQL_NULL_HSTMT;
SQLAllocHandle(SQL_HANDLE_STMT, hDBC, &hSTMT);
```

Preparing And Executing A SQL Statement

Now you have a number of choices. You can choose, at runtime, to prepare and execute a SQL statement in a single step or to prepare it once and execute it multiple times. Other choices available are database stored procedures and driver functions that can be called. Here's an example of a SQL statement that is prepared and executed at runtime in a single step:

```
SQLExecDirect(hSTMT,
        reinterpret_cast<SQLCHAR *>("SELECT * FROM authors"),
        SQL_NTS);
```

The preceding SQL statement defines a query that returns a block of data, called a *rowset*. This rowset consists all columns of all rows in the authors table.

Visual Basic and Access use the term *recordset* instead of *rowset*. Probably to be consistent with VB and Access, much of the Visual C++ documentation also uses the term *recordset*. However, the VC++ documentation isn't consistent, and both terms are used. The VC++ glossary makes a subtle distinction between them. It defines a rowset as "in ODBC, one or more rows returned by a single fetch operation," and it defines a recordset as "a set of records selected from a data source. The records can be from a table, a query, or a stored procedure that accesses one or more tables." The term *result set* is also used. It's defined as "a collection of data returned by an SQL query on a database."

Processing The Data

After the preceding SQL statement has been executed, you need to get the results. Here you have three options involving the use of **SQLBindCol()** and **SQLGetData()**. Assume you don't want to bind each column in the result set to a program variable. You would first call **SQLFetch()** to retrieve a row of information and then call **SQLGetData()** from each data item you wish to retrieve. **SQLGetData()** copies the data from a specific result set column to a specific program variable. Here's a snippet of code that retrieves the information and prints the first name, last name, and phone number for each entry in the authors table.

```
for(RETCODE rCode = SQLFetch(hSTMT);
    SQL_SUCCEEDED(rCode);
    rCode = SQLFetch(hSTMT))
{
  char szLastName[MAXLASTNAME];
  char szFirstName[MAXFIRSTNAME];
```

```
char szPhone[MAXPHONE];
SQLINTEGER len;
SQLGetData(hSTMT, 2, SQL_C_CHAR,
           szLastName, MAXLASTNAME, &len);
SQLGetData(hSTMT, 3, SQL_C_CHAR,
           szFirstName, MAXFIRSTNAME, &len);
SQLGetData(hSTMT, 4, SQL_C_CHAR,
           szPhone, MAXPHONE, &len);
Display(szFirstName, szLastName, szPhone);
}
```

Committing Or Rolling Back The Transactions

Because no statements were executed that would make changes to the database, this step is not needed here. However, if you executed a statement that changed, deleted, or added data to the database, you would need to call **SQLEndTran()** to commit or roll back the transaction.

Disconnecting From The Data Source

After you are finished with the database, you need to disconnect and free all of the handles:

```
SQLFreeHandle(SQL_HANDLE_STMT, hSTMT);
SQLDisconnect(hDBC);
SQLFreeHandle(SQL_HANDLE_DBC, hDBC);
SQLFreeHandle(SQL_HANDLE_ENV, hEnv);
```

SQLFreeHandle() is an ODBC 3.0 generic function that replaces the ODBC 2.0 functions **SQLFreeEnv()**, **SQLFreeConnect()**, and **SQLFreeStmt()**.

ODBC MFC Programming

MFC provides two wrapper classes for the ODBC API. The **CDatabase** class represents the database source, and **CRecordset** represents the data itself. There are also two other classes that can be used with ODBC MFC applications. **CDBException** objects are thrown by almost all of the CDatabase classes' member functions if an exception condition occurs. **CRecordView**, which is derived from **CView**, is directly connected to a **CRecordset** object and can display database records using dialog controls.

CDatabase, CRecordset, CDBException, and **CRecordView** are defined in afxdb.h.

CDatabase

Although a **CDatabase** object can be used by itself, it is normally used with one or more **CRecordset** objects. Because a **CDatabase** class object represents a connection to a data source, very seldom will you need to derive a class from **CDatabase.** Here's a snippet of code that inserts a new author into the pubs database:

```
CDatabase db;
try
{
  db.Open(_T("ODBC;DSN=pubs;UID=sa;PWD="));
  db.ExecuteSQL(_T("INSERT INTO authors "
    "(au_id, au_lname, au_fname, phone, "
    "address, city, state, zip, contract)"
    "VALUES ('404-24-4472', 'James', 'Jesse', "
    "'908 840-4098', '1231 First Street', 'Boston', "
    "'MA', '01052', 1)"));
  db.Close();
}
catch(CDBException *pe)
{
  MessageBox(pe->m_strError, "Database Error");
  pe->Delete();
}
```

CRecordset

A **CRecordset** object represents a set of records retrieved from a data source. The **CRecordset** class supports several types of recordsets, but two are generally used: snapshots and dynasets. A *snapshot* is a static picture of the data taken at the time the recordset was filled; it isn't affected by changes made by other users of the data source. A *dynaset*, on the other hand, is dynamic. It stays synchronized with changes made by other users.

The easiest way to create a recordset class is to use the ClassWizard to generate a class. The ClassWizard will display the Database Options dialog box, shown in Figure 21.3, so that you can specify many of the characteristics that

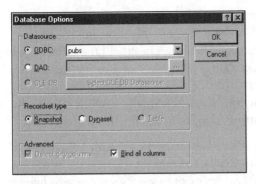

Figure 21.3   The Database Options
dialog box.

will be used to define your **CRecordset**-derived class. For this data source, two additional dialog boxes are displayed. The first allows you to specify login information, and the second lets you select the data source.

After you have a **CRecordset**-derived class, you can use it to execute SQL statements against the data source. Here's a snippet of code that retrieves the authors table and displays the first name, last name, and phone number of each entry in the table:

```
CDatabase db;
try
{
  if(db.Open(_T("ODBC;DSN=pubs;UID=sa;PWD="")))
  {
    CAuthorsSet authorset(&db);
    authorset.Open(CRecordset::snapshot,
            _T("SELECT * FROM authors ORDER BY au_lname"));
    for( ; ! authorset.IsEOF(); authorset.MoveNext())
    {
      Display(authorset.m_au_fname,
              authorset.m_au_lname,
              authorset.m_phone);
    }
    db.Close();
  }
}
catch(CDBException *pe)
{
  MessageBox(pe->m_strError, "Database Error");
  pe->Delete();
}
```

The **CRecordset** provides a number of features that make performing queries easier. First, if you don't pass a **CDatabase** object to the **CRecordset** constructor, **CRecordset::Open()** will create a **CDatabase** object, call the **CRecordset** virtual function **GetDefaultConnect()** to get the data source connection string, and then pass the string to **CDatabase::Open()**. ClassWizard provides this function for your **CRecordset**-derived class. You might want to modify the ClassWizard-provided connect string to include the user ID and password.

ClassWizard also provides your **CRecordset**-derived class with a **GetDefault SQL()** function, which the framework calls. You can edit this function as you see fit. For example, you can use a **CALL** statement to specify a predefined query: {CALL GetAuthorizationByUserID}. When ClassWizard generates your **CRecordset**-derived class, it provides a data member for each of the columns in the data source. These data members are tied to the corresponding columns in the data source by the **DoFieldExchange()** function. The framework calls this function to move data from the data source to your data members or vice versa. This partial implementation of a **CRecordset**-derived class is used to query the authors table for the first name, last name, and phone columns.

```
CNameAndPhone::CNameAndPhone(CDatabase* pdb)
  : CRecordset(pdb)
{
  //{{AFX_FIELD_INIT(CNameAndPhone)
  m_au_lname = _T("");
  m_au_fname = _T("");
  m_phone = _T("");
  m_nFields = 3;
  //}}AFX_FIELD_INIT
  m_nDefaultType = snapshot;
}


CString CNameAndPhone::GetDefaultConnect()
{
  return _T("ODBC;DSN=pubs;uid=sa;pwd=");
}


CString CNameAndPhone::GetDefaultSQL()
{
  return _T("[dbo].[authors]");
}


void CNameAndPhone::DoFieldExchange(CFieldExchange* pFX)
{
  //{{AFX_FIELD_MAP(CNameAndPhone)
```

```
    pFX->SetFieldType(CFieldExchange::outputColumn);
    RFX_Text(pFX, _T("[au_lname]"), m_au_lname);
    RFX_Text(pFX, _T("[au_fname]"), m_au_fname);
    RFX_Text(pFX, _T("[phone]"), m_phone);
    //}}AFX_FIELD_MAP
}
```

Two frequently used **CRecordset** data members are **m_strFilter** and **m_strSort**. These data members are used to specify, respectively, the selection criteria and how the records are to be sorted. Following is a snippet of code that returns the first name, last name, and phone of the authors with an area code of 415. The recordset is sorted by last name in ascending alphabetically order.

```
try
{
    CNameAndPhone authorset;
    authorset.m_strFilter = "phone LIKE '415 %'";
    authorset.m_strSort = "au_lname ASC";
    authorset.Open();

    for( ; ! authorset.IsEOF(); authorset.MoveNext())
    {
        Display(authorset.m_au_fname,
                authorset.m_au_lname,
                authorset.m_phone);
    }
}
catch(CDBException *pe)
{
    MessageBox(pe->m_strError, "Database Error");
    pe->Delete();
}
```

ADO

ActiveX Data Objects are a collection of dual-interface objects used to connect to and manipulate data. The ADO model, shown in Figure 21.4, consists of seven objects (**Connection, Command, Recordset, Error, Property, Parameter,** and **Field**) and four collections (**Errors, Properties, Parameters,** and **Fields**), which makes it fairly simple to understand. ADO is housed in MSADO15.DLL and has a type library that you can view using the OLE/COM Object Viewer (see Figure 21.5).

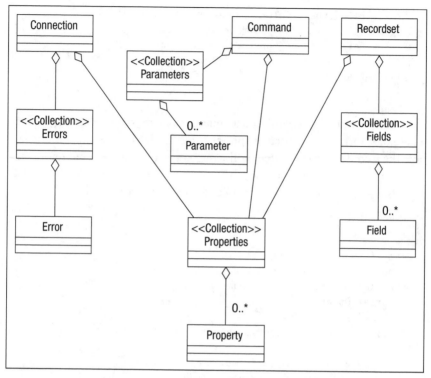

Figure 21.4 The ADO object model.

As of this writing, the MDAC 2.5 SDK Beta documentation indicates that two additional objects will be added to the model: **Record** and **Stream**.

You bring ADO into your program by the **#import** directive, as in the following:

```
#import "c:\Program Files\Common Files\System\ADO\msado15.dll"
```

The type library contained in msado15.dll is defined in the ADODB namespace. If you want, you can place it in another namespace by using the **rename_namespace** attribute. Or, you can use the **no_namespace** attribute, which tells the compile to not generate a namespace at all. There is also a potential problem with the preceding **#import** statement. The type library header generated will contain a definition of EOF, which will conflict with an EOF definition in ios.h.

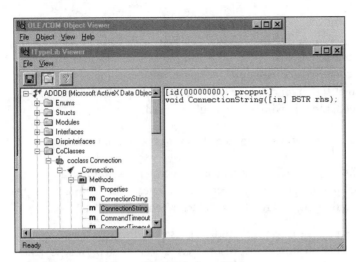

Figure 21.5   Viewing the ADO type library.

To avoid this conflict, you need to use the **rename** attribute. Here's one possible way you might change the **#import** directive:

```
#import "C:\Program Files\Common Files\system\ado\MSADO15.DLL" \
    rename_namespace("ADOCG") rename("EOF", "EndOfFile")
using namespace ADOCG;
```

The Connection Object

The **Connection** object has one primary purpose: to manage a physical connection to the database. With the **Connection** object, you can access simple nonrelational data, such as files on a server, or more-robust data, such as a relational database. The **Connection** object allows you to do the following:

➤ Open a connection to a data source

➤ Execute SQL statements or database stored procedures

➤ Establish transactions for data updates

Although it's not required that you establish a connection first, it's usually the wise thing to do because there's significant overhead involved in connecting to a data source. Creating the **Connection** object is very simple using the type library-produced smart pointer. You only have to declare a smart pointer and pass the **Connection** object's **CLSID** into its constructor, as follows:

```
_ConnectionPtr spConn(__uuidof(Connection));
```

To initiate the connection, you call **Open()**, passing a connection string that specifies the data source, the user ID, and the password required for the connection. The connection string can be as simple as the ODBC data source name, or it can contain extra parameters separated by semicolons. For example, to connect to an SQL Server database named Development located on a server named Appleseed, the following string could be used:

```
"driver={SQL Server};server=Appleseed;database=Development"
```

When you are finished with the data source connection, you simply call **Close()**. When the smart pointer goes out of scope, it will release the **Connection** object. The **Connection** object's methods are described in Table 21.1.

The **Connection** object's **Execute()** method is used to directly execute a query and return a minimally featured **Recordset** object. The method prototype (taken from .tlh) looks like this:

```
_RecordsetPtr Execute (_bstr_t CommandText,
                       VARIANT * RecordsAffected,
                       long Options );
```

CommandText is a SQL statement, table name, stored procedure, or some other provider-specific command text. *RecordsAffected* returns how many records were affected by the command. (It returns -1 if an error occurs.) Here, *Options* indicates how the provider evaluates the *CommandText* argument. It can be one or more of **CommandTypeEnum** or **ExecuteOptionEnum**.

Table 21.1   The Connection object's methods.

Method	Description
BeginTrans	Assists in transaction management. Use this method when you want to group a series of data source changes into a single unit.
Cancel	Cancels the current asynchronous operation (**Execute()** or **Open()**).
CommitTrans	Assists in transaction management. Use this method to make all changes within the current transaction permanent.
Execute	Executes a **Connection** object's command directly.
Open	Establishes the connection to the data source.
OpenSchema	Returns schema information, such as table structures, from the database.
RollbackTrans	Assists in transaction management. Use this method to undo all changes within the current transaction.

The possible values for **CommandTypeEnum** are as follows:

➤ **adCmdUnspecified**—Not specified.

➤ **adCmdUnknown**—An unknown command type (default).

➤ **adCmdText**—A simple SQL command or query.

➤ **adCmdTable**—A database table name.

➤ **adCmdStoredProc**—A database stored procedure.

➤ **adCmdFile**—The name of a file that is a persistent recordset.

➤ **adCmdTableDirect**—A table with all columns selected.

The possible values for **ExecuteOptionEnum** are as follows:

➤ **adOptionUnspecified**—How the provider should execute the command is unspecified.

➤ **adAsyncExecute**—Indicates that the command should execute asynchronously.

➤ **adAsyncFetch**—After the initial rows are fetched, the remaining rows will be fetched asynchronously.

➤ **adAsyncFetchNonBlocking**—The main thread will never block.

➤ **adExecuteNoRecords**—Discards the recordset normally returned from **Execute()**.

The **Connection** object's properties are described in Table 21.2.

Here's a snippet of code that uses a smart pointer to create a **Connection** object and then opens the pubs database:

```
_ConnectionPtr spConn(__uuidof(Connection));
spConn->ConnectionString = "Data Source=pubs;uid=sa;pwd=";
spConn->Open("", "", "", adConnectUnspecified);
```

Rather than using the **ConnectionString** property the information can be passed as arguments, like so:

```
spConn->Open("pubs",                     // Using a DSN
            "sa",                        // User ID
            "",                          // Password
            adConnectUnspecified);       // Options
```

The last parameter can be one of two values; **adConnectUnspecified** opens the connection synchronously and **adAsyncConnect** opens it asynchronously.

Table 21.2	The Connection object's properties.
Property	**Description**
Attributes	Used to change the type of transactions used in the session.
CommandTimeout	Specifies the number of seconds to wait before a command times out and generates an error. The default is 30 seconds.
ConnectionTimeout	Specifies the number of seconds to wait before a connection attempt times out and generates an error. The default is 15 seconds.
ConnectionString	The session's connection string.
CursorLocation	Indicates whether recordset cursors (indicating the current record) should reside with the client or server. The default is **adUseServer**, which specifies that the server will manage the cursor. For large recordsets, this is more efficient, and the cursor is more sensitive to changes made by other users. The value **adUseClient** specifies that the a local (client-side) cursor will be used. The local cursor provides the most flexibility of the two.
DefaultDatabase	Indicates the default database of a **Connection**. This property isn't available with all OLE DB providers.
IsolationLevel	An enumerated value that allows you to change the isolation level. The most frequently used values are **adXactCursorStability**, which specifies that your transaction can't see the uncommitted changes of other transactions, and **adXactChaos**, which specifies that your transaction can't overwrite pending changes of more highly isolated cursors. Other values are **adXactUnspecified, adXactReadUncommitted, adXactBrowse, adXactReadCommitted, adXact RepeatableRead, adXactIsolated,** and **adXact Serializable**.
Mode	An enumerated value that enables you to set (or find) a set of permissions. The possible values are **adMode Unknown, adModeRead, adModeWrite, adMode ReadWrite, adModeShareDenyRead, adModeShare DenyWrite, adModeShareExclusive, adModeShare DenyNone,** and **adModeRecursive**.
State	Indicates the state of the connection, such as open (**adStateOpen**) or closed (**adStateClosed**).
Version	The ADO version.

The Command Object

The **Command** object is one of the most useful ADO objects. With it you can do a number of necessary and powerful tasks. For example, you can do the following:

➤ Execute SQL statements or stored procedures.

➤ Define and execute repetitive SQL commands that require a set of SQL parameters.

➤ Use a **Command** object to source a recordset.

There are some properties you must set before you can execute a command; others are optional. Table 21.3 describes the **Command** object's properties.

The **Command** object has several methods, and like the **Connection** object, it has an **Execute()** method. However, their signatures are different. Compare the following prototype for the **Command** object's **Execute()** method to the **Connection** object's **Execute()** method shown in the previous section, "The Connection Object."

```
_RecordsetPtr Execute(VARIANT * RecordsAffected,
                      VARIANT * Parameters,
                      long Options );
```

The first parameter, **RecordsAffected**, is used to receive the number of rows affected by the command. The second parameter is used to pass an array of SQL parameters stored in a **VARIANT**-filled **SafeArray** wrapped by a **VARIANT**. Setting this up is not trivial. Fortunately, an easier method exists. First, store each parameter in a **Parameter** object and add the **Parameter** objects to the **Command** object's **Parameters** collection object. Then pass **NULL** as the second parameter, indicating that the parameters to the SQL statement are to be taken from the **Parameters** collection object. (A discussion of both the **Parameters** collection object and the **Parameter** object is coming up.)

In case you didn't set the **CommandType** property, you can use the last parameter to indicate the command type. The value can be one or more of **Command TypeEnum** or **ExecuteOptionEnum** values.

The Parameters Collection And Parameter Object

A **Parameter** object is used to specify information about the data transferred to or from the data source when your command object is executed. Suppose you have the following query:

```
SELECT * FROM authors WHERE state = ?
```

Table 21.3	**The Command object's properties.**

Property	Description
ActiveConnection	A mandatory pointer to the **Connection** object associated with the current session.
CommandText	A mandatory text string that contains the SQL statement to be executed. It can also be a table name, a stored procedure, or another command recognized by the data provider.
CommandTimeout	Specifies how many seconds the command can execute before generating an error. A value of zero specifies no timeout. Defaults to 30 seconds.
CommandType	A value that describes the type of command that the **CommandText** property contains. The possible value can be one or more **CommandTypeEnum** values and **adExecuteNoRecords** from the **ExecuteOptionEnum**. Refer to the **Connection** object's **Execute()** method in Table 21.1.
Name	Indicates a name for a command.
Parameters	A pointer to the **Parameters** collection, which can be used set up SQL parameters for the command.
Prepared	**True** causes the data provider to prepare (compile) the command on the first invocation and then use the compiled command subsequently.
State	Indicates the object's current state. **adStateClosed** indicates that it is closed, whereas **adStateOpen** indicates that it is open. **adStateConnecting** indicates that the object is connecting, and **adStateExecuting** indicates that an asynchronously executing command is still executing. **adStateFetching** indicates that the rows of the object are being fetched. This property can have a combination of values. The default state is **adStateClosed**.

The question mark is a placeholder for a parameter to be supplied as a property of a **Command** object, as seen in this example:

```
_CommandPtr spCmd("ADODB.Command");
spCmd->ActiveConnection = spConn;
spCmd->CommandText = "SELECT * from authors WHERE state = ?";

_ParameterPtr spState = spCmd->CreateParameter("state",
                                               adChar,
                                               adParamInput,
                                               2, "KS");
spCmd->Parameters->Append(spState);
```

First, using a smart pointer, a **Command** object is created, and then the active connection is assigned. Next, the query statement is stored in the **Command** object's **CommandText** property. After that, a **Parameter** object is created and added to the **Command** object's **Parameters** collection using the **Append()** method.

The **Command** object's **CreateParameter()** method takes five arguments. Its prototype looks like this:

```
_ParameterPtr CreateParameter (
        _bstr_t Name,
        enum DataTypeEnum Type,
        enum ParameterDirectionEnum Direction,
        long Size,
        const _variant_t & Value = vtMissing );
```

The **Parameters** collection has two other methods besides **Append()**. One is **Delete()**, which does just what its name indicates. The other, **Refresh()**, tells ADO to examine both the query and the database to determine what data type to use and so on.

The **Parameters** collection has only two properties: **Count** and **Item**. **Count** contains the number of **Parameter** objects that the collection contains, and **Item** is an array that contains the **Parameter** objects.

The **Parameter** object has only one method: **AppendChunk()**. When you first call this method, any data in the **Parameter** object is overwritten. Subsequent calls add data to the end of the existing data. You use this method to fill the **Parameter** object with a large binary object. Be sure that the **Attributes** property has **adParamLong** set before you use **AppendChunk()**. The **Parameter** object's properties are described in Table 21.4.

The Recordset Object

Although you can carry out all your database operations using discrete SQL statements, it would become very laborious. Instead, the ADO **Recordset** object is specifically designed to manipulate data held in a data source. The **Recordset** object—the most robust of all the ADO objects—represents a set of records from the data provider. This object provides the capability to scroll through the records, as well as add, edit, and delete them. Each record consists of one or more fields. If the data source is a database, then the records represent table rows and the fields represent columns.

Table 21.4	The Parameter object's properties.
Property	**Description**
Attributes	Describes whether the parameter can be NULL (**adParamNullable**), signed (**adParamSigned**), or long binary object (**adParamLong**).
Direction	Specifies the direction of transfer or if the parameter is a return value. Can be **adParamInput**, **adParamOutput**, **adParamInput Output**, or **adReturnValue**.
Name	Indicates a name for a parameter.
NumericScale	Indicates the number of digits to the right of the decimal place.
Precision	Indicates the number of digits used to represent a numeric value.
Size	Indicates the maximum size of the parameter.
Type	An enumerated value that specifies the type of data. Common types are **adBinary**, **adBoolean**, **adBSTR**, **adChar**, **adCurrency**, **adGUID**, **adDBTimeStamp**, **adDouble**, **adNumeric**, **adInteger**, **adVarChar**, and **adWChar**.
Value	Indicates the actual value held by the parameter.

The **Recordset** object works by retrieving records and then letting you manipulate each specific record indicated by a cursor position. You can access a
record's data using the **Recordset** object's **Fields** collection. ADO provides
four types of recordset cursors; each type affects the way that your data is updated. A **CursorTypeEnum** value specifies the cursor type. Table 21.5 describes
the four cursor types.

Make sure you understand the various cursors. The exam will
undoubtedly present you with a set of requirements and then
have you select a cursor type.

The **Recordset** object has a number of properties and methods. Table 21.6
presents the **Recordset** object's key properties. (Table 21.10 presents some more
common methods.)

The **Filter** and **Sort** properties affect the data in the **Recordset**;
they don't modify the SQL statement. The **Filter** property is
not the same as the SQL **WHERE** clause, nor is the **Sort**
property the same as the SQL **ORDER BY** clause.

Table 21.5   The ADO cursor types properties.

Cursor Type	CursorTypeEnum	Description
Dynamic	**adOpenDynamic**	Allows unrestricted movement through the recordset. You can add, modify, or delete records. Records added, modified, or deleted by other users are visible. Depending on the data provider, you may or may not be able to use bookmarks. A bookmark allows you to easily and quickly move to a row.
Keyset	**adOpenKeyset**	Is similar to dynamic. Changes made by other users are incorporated into your recordset, but additions and deletions aren't.
Forward	**adOpenForwardOnly**	Is identical to dynamic, except it only allows forward movement through the records. This speeds up access to the data. This is the default cursor type.
Static	**adOpenStatic**	Allows you to add, modify, or delete records. However, changes made by other users are not visible.

The Fields Collection And Field Object

Each recordset has a **Fields** collection that contains **Field** objects. Each **Field** object represents an individual field in the recordset. The **Field** object contains basic information about the field, such as value, data type, and size. The **Field** object has only two methods: **GetChunk** and **AppendChunk**. Both are used to manipulate long binary data. The **Field** object's properties are described in Table 21.11.

When you create a new **Recordset** object, its **Fields** collection will be empty. **Field** objects can then be appended to the **Fields** collection. This will happen automatically when you call the **Recordset** object's **Open()** method. You can also append **Field** objects programmatically by calling the **Fields** collection's **Append()** method. Before calling **Append()**, you must set the **Recordset** object's **CursorLocation** property to **adUseClient**. In addition to the **Append()** method, the **Fields** collection has two more methods: **Delete()** and **Refresh()**. The Fields collection has two properties: **Count** and **Item**.

Table 21.6   The Recordset object's properties.

Property	Description
BOF	If true, the current cursor position is at the start of the recordset. If there are no records, **BOF** is true.
Bookmark	Identifies the current cursor position. You can save a bookmark in a variable and then later use it to quickly return to that record after moving to a different record.
CursorLocation	Sets the client-side or server-side cursor (**adUseClient** or **adUseServer**).
CursorType	Sets recordset type. Must be one of the **CursorTypeEnum** values specified in Table 21.5.
EditMode	Indicates current editing mode of the current record: **adEdit None**, **adEditInProgress**, **adEditAdd**, or **adEditDelete**.
EOF	If true, the current cursor position is at the end of the recordset. If there are no records, **EOF** is true. You usually need to rename this property in the **#import** directive. **EndOfFile** and **adoEOF** are commonly used.
Fields	Accesses the **Fields** collection for manipulating the data in the current record.
Filter	Allows you to specifiy which records in a recordset can become current. You can use a filter such as "state = 'CA' or state = 'OR'" to cause only records meeting the criterion to be displayed. You can also set **Filter** to one of the **FilterGroup Enum** values shown in Table 21.7.
LockType	Sets the type of record locking using one of the **LockType Enum** values (see Table 21.8).
MaxRecords	Limits the maximum number of records retrieved.
RecordCount	Returns the number of records in the recordset. Will be -1 if ADO cannot determine the number of records.
Sort	Allows you to sort the recordset by any field after retrieval. You can optionally use **ASC** or **DESC** to specify the sorting order. The default sort order is ascending.
Source	Contains the source of the data, such as the SQL **SELECT** statement or the name of the stored procedure.
State	Indicates the current state of the **Recordset**. It can be any of the **ObjectStateEnum** values: **adStateClosed**, **adStateOpen**, **adStateConnecting**, **adStateExecuting**, or **adStateFetching**.
Status	Returns a combination of **RecordStatusEnum** values. See Table 21.9.

The **Recordset** object and its associated **Fields** collection provides you with a flexible data structure that you can use for buffering and saving (persist) data, which can really simplify the task of moving legacy data, stored in flat files, into a database.

Table 21.7   The FilterGroupEnum values.

Value	Description
adFilterNone	Removes all filtering.
adFilterPendingRecords	Used to view only records changed but not yet saved to the server. Used only in batch mode.
adFilterAffectedRecords	Used to view only records affected by the last **CancelBatch**, **Delete**, **Resync**, or **UpdateBatch** method.
adFilterFetchedRecords	Used to view only the most recently cached records.
adFilterConflictingRecords	Used to view only records that failed the last **UpdateBatch** attempt.

Table 21.8   The LockTypeEnum values.

Value	Description
adLockReadOnly	The data can't be altered. This is the default.
adLockPessimistic	The record is locked as soon as you start to edit it.
adLockOptimistic	The record is locked only as it is sent back to the database.
adLockBatchOptimistic	The records are locked when a batch of records are updated.

Make sure that you understand the different locking types. Give special attention to **adLockPessimistic** and **adLock Optimistic**. Know when the lock starts and when it's released.

Table 21.9   The RecordStatusEnum values.

Value	Description
adRecOK	Record was successfully updated.
adRecNew	Record is new.
adRecModified	Record was modified.
adRecDeleted	Record was deleted.
adRecUnmodified	Record was not modified.
adRecInvalid	Because its bookmark is invalid, record was not saved.
adRecMultipleChanges	Because it would have affected multiple records, record was not saved.
adRecPendingChanges	Because it refers to a pending insert, record was not saved.
adRecCanceled	Because the operation was canceled, record was not saved.
adRecCantRelease	Because of existing record locks, record was not saved.
adRecConcurrencyViolation	Because optimistic concurrency was in use, record was not saved.
adRecIntegrityViolation	Because the user violated integrity constraints, record was not saved.
adRecMaxChangesExceeded	Because there were too many pending changes, record was not saved.
adRecObjectOpen	Because of a conflict with an open storage object, record wasn't saved.
adRecOutOfMemory	Because the computer has run out of memory, record wasn't saved.
adRecPermissionDenied	Because the user has insufficient permissions, record was not saved.
adRecSchemaViolation	Because it violates the structure of the underlying database, record was not saved.
adRecDBDeleted	Record has already been deleted.

Table 21.10	**The Recordset object's methods.**

Method	Description
AddNew	Adds a new record. You can optionally specify some or all of the **Fields** and **Values** arguments.
CancelUpdate	Cancels pending changes.
Clone	Creates a copy of a **Recordset**.
Close	Closes the **Recordset** object.
Delete	Deletes the current record. Pass it **adAffectGroup** to delete all the records that meet the current **Filter** criteria.
Find	Starting at the current record, searches for a record that satisfies the specified criteria. The criteria is a valid SQL **WHERE** clause.
Move	Allows you to move an absolute number of records forward or backward.
MoveFirst	Allows you to move to the first record in the recordset.
MoveLast	Allows you to move to the last record in the recordset.
MoveNext	Allows you to move forward by one record in the recordset.
MovePrevious	Allows you to move backward by one record in the recordset.
Requery	Refreshes the recordset by reissuing the query.
Resync	Refreshes the recordset to reflect the changes of any other users.
Save	Allows you to persist (save to a file) the recordset.
Update	Saves changes made to the current record. As with the **AddNew** method, you can optionally set values using the **Fields** and **Values** arguments.

Here's a snippet of code that opens a recordset on a client-side cursor. It then sorts the records by last name in ascending alphabetically order. Finally, it moves through the recordset one record at a time and displays the first name, last name, and phone number for each of the authors in the recordset.

```
_RecordsetPtr spRs(__uuidof(Recordset));
spRs->CursorLocation = adUseClient;
spRs->Open((IDispatch *) spCmd, vtMissing,
       adOpenStatic, adLockBatchOptimistic, adCmdUnspecified);

spRs->Sort = "au_lname ASC";

for(spRs->MoveFirst(); !spRs->EndOfFile; spRs->MoveNext())
```

```
{
  _bstr_t bstrFirstName =
             spRs->GetFields()->GetItem("au_fname")->Value;

  _bstr_t bstrLastName =
             spRs->GetFields()->GetItem("au_lname")->Value;

  _bstr_t bstrPhone =
             spRs->GetFields()->GetItem("phone")->Value;
  Display(bstrFirstName, bstrLastName, bstrPhone);
}
```

Exceptions And Error Processing

Most database operations are capable of throwing a number of errors. ADO stores each of these errors in the **Errors** collection. You can obtain these from your **Connection** object by calling the **GetErrors()** method. Once you have the **Errors** collection object, you can iterate through the **Error** objects. The **Error** object has several properties and no methods. The properties are described in Table 21.12.

Table 21.11 The Field object's properties.	
Property	**Description**
ActualSize	Returns the number of bytes actually stored in the **Field** object.
Attributes	Describes characteristic of the **Field** object. It can hold one or more **FieldAttributeEnum** values.
DefinedSize	Returns the maximum number of bytes that can be stored in the **Field** object.
Name	Provides the name of the field as stored on the database or as specified in the command that retrieved the data.
NumericScale	Indicates the number of digits to the right of the decimal place.
OriginalValue	Contains the value of **Field** when first retrieved from the database.
Precision	Indicates the number of digits used to represent a numeric value.
Type	Contains one of the **DataTypeEnum** values.
UnderlyingValue	Returns the current data value.
Value	Indicates the actual value held by the **Field** object.

Table 21.12	The Error object's properties.
Property	**Description**
Description	A text description of the error
HelpContextID	A context ID identifying the help topic
HelpFile	A Windows help file associated with the error
NativeError	Specifies the data provider's own error number
Number	A unique numeric error code
Source	The name of the object that caused the error
SQLState	Corresponds to the ODBC SQL state, as documented in the ANSI SQL standards

The **Description** and **Number** properties are probably the most useful because you can use them to find out what caused the error and then take the appropriate action. Here's an example of how you might catch and report errors.

```
...
_ConnectionPtr spConn(__uuidof(Connection));
  try
  {
    // your code goes here
  }
  catch (_com_error &e)
  {
    DumpComError(e);
    DumpADOError(spConn->GetErrors());
  }

  // more code here

void DumpComError(_com_error &e)
{
  cout << "\nCOM Error:\nCode = " << hex << e.Error()
       << "\nCode meaning = " << e.ErrorMessage()
       << "\nSource = "
       << static_cast<LPCSTR>(e.Source())
       << "\nDescription = "
       << static_cast<LPCSTR>(e.Description())
       << endl;
}

void DumpADOError(ErrorsPtr spErrors)
{
```

```
for(int i = 0; i < spErrors->GetCount(); i++)
{
  _variant_t vtItem((long) i);
  ErrorPtr spError(spErrors->Item[vtItem]);
  cout << "\nADO Error:\nCode = "
       << hex << spError->GetNumber()
       << "\nSource = "
       << static_cast<LPCSTR>(spError->GetSource())
       << "\nDescription = "
       << static_cast<LPCSTR>(spError->GetDescription())
       << endl;
}
cout << endl;
}
```

Practice Questions

Question 1

Assume that you are developing a geophysical application and you need to store a number of large bitmaps in the database. Which ADO method would you use?

- ○ a. AppendBlob
- ○ b. PutData
- ○ c. AppendChunk
- ○ d. AppendLongBinary

The correct answer is c. The **AppendChunk()** method is used to store large binary objects in a **Field** object. Answers a, b, and d are incorrect because they do not exist.

Question 2

Which of the following statements are true? [Check all of the correct answers]

- ❏ a. DAO is an object model for accessing relational data through ODBC.
- ❏ b. ADO is an object model for accessing all types of data through OLE DB.
- ❏ c. The MDAC toolkit includes ADO, OLE DB, and ODBC.
- ❏ d. RDO is an object model for accessing local and SQL data through Microsoft Jet.

The correct answers are b and c. ADO is a collection of COM objects that use OLE DB to access relational and nonrelational data. MDAC consists of the latest versions of ADO, OLE DB, and ODBC, as well as ODBC drivers and OLE DB providers. Answer a is incorrect because DAO accesses data through Microsoft Jet, not through ODBC. Answer d is incorrect because RDO accesses data through ODBC, not through Microsoft Jet.

Question 3

Which of the following ADO objects has an Open() method? [Check all of the correct answers]

❑ a. Connection

❑ b. Command

❑ c. Recordset

❑ d. Field

The correct answers are a and c. The **Connection** object's **Open()** method is used to open a connection to a data source. The **Recordset** object's **Open()** method is used to open a cursor that represents records of a data source. Answer b is incorrect because the **Command** object is used to define a command that can be executed against a data source. Answer d is incorrect because a **Field** represents a column of data.

Question 4

Which of the following are valid ways to populate an ADO Recordset object? [Check all of the correct answers]

❑ a. Pass a SQL statement to the Recordset object's Open() method.

❑ b. Pass a SQL statement to the Connection object's Open() method.

❑ c. Store a SQL statement in the Command object's CommandText property and then call its Execute() method.

❑ d. Store a SQL statement in the Recordset object's Source property and then call its Execute() method.

The correct answers are a and c. The **Recordset** object's **Open()** method, as well as the **Execute()** method, for either the **Command** object or the **Connection** object can be used to populate a **Recordset** object. The one you use depends on the type of recordset you wish to create. For example, when calling the **Recordset** object's **Open()** method, you can pass it an SQL statement, a table name, a stored procedure call, a valid **Command** object, or even an URL. You can also choose to pass it a string, in which case it will use the **Source** property that must contain a string or a valid **Command** object. When calling the **Connection** object's **Execute()** method, you can pass it the same things you can pass to the **Recordset** object's **Open()** method, plus you can pass it provider-specific text to execute. The **Command** object's **Execute()**

method always executes what is stored in the **CommandText** property, which can be a SQL statement or any other type of command statement recognized by the provider.

Answer b is incorrect because you cannot pass an SQL statement to the **Connection** object's **Open()** method. Answer d is incorrect because the **Recordset** object doesn't have an **Execute()** method. However, it does have a **Source** property that is used with its **Open()** method as described in the previous paragraph.

Question 5

> Which of the following are valid ADO collections? [Check all of the correct answers]
>
> ❑ a. Field
> ❑ b. Parameters
> ❑ c. Properties
> ❑ d. Connections

The correct answers are b and c. **Parameters** and **Properties** are valid collections (as are **Errors** and **Fields**). Answer a is incorrect because **Fields** is the collection, not **Field**. Answer d is incorrect because **Connection** is a standalone object; **Connections** does not exist.

Need To Know More?

 Esposito, Dino. "With Further ADO: Coding Active Data Objects 2.0 with Visual Studio 6.0." *Microsoft Systems Journal*, February 1999. This is a well-written article that provides a good overview of ADO and quite a bit of detail on the **Recordset** object.

 Kruglinski, David J., George Shepherd, and Scot Wingo. *Programming Microsoft Visual C++*, 5th ed. Microsoft Press, Redmond, WA: 1998. ISBN 1-57231-857-0. Chapter 32 provides a good introductory coverage of ODBC with MFC. If you are interested in DAO, Chapter 32 provides a good introduction.

 Robison, Lyn. *Teach Yourself Database Programming with Visual C++ 6 in 21 Days*. Sams Publishing, Indianapolis, IN: 1999. ISBN 0-672-31350-2. On Amazon.com the author describes this book like this: "The book covers VC++ programming for ADO, RDS, OLE DB, ODBC, MTS, COM, as well as DAO and the MFC ODBC classes. The book teaches how to choose the best database model/technology for your application, how to do database design, ways to leverage a database server, how to create C++ component software for database apps, and tools and strategies for multitier application development. The book contains detailed source code examples, as well as practical advice for building real-life database applications."

This is a tall order for one book. However, I believe this well-written book does a good job of showing how to use Visual C++ to write database programs. It's easy to follow, and the example code works. It's a good introductory book to get you started.

 Sussman, Dave. *ADO 2.1 Programmer's Reference*. Wrox Press Ltd., Birmingham, UK: 1999. ISBN 1861002688. This handy reference book is well organized and easy to use. Each major ADO object is given its own chapter. Although, like Microsoft's online documentation, everything in the book is in Visual Basic, it provides a convenient source of information on methods, properties, and **enum** values.

MSDN Library, Platform SDK\Data Access Services\Microsoft Data Access Components (MDAC) SDK\Microsoft ActiveX Data Objects (ADO). This provides the best coverage of ADO that I've found. The Programmer's Reference provides a good description of the features and very good API reference. A number of solid samples are provided, and there is a tutorial to get the beginner started. Although the API reference is aimed at a Visual Basic programmer, there are sample programs for VC++.

 MSDN Library, Platform SDK\Data Access Services\Microsoft Data Access Components (MDAC) SDK\Microsoft Data Access Technical Articles. This subset of the MSDN Library provides a number of good articles. It includes articles on ODBC, UDA, ADO, and OLE DB.

 MSDN Library, Technical Articles. Here, you'll find a number of good articles on UDA and ADO. Many are somewhat dated, but because they mostly deal with strategy more than implementation, they're still relevant.

 Microsoft's Universal Data Access Web site at **www.microsoft. com/data** provides a wealth of information on ODBC, ADO, and OLE DB. You'll find links to articles, sample code, and downloads to the most current releases of the MDAC components.

Debugging And Testing Your Application

Terms you'll need to understand:

√ Call Stack

√ Breakpoint

√ Memory leak

√ Assertion statement

√ Exception

√ Remote debugging

√ Debug heap

√ Unit testing

√ Integration testing

√ Regression testing

√ Stress testing

√ Beta testing

Techniques you'll need to master:

√ Building a debug version of your program.

√ Using the debug libraries to locate memory leaks.

√ Performing remote debugging.

√ Understanding the differences between unit, regression, beta, and integration testing.

A certain level of congratulations is in order when you reach the point at which you believe you should start debugging your project. From the 50,000-foot level of design, code, debug, and test, it may appear that you're more than halfway to delivering a product. If it only were that simple. Just be thankful that you probably only have to deal with 32-bit operating systems. This chapter leads you through a review of the debug topics that you're probably already familiar with and perhaps a few that you may not have known about.

Debugging And The IDE

The Visual C++ application incorporates a powerful debugging environment. The debugger supports the various executable forms that the development environment can create, including DLLs and COM components.

Debug Build

The first step when debugging an application is creating a debug build of the project. A *debug build* generally differentiates itself from a *release build* in that it contains symbolic debug information, and compiler optimization of the code is not performed.

The following characteristics generally apply to debug builds of your program:

➤ Compiler optimization is not enabled.

➤ The _DEBUG symbol is defined.

➤ Your program is linked with debug versions of the runtime and/or MFC libraries.

➤ Symbolic debugging information is produced for the project.

Commands

The Visual C++ integrated development environment (IDE) incorporates a sophisticated source-level debugger. In addition to a graphical user interface offering windows, menus, and toolbars, direct interaction between UI components is supported with drag-and-drop capability. Thus, memory address locations may be dragged between Watch, Variable, or Memory windows.

Go

The **Go** command begins the debugging process, continuing through to the end of the program until a breakpoint is encountered or until you issue the **Break** command from the debugger to suspend execution. (Breakpoints are detailed later in the chapter.)

Step Over

This command is the most common debug command, allowing you to proceed to the next statement.

Step Into/Out

This command instructs the debugger to enter the pending function or step out of the current function.

Run To Cursor

Similar to the **Go** command, this command instructs the debugger to stop at the cursor location.

Windows

The Visual C++ debugger comprises quite a number of windows. Each of these windows can either float within the IDE frame window or be docked in almost any configuration imaginable.

Registers

The Registers window is not displayed by default when you first debug a project; however, once displayed, it becomes part of your project settings for your debug session and is subsequently displayed for future debugging. You can directly edit register values by typing over the display. You may also drag register contents to the Watch or Memory windows for content viewing.

 You can change the **EIP** (instruction pointer) register during a debugging session to jump around code you do not want to execute.

 The return value of a function is often placed in the **EAX** register. You may change this value and affect program flow accordingly.

Although technically not a register, the Visual C++ debugger offers a *pseudoregister*, whose label is **ERR**, to view the last error code for the current thread. Enter this label in a Watch window, using the **hr** format specifier, as shown:

```
ERR, hr
```

Memory

The Memory window allows you to view the contents of large portions of contiguous memory. This is useful when you want to inspect large character buffers or string contents. The default is to view the memory contents in base 10; however, it is possible to set an option to view the buffer as Unicode.

Watch

The Watch window consists of four tab views into which you may either type the name of variables to display or drag variable labels from other debug windows. The debugger allows you to supply a format argument to ease interpretation of watch variables. Variables and expressions in the Watch window can operate on any variable or object that is in scope. The syntax for formatting a variable requires you to place a comma and then the format symbol after the variable. Hence, the line

```
result, hr
```

formats the variable whose name is **result** as an **HRESULT**. As such, a value of 0x00000000L will appear as the "decoded" text **S_OK**. Similarly, formatting a variable with the Window message flag will display an 0x000F value as **WM_PAINT**.

The following list summarizes common watch formatting codes:

➤ *d, i*—Signed decimal integer

➤ *u*—Unsigned decimal integer

➤ *o*—Unsigned octal integer

➤ *x,X*—Hexadecimal integer

➤ *l,h*—Long or short prefix for d, i, u, o, x, X

➤ *f*—Signed floating-point numeric

➤ *e*—Signed scientific notation

➤ *g*—Signed floating-point numeric or signed scientific notation, whichever is shorter

- ➤ *c*—Single character

- ➤ *s*—String

- ➤ *su*—Unicode string

- ➤ *st*—Unicode string or ANSI string, depending on Unicode Strings setting in autoexp.dat

- ➤ *hr*—**HRESULT** or Win32 error code

- ➤ *wc*—Window class flag

- ➤ *wm*—Windows message numbers

> The autoexp.dat file contains rules for expanding variables in the Data Tips, Variable, and Watch windows.

QuickWatch

The QuickWatch window is a valuable tool when you don't want to occupy screen real estate with a docked Watch window. This window is similar to the Watch window except that it can only display a single variable or evaluate a single expression.

Disassembly

The Disassembly window can be used to view the optimizations that may cause problems in release builds that are not seen in nonoptimized debug projects. Additionally, you may step between statements that appear on a single line of C/C++ source code.

Call Stack

The Call Stack window displays those functions through which the program has entered and not yet returned.

> The Call Stack window allows you to set breakpoints using exactly the same commands as in the editor.

Variables

The Variables window is a tabbed display that contains a view to variables that are in scope. The tabs further scope context variables in the following manner:

➤ *Auto*—This is the default view, displaying variables for the previous and current statement.

➤ *Locals*—This view displays all variables that have context for the current function.

➤ *This*—This view only displays class variables.

Output

The Output window includes Build, Debug, Results, and SQL Debugging tab views. The lines that contain compiler errors or warnings may be quickly navigated to by double-clicking on the build entry. Additionally, you can click on Build Error Numbers in the Output window and display a description of the error by pressing F1.

DataTips

The Visual C++ IDE allows you to "hover" over variables and expressions to present a pop-up window containing the appropriate values. This feature is available when you have stopped at a breakpoint and the values and expressions are in scope.

Threads

A thread management dialog box is available from the Debug menu and is available if your project is multithreaded. Using this dialog box, you may set the focus on a thread, as well as suspend and resume thread operations.

Files

There are two very important file types that are instrumental in debugging your project: the debug files and the program database file.

Debug Files (DBG)

The debug files that the Visual C++ creates are in the Portable Executable (PE) format. In addition to CodeView information, this file also contains COFF and Frame Pointer Optimization (FPO) symbol data.

Program Database File (PDB)

The program database file contains the following information:

➤ Debugging data

➤ Project state information

➤ Incremental link data

AfxDumpStack

The **AfxDumpStack** function is new to Visual C++ 6 and allows you to obtain stack information about misbehaving MFC programs built in release mode—without needing a debugger. This function sounds like a programmer's dream come true—and it is, considering how easy it is to implement. The function accepts a single argument, indicating the target. Its prototype is as follows:

```
void AFXAPI AfxDumpStack(DWORD dwTarget =
AFX_STACK_DUMP_TARGET_DEFAULT);
```

The **dwTarget** argument is defined as any of the following constants. Combinations of these options may be supplied using the **bitwise OR** operation:

➤ **AFX_STACK_DUMP_TARGET_DEFAULT**—This is the default value defined in the function prototype, sending dump output to the default output context. The output for debug builds uses the **TRACE** macro, whereas release builds use the clipboard.

➤ **AFX_STACK_DUMP_TARGET_TRACE**—This option directs all output to the **TRACE** macro for both release and debug builds. Thus, there is no output context for release builds, because **TRACE** is ignored.

➤ **AFX_STACK_DUMP_TARGET_CLIPBOARD**—With this option, output is always directed to the clipboard using the **CF_TEXT** format.

➤ **AFX_STACK_DUMP_TARGET_BOTH**—This option provides dump information to both the clipboard and the **TRACE** macro.

➤ **AFX_STACK_DUMP_TARGET_ODS**—The ODS abbreviation identifies the **OutputDebugString** Win32 function. As such, this option supplies debug information to both release and debug builds, either of which may be "attached" to a debugger.

For each stack entry that this method generates, the following information will be provided:

➤ The return address of the last function call

➤ The module and full path containing the function

➤ The function's prototype

➤ The offset in bytes from the function prototype to the return address

Note: To function properly, this feature requires the IMAGEHLP.DLL to be installed; otherwise, an error message displays when this function is called.

Edit And Continue

New to Visual C++ 6 is the Edit and Continue debug option. As the name says, you can make changes to your code while debugging, and then continue running (or debugging) your program on the fly. To use this feature, you must be running your project in the debugger; however, your program need not be stopped in the debugger. Use the editor to change the code as necessary (see the limitations that follow), and then select the Apply Code Changes option from the Debug menu. The Output window displays output similar to the following:

```
Compiling...
mfc.cpp
Applying Code Changes...
Edit and Continue - 0 error(s), 0 warning(s)
```

Assuming that you receive no errors, your program executes according to the changes you implemented.

Limitations

While Edit and Continue is a powerful extension to the development environment, you may not be able to perform every code change you want and expect to continue executing your program. The following limitations apply:

➤ Changes may not be made to resource or read-only files.

➤ Exception handling blocks may not be modified.

➤ You may not change data types or introduce new data types.

➤ You may not remove or change function prototypes.

➤ Changes are not permitted on global or static code.

➤ Code changes may not be made to code using any optimization settings, including /O1, /O2, /Og, /Ox, /Ob1, and /Ob2.

Breakpoints

A *breakpoint* pauses execution of a program in the debugger. When the program is paused, the current stack, registers, and function variables may be inspected and/or modified.

If you are having problems setting breakpoints or they are not behaving as expected, you might want to check the items detailed in this section.

A breakpoint can only be set from source code if its symbolic data is available to the debugger. First, make sure that the code you are attempting to debug was compiled with the debug flag or you have symbolic information available. Second, if the code is contained in a DLL or an ActiveX component, the symbolic information may not yet be loaded. Specify additional DLLs and COM servers in the Additional DLLs field of the Debug Options dialog box.

You should already be familiar with common breakpoint operations, including when a variable or expression changes value. However, it may be important to review some advanced breakpoint settings, especially those set from the Data tab:

➤ *Array Element*—To break when any element in an array changes, enter the *first* element of the array in the Expression field and enter the number of elements in the Number Of Elements field.

➤ *Pointer*—Breaking at the address pointed to by a pointer requires a dereference of the pointer name in the Expression field, whereas the location value of a pointer simply requires the pointer's name.

➤ *Conditional Breakpoints*—Using the conditional breakpoint option, you can debug conditions where a function fails after succeeding many times prior. Therefore, you can set the **Skip Count** value to indicate the number of times the debugger passes over the breakpoint before stopping.

The Breakpoint dialog box also supports breaking at specific memory addresses, and a specific **WndProc** receives designated Windows messages.

COFF And Exports

The default setting for the Visual C++ debugger is to employ debug information in a CodeView-compatible format. However, the debugger is capable of offering debug support to programs that provide either **COFF** or **Export** information.

➤ *COFF*—The **COFF** debug format is used by other debuggers.

➤ *Export*—Symbolic information may be acquired by analyzing the export tables of a DLL.

The Debug tab of the Options dialog box provides a Load COFF & Exports checkbox to enable this feature.

Just-In-Time Debugging

The Just-in-Time debug option refers to the capability to debug a program that you are not currently working on in the Visual C++ environment. At the time that an application faults on your computer, the Visual C++ debugger can be started automatically. This option is available from the Debug selection of the Tools menu.

Symbols

The _DEBUG is defined upon specifying the /Mtd or /Mdd compiler options. As such, code blocks that appear between **#ifdef _DEBUG** and **#endif** are compiled.

Debugging Strategies

Just as common programming strategies have been identified as "patterns," so too can you identify categories of programming faux pas. Detailing all of the ways a developer can wreak havoc inside a program's process space is beyond the scope of this book, so the list has been narrowed to some of the more common misprogramming practices and ways to debug them.

MFC Memory Leaks

A *memory leak* occurs when heap memory is allocated and not de-allocated before the program ends. Although it's usually simple to identify cases that allocate memory in your program's **InitInstance** function and free the memory in **ExitInstance**, it is the memory that is continually recycled during program operation that can be difficult to track and cause you to exhaust the heap.

Tracking memory allocation in MFC programs can be made simpler, and the Wizards do this for you automatically, by defining the **DEBUG_NEW** macro as shown:

```
#define new DEBUG_NEW
```

By defining the preceding macro at the top of your source files, you can track the file and line number of each allocation. Use the **DumpAllObjectsSince** function to output all of the objects that are currently allocated. MFC uses the same debug heap and memory allocator as the C runtime library. (Debug heaps are detailed later in the chapter.)

Although identifying memory allocations may be appropriate for some situations, MFC offers more-powerful functions, **Checkpoint** and **Difference**, which build on memory tracking and help pinpoint leaks. Used in conjunction with the **CMemoryState** object, these methods allow you to take a "snapshot" of memory and identify memory allocation differences at a later time.

Assertion Statements

Many programmers place assertion statements at the top of their functions to verify the assumption that the arguments that are being passed exist and/ or are correct according to some constraint. For example, if a function is designed to draw a line and one argument is a handle to a device context (hDC), an assertion statement—or assert—may be placed at the top of the function, verifying that a non-NULL value is passed in. Asserts that fail result in the display of a dialog box. Visual C++ supports three general assertion statement categories:

➤ C runtime library asserts

➤ MFC assert macros

➤ ANSI C/C++ assert functions

 Any flavor of assertion only compiles when the **_DEBUG** flag is defined. Otherwise, the compiler treats the assert as a NULL statement, introducing no additional overhead.

Common uses for assertion statements include the following:

➤ Verifying input parameters

➤ Testing for error conditions

➤ Validating operation results

Programs that employ objects that derive from **CObject** can benefit from the use of the **ASSERT_VALID** macro. This macro performs a check of the object's internal consistency, and as with the traditional assertion statements, this statement has no effect in a release build. MFC offers programmers an **ASSERT** statement that outputs file and line-number information on expression evaluation failure.

 The **VERIFY** macro is similar to the **MFC ASSERT** macro, except that it evaluates the expression in release builds as well as debug builds.

Threads

The Debug menu offers a Threads dialog box selection. Using this dialog box, you may set focus on a thread and suspend or resume thread execution.

Exceptions

Execution of code outside the normal flow of control identifies an *exception*. By default, the Visual C++ debugger writes exception messages to the Output window; however, your program is not halted, unless a handler is not provided for the exception, and with the exception of Ctrl+C and Ctrl+Break key combinations (by default). The Exceptions dialog box is available from the Tools menu, allowing you to specify either of two states, Stop Always or Stop If Not Handled, for nearly 30 exception conditions.

Debugging Without The Project

It's possible to debug both DLLs and EXEs even if you don't have the project or workspace that they were built in. As long as you have the source code for the module you are trying to debug, the steps to debug either type are essentially the same. A temporary workspace is created when you debug in this manner. You have the option of saving the project settings when you leave Visual C++.

Debugging EXEs

To begin debugging an executable, use the **Open** command or **Open Workspace** command from the File menu, and select the executable you want to debug. The file should have been compiled with debug information that either resides in the EXE or in a program database file. Activate the debugger in the same manner you would if you had a project workspace: by selecting Start Debug from the Debug menu or by clicking on **Go** in the debug toolbar.

Debugging DLLs

Open and select the DLL you want to debug using either the **Open** command or **Open Workspace** command from the File menu. Specify the executable you want to load the DLL using the Executable For Debug Session field in the Debug tab of the Project Settings dialog box. Start debugging with Start Debug from the Debug menu.

As with an EXE, it is also possible to debug a DLL without having an associated project or workspace.

Remote Debugging

Visual C++ supports a debug mode called *remote debugging*. Using this option, you can run the program that is being debugged on one computer while the

IDE "debugging" the application runs on a different computer. This procedure might be necessary if, for example, the failure that is being "flushed out" isn't present on the debug machine, the target machine doesn't possess the resources to run the IDE, a local IDE interferes with the UI, or the target machine exists in a different locale but is visible on a LAN.

The target machine (the one that is going to run the program being debugged—not the debugger) must have access to the MSVCMON.EXE utility. This utility provides a dialog box in that you identify the debugging host.

The machine that contains the Visual C++ IDE must have the Debugger Remote Connection specified from the Build menu. In addition, you must identify the target machine. The debugger's **Go** command causes the application under test to launch on the target machine.

Active Process

It is possible to "attach" the Visual C++ debugger to any process running locally on the machine, including services, although you have to be properly permissioned. From the Build menu, select the Start Debug option, which displays a submenu containing four items; one of these submenu items is Attach To Process. Selecting this menu displays an Attach To Process dialog box, which contains a list of processes and (optionally) system processes running on the computer. Just selecting a process and clicking on OK will begin a debugging session.

ActiveX

Although ActiveX controls may be debugged in the Visual C++ IDE, the Test Container utility that Microsoft provides is a perfect example of a container application to use to exercise your control. Menus are provided to invoke methods, change properties, and fire events on your control.

If you are on the other side of the fence—writing an ActiveX container—your job is simpler because you can debug the container as you would any MFC application.

Optimized Code

A number of compiler options are available to optimize code. During this process, the compiler rearranges machine instructions to make better use of the processor's available registers and/or attempt to produce code that can remain in cache.

Although you should make every attempt to debug code that has not been optimized, there are situations where optimization can result in runtime errors. In such cases, it is recommended that you do the following:

➤ Use the /Zi compiler switch to obtain symbolic information of variable names and types, as well as function and line numbers.

➤ Display the Registers and Disassembly windows to set breakpoints and analyze the resulting machine code for the best place to set breakpoints.

DLLs

There are different debug configurations that you may encounter when debugging a DLL:

➤ *Calling program and DLL projects and source*—Load the calling program's project and set breakpoints in the DLL as you normally do for the project. If you load the DLL dynamically, specify the DLL using the Additional DLLs debug option field.

➤ *DLL project and source*—You must supply the Executable For Debug Session field in the Debug Option dialog box.

Debug Heap

When writing C++ code, there is nothing more tedious than keeping track of memory allocation and release with the **new** and **delete** commands. For C++ projects, defining the **_CRTDBG_MAP_ALLOC** symbol will direct heap functions to their corresponding debug versions, outputting source file and line number information.

The *debug heap* adds some overhead in both performance and resource consumption by performing various overwrite checks and allocating more memory than the amount that was requested. The compiler "marks" memory on either side of an allocation request with a "no man's land," filling this area with 0xFD bytes. An operation that causes a memory overrun ventures into this marked area, thus allowing the detection of faulty code. New memory requests are populated with 0xCD bytes, and memory-free operations are filled with 0xDD bytes.

 You can validate the integrity of the heap at any time, from within your code, by calling **_CrtCheckMemory**. In addition, a number of heap-checking properties may be set using the **_CrtSetDbgFlag** function. The C runtime library provides a number of API calls that can be used when debugging. Be sure to familiarize yourself with these calls.

General MFC

There are a number of things that you can do when debugging an MFC-based application that can make your task easier.

Window Arrangement

If possible, you should try to arrange your debugger and debug application so that they don't overlap. This is important when attempting to solve focus issues and identifying the contents of a device context during GDI development.

Tracing

The MFC **TRACE** macros can be instrumental in identifying program problems, especially those where timing is involved and breakpoints hamper the "natural flow" of the code. There are four trace macros: **TRACE0, TRACE1, TRACE2**, and **TRACE3**. Each takes zero to three arguments, respectively, in a manner similar to **printf**. Additionally, there are two global variables that modify the **TRACE** macro behavior:

➤ **afxTraceEnabled**—This variable may be set to true or false, depending on whether or not you want to product trace output.

➤ **afxTraceFlags**—This variable may be set under program control but is more easily set using the TRACER.EXE utility, which offers a user-friendly description of the possible bit field options.

Object Dump

It is possible to dump the state of any **CObject**-derived object during a debug session by calling its **Dump** function. The **CObject** class provides a virtual function, **Dump**, that you should override to provide state information. The state information is written to a **CDumpContext** stream that is passed into the function as an argument.

Afx Diagnostic Functions

Although there are more than a dozen **Afx** routines that offer debugging services, you should be aware of some of the more commonly used functions:

➤ **AfxCheckError**—This method accepts a single argument, an SCODE, and is used to check OLE function call return codes and throw the correct MFC exception as required.

➤ **AfxCheckMemory**—This is an expensive function that validates the available heap, printing inconsistency messages to the debugger's output window. This function accepts no arguments and returns a Boolean status value.

➤ **AfxEnableMemoryTracking**—Accepting a single Boolean argument, use this function to disable memory tracking in the Debug version of the MFC library.

> ➤ **AfxIsMemoryBlock**—This diagnostic function verifies if the supplied pointer and block length arguments are consistent with those of an allocation that occurred using the debug version of the **new** operator.

> ➤ **AfxIsValidAddress**—Among the most common MFC diagnostic functions, this function accepts a pointer and a number of bytes to test as valid within the calling program's process space. An optional third argument specifies whether the memory is for reading and writing, or just accessed for reading.

> ➤ **AfxIsValidString**—This function verifies that the supplied pointer is a valid string. A second argument, indicating that the length of the string defaults to −1, identifies the string as null-terminated.

> ➤ **AfxSetAllocHook**—This function accepts a single argument of type **AFX_ALLOC_HOOK**. Use this function to specify a callback function that is called before memory allocation occurs. The prototype for the callback function is as follows:

```
BOOL AFXAPI AllocHook(size_t nSize, BOOL bObject, LONG
lRequestNumber);
```

Debugging Tools

Over the years, Microsoft has provided a number of tools whose purpose is to help locate programming problems, test program features, or identify differences among the various supported platforms. Programs that you used for the 16-bit development, such as Heap Walker and Shaker, have been gracefully retired, leaving room for a new breed of debug and testing tools.

Depends (Dependency Walker)

The purpose of the Dependency Walker utility is to recursively investigate all the DLLs/modules that make up an executable and produce a report that contains the following information:

> ➤ *Missing Files*—Generally indicates that the DLL isn't on the path and cannot be located.

> ➤ *Invalid Files*—The format of the file is not compatible with the Windows operating system.

> ➤ *Unresolved External*—Checks to make sure that function import requirements are addressed as exports of the specified module.

➤ *Circular Dependency*—Considered to be rare; however, forward-referenced functions may cause problems under some circumstances.

➤ *Machine Build Mismatch*—Detects instances where one type of machine tries to load DLLs built for a different processor architecture.

Spy++

Among the most useful tools for performance tuning is the Spy++ utility. This update of the original Spy program allows you to monitor window activity and messages. Spy++ allows you to view system processes and threads. The Spy++ utility is designed as an MDI application, allowing you to open one or more windows in the four categories discussed previously in the chapter. Spying on Windows or Messages requires you to drag a locator icon out of the Find dialog box and onto a window to identify the source application.

When set on Windows, you can define the origin of window messages. When set on Messages, you can do the following:

➤ Define the scope of messages you want to view

➤ Identify messages registered using **RegisterWindowMessage**

➤ View "unknown" messages

Debugging COM Clients And Servers

The client server application debugging process of can be trying. Microsoft's RPC (Remote Procedural Call) debugger option removes some of the pain by allowing you to step between client and server code with no effort. For in-process servers, the debugger switches between client and server debugging. For out-of-process servers, a second instance of the debugger launches.

RPC Debugging

Before you can use RPC debugging for client/server applications that employ COM, you must enable the option. Choose Tools|Options, Debug. The OLE RPC Debugging option must be checked.

Testing

If one rule summarizes the testing process, it's that testing becomes increasingly (almost exponentially) more expensive to identify and correct program flaws the further out in the design, code, debug, and test lifecycle that they are identified.

Unit

Unit testing is generally the easiest testing to perform and probably the most overlooked. Simply stated, a unit test exercises a small piece of code, usually a function; however, when dealing with MFC, OLE, and Windows, this may be a test of a message event or an ActiveX property or method. Such tests, in a formal sense, are generally ignored. That is, most developers do not build test harnesses or expose entry points to a test program for the purpose of exercising single functions. Also, it may be difficult to exercise functions that rely on a certain state or complex data arguments, because for a test program to reconstitute the needed state or to build the required data, parameters may be extremely difficult. Proper unit testing strives to execute every code path that exists in a function.

Integration

The purpose of *integration testing* is to validate that the components, which may behave correctly in a standalone manner, still operate appropriately when working together. Thus, functions and events that pass unit testing may fail during integration test, because certain function outputs feed other methods unexpected data values.

Regression

Regression testing strives to identify seemingly unrelated bugs that are introduced during a code-build-debug-release cycle. Regression testing runs tests that encompass not only those areas into which change was introduced, but other parts of the application as well. A regression test suite is usually performed as a "smoke test" before releasing the program to a larger testing audience.

Stress

Stress testing refers to application testing that is performed while operating system resources are consumed in a manner that taxes the machine. Stress testing an application may attempt to exhaust the following resources:

➤ Global heap

➤ Windows GDI resources

➤ File handles

➤ Available disk space

➤ Network bandwidth and other resources

The purpose of such testing is to cause the program under test to execute exception, or other fault protection logic, if it exists. Otherwise, such testing results in the identification of conditions that cause the program to fail in an unrecoverable manner. Microsoft offers a utility named STRESS.EXE that can exercise an operating system in many of the ways listed in this section.

Beta

The *beta testing* stage opens the testing process to a larger audience and usually begins when the product is feature-complete and stable enough to be made available to persons not in the quality assurance department.

Make sure that you understand the differenty types of testing and the sequence in which they are conducted. The test writers love to present a scenario and then ask a question about what type of test to use or what test sequence to follow.

Practice Questions

Question 1

> Which register do you modify when your program is stopped in the debugger in order to step around code you believe will cause a general protection fault?
>
> ○ a. EIP
>
> ○ b. EAX
>
> ○ c. ERR
>
> ○ d. ST0

The correct answer is a. Changing the value of the instruction pointer register identifies the next "statement" that the processor executes. The **EAX** register can be used to identify the return value of a function. **ERR** is a pseudoregister that contains the current thread's last error code. **ST0** is a floating-point register.

Question 2

> Which of the following correctly identifies the watch window syntax to display the contents of a Unicode string whose variable name is "stringOut"?
>
> ○ a. su, stringOut
>
> ○ b. stringOut, su
>
> ○ c. stringOut su
>
> ○ d. stringOut %su

The correct answer is b. The syntax for formatting a variable requires the placement of a comma after the variable name, followed by the format symbol. All the other variations are incorrect; therefore, answers a, c, and d are incorrect.

Question 3

Which debug feature activates the debugger when any program on your computer faults?

○ a. Edit and Continue

○ b. Just-in-Time debugging

○ c. COFF debug information

○ d. Any program compiled with the _ACTIVEDEBUG flag set

The correct answer is b. The Just-in-Time debugger can be enabled in the Debug tab of the Options dialog, available from the Tools menu. The Edit and Continue feature allows you to modify code on the fly during a debug session, so answer a is incorrect. The **COFF** format is a different way of storing debug information, so answer c is incorrect. There is no _**ACTIVEDEBUG** flag, so answer d is incorrect.

Question 4

Which use for assertion statements is not valid?

○ a. Verify input parameters

○ b. Test for error conditions

○ c. Validate operation results

○ d. Output a message to the dump context

The correct answer is d. A dump context object may not be specified for assert statements. Answers a, b, and c are valid assertion statements.

Question 5

Which statements are valid with respect to the use of the Dependency Walker utility? [Check all of the correct answers]

❑ a. Warns of DLLs that cannot be loaded

❑ b. Identifies rare circular reference issues

❑ c. Reports unresolved external conditions

❑ d. Displays an address fix-up table

The correct answers are a, b, and c. The Dependency Walker utility doesn't display fix-up information, so answer d is incorrect.

Need To Know More?

 Kruglinski, David J., George Shepherd, and Scot Wingo. *Programming Microsoft Visual C++*. 5th ed. Microsoft Press, Redmond, WA, 1998. ISBN 1-57231-857-0. This book strikes a good balance between theory and practical application. It's divided into six parts and covers nearly every aspect of MFC programming, from the basics to database management and the Internet.

 Zacker, Craig. *Zero Administration for Windows*. Seastaopol, CA 95472: 1999. ISBN 1-56592-508-4. This book is aimed primarily at system administrators. It focuses on the methodologies used by ZAK. Topics include planning, deployment, installation, profiles and policies.

 MSDN, Platform SDK\Management Services.

Deploying Your Application

Terms you'll need to understand:

√ Files and file groups

√ Components and subcomponents

√ ZAW

√ TCO

√ Cabinet

√ Sign

√ Certificate

√ **<Object>** tag

Techniques you'll need to master:

√ Creating installation scripts

√ Identifying when to use SMS to distribute applications

√ Understanding the design goals of ZAW

√ Constructing and signing CAB files for Internet code deployment

InstallShield Packaging Concepts

Applications created using Visual C++ can be deployed using InstallShield, which ships on the Visual C++ disk but must be installed separately. You should be familiar with InstallShield's packaging scheme before generating a setup script. The building blocks for an install script are files and file groups, and components and subcomponents.

Files And File Groups

Files identify any file that you wish to ship as part of the install set—for example, executables, dynamic-link libraries, and help files. File groups are defined as those files with similar characteristics, including shared/not shared, compressed/uncompressed, or NT only/Windows 95/98 only.

Components And Subcomponents

The other packaging building blocks are components and subcomponents, which most closely relate to the installable items that the user checks or unchecks during the setup program, identifying what is to be installed during the setup process. Thus, components for an office productivity suite may include word processor, spreadsheet, and database, whereas subcomponents constitute sample files, tutorials, and templates.

InstallShield Package And Deployment Wizard

Setup Panel One

The first wizard step captures basic information regarding your application and company.

Application Name

The application name appears in the title and caption bar of the setup window, as well as for the base Registry key under which additional information regarding this application's setup procedure appears.

Company Name

The company name also appears in Registry entries for the application. This option appears in InstallShield shipped with the Enterprise Edition of Visual C++ 6.

Development Environment

InstallShield for Visual C++ only provides a single selection: Visual C++.

Application Type

The application type identifies common product categories, including database application and Internet application.

Application Version

The version number of the program is provided in an edit field and is available at runtime from the file's property sheet.

Application Executable

The setup script must know the name of your executable, thus identifying the program to run at the completion of the client install procedure.

Choose Dialogs Panel

The resulting installation script will appear as a wizard with one or more dialog box steps. Use this dialog box to select those "steps" you want to include as part of your setup procedure. The following list details these options:

➤ *Welcome Message*—The welcome message is simple enough. As the first page of the wizard, it identifies the application being installed, as well as the authoring company and/or copyright warnings.

➤ *Software License Agreement*—A paragraph that explains your license agreement is displayed in this dialog box. Typically, the user is prompted either to agree with the terms, in which case the next step of the wizard is presented, or to cancel the installation process.

➤ *Readme*—The Readme panel allows you to paste the text of the readme.txt file that usually ships with your application into a scrollable editbox.

➤ *User Information*—This panel contains fields for end users to enter their name, company, and product serial number.

➤ *Install Location*—The default installation location is to use the company name information that you presented in the first wizard panel as the subdirectory name under the C:\Program Files directory.

➤ *Setup Type*—A typical install kit contains Typical, Compact, and Custom setup configurations. This panel offers these three common choices. If the user selects the Custom install, the next wizard step will be one that allows the selection of installable components.

➤ *Destination Folder*—This standard wizard step allows the end user to define the name of the desktop folder into which the program icons will be placed.

➤ *Summary*—The summary panel generally contains a paragraph that describes the selected options, install directory, program folder, and so on.

➤ *Complete*—The last wizard panel offers to display the readme file and/or launch the successfully installed application.

Target Platform

The second step in the install creation wizard is to identify the platform(s) that the setup script will target. Such targets include the following:

➤ Windows 95/98

➤ Windows NT 3.51 (Intel, MIPS, Alpha)

➤ Windows NT 4.0 (Intel, MIPS, Alpha)

> *Note: InstallShield for Visual C++ does not allow the creation of setups for 16-bit Windows operating systems.*

Languages

The languages wizard panel allows you to define the language(s) that you want the resulting setup to support. InstallShield for Visual C++ allows only English as the language; however, you may purchase dozens of languages and sublanguage (dialects) resources.

Setup Types

The next wizard panel allows you to select one or more setup types to include in your installation script. By default, Compact, Typical, and Custom are selected; however, you may also choose one or more of the others, including the following:

➤ Network

➤ Administrator

➤ Network (Best Performance)

➤ Network (Efficient Space)

Components

The next step is the Specify Components panel, allowing you to select the components that constitute your setup types. Components are modifiable at any stage of the install definition process, where the term "component" refers to the InstallShield term defined at the beginning of this section. Typical components include the following:

➤ Program files

➤ Example files

➤ Help files

➤ Shared DLLs

File Groups

The second-to-last wizard panel allows you to select the file groups, which you defined earlier, to be included in the install set. Typical file groups include the following:

➤ Program executable files

➤ Program DLLs

➤ Example files

➤ Help files

➤ Shared DLLs

Summary

The final dialog box offers a summary of all of the wizard selections that you made to define the install script for this project.

Systems Management Server

Microsoft offers the System Management Server (SMS) product in order to provide a centralized distribution and monitoring of workstation and server software. SMS is tightly integrated with Microsoft SQL Server and NT Server, using the Microsoft Management Console (MMC) as an administrative user interface. Finally, SMS adheres to industry standard data formats: Desktop Management Task Force (DMTF) and Management Information Format (MIF).

Identifying Features

Systems Management Server offers a number of features that extend ZAW (Zero Administration for Windows) beyond that which is offered by the operating system. These additional features include the following:

➤ *Configuration Discovery*—SMS can "discover" information regarding the hardware and software that is on the network.

➤ *Granular Software Distribution*—Sophisticated scripts can be created using SMS that define the distribution of software based upon hardware configuration and software inventory properties.

➤ *Unattended Configuration*—This feature allows remote, synchronized, and timed distribution of client and server software.

➤ *Dry-run*—This unique feature allows an administrator to test the likelihood of installation success on machines under management, without actually disturbing the operating behavior of the target machines.

➤ *Roll-back*—In the event a software rollout encounters difficulty, SMS may be instructed to roll back all or specified clients.

➤ *Patch*—Rather than requiring the download of an entire software component, it is possible to transmit just the binary's "delta" to a target machine.

➤ *Heterogeneous Interoperability*—SMS is capable of managing hardware and distributing software to platforms other than Intel and Windows.

➤ *Remote Diagnostics*—Client machines that are experiencing trouble may be remotely diagnosed, and necessary configuration changes may be made accordingly.

Ease Of Use

SMS addresses the ZAW ease-of-use requirement by leveraging the Microsoft Management Console (MMC). MMC centralizes system administrative tasks by offering an extensible architecture into which applications supply "snap-ins." Management snap-ins exist for most BackOffice products, including SMS, MTS, and SQL Server.

System Requirements

Microsoft recommends a Pentium II-class computer, with 128MB RAM and 1GB of hard disk space as the hardware platform for SMS. The host operating system must be a minimum of NT4 with Service Pack 4 installed. Additionally, SMS requires SQL Server to be present. Again, the minimum configuration involves SQL Server 6.5 with Service Pack 4, although SMS 2 is also compatible with SQL Server 7.

Software Distribution With SMS

Distributing software using SMS requires a setup script that provides a Package Definition File (PDF). The PDF file is an ASCII text file that defines a software package that is to be distributed by the server. The PDF file, in conjunction with information that is stored in the SMS database, is used by the Package Control Manager (PCM) to execute software installs.

Package Definition File

The PDF file contains information in value-name pair format that identifies properties that define a package. This file contains three predefined package settings:

➤ Workstation

➤ Sharing

➤ Inventory

SMS API

You can design your application to take advantage of the services that SMS offers by programming to the SMS API. An SMS-aware application may leverage SMS for the following information:

➤ Inquire as to the properties of any object in SMS inventory.

➤ Create, modify, or delete software distribution packages.

➤ Create, modify, or delete software distribution command jobs.

➤ Create, modify, or delete SMS object queries.

➤ Access existing machine and site groups, which act as aliases for groups of target machines and sites for software distribution.

Zero Administration Initiative

From a business operations perspective, there are two costs associated with purchasing a computer. The first continues to fall: This is the actual cost of the computer hardware itself. The second cost, which may not be immediately apparent to software developers, is the price to support the machine once it is purchased and placed on a user's desk. In addition to the licensing fees that must be paid for the user's software, there are costs involved in setting up network access, establishing an email account, and providing help desk services. Microsoft's ZAW initiative is an attempt to lower what is commonly referred to as total cost of ownership (TCO). One of the most apparent reductions of TCO for an enterprise's computer network will be the savings involved with remote management. Rather than having a person physically interact with a computer to perform common configuration tasks, the tasks can be performed from a remote central location.

Note: The ZAW initiative is a superset of Microsoft's current ZAK (Zero Administration for Windows Kits) procedures. Although some of the goals of ZAK are common to ZAW, its technology is based on the Windows 95/98 and NT 4.0 platform offerings, whereas a more full realization of ZAW will begin seeing light on the Windows 2000 operating systems.

Design Goals

There are a number of features that identify the ZAW initiative. The following list details each of these features:

➤ *Ease of use*—Creating software and systems that are easy to use has been a design goal for almost every piece of hardware and software ever created. In the ZAW context, this implies software that can detect its environment and configure itself based on a set of provided rules.

➤ *Remote management*—By far the most ambitious goal set to reduce ownership cost is the remote management and configuration of hardware and software. In this manner, scripts can be defined that identify the applications, desktop settings, and data files that should be installed on a machine, regardless of which computer a user logs in on.

➤ *Transparency*—A final goal of ZAW is to integrate seamlessly with existing hardware and software. It would be senseless to offer a technology that is supposed to decrease TCO, while itself requiring a steep learning curve and additional user training.

Core OS Features

The following "core operating system features" are being made in Windows 2000 to support the ZAW initiative:

➤ Remote, centralized, policy-based management

➤ Simplified installation and maintenance of the Windows operating system

➤ Application management and deployment

➤ Mobile and roaming user support

➤ Side-by-side machine replacement with no loss of user data

➤ Remote boot

➤ Improved supportability

Active Directory

Active Directory is a fundamental technology for solving the location transparency issues that face many of the ZAW initiatives. Active Directory service is included with Windows 2000 Server and provides secure, distributed, partitioned, and replicated storage objects. A fundamental difference between Active Directory and traditional directory services is that the construction of the directory tree is performed "from the bottom up." This allows the construction of a large tree with domains subdivided into organization units (OU) for the purposes of administration.

Internet/Intranet Delivery

If you want to deploy your application or control using a Web-based delivery mechanism, such as embedding the object in a Web page, you will need to understand Microsoft's CAB file architecture. In a nutshell, the steps to creating and signing a CAB file are as follows:

➤ Acquire a certificate, either by purchasing one from a CA or generating a test certificate.

➤ Create the CAB file containing the files you want to distribute.

➤ Sign your files.

CAB File

The CAB file format is useful when you want to deliver code to an end user's computer in a single package, via the Internet or company intranet, and have it automatically install and register itself. The CAB file format is a perfect vehicle for delivering MFC and ATL projects that you create using Visual C++. A CAB file contains all of an executable's components in a compressed form, as well as the instructions necessary to perform the installation. Cabinet files can contain an inventory file that has a .OSD extension. The OSD file instructs Internet Explorer's Package Manager how to install the cabinet's contents.

Signing And Certificates

Having executables download, install, and execute on your computer is an obvious security concern. One mechanism that is available to protect your computer from malicious programs is only allowing those programs that are signed and verified by a trusted source to execute on your computer. Although you may "sign" individual DLLs and EXEs, it is more common to create a CAB file and sign this single file. Signing a file associates it with a digital certificate and ensures that the code the end user receives has not been tampered with.

A certificate, provided by a certificate authority (CA), must be obtained before you can sign your code. The CA acts as a trusted intermediary between the software publisher and the end user. (VeriSign is a well-known CA.) The certificate that the CA issues is called a software publisher certificate, and it must conform to the X.509 standard, employing public-key encryption. The certificate consists of two parts: the certificate file and the private key. You sign your files using the private key, and the user verifies the authenticity of the received file by obtaining the public key from the CA. It is also possible to generate a test certificate using the MAKECERT utility.

A certificate contains the following information:

➤ *Version*—Identifies the format of the certificate.

➤ *Serial Number*—The CA assigns a unique value.

➤ *Algorithm Identifier*—Identifies the algorithm used to sign the certificate.

➤ *Issuer*—Identifies the CA.

➤ *Period of Validity*—The date the certificate is valid and the date the certificate expires.

➤ *Subject*—The name of the user.

➤ *Subject's Public Key*—Contains the public-key algorithm name and the public key.

➤ *Signature*—The CA's signature.

INF File

The INF file identifies the components of the install set for the CAB file. These components may include DLLs, EXEs, help files, and so on. The INF instructs the CAB extraction utility how to deal with platform differences and file versioning issues. By default, newer versions of files on the target system overwrite older-version files.

Note: An INF file is not a CAB file requirement. Its purpose is to instruct a Windows operating system how to load and register a bundled control. An OSD file may be present in the CAB instead of an INF file, identifying the various bundled components and their installation.

The following INF file defines a cabinet that contains two files: MY COMPONENT.DLL and ADDITIONAL.DLL. The file identifies MYCOMPONENT.DLL as a COM server, specifying a CLSID and requiring registration.

```
; Sample INF file for MYCOMPONENT.DLL
[version]
; version signature (same for both NT and
                     Win95) do not removesignature="$CHICAGO$"
AdvancedINF=2.0
[Add.Code]
mycomponent.dll=mycomponent.dll
additional.dll=additional.dll
; needed DLL
[additional.dll]
file-win32-x86=thiscab
FileVersion=1,0,1,1
DestDir=10
RegisterServer=yes
[mycomponent.dll]
file-win32-x86=thiscab
clsid={632BBD12-11EE-1220-A97A-000000001231}
FileVersion=1,0,0,1
RegisterServer=yes
; end of INF file
```

The following section definitions appear in a CAB file.

➤ *Version*—The version tag identifies the operating system(s) that the CAB is compatible with. These options include Windows 95/98, Windows NT 4.0, and Windows 2000 and/or later.

➤ *Add. Code*—The Add.Code section contains a list of files that are contained in the CAB and associates each to a subsection in the INF file.

➤ *Subsection*—Each subsection must be associated with a file (defined in the section above). Values tags that may appear in this section include the CLSID of the control, the component's version number, and a flag that indicates that the component requires OLE registration.

Cabinetry

The files necessary to create, view, and sign CAB files are available in Microsoft's Cabinet Software Development Kit. The SDK includes the following:

➤ Utilities to create and extract CAB files

➤ Compression and decompression libraries and header files

➤ Documentation and code samples

Creating A CAB

If you have installed the SDK and have created an INF file, you can create a CAB file. The following line uses the Cabarc.exe utility and the INF file defined in the preceding code to create a CAB file named My.CAB containing a compressed Intel-compatible binary that allows 6,248 bytes for the digital certificate.

```
Cabarc.exe -s 6144 N My.cab MyComponent.dll additional.dll My.inf
```

Signing A CAB

Signing CAB files requires tools that are part of Microsoft's CryptoAPI Tools and Authenticode technology. The utilities that are part of this suite include those that can digitally sign files, view certificates, and modify certificates. The first step of signing a CAB files requires the Makecert.exe program. This utility creates a key pair, consisting of a private and public key. Additionally, the key pair is associated with an X.500 distinguished name, and the resulting X.509 certificate is signed by the private key.

```
Makecert.exe -u:mykey -n:CN=strattonassociates cert.cer
```

The final step is to use the Signcode.exe utility to sign the CAB file and embed a PKCS7 certificate.

```
Signcode-spc cert.spc -k mykey mycab.cab
```

> *Note: The Certification File Validity Utility (chktrust) is a useful tool to have in your Internet-development arsenal. It allows you to extract certificates from signed objects, and it's useful in proving that you accomplished what you set out to do with such arcane tools.*

Network Dispersal

Now that your component has been created, signed, and packaged, it's time to get it out to its intended audience of users. One of the simplest and most common dispersal mechanisms is embedding component in a Web page.

ActiveX

Distributing components for remote activation or for use by remote clients can easily be resolved using ActiveX technology. ActiveX was Microsoft's answer to a competing component technology in Java known as JavaBeans. The original ActiveX specification was a variation, actually a superset of OLE control functionality. For a COM server to consider itself an OLE control, it had to implement a dozen or so interfaces. This specification has since been revised to categorize an ActiveX control as one that performs self-registration and exposes IUnknown. This relaxation of the ActiveX definition identifies almost any COM server as an ActiveX component. As such, it is now possible to distribute any COM server using ActiveX technology and use DCOM for these components to communicate with each other.

The key to delivering ActiveX enabled content within standard HTML pages is the **Object** tag. The **Object** tag, whose origin may have been well-intentioned, has become a catchall for datatypes that were not envisioned during the design of HTML. The **Object** used to embed an ActiveX control appears in the following code:

```
<OBJECT
    ID=MYCONTROL
    TYPE="application/x-oleobject"
    CLASSID="clsid:ADD870B6-A8EE-11AF-9377-00BB004A7F12"
    CODEBASE="http://websvr/MYCONTROL.CAB"
    WIDTH=12
    HEIGHT=12>
    <PARAM NAME="Start Command" VALUE="Index">
    <PARAM NAME="Result Set Size" VALUE="100">
    <PARAM NAME="Query" VALUE="Author=Olafsen">
</OBJECT>\
```

Although the **Object** tag supports almost two dozen modifiers, it is important to understand those that are necessary for ActiveX creation and initialization.

➤ *CODEBASE*—Identifies the path used to retrieve the object.

➤ *CLASSID*—Contains the CLSID for the object.

➤ *TYPE*—The MIME type for ActiveX controls is "application/x-oleobject".

➤ *PARAM NAME*—Arguments that are passed to the component are prefaced by this tag. The parameter values may either be hard-coded in the HTML or the result of browser-side scripting operations.

Practice Questions

Question 1

> Which is not an InstallShield "building block" concept?
>
> ○ a. File groups
>
> ○ b. Components
>
> ○ c. Subcomponents
>
> ○ d. DLLs

The correct answer is d. InstallShield packaging identifies files and file groups, as well as components and subcomponents. Therefore answers a, b, and c are incorrect choices.

Question 2

> InstallShield would identify a grouping of install options such as tutorials, templates, and sample graphics as what? [Check all the correct answers]
>
> ❑ a. Components
>
> ❑ b. Subcomponents
>
> ❑ c. Files
>
> ❑ d. File Groups

The correct answers are a and b. Components and subcomponents identify those options that are presented to the user in a custom setup and allow the end users to select only those that they want to install. The component organization must always result in a program that actually runs, regardless of the user's custom selections. Therefore, answers c and d are incorrect.

Question 3

> Which are identifying features of SMS? [Check all of the correct answers]
>
> ❑ a. Granular Software Distribution
>
> ❑ b. Remote Diagnostics
>
> ❑ c. Configuration Discovery
>
> ❑ d. Failed Install Retry

The correct answers are a, b and c. If an install fails to complete, a rollback is performed on the target machine, guaranteeing the machine is in its previous operable state. Therefore, answer d is incorrect

Question 4

> What information is part of an X.509 certificate?
>
> ○ a. Expiration information
>
> ○ b. Certificate destination
>
> ○ c. Issuer identification
>
> ○ d. A serial number

The correct answer is b. The certificate is issued to the entity that creates either the message or the code. The issuing CA does not have to know who will receive the signed data; therefore, answers a, c, and d are incorrect.

Question 5

> Which are design goals of Microsoft's Zero Administration for Windows initiative? [Check all of the correct answers]
>
> ❑ a. Ease of use
>
> ❑ b. Seamless integration
>
> ❑ c. Employ Internet delivery
>
> ❑ d. Remote management

The correct answers are a, b, and d. SMS is not designed to work over the Internet; therefore, answer c is incorrect.

Question 6

What information does not appear in any section of an INF definition for a CAB file?

○ a. File version information

○ b. Destination directory

○ c. Auto-registration of COM server

○ d. License key information

The correct answer is d. License key, if required by the COM server, is handled in the IClassFactory2 interface.

Need To Know More?

 Li, Sing, and Panos Economopoulos. *Professional Visual C++ 5 ActiveX/Com Control Programming.* Wrox Press Ltd, Olton, Birmingham, Canada: 1997. ISBN: 1-861000-37-5. This book offers comprehensive discussions on developing and deploying ActiveX components.

 Pinnock, Jonathan. *Professional DCOM Application Development.* Wrox Press Ltd, Olton, Birmingham, Canada: 1998. ISBN: 1-861001-31-2. This book provides chapters that explain digital certificate technology as well as the various mechanisms available to deploy distributed applications.

Sample Test

In this chapter, I provide pointers to help you develop a successful test-taking strategy, including how to choose proper answers, how to decode ambiguity, how to work within the Microsoft testing framework, how to decide what you need to memorize, and how to prepare for the test. At the end of the chapter, 50 questions on subject matter pertinent to Microsoft Exam 70-016, "Designing and Implementing Desktop Applications Using Microsoft Visual C++ 6.0," are included.

Questions, Questions, Questions

There should be no doubt in your mind that you are facing a test full of specific and pointed questions. If the version of the exam that you take is fixed-length, it will include 43 questions, and you will be allotted 90 minutes to complete the exam. If it's an adaptive test (the software should tell you this as you begin the exam), it will consist of somewhere between 25 and 35 questions (on average) and take somewhere between 30 and 60 minutes.

Whichever type of test you take, for this exam, questions belong to one of five basic types:

➤ Multiple choice with a single answer

➤ Multiple choice with multiple answers

➤ Multipart with a single answer

➤ Multipart with multiple answers

➤ Simulations whereby you click a GUI screen capture to simulate using the Visual C++ interface

Always take the time to read a question at least twice before selecting an answer, and you should always look for an Exhibit button as you examine each question. Exhibits include graphics information related to a question. An *exhibit* is usually a screen capture of program output or GUI information that you must examine to analyze the question's contents and formulate an answer. The Exhibit button brings up graphics and charts used to help explain a question, provide additional data, or illustrate page layout or program behavior.

Not every question has only one answer; many questions require multiple answers. Therefore, you should read each question carefully, determine how many answers are necessary or possible, and look for additional hints or instructions when selecting answers. Such instructions often occur in brackets, immediately following the question itself (multiple-answer questions).

Picking Proper Answers

Obviously, the only way to pass any exam is to select enough of the right answers to obtain a passing score. However, Microsoft's exams are not standardized like the SAT and GRE exams; they are far more diabolical and convoluted. In some cases, questions are strangely worded, and deciphering them can be a real challenge. In those cases, you may need to rely on answer-elimination skills. Almost always, at least one answer out of the possible choices for a question can be eliminated immediately because it matches one of these conditions:

➤ The answer does not apply to the situation.

➤ The answer describes a nonexistent issue, an invalid option, or an imaginary state.

➤ The answer is inconsistant with information in the question itself.

After you eliminate all answers that are obviously wrong, you can apply your retained knowledge to eliminate further answers. Look for items that sound correct but refer to actions, commands, or features that are not present or not available in the situation that the question describes.

If you're still faced with a blind guess among two or more potentially correct answers, reread the question. Try to picture how each of the possible remaining answers would alter the situation. Be especially sensitive to terminology; sometimes the choice of words ("remove" instead of "disable") can make the difference between a right answer and a wrong one.

Only when you've exhausted your ability to eliminate answers but remain unclear about which of the remaining possibilities is correct should you guess at an answer. An unanswered question offers you no points, but guessing gives you at least some chance of getting a question right; just don't be too hasty when making a blind guess.

 If you're taking a fixed-length test, you can wait until the last round of reviewing marked questions (just as you're about to run out of time or out of unanswered questions) before you start making guesses. If you're taking an adaptive test, you'll have to guess in order to move on to the next question if you can't figure out an answer some other way. Either way, guessing should be a last resort.

Decoding Ambiguity

Microsoft exams have a reputation for including questions that can be difficult to interpret, confusing, or ambiguous. In my experience with numerous exams, I consider this reputation to be completely justified. The Microsoft exams are tough, and they're deliberately made that way.

The only way to beat Microsoft at its own game is to be prepared. You'll discover that many exam questions test your knowledge of things that are not directly related to the issue raised by a question. This means that the answers you must choose from, even incorrect ones, are just as much a part of the skill assessment as the question itself. If you don't know something about most aspects of Visual C++ 6, you may not be able to eliminate obviously wrong answers because they relate to a different area of Visual C++ than the one that's addressed by the question at hand. In other words, the more you know about the software, the easier it will be for you to tell right from wrong.

Questions often give away their answers, but you have to be Sherlock Holmes to see the clues. Often, subtle hints appear in the question text in such a way that they seem almost irrelevant to the situation. You must realize that each question is a test unto itself and that you need to inspect and successfully navigate each question to pass the exam. Look for small clues, such as the mention of times, group permissions and names, and configuration settings. Little things such as these can point to the right answer if properly understood; if missed, they can leave you facing a blind guess.

Another common difficulty with certification exams is vocabulary. Microsoft has an uncanny knack for naming some utilities and features entirely obviously in some cases and completely inanely in other instances. Be sure to brush up on the key terms presented at the beginning of each chapter of this book. You may also want to read through the glossary at the end of this book the day before you take the test.

Working Within The Framework

The test questions appear in random order, and many elements or issues that receive mention in one question may also crop up in other questions. It's not uncommon to find that an incorrect answer to one question is the correct answer to another question, or vice versa. Take the time to read every answer to each question, even if you recognize the correct answer to a question immediately. That extra reading may spark a memory, or remind you about a Visual C++ 6.0 feature or function, that helps you on another question elsewhere in the exam.

If you're taking a fixed-length test, you can revisit any question as many times as you like. If you're uncertain of the answer to a question, check the box that's provided to mark it for easy return later on. You should also mark questions you think may offer information that you can use to answer other questions. On fixed-length tests, you'll usually mark somewhere between 25 and 50 percent of the questions on exams you take. The testing software is designed to let you mark every question if you choose; use this framework to your advantage. Everything you'll want to see again should be marked; the testing software can then help you return to marked questions quickly and easily.

For fixed-length tests, the author strongly recommends that you first read through the entire test quickly, before getting caught up in answering individual questions. This will help to jog your memory as you review the potential answers and can help identify questions that you want to mark for easy access to their contents. It will also let you identify and mark the tricky questions for easy return. The key is to make a quick pass over the territory to begin with—so that you know what you're up against—and then to survey that territory more thoroughly on a second pass, when you can begin to answer all questions systematically and consistently.

If you're taking an adaptive test and you see something in a question or one of the answers that jogs your memory on a topic, or that you feel you should record if the topic appears in another question, write it down on your piece of paper. Just because you can't go back to a question in an adaptive test doesn't mean you can't take notes on what you see early in the test, in hopes that it might help you later in the test.

For adaptive tests, don't be afraid to take notes on what you see in various questions. Sometimes, what you record from one question, especially if it's not as familiar as it should be or reminds you of the name or use of some utility or interface details, can help you on other questions later on.

Deciding What To Memorize

The amount of memorization you must undertake for an exam depends on how well you remember what you've read and how well you know the software by heart. If you're a visual thinker and can see the drop-down menus and dialog boxes in your head, you won't need to memorize as much as someone who's less visually oriented. However, the exam will stretch your abilities to memorize product features and functions, interface details, and proper application design, development, and maintenance approaches, as well as how they all relate to Visual C++ 6.

At a minimum, you'll want to memorize the following kinds of information:

➤ MFC

➤ COM components

➤ ATL

➤ ActiveX

➤ ADO

➤ DLLs

➤ Debugging

➤ Development tools

If you work your way through this book while sitting at a machine with Visual C++ 6 installed and try to manipulate this environment's features and functions as they're discussed throughout, you should have little or no difficulties mastering this material. Also, don't forget that The Cram Sheet at the front of the book is designed to capture the material that's most important to memorize; use this to guide your studies as well.

Preparing For The Test

The best way to prepare for the test—after you've studied—is to take at least one practice exam. One is included here in this chapter for that reason; the test questions are located in the pages that follow (and unlike the preceding chapters in this book, the answers don't follow the questions immediately; you'll have to flip to Chapter 25 to review the answers separately).

Give yourself 105 minutes to take the exam, and keep yourself on the honor system—don't look at earlier text in the book or jump ahead to the answer key. When your time is up or you've finished the questions, you can check your work in Chapter 25. Pay special attention to the explanations for the incorrect answers; these can also help to reinforce your knowledge of the material. Knowing how to recognize correct answers is good, but understanding why incorrect answers are wrong can be equally valuable.

Taking The Test

Relax. Once you're sitting in front of the testing computer, there's nothing more you can do to increase your knowledge or preparation. Take a deep breath, stretch, and start reading that first question.

You don't need to rush either. You have plenty of time to complete each question, and if you're taking a fixed-length test, you'll have time to return to those questions that you skipped or marked for return. If you read a question on a fixed-length test twice and you remain clueless, you can mark it; if you're taking an adaptive test, you'll have to guess and move on. Both easy and difficult questions are intermixed throughout the test in random order. If you're taking a fixed-length test, don't cheat yourself by spending too much time on a hard question early on in the test, thereby depriving yourself of the time you need to answer the questions at the end of the test. If you're taking an adaptive test, don't spend more than five minutes on any single question—if it takes you that long to get nowhere, it's time to guess and move on.

On a fixed-length test, you can read through the entire test, and before returning to marked questions for a second visit, you can figure out how much time you've got per question. As you answer each question, remove its mark. Continue to review the remaining marked questions until you run out of time or complete the test.

On an adaptive test, set a maximum time limit for questions and watch your time on long or complex questions. If you hit your limit, it's time to guess and move on. Don't deprive yourself of the opportunity to see more questions by taking too long to puzzle over questions, unless you think you can figure out the answer. Otherwise, you're limiting your opportunities to pass.

That's it for pointers. Here are some questions for you to practice on.

Good luck!

Sample Test

Question 1

Which of the following functions allow you to act on menu items? [Check all of the correct answers]

- ❑ a. CCmdUI::SetCheck()
- ❑ b. CCmdUI::DrawItem()
- ❑ c. CMenu::SetText()
- ❑ d. CCmdUI::Enable()
- ❑ e. CMenu::SetRadio()

Question 2

When you initially created your application, at Step 4 of 6 you deselected the Initial Status Bar option. Now you have decided you would like your application to have a status bar. Where do you need to add code to create and display the status bar?

- ○ a. In InitInstance() of your application class
- ○ b. In OnCreate() of CMainFrame
- ○ c. In PreCreateWindow() of CMainFrame
- ○ d. In OnDraw of your view class

Question 3

Which is not a window that the IDE provides for debugging?

- ○ a. Registers
- ○ b. Memory
- ○ c. Watch
- ○ d. Inspect

Question 4

Which statement is true?

○ a. Win32 operating systems provide two types of threads: worker threads and UI threads.

○ b. User-interface threads are represented by CWinThread, but worker threads are represented by AfxThread.

○ c. Worker threads must always be created by the primary thread.

○ d. Worker threads do not require a message handler.

Question 5

You are implementing a COM server using MFC. Which of the following statements are true? [Check all of the correct answers]

❑ a. The METHOD_PROLOGUE() macro is placed in the implementation of an interface function to provide access to the IUnknown interface.

❑ b. The STDMETHOD() and STDMETHOD_() macros are placed between the BEGIN_INTERFACE_MAP() and END_INTERFACE_MAP() macros.

❑ c. BEGIN_INTERFACE_PART() generates function prototypes for QueryInterface(), AddRef(), and Release().

❑ d. The COM_INTERFACE_ENTRY() macro is placed between the BEGIN_COM_MAP() and END_COM_MAP() macros.

Question 6

The purpose of the IConnectionPoint::Advise() method is to:

○ a. Notify the sink of an event

○ b. Inform the client of the IID of the outgoing interface

○ c. Set up a connection between a connection point and a sink

○ d. Provide the connection point object with a cookie that uniquely identifies the connection

Question 7

Which of the following ADO cursor types makes changes by other users available after the connection is established? [Check all of the correct answers]

❏ a. adOpenDynamic

❏ b. adOpenKeyset

❏ c. adOpenForwardOnly

❏ d. adOpenStatic

Question 8

Which is not information collected by InstallShield when constructing an install script?

○ a. Application name

○ b. Application version

○ c. Application's executable file

○ d. Application's size in bytes

Question 9

Which is not a valid Afx diagnostic function?

○ a. AfxIsValidAddress

○ b. AfxSetAllocHook

○ c. AfxEnableMemoryTracking

○ d. AfxDefragHeap

Question 10

A DDX_ function is used to move data between which of the following? [Check all of the correct answers]

❏ a. A dialog box and its parent window

❏ b. A document object and a dialog box

❏ c. A dialog box and a control

❏ d. A document object and a view object

Question 11

Which of the following statements best describes what COFF is?

○ a. A debug format used by other debuggers

○ b. A debug link option

○ c. A runtime library specification

○ d. A necessity for on-the-fly debugging to occur

Question 12

Using SDK, you are implementing a COM object that supports aggregation. Which statement is true?

○ a. The outer object must provide wrapper functions for each of the inner object methods that the outer object wishes to make available to its clients.

○ b. When creating the inner object, the outer object calls CoCreate InstanceEx(), passing the this pointer.

○ c. The inner object must delete itself when the delegating unknown's reference count goes to zero.

○ d. When the outer object creates the inner object, it can ask for any of the inner object's interfaces.

Question 13

The Windows NT Registry contains five root keys. Which of the following statements are true of the HKEY_CURRENT_CONFIG key?

○ a. It contains the changes to the standard configuration information kept under the HKEY_LOCAL_MACHINE root key.

○ b. It contains all of the actively loaded user profiles.

○ c. It contains an entry that contains the user profile for the user who is currently logged on to the local computer.

○ d. Answers b and c.

Question 14

Which is Microsoft's preferred file distribution format?

○ a. ZIP

○ b. JAR

○ c. CAB

○ d. _CMPRSS

Question 15

Assume that you work for Acme Travel and are enhancing a COM application that includes the following code:

```
COSERVERINFO csi = { 0, NULL, NULL, 0 };
MULTI_QI mqi[] =
  {
    {&IID_IAirlines, NULL, S_OK},
    {&IID_ILodging, NULL, S_OK},
    {&IID_IRentalCars, NULL, S_OK},
    {&IID_ICruises, NULL, S_OK},
    {&IID_IResorts, NULL, S_OK}
  };
HRESULT hr = CoCreateInstanceEx(
                CLSID_TravelAgencyServer,
                NULL, CLSCTX_SERVER, &csi,
                sizeof(mqi)/sizeof(mqi[0]),
                mqi);
```

Which of the following statements are true? [Check all of the correct answers]

❑ a. If the object is located on a remote computer, CoCreateInstance Ex() will return an error code.

❑ b. If everything works correctly, the MULTI_QI structure will contain five interface pointers.

❑ c. If the object is located on a remote computer, the CLSCTX_SERVER argument must be changed to CLSCTX_REMOTE_SERVER.

❑ d. All of the above are correct.

Question 16

What does MDAC stand for?

○ a. Microsoft Distributed Architecture for Computers

○ b. Microsoft Data Access Components

○ c. Microsoft Data Access Control

○ d. Microsoft Does Act Cautious

Question 17

You recently built an Automation server. Your server provides rich error information using the Automation-defined error object mechanism. To implement this error reporting, you had to implement which of the following interfaces? [Check all of the correct answers]

❑ a. ICreateErrorInfo

❑ b. IErrorInfo

❑ c. ISupportErrorInfo

❑ d. All of the above

❑ e. Both a and c

Question 18

You are developing an application that uses ADO to access a SQL Server database. Some of the requirements for the application are as follows:

• Support for up to 250 concurrent users.

• As new records are added to the database, the additions must be immediately visible to all users.

• The possibility of users viewing inconsistent data must be guarded against.

Which of the following would be best for updating a single record?

○ a. CursorType of adOpenKeyset and LockType of adLockPessimistic

○ b. CursorType of adOpenDynamic and LockType of adLockPessimistic

○ c. CursorType of adOpenKeyset and LockType of adLockOptimistic

○ d. CursorType of adOpenDynamic and LockType of adLockOptimistic

Question 19

You are developing an MDI MFC application and have decided to provide the user with two toolbars unique to your application. In which function would you normally create the toolbars?

○ a. CWinApp:: InitInstance()

○ b. CMainFrame::PreCreateWindow()

○ c. CDocument::OnNewDocument()

○ d. CMainFrame::OnCreate()

Question 20

Examine the following table named "Employees":

EmpNumber	EmpName	EmpSalary
10	Ann	34925
20	Sue	37900
30	Bob	40100
40	John	32500
50	Kathy	39000

If the following code example is run, who will be the highest-paid employee?

```
_ConnectionPtr spConn(__uuidof(Connection));
try
{
  spConn->ConnectionString =
    "Data Source=ExamCram;uid=sa;pwd=";
  spConn->Open("", "", "",
               adConnectUnspecified);

  _CommandPtr spCmd(__uuidof(Command));
  spCmd->ActiveConnection = spConn;
  spCmd->CommandText =
    "SELECT * from employees "
    "WHERE EmpSalary < ?";

  _ParameterPtr spSalary =
    spCmd->CreateParameter("EmpSalary",
                           adCurrency,
```

(continued)

Question 20 *(continued)*

```
                        adParamInputOutput,
                        6,
                        40000.00);
  spCmd->Parameters->Append(spSalary);


  _RecordsetPtr spRs(__uuidof(Recordset));
  spRs->CursorLocation = adUseClient;
  spRs->Open((IDispatch *) spCmd, vtMissing,
    adOpenStatic, adLockBatchOptimistic,
    adCmdUnspecified);


  for(spRs->MoveFirst();
      !spRs->EndOfFile;
      spRs->MoveNext())
  {
    double salary =
      spRs->GetFields()->
      GetItem("EmpSalary")->Value;
    if(salary >= 38000.0)
      salary *= 1.03;
    else if(salary >= 35000.0)
      salary = salary * 1.04 + 1000;
    else if(salary >= 30000.0)
      salary = salary * 1.05 + 1500;
    else
      salary = salary * 1.06 + 2000;
  }
  spRs->UpdateBatch(adAffectAll);
  spRs->Close();
}
catch (_com_error &e)
{
...
```

○ a. Ann

○ b. Sue

○ c. Bob

○ d. Kathy

Question 21

You recently purchased an out-of-process component from a third party. The component's file name is COMPLEX.EXE. You now want to use this component with an application you are developing. Which of the following command lines can you use to register the component on your development system?

○ a. RegSvr32 COMPLEX.EXE

○ b. COMPLEX.EXE -regserver

○ c. RegEdit.EXE COMPLEX.EXE

○ d. RegEdit32.EXE COMPLEX.EXE

Question 22

Which are contained in a certificate? [Check all of the correct answers]

❑ a. A serial number

❑ b. An expiration date

❑ c. A bitmap image file

❑ d. An algorithm identifier

Question 23

You are developing a COM object using the SDK. You are implementing the IPersistStorage interface. Which method must you implement so that clients can make the object persist?

○ a. Write

○ b. SaveObject

○ c. Persist

○ d. Save

Question 24

Which statement is true concerning COM threading?

○ a. A single process can have only one single-threaded apartment.

○ b. A single process can have any number of multithreaded apartments.

○ c. A single process can have either a single-threaded apartment or a multithreaded apartment, but not both.

○ d. A single process can have one multithreaded apartment and one or more single-threaded apartments.

Question 25

The Interface Definition Language (IDL) provides constructs that allow you to create user-defined types. Which of the following constructs does the IDL support? [Check all of the correct answers]

❑ a. class

❑ b. enum

❑ c. struct

❑ d. union

Question 26

Which changes are not valid when using the Edit and Continue debug option? [Check all of the correct answers]

❑ a. Exception block modification

❑ b. Function prototype changes

❑ c. Modification of conditional statements

❑ d. Introduction of a new data type

Question 27

Assume you work for Acme Software. You develop an MFC MDI application that includes the following code:

```
SetRegistryKey(_T("Acme Software"));
LoadStdProfileSettings();
```

Which of the following statements are true? [Check all of the correct answers]

❑ a. The standard INI file will be loaded.

❑ b. The list of most recently used files are kept in the Registry under HKEY_CURRENT_USER\Software\Acme Software\.

❑ c. The code is located in the InitInstance() member function of your CWinApp-derived class.

❑ d. The code is located in the CFrameWnd constructor.

Question 28

You are developing a COM component. You want the component to be a connectable object. Which statement is true?

○ a. Your component must implement the IConnectionPoint interface. The client must implement the IConnectionPointContainer interface.

○ b. Your component must implement both the IConnectionPoint and the IConnectionPointContainer interfaces.

○ c. Your component must implement the IConnectionPointContainer interface, and the client must implement the IConnectionPoint interface.

○ d. Your component must implement the ISupportConnectionPoints. The client must implement both the IConnectionPoint and the IConnectionPointContainer interfaces.

Question 29

Which are members of the Workspace window's Resource View?

❑ a. Accelerator tables

❑ b. Dialog boxes

❑ c. Windows

❑ d. Cursors

Question 30

Examine the following code:

```
class A
{
public:
  A()  { cout << "ctor A\n"; }
  ~A() { cout << "dtor A\n"; }
};

class B : public A
{
public:
  B() { cout << "ctor B\n"; }
  ~B() { cout << "dtor B\n"; }
};

class C : public B
{
public:
  C() { cout << "ctor C\n"; }
  ~C() { cout << "dtor C\n"; }
};

int main()
{
  C c;            // object 1
  A *a = new C;   // object 2
  delete a;
  return 0;
}
```

(continued)

Question 30 *(continued)*

```
What is displayed?

O a. ctor A
     ctor B
     ctor C
     ctor C
     dtor C
     dtor C
     dtor B
     dtor A


O b. ctor A
     ctor B
     ctor C
     ctor A
     ctor B
     ctor C
     dtor C
     dtor B
     dtor A
     dtor C
     dtor B
     dtor A


O c. ctor A
     ctor B
     ctor C
     ctor A
     ctor B
     ctor C
     dtor A
     dtor B
     dtor C
     dtor A
     dtor B
     dtor C
```

(continued)

Question 30 *(continued)*

```
○ d.  ctor  A
       ctor  B
       ctor  C
       ctor  A
       ctor  B
       ctor  C
       dtor  A
       dtor  C
       dtor  B
       dtor  A
```

Question 31

A certificate that Microsoft and most vendors recognize is in what format?

○ a. X.500

○ b. X.509

○ c. ZIP

○ d. PCMCIA

Question 32

Which of the following attributes can be used to decorate an IDL interface declaration? [Choose three]

❑ a. oleautomation

❑ b. object

❑ c. pointer

❑ d. dual

Question 33

Which kinds of files can SourceSafe manage?

○ a. Text

○ b. Binary

○ c. Image

○ d. Resource

○ e. All of the above

○ f. Answers a and b only

Question 34

You are building a COM object that supports aggregation. Which of the following statements are true? [Check all of the correct answers]

❑ a. Other objects will be able to reuse your object by aggregation, but not by containment.

❑ b. Your object must be packaged into an in-process server.

❑ c. When other objects reuse your object by aggregation, they will be able to selectively choose the interfaces that are exposed.

❑ d. All of the above are correct.

Question 35

Your application has opened an ADO Recordset. Which of the following conditions are true if there are no records?

○ a. BOF is true and EOF is false.

○ b. BOF is false and EOF is false.

○ c. BOF is true and EOF is true.

○ d. BOF is false and EOF is true.

Question 36

You are building a Sales component that you want to be able to use with scripting languages. Because the component will also be used by C++ applications, you decide to implement a dual interface. You plan to provide a number of operations as part of the ISales interface. As a minimum, you will need to implement methods for which of the following interfaces?

○ a. IUnknown

○ b. ISales

○ c. IDispatch

○ d. All of the above

○ e. Answers a and b

Question 37

Which of the following is a complete list of IDL primitive or base data types?

○ a. boolean, byte, char, double, float, hyper, int, long, short, small, void, wchar_t

○ b. boolean, byte, char, double, enum, float, hyper, int, long, short, struct, small, union, void, wchar_t

○ c. boolean, byte, char, double, float, hyper, int, long, short, void, wchar_t

○ d. byte, char, double, float, hyper, int, long, short, small, void, wchar_t

Question 38

Which switches determine the calling convention that the compiler uses? [Check all of the correct answers]

❑ a. /Gd

❑ b. /Gr

❑ c. /GX

❑ d. /Gz

Question 39

Within the MFC framework, which of the following statements are true? [Choose two]

- ❑ a. Standard controls send notifications to their parents using WM_COMMAND.
- ❑ b. Menu items send notifications using WM_MENU_CHANGE.
- ❑ c. Most common controls enclose their notifications in WM_NOTIFY.
- ❑ d. Buttons send notifications using WM_BTN_CLICKED.

Question 40

You are developing an application that will use a COM object that has 25 interfaces. You know that the object will be located on the server, and you need to minimize network traffic. Which of the following functions would you use when creating the object?

- ○ a. CoGetClassObject()
- ○ b. CoCreateInstance()
- ○ c. CoCreateInstanceEx()
- ○ d. OleGetClassObject()

Question 41

You are implementing an SDI MFC application that uses context-sensitive help. When you distribute your application, files with which of the following extensions will you need to include as part of the installation? [Check all of the correct answers]

- ❑ a. EXE
- ❑ b. CNT
- ❑ c. HLP
- ❑ d. RTF

Question 42

Examine the following table named "Employees", which is stored in a SQL Server 7 database:

EmpNumber	EmpName	EmpSalary
10	Ann	34925
20	Sue	37900
30	Bob	40100
40	John	32500
50	Kathy	39000

You have two valid ADO smart pointers. The first one, spCmd, points to a Command object, and the other one, spRsEmp, points to a Recordset object. Which of the following code examples will locate Bob?

```
// Example 1
  spCmd->CommandText =
    "SELECT * from employees ";
  spRsEmp->Open((IDispatch *) spCmd,
    vtMissing, adOpenForwardOnly,
    adLockReadOnly, adCmdText);
  spRsEmp->MoveFirst();
  _bstr_t bstrFind("EmpNumber = 30");
  spRsEmp->Find(bstrFind, 0,
              adSearchForward);


// Example 2
  spCmd->CommandText =
      "SELECT * from employees "
      "WHERE EmpNumber = ?";
  long id = 30;
  ParameterPtr spNumber =
    spCmd->CreateParameter("EmpNumber",
                adInteger, adParamInput,
                4, id);
  spCmd->Parameters->Append(spNumber);
  spRsEmp->Open((IDispatch *) spCmd,
      vtMissing, adOpenForwardOnly,
      adLockReadOnly, adCmdText);
```

(continued)

Question 42 *(continued)*

```
// Example 3
   spCmd->CommandText =
      "SELECT * from employees ";
   spRsEmp->Open((IDispatch *) spCmd,
         vtMissing, adOpenForwardOnly,
         adLockReadOnly, adCmdText);
   spRsEmp->MoveFirst();
   spRsEmp->Find("EmpNumber = 30", 0,
            adSearchForward);

// Example 4
   spRsEmp->Open(
   "SELECT * from employees "
   "WHERE EmpNumber = 30",
   "Data Source=ExamCram;uid=sa;pwd=",
   adOpenForwardOnly, adLockReadOnly,
   adCmdText);
```

○ a. Examples 1 and 2

○ b. Example 3 and 4

○ c. Examples 1 and 3

○ d. Examples 2 and 4

○ e. All four examples

○ f. None of the examples

Question 43

When using ODBC with MFC, which class encapsulates a connection with the data source?

○ a. CDatabase

○ b. CDataSource

○ c. CConnection

○ d. CODBCConnection

Question 44

Which are common debugger commands available from both the toolbar and menu? [Check all of the correct answers]

❑ a. Go

❑ b. Step Over

❑ c. Step Into

❑ d. Step Around

Question 45

You are writing an MFC SDI database application. You have a form where users can update records. You are concerned that the user might try to exit the program without saving changes to the database. The default MFC procedure allows users to save document changes to a file, not to the database. This is not what you want. Which function do you need to override to provide the correct functionality?

○ a. CRecordset::Update()

○ b. CDocument::SaveModified()

○ c. CView::OnUpdate()

○ d. CWnd::SaveModified()

Question 46

Which are two valid ways of acquiring a certificate?

❑ a. Generate a test certificate using the MakeCert utility

❑ b. Purchase a certificate from a CA

❑ c. Use any certificate that is posted publicly

❑ d. Create a certificate using the ChkTrust utility

Question 47

You work for a software company that specializes in MFC. The company's mission is to provide custom software development for small- to medium-sized companies. Your firm just signed a contract with the Exotic Places travel agency to develop a new reservation system. Here is the information you have been given:

- The Exotic Places travel agency employs 75 people. Thirty-nine of the employees are agents who provide customers with travel information such as flights, lodging, and cruises. These agents will also make arrangements and reservations. Twenty-five of the employees are managers. Fifteen of the managers supervise the agents. Five employees are accountants and financial managers. The remaining employees provide clerical support.

- The agents and supervisors need to use the new application as a standalone application. The accountants will need to access some of the services it provides through an application that will be built at a later time.

- It's anticipated that the number of users will double over the next two years.

- The Exotic Places agency currently has five branch offices. Each branch office has its own database; most of these databases are MS Access. The agency is in the process of networking the branch offices together. They also hired a firm to install a center SQL Server database and migrate their data. Your application will be required to use the SQL Server database.

- The financial/accounting system that might be developed uses Visual C++. However, there is a possibility that it will be built using Visual Basic.

What type of project will you create?

○ a. MFC EXE with Automation enabled

○ b. Win32 EXE

○ c. MFC DLL with Automation enabled

○ d. Either a or c

Question 48

An ActiveX control sends its container by which of the following techniques?

○ a. Send a WM_COMMAND message

○ b. Send a WM_EVENT message

○ c. Send a WM_NOTIFY message

○ d. Call a container implemented method

Question 49

You have developed an SDI MFC application with a CFormView. You have added menu items and placed their handlers in your CFormView-derived class. Which class performs the message map lookup?

○ a. Your CFormView-derived class

○ b. CMainFrame

○ c. CCmdTarget

○ d. CWinApp

Question 50

Which Visual C++ editions allow linking to the dynamic MFC libraries? [Check all of the correct answers]

❏ a. Standard

❏ b. Professional

❏ c. Enterprise

❏ d. Personal

25

Answer Key

. . . .

1. a, d	16. b	31. b	46. a, b
2. b	17. c	32. a, b, d	47. a
3. d	18. a	33. e	48. d
4. d	19. d	34. b, c	49. c
5. a, c	20. c	35. c	50. b, c
6. c	21. b	36. d	
7. a, b	22. a, b, d	37. a	
8. d	23. d	38. a, b, d	
9. d	24. d	39. a, c	
10. c	25. b, c, d	40. c	
11. a	26. a, b, d	41. a, b, c	
12. b	27. b, c	42. e	
13. a	28. b	43. a	
14. c	29. a, b, d	44. a, b, c	
15. b	30. d	45. b	

Question 1

The correct answers are a and d. Answer b is incorrect because **DrawItem()** is a member function of **CMenu**. It is called by the framework when a visual aspect of an owner-drawn menu changes. Answers c and e are incorrect because **SetText()** and **SetRadio()** are members of **CCmdUI**, not **CMenu**.

Question 2

The correct answer is b. **InitInstance()** of the application class instantiates the document template, adds the template to the list of document templates, and processes the command-line parameters. When **ProcessShellCommand()** is called, it, among other things, calls **CWinApp::OnFileNew()** or **CWinApp:: OpenDocumentFile()** to start the application. It's during this phase of the program execution that the framework creates the document, frame window, and view. When the frame window is created, **CMainFrame::OnCreate()** is called. **CMainFrame::OnCreate()** is where the status bar needs to be created and attached to the frame.

Question 3

The correct answer is d. Debug windows include Registers, Memory, Watch, Variables, and Call Stack.

Question 4

The correct answer is d. To the Win32 operating systems, only one type of thread exists. The only distinction the operating system makes among threads is their scheduling priorities. MFC distinguishes two types of threads: user-interface threads and worker threads. All threads in MFC applications are represented by **CWinThread** objects. In most situations, you don't even have to explicitly create these objects; instead, you can call the framework helper function **AfxBeginThread**, which creates the **CWinThread** object for you, starts it, and returns its address so you can refer to it later. Your application can have multiple concurrent threads of execution running simultaneously. The operating system creates a process and begins executing the primary thread of that process. This primary thread can create additional threads. Each thread created by the primary thread can, in turn, create additional threads.

Worker threads are commonly used to handle background tasks the user doesn't need to know or care about. As such, there is usually no interaction, and a message pump isn't required.

Question 5

The correct answers are a and c. The **METHOD_PROLOGUE()** macro creates the **pThis** pointer, which can be used to access the **IUnknown** interface implemented by the **CCmdTarget**-derived class. **BEGIN_INTERFACE_ PART()** and **END_INTERFACE_PART()** are placed in the header file. Together, they create an interface as a nested class, create an instance of the interface, and generate function prototypes for **QueryInterface()**, **AddRef()**, and **Release()**. Answer b is incorrect because the **STDMETHOD()** and **STDMETHOD_()** macros are placed between the **BEGIN_INTERFACE_ PART()** and **END_INTERFACE_PART()** macros, not between the **BEGIN_INTERFACE_MAP()** and **END_INTERFACE_MAP()** macros. Answer d is incorrect because the macros are not used with MFC; they're used with ATL.

Question 6

The correct answer is c. The client calls **IConnectionPoint::Advise()**, passing the connectable object a pointer on which the client's sink can receive outgoing calls. Answer a is incorrect because the object notifies the sink of an event by calling a method on the client's sink interface. Answer b is incorrect because the client obtains the **IID** of the outgoing interface a connect point supports by calling **IConnectionPoint::GetConnectionInterface()**. Answer d is incorrect because **IConnectionPoint::Advise()** returns a cookie to the caller. This cookie uniquely identifies the connection and must be used by the caller to delete the connection.

Question 7

The correct answers are a and b. The **adOpenDynamic** cursor makes all additions, changes, and deletions made by other users visible. The **adOpenKeyset** cursor makes changes to existing records and deleted records visible. Answers c and d are incorrect because changes made by other users are not visible with **adOpenForwardOnly** and **adOpenStatic** cursors.

Question 8

The correct answer is d. The install script will determine the size of the executable, and InstallShield will identify available disk capacity problems.

Question 9

The correct answer is d. An **Afx** function is not provided to reduce heap fragmentation.

Question 10

The correct answer is c. When using the **DDX** mechanism, you set the initial values of the dialog object's member variables, typically in your **OnInitDialog** handler or the dialog constructor. Immediately before the dialog is displayed, the framework's **DDX** mechanism transfers the values of the member variables to the controls in the dialog box, where they appear when the dialog box itself appears in response to **DoModal** or **Create**. The default implementation of **OnInitDialog** in **CDialog** calls the **UpdateData** member function of class **CWnd** to initialize the controls in the dialog box.

The same mechanism transfers values from the controls to the member variables when the user clicks the OK button (or whenever you call the **UpdateData** member function with the argument **TRUE**). The dialog data validation mechanism validates any data items for which you specified validation rules.

Question 11

The correct answer is a. COFF is actually a standard file format for containing multiple object files; debugging information is incidental to that. However, given the possible choices, a is the best answer. This is not the preferred format for Microsoft's debug information; however, the Visual Studio debugger will recognize and use the format if available.

Question 12

The correct answer is b. COM requires that the outer object pass its **this** pointer, which represents the outer object's **IUnknown**. This allows the inner object to detect that it is being aggregated. Answer a is incorrect because this is a requirement for containment, not for aggregation. Aggregation allows a client, after obtaining an inner object interface, to directly call methods implemented by the inner object. Answer c is incorrect because to inner object's delegating unknown must route all calls to **Release()** outward to the outer object's **IUnknown**—this is also true for calls to **QueryInterface()** and **AddRef()**. The inner object, therefore, has no knowledge of the reference count. Answer d is incorrect because the outer object is only permitted to ask for the inner object's implicit **IUnknown**. If it were to ask for any other interface, the inner object would delegate the request outward, thereby causing an infinite recursion.

Question 13

The correct answer is a. The HKEY_CURRENT_CONFIG root key contains sets of changes to the standard configuration of services and devices established in the Software and System keys under HKEY_LOCAL_ MACHINE. Answer b is incorrect because it is HKEY_USERS that contains all of the actively loaded user profiles, not HKEY_CURRENT_CONFIG. Answer c is incorrect because HKEY_CURRENT_USER contains the user profile for the user who is currently logged on. Answer d is incorrect because both b and c are incorrect.

Question 14

The correct answer is c. The ZIP and JAR file formats are popular for Java; however, Microsoft tools and browsers also allow such code to be delivered in CAB files. There is no such thing as the _CMPRSS format.

Question 15

The correct answer is b. The **MULTI_QI** structure allows a set of interface pointers to be returned from the same object in a single round-trip to the server. Answer a is incorrect because the **COSERVERINFO** structure doesn't contain a specific machine, which causes COM to look in the Registry under the class's **RemoteServerName** named value to determine the specific computer where the object is located. Answer c is incorrect because the **CLSCTX_SERVER** code is defined as the logical OR of **CLSCTX_ INPROC_SERVER, CLSCTX_ LOCAL_SERVER**, and **CLSCTX_REMOTE_SERVER**. Answer d is incorrect because answers a and c are incorrect.

Question 16

The correct answer is b. The NT Option Pack supplies the most recent data access components, providing support for ActiveX Data Objects (ADO), OLE DB, and ODBC drivers and services.

Question 17

The correct answer is c. **ICreateErrorInfo** and **IErrorInfo** are implemented by an error object supplied to you by the operating system when you call the API function **CreateErrorInfo()**. You place error information in the error object by using the **ICreateErrorInfo** interface and then call the API function **SetErrorInfo()**, passing the **IErrorInfo** interface. **SetErrorInfo()** sets the error object as the current error object for the current thread. You then return the **HRESULT** to the client. The client can then ask to use your object's **ISupportErrorInfo** to find out if the error information is supported for a specific IID. If yes, the client then calls **GetErrorInfo()** to obtain the **IErrorInfo** interface, which it uses to retrieve the error information.

Question 18

The correct answer is a. The question first presents the requirements and asks you to make a choice for a specific case. In the case presented, not all requirements are germane. The important requirement in this case are the first and third bullet. If you are updating only one record, you don't need to view additions made by other users. However, it's important that the **CursorType** use as few resources as possible. Here, because only two types of cursors were presented, you need to choose the better of the two—that is, the one using the least amount of resources—which is **adOpenKeyset**. Probably more important in this case is the type of lock used. Because **adLockPessimistic** causes the data to be locked from the beginning of the modification through the call to **Update()**, it is the correct choice.

Question 19

The correct answer is d. The standard toolbar is created in **CMainFrame:: OnCreate()**, and it makes the most sense to create your unique toolbars here also. Although you can create your toolbars in a different manner, the way the framework is constructed makes using **CMainFrame::OnCreate()** the most logical and easiest alternative.

Question 20

The correct answer is c. This is a nasty question. It requires you to read the code very carefully. There is a lot of code, and it's easy to get caught up in all the calculations. The key to answering this question is to notice that **salary** is never placed in the recordset, so the database doesn't get updated. Here is the missing line of code:

```
else
    salary = salary * 1.06 + 2000;
    spRs->GetFields()->GetItem("EmpSalary")->
    Value = salary;
}
spRs->UpdateBatch(adAffectAll);
```

Question 21

The correct answer is b. Answer a is incorrect because RegSvr32.EXE is used to register in-process components. Answers c and d are incorrect because both RegEdit.EXE and RegEdit32.EXE are used to view and change settings in your system Registry.

Question 22

The correct answers are a, b, and d. The CA supplies a serial number for the certificate, and the expiration date and encryption algorithm are also necessary. A bitmap image is not part of a certificate.

Question 23

The correct answer is d. **IPersistStorage::Save()** saves an object, along with any nested objects that it contains. Answers a, b, and c are incorrect because these methods don't exist.

Question 24

The correct answer is d. In order for a process to use COM, it must have at least one apartment. The types of apartments a given process can have are as follows:

➤ *One single-threaded apartment (STA).* The apartment is known as the "main STA." Because only one thread can occupy an STA, the process will only have one thread using COM.

➤ *One or more STAs.* The first STA being the main STA will run the main thread. All other threads will run in their own STA.

➤ *One multithreaded apartment (MTA).* There can only be one MTA per process, which can host any number of threads.

➤ *One MTA and one or more STAs.* In this situation, the process can run multiple threads in the one MTA. It can also run multiple STA threads, but each STA can host at most one thread.

Question 25

The correct answers are b, c, and d. Because of its historical roots, the IDL is based on C syntax and, like C, supports **enum**, **struct**, and **union**. C has no concept of a **class** and neither does the IDL.

Question 26

The correct answers are a, b, and d. Such fundamental changes to a class, function, or application are not permitted. You may, however, change conditional branching statements as long as they don't conflict with the limitations identified by the other answers a, b, and d.

Question 27

The correct answers are b and c. Answer a is incorrect because **SetRegistryKey()** causes application settings to be stored in the Registry instead of the INI file. Answer d is incorrect because **SetRegistryKey()** and **LoadStdProfileSettings()** are members of **CWinApp**, not **CFrameWnd**.

Question 28

Answer b is correct. The other answers are incorrect because b is correct. Answer d also includes the name of a nonexistent interface to add confusion.

Question 29

The correct answers are a, b, and d. There are editors for these resource types. A Resource Editor is not available for a generic window.

Question 30

The correct answer is d. To correctly answer this question, you must know the order in which objects are constructed and destructed, as well as understand polymorphic behavior. Objects are constructed from the top down (base class to most derived) and destructed from the bottom up. Polymorphic behavior by a function requires that the function be declared **virtual** in a base class, which can be overridden in a derived class, and that the virtual function is called through a pointer or a reference. Answer a is incorrect because the construction of object 2 doesn't invoke the constructors for classes A and B. Answer b is incorrect because the destruction of object 2 invokes the destructors for classes B and C. Because the base class (class A) destructor is not virtual, only the destructor for class A is invoked. Answer c is incorrect because the order of destruction is wrong. Answer c is also incorrect because object 2's destructors for classes B and C are invoked.

Question 31

The correct answer is b. The X.509 specification identifies the format of the most commonly employed certificates. The X.500 convention describes, among other things, a distinguished name, whereas ZIP is a compression format and PCMCIA is a hardware/software-driver specification.

Question 32

The correct answers are a, b, and d. Answer a, **oleautomation**, is used to indicate an Automation-compatible interface. Answer b, **object**, identifies the interface as a COM-style, rather than a RPC-style interface. Answer d, **dual**, indicates that the interface supports both Automation and vtable binding. Answer c is incorrect because there is no interface attribute named "pointer."

Question 33

The correct answer is e. This question tries to trick you by listing Resource files and Image files separately from binary files. Recall that using SourceSafe, you can manage both text and binary data files. Because Resource files and Image files are actually binary files, they too can be managed using SourceSafe.

Question 34

The correct answers are b and c. An out-of-process server is a standalone executable that runs in a different apartment than the client executable. Because aggregation doesn't work across apartments, your object must be an in-process server. Also, because all interface queries are made to the outer object, it can selectively screen out requests for any interface it chooses to. Answer a is incorrect because there are no special requirements that need to be met in order for an object to be reused by containment. Therefore, all COM objects can be reused by containment. Answer d is incorrect because answer a is incorrect.

Question 35

Answer c is correct. When both **BOF** and **EOF** are **true**, the recordset has no record. Answers a, b, and d are incorrect because either or both **BOF** and **EOF** are **false**.

Question 36

The correct answer is d. The **IUnknown** interface must be implemented because it is the root of all COM interfaces. Scripting languages like VBScript and JScript require dynamic invocation, more commonly called "late binding." In COM, dynamic invocation is called "Automation" and is supported by the **IDispatch** interface. Therefore, the **IDispatch** interface must be implemented. Because the **ISales** interface is the interface that provides the unique functionality for this component, its methods must be implemented. Answer e is incorrect because it doesn't include all three interfaces.

Question 37

The correct answer is a. Answer b is incorrect because **enum, struct,** and **union** are not primitive types. Answer c is incorrect because it does not include the **small** data type. Answer d is incorrect because it does not include the **boolean** data type.

Question 38

The correct answers are a, b, and d. The **/Gd** option is the default __cdecl calling convention. **/Gr** instructs the compiler to use __fastcall, whereas **/Gz** employs __stdcall.

Question 39

Answers a and c are correct. Answer b is incorrect because menu items use the **WM_COMMAND** message to send notifications. There is no **WM_MENU_ CHANGE** message. Answer d is incorrect because buttons use the **BN_CLICKED** control-notification message when clicked by a user.

Question 40

The correct answer is c. To avoid network traffic, the **CoCreateInstanceEx()** method supports the request for multiple interface pointers in one network round-trip. Answer a is incorrect because it is incomplete. **CoGetClassObject()** returns a pointer to the class factory interface. You then use this interface to actually create the COM object. Answer b is incorrect because **CoCreate In-stance()** can only request a single interface pointer. Answer d is incorrect because there is no such function.

Question 41

The correct answers are a, b, and c. Answer a is correct because EXE is the extension of the application itself. Answer b is correct because CNT is the extension of the contents file. This file must be installed in order for WinHelp to provide a tree-view table of contents. Answer c is the extension of the help file, so it too must be installed. Answer d is incorrect because it is the extension of the Help source file.

Question 42

The correct answer is e. All four code examples will return **Bob**. This is another nasty question. You must read every line of code very carefully to ensure everything is as it should be. When taking the exam, you should pass over this kind of question the first time through. Then, if you have time, you should come back to it. Examples 1 and 3 both correctly use the **Recordset** object's **Find** method. They only differ by how the command is passed to the **Find** method. Example 2 uses a **Parameter** object to specify the criteria for the **WHERE** clause. Example 4 is about as simple as it gets; the **SELECT** statement and the connection string are both passed to the **Recordset** object's **Open** method.

Question 43

The correct answer is a. Answer b is incorrect because the **CDataSource** class corresponds to an OLE DB data source object. Answers c and d are incorrect because they are not legal MFC classes.

Question 44

The correct answers are a, b, and c. There is no command to skip over a function or statement. You can, however, accomplish the same results by using Set Next Statement.

Question 45

The correct answer is b. Before the framework closes a modified document, it calls **CDocument::SaveModified()**. The default implementation displays a message box asking the user whether to save the document. If the user chooses YES, the framework saves the document. You override **CDocument::Save Modified()** when the default behavior is not what you want. Answer a is incorrect because

CRecordset::Update() is used to save new or edited data on the data source. Answer c is incorrect because **CView::OnUpdate()** is called by the framework to update the view after the document has been modified. Answer d is incorrect because **CWnd::SaveModified()** doesn't exist.

Question 46

The correct answers are a and b. Using a publicly posted certificate (if you can find one) is not a wise idea, because the private-key information must be posted to be of use. Once the information is posted, there is little value in having the certificate. The ChkTrust utility is used to check the validity of a signed file.

Question 47

The correct answer is a. This question tries to mislead you with irrelevant information. You will probably see a few questions like this on the exam. The key is the second bullet, which requires your new application to run standalone and, at some time in the future, provide services to an as-yet-unknown client. It's possible to use the SDK to develop a Win32 EXE that could satisfy the requirements. However, you specialize in MFC, so using the SDK would not be prudent. An MFC DLL is not an acceptable choice because your application must run standalone. Answer d is incorrect because it includes answer c.

Question 48

The correct answer is d. ActiveX controls exploit the Connectable Objects technology to provide events. The control typically implements the **IConnectionPointContainer, IConnectionPoint,** and **IProvideClassInfo** interfaces. Through these interfaces the container determines the events that the control supports. The container implements a method for each of the events it wants to receive and provides the control with a pointer to the interface. Then, whenever the control wants to send an event to the container, it uses the pointer to invoke the method in the container that corresponds to the events. Answers a and c are incorrect because they indicate that a Windows message is being sent. Answer b is incorrect because **WM_EVENT** does not exist, and if it did, the answer would be incorrect for the same reason that a and c are incorrect.

Question 49

The correct answer is c. **CCmdTarget** is MFC's base class for the message map architecture, and it performs the actual message map lookup.

Question 50

The correct answers are b and c. The Standard edition only allows static linking, and there is no Personal edition.

Glossary

. . . .

Activation—The process of loading an object in memory, which puts it into its running state.

ActiveX—A set of technologies that enables software components to interact with one another in a networked environment, regardless of the language in which they were created. ActiveX is built on the Component Object Model (COM).

ActiveX component—A physical file that contains classes, which are definitions of objects. Classes were formerly known as "OLE Automation servers" and "OLE Automation controllers."

ActiveX control—An object that you place on a form to enable or enhance a user's interaction with an application. ActiveX controls have events and can be incorporated into other controls.

ActiveX object—An object can meet the requirements of the ActiveX specification by implementing only the **IUnknown** interface. However, in practical terms one usually thinks of an ActiveX object as an object exposed to other applications or programming tools through Automation interfaces.

ActiveX Data Objects (ADO)—A collection of dual interface objects and their properties, methods, and events that allows you to connect to and manipulate data. ADO uses OLE DB to access the data and presents the developer with an easy to use interface. See *OLE DB*.

Aggregate object—A COM object that is made up of one or more other COM objects. One object in the aggregate is designated the controlling object, which controls which interfaces in the aggregate are exposed and which are private. This controlling object has a special implementation of **IUnknown** called the controlling **IUnknown**. All objects in the aggregate must pass calls to **IUnknown** methods through the controlling **IUnknown**. See also *Aggregation*.

Aggregation—A composition technique for implementing COM objects. It allows you to build a new object by using one or more existing objects that support some or all of the new object's required interfaces. The aggregate object chooses which interfaces to expose to clients, and the interfaces are exposed as if they were implemented by the aggregate object. Clients of the aggregate object think they communicate only with the aggregate object. See also *Aggregate object*.

Ambient property—A runtime property that defines a container's surroundings, including default colors, fonts, and alignment. Controls use ambient properties to assume the look and feel of its surrounding environment.

Apartment—In COM, objects with different concurrency semantics are separated into distinct execution contexts, called apartments. Apartments help programmers manage thread concurrency with respect to their COM objects. COM's apartment models provides a simple set of rules, which when followed, programmers will receive the concurrency behavior they expect from the COM environment. See also *Single-threaded apartment (STA) model* and *Multithreaded apartment (MTA) model*.

Apartment thread—See *Main thread* and *Single-threaded apartment (STA) model*.

Apartment threading model—See *Main thread* and *Single-threaded apartment (STA) model*.

Application Programming Interface (API)—A set of routines that an application uses to request and carry out lower-level services. The ODBC API is composed of the ODBC functions.

Automation—COM-based technology that enables interoperability among components. Automation is typically used to create applications that expose objects to programming tools and macro languages, to create and manipulate one application's objects from another applications, or to create tools for accessing and manipulating objects.

Automation object—An object that is exposed to other applications or programming tools through Automation interfaces.

Bookmark—A value that identifies a row in a rowset. Bookmarks are saved by the consumer and used later in the life of the rowset to retrieve a particular row.

Breakpoint—A location in a program at which execution is halted so that a programmer can examine the program's status, the contents of variables, and so on. A breakpoint is set and used within a debugger and is usually implemented by inserting at the point some kind of jump, call, or trap instruction that transfers control to the debugger.

Binary string (BSTR)—A pointer to a null-terminated character string in which the string length is stored with the string.

Cabinet file—A file that contains compressed files. The CAB file format is useful when you want to deliver code to an end user's computer in a single package, via the Internet or company intranet, and have it automatically install and register itself.

Cache—A buffer used to hold data during input/output (I/O) transfers between disk and random access memory (RAM).

Call-level interface (CLI)—The interface supported by ODBC for use by an application.

Catalog—The Microsoft Transaction Server data store that maintains configuration information for components, packages, and roles. You can administer the catalog by using the Microsoft Transaction Server Explorer.

Class—The formal definition of an object. The class acts as the template from which an instance of an object is created at runtime, and it defines the properties of the object and the methods used to control the object's behavior.

Class factory—A COM object that implements the **IClassFactory** or **IClassFactory2** interface and that creates one or more instances of an object identified by a given class identifier (CLSID). See also *Class identifier (CLSID)*.

Class ID—See *Class identifier (CLSID)*.

Class identifier (CLSID)—A globally unique identifier (GUID) that identifies a COM component. Each COM component has its CLSID in the Windows Registry so that it can be loaded by other applications. See also *Globally Unique Identifier (GUID)*, *Class*, and *Class factory*.

Class object—In object-oriented programming, an object whose state is shared by all the objects in a class and whose behavior acts on that class-wide state data. In COM, class objects are called class factories, and typically have no behavior except to create new instances of the class. See also *Class factory*.

Client—An application or process that requests a service from some process or component.

Client cursor—In database programming a cursor implemented on the client. The entire result set is first transferred to the client, and the client application programming interface (API) software implements the cursor functionality from this cached result set. Client cursors typically do not support all types of cursors, only static and forward-only cursors. See also *Server cursor*.

CLSID—See *Class identifier.*

Coclass—An implemented COM object. Coclasses are useful in COM only for creating the instance. The new instance's functionality is contained in the COM interfaces it implements.

Collection—An object that contains a set of related objects.

Column—In a relational database table, the area, sometimes called a field, in each row that stores the data about an attribute of the entity represented by the table.

Column ID—A structure used to identify a column, primarily in a command where there are no stable ordinals or column names.

COM—See *Component Object Model.*

COM object—An object that conforms to the Component Object Model (COM) architecture. A COM object is an instance of an object definition (class), which specifies the object's data and one or more implementations of interfaces on the object. Clients interact with a COM object only through its interfaces. See also *Component Object Model (COM)* and *Interface.*

Command—An ADO object that encapsulates a command.

Command text—The text command associated with a command object. Although it is not required to be, this is usually a SQL statement.

Commit—The capability to persistently save any changes made to a database or a storage or stream object since it was opened or changes were last saved. A SQL **COMMIT** statement guarantees that all or none of a transaction's modifications are made a permanent part of the database. See also *Roll back.*

Component—A discrete unit of code built on COM technology that provides a well-specified set of publicly available services through well-specified interfaces. Components provide the objects that clients request at runtime.

Component Object Model (COM)—A software architecture that allows components made by different software vendors to be combined into a variety of applications. COM defines a standard for component interoperability, is not dependent on any particular programming language, is available on multiple platforms, and is extensible. COM is the programming model and binary standard on which ActiveX and Automation technologies are based. See also *Interface.*

Concurrency—A mode of operation that allows multiple users to access and change shared data at the same time.

Connectable object—A COM object that implements, as a minimum, the **IConnectionPointContainer** interface, for the management of connection-point objects. Connectable objects support communication from the server to the client. A connectable object creates and manages one or more connection-point objects, which receive events from interfaces implemented on other objects and send them on to the client. See also *Connection-point object*.

Connection—A particular instance of a driver and data source.

Connection-point object—A COM object that is managed by a connectable object and that implements the **IConnectionPoint** interface. One or more connection-point objects can be created and managed by a connectable object. Each connection-point object manages incoming events from a specific interface on another object and sends those events on to the client. See also *Connectable object*.

Container—An application or object that can contain other objects, and which interacts with the contained objects through Automation.

Container application—An application that supports compound documents. The container application provides storage for an embedded or linked object, a site for its display, access to the display site, and an advisory sink for receiving notifications of changes in the object.

Consistency—A state where durable data matches the state expected by the business rules that modified the data.

Control—An object that you can place on a form or designer and that has its own set of recognized properties and events. Controls can receive user input, display output, and trigger event procedures. You can manipulate most controls by using methods.

Control container—An object that provides sites that can contain controls. Typically, these sites all exist on the same document or form. The control container implements entry points for controls and exposes ambient properties to them. In COM, an application that supports embedding of controls by implementing the **IOleControlSite** interface. See also *Control*.

Controlling IUnknown—A special instance of the **IUnknown** interface that is implemented in an aggregate object.

Current row—The row currently pointed to by the cursor. Positioned operations act on the current row.

Cursor—A database object used by applications to manipulate data by rows. Using cursors, multiple operations can be performed row by row against a result set; with or without returning to the original table.

Custom interface—A user-defined COM interface that isn't defined as part of COM.

Data source name (DSN)—The name assigned to an ODBC data source. Applications can use data source names (DSNs) to request a connection to a system ODBC data source, which specifies the computer name and (optionally) the database to which the DSN maps. A DSN can also refer to an OLE DB connection.

Data transfer object—An object that implements the **IDataObject** interface and contains data to be transferred from one object to another through either the Clipboard or drag-and-drop operations.

Database—A collection of information, tables, and other objects organized and presented to serve a specific purpose, such as to facilitate searching, sorting, and recombining data. Databases are stored in files. A database is also a discrete collection of data in a DBMS.

Database Management System (DBMS)—A repository for the collection of computerized data files that enables users to perform a variety of operations on those files, including retrieving, appending, editing, updating, and generating reports. A DBMS provides a layer of software between the physical database and the user and manages all access to the database.

Debugger—A program designed to aid in finding errors in another program by allowing the programmer to step through the program, examine the data, and monitor conditions, such as the values of variables.

Design-time object—An object used at design time within a host's development environment. See also *Runtime object*.

Document view—A particular presentation of a document's data. A single document object can have one or more views, but a single document view can belong to one (and only one) document object.

Dynamic cursor—A mechanism that allows unrestricted movement through a recordset. Updates, deletes, and inserts made by users are reflected in the dynamic cursor. See also *Keyset cursor*, *Static cursor*, and *Forward-only cursor*.

Dynamic link library (DLL)—A executable file that contains one or more functions that are compiled, linked, and stored separately from the processes that use them. The operating system maps the DLLs into the address space of the calling process when the process is starting or while it's running.

Enumerator—A COM object that searches for data sources and other enumerators.

Error—A condition in which a fatal error occurred. Also used to refer to any error, whether or not it is fatal.

Error code—A class of return code, of the type **HRESULT**, that begins with **E_** or **DB_E_** and indicates that the method failed completely and was unable to do any useful work.

Error object—An object that contains detailed information about an error.

Event sink—An event sink implements the member functions for a set of events.

Event source—An event source calls the interface that handles events.

Exception—An abnormal condition or error that occurs during the execution of a program and that requires the execution of software outside the normal flow of control.

Field—See *Column*.

Filter—A set of criteria applied to records to show a subset of the records.

Forward-only cursor—A mechanism that can only move forward through the recordset; rows can be read only in sequence from the first row to the last row. See also *Dynamic cursor*, *Keyset cursor*, and *Static cursor*.

Free threading model—See *Multithreaded apartment (MTA) model*.

Globally Unique Identifier (GUID)—In COM, a 16-byte value that uniquely identifies something, usually the software that implements one or more objects or an interface on one of those objects. Microsoft's implementation of the Open Software Foundation (OSF) distributed computing environment (DCE) Universally Unique Identifier (UUID).

HRESULT—A 32-bit integer value that provides error information. It consists of four parts: severity (bit 31), reserved (bits 29 and 30), facility code (bits 16 to 28), and return code (bits 0 to 15). The predefined severity constants are **SEVERITY_SUCCESS** (zero) and **SEVERITY_ERROR** (one).

In parameter—A parameter that is allocated, set, and freed by the caller of a function or interface method. An In parameter is not modified by the called function. See also *In/Out parameter* and *Out parameter*.

In/Out parameter—A parameter that is initially allocated and freed by the caller of an interface method. See also *In parameter* and *Out parameter*.

In-process server—A server implemented as a DLL that runs in the process space of the client. A component is said to be running as an in-process server when it provides objects from within another component or application's process space. See also *Out-of-process server*, *Local server*, and *Remote server*.

Instance—An object for which memory is allocated or which is persistent.

Instantiate—To create an instance of an object.

Interface—A group of semantically related functions that provide access to a COM object. Each interface defines a contract that allows objects to interact according to the Component Object Model (COM). See also *Component Object Model* and *COM object*.

Interface definition language (IDL)—Used to specify a COM interface. The interface includes the set of data types and the set of functions to be executed. Interfaces specify the function prototypes for remote functions. These prototypes, in turn, define many aspects of the behavior interface that users can expect from these functions.

Interface identifier (IID)—A globally unique identifier (GUID) associated with an interface. Some functions take IIDs as parameters to allow the caller to specify which interface pointer should be returned.

IPersistxxx object—A COM object that supports **IPersistStream, IPersist Stream Init**, or **IPersistStorage**.

Keyset cursor—A mechanism that allows unrestricted movement through a recordset. Updates made to its member rows by other users are reflected in the keyset cursor, but it doesn't show the effects of inserts or deletes. See also *Dynamic cursor, Static cursor*, and *Forward-only cursor*.

License key—A string that, if present, allows a software component to be created.

Licensing—A feature of COM that provides control over object creation. Only clients authorized to use licensed objects can create them. Licensing is implemented in COM through the **IClassFactory2** interface and by support for a license key that can be passed at runtime.

Local server—An out-of-process server implemented as an EXE application running on the same machine as its client application. See also *In-process server, Out-of-process server*, and *Remote server*.

Lock—A restriction on access to a resource in a multi-user environment. SQL Server locks users out of a specific record, field, or file automatically to maintain security or prevent concurrent data manipulation problems.

Locking—The process by which a DBMS restricts access to a row in a multi-user environment. The DBMS usually sets a bit on a row or the physical page containing a row that indicates the row or page is locked.

Main thread—A single thread used to run all objects of components marked as "single threaded." See also *Single-threaded apartment (STA) model.*

Marshaling—The process of packaging and sending interface method calls across thread, process, or machine boundaries. See also *Unmarshaling, Proxy,* and *Stub.*

Method—A procedure (function) that acts on an object.

Microsoft ActiveX Data Objects (ADO)—An easy-to-use, application programming interface (API) wrapping OLE DB for use in languages, such as Visual Basic, Visual Basic for Applications, Active Server Pages, and Microsoft Internet Explorer Visual Basic Scripting.

MIDL—Microsoft Interface Definition Language; a compiler (Midl.exe).

Moniker—An object that acts as the name that uniquely identifies a specific COM object instance. Each moniker knows how to create and initialize a COM object of the type it represents. A moniker object implements the **IMoniker** interface.

Multithreaded apartment (MTA) model—In COM, the MTA model allows multiple threads to operate within the same thread-safe "box." This model is sometimes referred to as the *free threading model* and occasionally as a *worker thread.*

Object—A combination of code and data that can be treated as a unit. A class defines a specific kind of object. In object-oriented programming, an object is an entity that has state, behavior, and identity. Its state consists of its attributes and the current values of those attributes. An object's behavior consists of the operations that can be performed on it and the corresponding changes in its state. An object's identity distinguishes it from other objects. In contrast, a COM object's behavior is defined by the interfaces it supports. A COM object's state is not explicitly specified, but is implied by its interfaces. A COM object is created by a component's class factory. See also *Component Object Model (COM), Interface,* and *Instance.*

Object Description Language (ODL)—Used to specify a COM interface. ODL was superseded by IDL. However, AppWizard still creates ODL files. See *Interface definition language (IDL).*

Object Linking and Embedding (OLE)—A mechanism that allows users to place content objects created by one application in documents created by another application.

ODBC—See *Open Database Connectivity.*

ODBC driver—A dynamic link library (DLL) that an ODBC-enabled application can use to access an ODBC data source. Each ODBC driver is specific to a database management system (DBMS). See also *Open Database Connectivity*.

OLE—See *Object Linking and Embedding*.

OLE DB—A COM-based application programming interface (API) for accessing data. OLE DB supports accessing any format data storage (databases, spreadsheets, text files, and so on) for which an OLE DB provider is available.

Open Database Connectivity (ODBC)—A relational database application programming interface (API) aligned with the American National Standards Institute (ANSI) and International Organization for Standardization (ISO) standards for a database Call Level Interface (CLI). ODBC supports access to any database for which an ODBC driver is available.

Out parameter—A parameter that is freed by the caller, but its value is set by the method being called. See also *In parameter* and *In/Out parameter*.

Out-of-process server—A server that runs outside the process of its client, either on the same machine or a remote machine. See also *Local server* and *Remote server*.

Package—A set of components that perform related application functions. All components in a package run together in the same Microsoft Transaction Server server process. A package is both a trust boundary that defines when security credentials are verified and a deployment unit for a set of components. You can create packages with the Transaction Server Explorer.

Package file—A file that contains information about the components and roles of a package. A package file is created using the package export function of the Transaction Server Explorer. When you create a pre-built package, the associated component files (DLLs, type libraries, and proxy-stub DLLs, if implemented) are copied to the same directory where the package file was created.

Persist—To save the current state of an object, such as to a file.

Persistent—Lasting between program sessions or renewed when a new program session is started.

Persistent storage—Storage of a file or object in a medium, such as a file system or database, so that the object and its data persist when the file is closed and then reopened later.

Programmatic identifier (progID)—A name that identifies a COM component.

Property—A named attribute of an object. Properties define object characteristics, such as size, color, and screen location, or the state of an object, such as enabled or disabled.

Property frame—The user-interface mechanism that displays one or more property pages for a control. A standard implementation of a property frame that can be accessed by using the **OleCreatePropertyFrame** helper function. See also *Control* and *Property page*.

Property page—A grouping of properties presented as a tabbed page of a property sheet. In COM, an object with its own CLSID that is part of a user interface, implemented by a control, and allows the control's properties to be viewed and set. Property page objects implement the **IPropertyPage** interface. See also *CLSID* and *Control*.

Property page site—The location within a property frame where a property page is displayed. The property frame implements the **IPropertyPageSite** interface, which contains methods to manage the sites of each of the property pages supplied by a control. See also *Property frame*.

Property set—A logically related group of properties that is associated with a persistently stored object. To create, open, delete, or enumerate one or more property sets, implement the **IPropertySetStorage** interface. If you are using compound files, you can use COM's implementation of this interface rather than implementing your own. See also *Persistent properties*.

Property set storage—A COM storage object that holds a property set. A property set storage is a dependent object associated with and managed by a storage object.

Property sheet—A specialized window through which users can modify the attributes of an external object, such as the current selection in a view. A property sheet has three main parts: the containing window, one or more property pages shown one at a time, and a tab at the top of each page that the user clicks to select that page. See also *Property page*.

Proxy—In COM, an interface-specific object that provides the parameter marshaling and communication required for a client to call a server object that is running in a different apartment. A proxy runs in the address space of the client and communicates with a corresponding stub in the server's address space. See also *Stub*, *Marshaling*, and *Unmarshaling*.

Query—A SQL statement. Sometimes used to mean a **SELECT** statement.

Record—In ADO, the record object represents a row in a Recordset, or a file or directory in a file system. See *Row*.

Recordset—In ADO, represents the entire set of records from a base table, query, or view. See *Result set*.

Reference counting—Keeping a count of each interface pointer held on an object to ensure that the object is not destroyed before all references to it are released. See also *Lock*.

Registry key—A unique identifier assigned to each piece of information in the system registration database.

Remote component—A component used by a client on a different computer. See *Remote server*.

Remote Procedure Call (RPC)—A standard that allows one process to make calls to functions that are executed in another process. The process can be on the same computer or on a different computer in the network.

Remote server—A server application running on a different machine from the client application using it. See also *In-process server*, *Local server*, and *Out-of-process server*.

Result set—The set of rows returned from a **SELECT** statement. The format of the rows in the result set is defined by the column-list of the **SELECT** statement.

Roll back—The capability to remove partially completed transactions after a database or other system failure. A SQL **ROLLBACK** statement discards all changes made to a database since the beginning of the transaction. See also *Commit*.

Row—A data structure that is a collection of columns, each with its own name and type. A row can be accessed as a collective unit of elements, or the elements can be accessed individually. A row is also known as a record. See also *Column*.

Running Object Table (ROT)—A globally accessible table on each computer that keeps track of all COM objects in the running state that can be identified by a moniker. Moniker providers register an object in the table, which increments the object's reference count. Before the object can be destroyed, its moniker must be released from the table.

Runtime object—An object created at runtime and used as part of an executable application. See also *Design-time object*.

SCODE—A 32-bit integer value used to return detailed information to the caller of an interface method or function. See also **HRESULT**.

SELECT—A SQL statement used to retrieve data from the database.

Self-registration—The process by which a server can perform its own registry operations.

Semaphore—A locking mechanism used inside resource managers or resource dispensers. Semaphores have no symbolic names, only shared and exclusive-mode access, no deadlock detection, and no automatic release or commit.

Server—A network computer that controls access to resources, such as files, printers, and communication devices. In COM, *server* is informal for Server application.

Server application—An application that can create COM objects. Container applications can then embed or link to these objects. See also *Container application*.

Server cursor—A cursor implemented on the server. The cursor is built at the server, and only the rows fetched by an application are sent to the client. See also *Client cursor*.

Single-threaded apartment (STA) model—In COM, this model allows multiple threads to be created, where each thread will belong to only one apartment. When instantiated, the COM object is placed in its own apartment and will automatically be thread-safe because the same thread is always used to call its methods. This model is sometimes referred to as the *apartment threading model* and occasionally as a *user-interface-style thread*.

Single-threading model—All of a component's methods are executed on the main tread only.

SQL—See *Structured query language*.

SQL-92—The latest version of the standard for SQL, published in 1992. The international standard is ISO/IEC 9075:1992 Database Language SQL. The American National Standards Institute (ANSI) also published a corresponding standard (Data Language SQL X3.135-1192), so SQL-92 is sometimes referred to as ANSI SQL in the United States.

Static cursor—A mechanism that allows unrestricted movement through a recordset. Static cursors don't reflect updates, deletes, or inserts made to underlying data while the cursor is open. Sometimes called snapshot cursors. See also *Dynamic cursor*, *Keyset cursor*, and *Forward-only cursor*.

Storage object—A COM object that implements the **IStorage** interface. A storage object contains nested storage objects or stream objects, resulting in the equivalent of a directory/file structure within a single file. See also *Stream object*.

Stream object—A COM object that implements the **IStream** interface. A stream object is analogous to a file in a directory/file system. See also *Storage object*.

Structured query language (SQL)—A database query and programming language developed by IBM for mainframe computers. It is widely used for accessing data, querying, updating, and managing relational database systems. There is now an ANSI-standard SQL definition for all computer systems. *See also* SQL-92.

Structured storage—COM's technology for storing compound files in native file systems. See also *Storage object* and *Stream object*.

Stub—In COM, an interface-specific object that unpackages the marshaled parameters and calls the required method. The stub runs in the receiver's address space and communicates with a corresponding proxy in the sender's address space. See also *Proxy*, *Marshaling*, and *Unmarshaling*.

System registry—A system-wide repository of information supported by Windows, which contains information about the system and its applications, including COM clients and servers.

System stored procedures—A precompiled collection of SQL statements. System stored procedures are provided as shortcuts for retrieving information from system tables or mechanisms for accomplishing database administration and other tasks that involve updating system tables. You can write stored procedures (called user-defined stored procedures), which can be executed from any database.

Thread—The basic (memory) entity to which the operating system allocates CPU time. A thread can execute any part of the application's code, including a part currently being executed by another thread. All threads of a process share the virtual address space, global variables, and operating-system resources of the process.

Thread safe—A resource or process that internally handles synchronization. Threads that need to access thread-safe resources can do so as if they were in a single-threaded environment.

Threading model, apartment—See *Single-threaded apartment (STA) model*.

Threading model, both—Objects that support the single-threaded apartment model and the multithreaded apartment model.

Threading model, free—See *Multithreaded apartment (MTA) model*.

Threading model, multithreading—See *Multithreaded apartment (MTA) model*.

Transaction—An atomic unit of work. The work in a transaction must be completed as a whole; if any part of the transaction fails, the entire transaction fails.

Type information—The information about an object's class provided by a type library. To provide type information, a COM object implements the **IProvideClassInfo** interface.

Type library—A file or component within another file that contains standard descriptions of exposed objects, properties, and methods.

Unicode—Unicode defines a set of letters, numbers, and symbols in a worldwide encode scheme. It symbol is represented by 16-bits. Unicode has more than 65,000 possible values and includes characters for most languages. Windows NT uses Unicode exclusively at the system level.

Uniform data transfer—A model for transferring data via the Clipboard, drag and drop, or Automation. Objects conforming to this model implement the **IDataObject** interface. This model replaces DDE (dynamic data exchange).

Universal resource locator (URL)—The identifier used by the Web for the names and locations of objects on the Internet.

Universally Unique Identifier (UUID)—See *Globally Unique Identifier (GUID)*.

Unmarshaling—Unpacking parameters that have been sent to a proxy across process boundaries. See also *Marshaling*, *Proxy*, and *Stub*.

Virtual Table (VTBL)—An array of pointers to interface method implementations. See also *Interface*.

Warning code—A class of return code, of the type **HRESULT**, that begins with **S_** or **DB_S_** and indicates success of the method but with a warning.

Index